Computing Essentials 2002-2003

Introductory Edition

Computing Essentials 2002-2003

Introductory Edition

Timothy J. O'Leary
Arizona State University

Linda I. O'Leary

McGraw-Hill
Irwin

Boston Burr Ridge, IL Dubuque, IA Madison, WI New York
San Francisco St. Louis Bangkok Bogotá Caracas Kuala Lumpur
Lisbon London Madrid Mexico City Milan Montreal New Delhi
Santiago Seoul Singapore Sydney Taipei Toronto

McGraw-Hill Higher Education

A Division of The **McGraw-Hill** *Companies*

COMPUTING ESSENTIALS 2002-2003: INTRODUCTORY EDITION
Published by McGraw-Hill/Irwin, an imprint of The McGraw-Hill Companies, Inc. 1221 Avenue of the Americas, New York, NY, 10020. Copyright © 2002 by The McGraw-Hill Companies, Inc. All rights reserved. No part of this publication may be reproduced or distributed in any form or by any means, or stored in a database or retrieval system, without the prior written consent of The McGraw-Hill Companies, Inc., including, but not limited to, in any network or other electronic storage or transmission, or broadcast for distance learning.

Some ancillaries, including electronic and print components, may not be available to customers outside the United States.

This book is printed on acid-free paper.

domestic   1 2 3 4 5 6 7 8 9 0 QPD/QPD 0 9 8 7 6 5 4 3 2
international 1 2 3 4 5 6 7 8 9 0 QPD/QPD 0 9 8 7 6 5 4 3 2

ISBN   0-07-249210-4

Publisher: *George Werthman*
Sponsoring editor: *Dan Silverburg*
Developmental editor I: *Sarah Wood*
Manager, Marketing and Sales: *Paul Murphy*
Project manager: *Laura Ward Majersky*
Manager, new book production: *Melonie Salvati*
Lead supplement producer: *Marc Mattson*
Senior producer, Media technology: *David Barrick*
Photo research coordinator: *David A. Tietz*
Photo researcher: *Deborah Bull Photosearch, Inc.*
Cover design: *Gino Cieslik*
Interior design: *Maureen McCutcheon*
Typeface: *10/12 New Aster*
Compositor: *Cecelia Morales*
Printer: *Quebecor World Dubuque Inc.*

Library of Congress Cataloging-in-Publication Data

O'Leary, Timothy J.
    Computing Essentials, 2002-2003 / Timothy J. O'Leary, Linda I. O'Leary.--Introductory ed.
      p. cm.
    Includes index.
    ISBN 0-07-249210-4 (alk. paper) -- ISBN 0-07-113150-7 (international)
      1. Computers. 2. Electronic data processing. I. O'Leary, Linda I.
    QA76.5 .O443 2002
    004--dc21   2002016518

INTERNATIONAL EDITION ISBN 0-07-113150-7
Copyright © 2002. Exclusive rights by The McGraw-Hill Companies, Inc. for manufacture and export.
This book cannot be re-exported from the country to which it is sold by McGraw-Hill. The International Edition is not available in North America.

www.mhhe.com

Information Technology at McGraw-Hill

At McGraw-Hill Higher Education, we publish instructional materials targeted at the higher education market. In an effort to expand the tools of higher learning, we publish texts, lab manuals, study guides, testing materials, software, and multimedia products.

At McGraw-Hill/Irwin (a division of McGraw-Hill Higher Education), we realize that technology has created and will continue to create new mediums for professors and students to use in managing resources and communicating information to one another. We strive to provide the most flexible and complete teaching and learning tools available as well as offer solutions to the changing world of teaching and learning.

InformationTechnology

McGraw-Hill/Irwin is dedicated to providing the tools for today's instructors and students to successfully navigate the world of Information Technology.

- **Seminar Series**—McGraw-Hill/Irwin's Technology Connection seminar series offered across the country every year demonstrates the latest technology products and encourages collaboration among teaching professionals.

- **McGraw-Hill/Osborne**—This division of The McGraw-Hill Companies is known for its best-selling Internet titles, *Internet & Web Yellow Pages* and the *Internet Complete Reference*. For more information, visit Osborne at **www.osborne.com**.

- **Digital Solutions**—McGraw-Hill/Irwin is committed to publishing digital solutions. Taking your course online doesn't have to be a solitary adventure, nor does it have to be a difficult one. We offer several solutions that will allow you to enjoy all the benefits of having your course material online. For more information visit **www.mhhe.com/solutions/index.mhtml.**

- **Packaging Options**—For more information about our discount options, contact your McGraw-Hill/Irwin sales representative at 1-800-338-3987 or visit our Web site at **www.mhhe.com/it**.

Brief Contents

Contents

Contents **xi**

9

Privacy, Security, Ergonomics, and the Environment 234

10

Your Future and Information Technology 266

Contents **xiii**

Preface

INTRODUCTION

The twentieth century not only brought us the dawn of the Information Age, but continued to bring us rapid changes in information technology. There is no indication that this rapid rate of change will be slowing—it may even be increasing. As we begin the twenty-first century, computer literacy will undoubtedly become prerequisite in whatever career a student chooses. The goal of *Computing Essentials, 2002-2003* is to provide students with the basis for understanding the concepts necessary for success in the Information Age. *Computing Essentials* also endeavors to instill in students an appreciation for the effect of information technology on people and our environment, and to give students a basis for building the necessary skill set to succeed in this new, twenty-first century.

ABOUT THE AUTHORS

Tim and Linda O'Leary live in the American Southwest and spend much of their time engaging instructors and students in conversation about learning. In fact, they have been talking about learning for over 25 years. Something in those early conversations convinced them to write a book, to bring their interest in the learning process to the printed page. Today, they are as concerned as ever about learning, about technology, and about the challenges of presenting material in new ways, both in terms of content and the method of delivery.

A powerful and creative team, Tim combines his years of classroom teaching experience with Linda's background as a consultant and corporate trainer. Tim has taught courses at Stark Technical College in Canton, Ohio, and at Rochester Institute of Technology in Upper New York state, and is currently a professor at Arizona State University in Tempe, Arizona. Tim and Linda have talked to and taught students from 8 to 80, all of them with a desire to learn something about computers and the applications that make their lives easier, more interesting, and more productive.

Each new edition of an O'Leary text, supplement, or learning aid has benefited from these students and their instructors who daily stand in front of them (or over their shoulders). *Computing Essentials, 2002-2003* is no exception.

A WORD FROM THE AUTHORS

Times are changing, technology is changing, and this text is changing too. Do you think the students of today are different from yesterday? Mine are and I'll wager that yours are as well. On the positive side, I am amazed how much effort students put toward things that interest them and things they are convinced are relevant to them. Their effort directed at learning application programs and exploring the Web seems at times limitless. On the other hand, it is difficult

to engage them in other equally important topics such as personal privacy and technological advances.

I've changed the way I teach and this book reflects that. I no longer *lecture* my students about how important certain concepts like microprocessors, input devices, and utility programs are. Rather, I begin by *engaging* their interest by presenting practical tips related to the key concepts, by *demonstrating* interesting applications that are relevant to their lives, and by *focusing* on outputs rather than processes. Then, I *discuss* the concepts and processes.

Motivation and relevance are the keys. This text has several features specifically designed to engage students and to demonstrate the relevance of technology in their lives. These elements are combined with a thorough coverage of the concepts and sound pedagogical devices.

SELECTED FEATURES OF THIS EDITION

- **Visual Chapter Openers** Each chapter begins with a two-page Visual Chapter Opener with large graphics and brief text. The graphics present the structure and organization of the chapter. The text relates the graphics to topics that are covered in the chapter and discusses their importance. The objective of the visual chapter openers is to engage students and provide relevancy and motivation.

- **On the Web Explorations** Within nearly every chapter, two or more On the Web Explorations are presented as marginal elements. These explorations encourage students to connect to carefully selected Web sites that provide additional information on key topics. The objective of the Web Explorations is to encourage students to expand their knowledge by using Web resources.

- **Tips** Within nearly every chapter, Tips are provided that offer advice on a variety of chapter-related issues such as how to efficiently locate information on the Web, how to speed up computer operations, and how to protect against computer viruses. One objective of the Tips is to provide students with assistance on common technology-related problems or issues. The other objective is to motivate students by showing the relevance of concepts presented in the chapter to their everyday lives.

- **Concept Checks** Every chapter contains strategically placed Concept Check boxes. Each box contains questions related to the material just presented. The objective of these Concept Checks is to provide students the opportunity to test their retention of key chapter concepts.

- **Making IT Work for You**  Based on student surveys, 12 special interest topics have been identified. These topics include downloading music from the Internet, creating personal Web sites, and using the Internet to place free long-distance telephone calls. Each of these 12 special interest topics is presented in a two-page Making IT Work for You section within the relevant chapter. The objective is to engage students by presenting high-interest topics and to motivate them to learn about related concepts in the chapter.

- **Demonstration Videos** Based on student interest and chapter content, several Making IT Work for You special interest topics have been selected for special attention. I have created seven short videos that bring these selected topics to life. These videos are available on CD and VHS tape for classroom viewing and on the Web for direct student viewing. One objective of this feature is to motivate students by animating and extending the static printed two page Making IT Work for You presentation in the textbook. The other objective is to provide instructors with a presentation tool for classroom demonstrations that are integrated and further supported by the textbook.

- **A Look to the Future**  Each chapter concludes with a brief discussion of a specific recent technological advance related to material presented in the chapter. The objective of this feature is to remind students that technology is always changing and to reinforce the importance of staying informed of recent changes.

- **Visual Chapter Summaries** Each chapter ends with a multipage visual chapter summary. Like the chapter openers, the summaries use graphics to present the structure of the chapter and text to provide specifics. Using a columnar arrangement, major concepts are represented by graphics followed by detailed text summaries. The objective of the visual chapter summaries is to provide a detailed summary of key concepts and terms in an engaging and meaningful way.

- **Using Technology** Every chapter has two Web-related end-of-chapter exercises that direct students to explore current  popular uses of technology. In most cases, the first question requires the student to view one of the Making IT Work for You Web-delivered demonstrations and to respond to a series of related questions. The other question requires Web research. One objective of the Using Technology feature is to provide support for instructors who would prefer their students to view the Making IT Work for You videos on the Web rather than in class. The other objective is to provide a powerful tool to engage and motivate students by providing assignments related to technology that directly relates to them.

- **Expanding Your Knowledge** Every chapter has two Web-related end-of-chapter exercises directing students to enhance their depth of knowledge on specific technologies introduced in the chapter. In most cases, the first question requires the students to use their free Interactive Companion CD-ROM and to respond to a series of related questions. The second question requires Web research into carefully selected topics. One objective of the Expanding Your Knowledge

feature is to provide support for instructors who want their students to effectively use the free Interactive CD-ROM. The other objective is to support instructors who want their students to obtain greater in-depth understanding of key technologies.

- **Building Your Portfolio** Every chapter has two Web-related end-of-chapter exercises directing students to prepare and to write a one- or two-page paper on critical technology-related issues. The first question requires students to summarize and analyze select emerging technologies addressed in the chapter. The second question focuses on a critical chapter-related privacy, security, and/or ethical issue. Students are required to consider, evaluate, and formulate a position. One objective of the Building Your Portfolio feature is to support instructors who want their students to develop critical thinking and writing skills. Another objective is to provide support for instructors who want their students to create written document(s) recording their technology knowledge. A third objective is to provide support for instructors who want their students to recognize, understand, and analyze key privacy, security, and ethical issues relating to technology.

- **Engaging Students** Having all these features is one thing. Making the students aware of them is another. Like almost all textbooks, Chapter 1 of this textbook provides an overview and framework for the following chapters. *Unlike other textbooks, this one also provides a discussion and overview of each of the above features.* One objective of this approach is to support instructors who want to focus their students' attention on any one or on a combination of features. The other objective is to motivate students by highlighting features that are visually interesting and relevant to their lives.

Instructor's Guide

RESOURCES FOR INSTRUCTORS

We understand that, in today's teaching environment, offering a textbook alone is not sufficient to meet the needs of the many different instructors who use our books. To teach effectively, instructors must have a full complement of supplemental resources to assist them in every facet of teaching from preparing for class; to conducting and lecture; to assessing students' comprehension. *Computing Essentials, 2002–2003* offers a complete, fully integrated supplements package, as described below.

Instructor's Resource Kit

The Instructor's Resource Kit contains an updated CD-ROM containing the Instructor's Manual in both MS Word and PDF formats, PowerPoint slides, and Brownstone's Diploma test generation software with accompanying test item files for each chapter. The distinctive features of each component of the Instructor's Resource Kit are described below.

- **Instructor's Manual** The Instructor's Manual contains a schedule showing how much time is required to cover the material in the chapter; a list of the chapter competencies; tips for covering difficult material; and answers to the Concept Checks. Also included are references to corresponding topics on the Interactive Companion CD-ROM, answers to all the exercises in the Chapter Review section and answers to the On the Web Exercises. The manual also includes a helpful introduction that explains the features, benefits, and suggested uses of the IM and an index of concepts and corresponding competencies.

- **PowerPoint Presentation** The PowerPoint presentation is designed to provide instructors with a comprehensive resource for use during lecture. It includes a review of key terms and definitions, figures from the text,

along with several new illustrations, anticipated student questions with answers, and additional resources that can be accessed in Internet-enabled classrooms. Also included with the presentation are comprehensive speaker's notes.

- **Testbank** The *Computing Essentials 2002–2003* edition testbank contains over 3,000 questions categorized by level of learning (definition, concept, and application). This is the same learning scheme that is introduced in the text to provide a valuable testing and reinforcement tool. The test questions are identified by text page number to assist you in planning your exams, and rationales for each answer are also included. Additional test questions, which can be used as pretests and posttests in class, can be found on the Online Learning Center, accessible through our Supersite (**www.mhhe.com/it**).

Making IT Work Video Series

Available on CD or the Web site, these videos provide cutting edge context to help students learn the concepts presented in the text. This series of brief video presentations features the author and corresponds to specific Making IT Work for You topics from the text, making it a flexible tool for in-class and Web-delivered demonstrations while engaging students by presenting high interest topics directly related to the concepts presented in the text. The series includes videos on:

- *CD-R Drivers and Music from the Internet*
- *Creating a Personal Web Site*
- *Creating an Active Desktop*
- *Instant Messaging*
- *Locating Jobs Online*
- *Using TV Tuner Cards and Video Clips*
- *Virus Protection*

Interactive Companion CD-ROM

This free student CD-ROM, designed for use in class, in the lab, or at home by students and professors alike includes a collection of interactive tutorial labs on some of the most popular topics in information technology. By combining video, interactive exercises, animation, additional content, and actual "lab" tutorials, we expand the reach and scope of the textbook.

Digital Solutions to Help You Manage Your Course

PageOut—PageOut is our Course Web Site Development Center that offers a syllabus page, URL, McGraw-Hill Online Learning Center content, online exercises and quizzes, gradebook, discussion board, and an area for student Web pages. For more information, visit the PageOut Web site (**www.pageout.net**).

Online Learning Centers—The Online Learning Center that accompanies *Computing Essentials* is accessible through our Information Technology Supersite (**www.mhhe.com/it**). This site provides additional learning and instructional tools developed using the same three-level approach found in the text and supplements. This offers a consistent method for students to enhance their comprehension of the concepts presented in the text.

Online Courses Available—OLCs are your perfect solutions for Internet-based content. Simply put, these Centers are "digital cartridges" that contain a book's pedagogy and supplements. As students read the book, they can go online and take self-grading quizzes or work through interactive exercises. These also provide students appropriate access to lecture materials and other key supplements.

Online Learning Centers can be delivered through any of these platforms:

McGraw-Hill Learning Architecture (TopClass)

Blackboard.com

ECollege.com (formally Real Education)

WebCT (a product of Universal Learning Technology)

O'Leary Series Applications Lab Manuals

Available separately, or packaged with *Computing Essentials*, is the O'Leary Series computer applications lab manuals for Microsoft Office. The O'Leary Series offers a step-by-step approach to developing computer applications skills and is available in both brief and introductory levels. The introductory level manuals are MOUS Certified and prepare students for the Microsoft Office User Certification Exam.

Skills Assessment

SimNet eXPert (Simulated Network Assessment Product)—SimNet provides a way for you to test students' software skills in a simulated environment. SimNet is available for Microsoft Office 97, Microsoft Office 2000, and Microsoft Office XP. SimNet provides flexibility for you in your course by offering:

- Pretesting options
- Posttesting options
- Course placement testing
- Diagnostic capabilities to reinforce skills
- Proficiency testing to measure skills
- Web or LAN delivery of tests
- Computer-based training tutorials (new for Office XP)
- MOUS preparation exams
- Learning verification reports
- Spanish version

For more information on skills assessment software, please contact your local sales representative, or visit us at **www.mhhe.com/it**.

PowerWeb for Concepts

PowerWeb is an exciting new online product available for *Computing Essentials 2002–2003*. A nominally priced token grants students access through our Web site to a wealth of resources—all corresponding to the text. Features include an interactive glossary; current events with quizzing, assessment, and measurement options; Web survey; links to related text content; and WWW searching capability via Northern Lights, an academic search engine. Visit PowerWeb at **www.dushkin.com/powerweb**.

STUDENT'S GUIDE TO THE O'LEARY LEARNING SYSTEM

Recently, at the end of the semester, some of my students stopped by my office to say they enjoyed the class and that they "learned something that they could *actually* use." High praise indeed for a professor! Actually, I had mixed feelings. Of course, it felt good to learn that my students enjoyed the course. However, it hurt a bit that they were *surprised* that they learned something useful.

> **Here's my promise to you:**
> *In the following pages you will find things that you can actually use now as well as that provide a foundation for understanding future technological advances.*

As you read the text, notice the "Tips" scattered throughout the book. These tips offer suggestions on a variety of topics from the basics of cleaning a monitor to how to make your computer run faster and smoother. Also, notice the "Making IT Work for You" sections that demonstrate some specific computer applications you might find interesting. For example, one demonstrates how to capture and use television video clips for electronic presentations and another shows how to capture, save, and play music from the Internet.

Many learning aids are built into the text to ensure your success with the material and to make the process of learning rewarding. In the pages that follow, we call your attention to the key features in the text. We also show you supplemental materials, such as the student Online Learning Center, that you should take advantage of to ensure your success in this course.

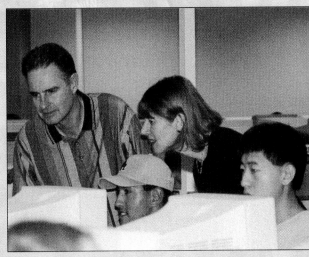

THE INTERNET, THE WEB, AND ELECTRONIC COMMERCE

COMPETENCIES

After you have read this chapter, you should be able to:

1 Describe Internet providers, connections, and protocols.

2 Discuss e-mail, mailing lists, newsgroups, chat groups, and instant messaging.

3 Describe search tools including search, metasearch, and specialized search engines.

4 Discuss electronic commerce including Web storefronts, auctions, and electronic payment.

5 Describe Web utilities: Telnet, FTP, plug-ins, and helper applications.

6 Discuss intranet

Visual Chapter Openers begin each chapter with two pages with large graphics and brief text. The graphics present the structure and organization of the chapter. The text relates the graphics to topics that are covered in the chapter and discusses their importance. The objective of the visual chapter openers is to engage students and provide relevancy and motivation.

Chapter 8

Want to communicate with a friend across town, in another state, or even in another country? Perhaps you would like to send a drawing, a photo, or just a letter. Looking for travel or entertainment information? Perhaps you're researching a term paper or exploring different career paths. Where do you start? For these and other information-related activities, try the Internet and the Web. They are 21st-century information resources designed for all of us to use.

The Internet is like a highway that connects you to millions of other people and organizations. Unlike typical highways that move people and things from one location to another, the Internet moves your **ideas** and **information**. Rather than moving through geographic space, you move through **cyberspace**—the space of electronic move-

ment of ideas and information. The Web provides an easy-to-use, exciting, multimedia interface to connect to the Internet and to access the resources available in cyberspace.

It has become an everyday tool for all of us to use. For example, you can create personal Web sites to share information with others and use instant messaging to chat with friends and collaborate on group projects.

Competent end users need to be aware of the resources available on the Internet and the Web. Additionally, they need to know how to access these resources, to effectively communicate electronically, to efficiently locate information, to understand electronic commerce, to use Web utilities, and to be knowledgeable about extranets, intranets, and security issues.

Key Terms Throughout the text, the most important terms are presented in bold type and are defined within the text. You will also find a list of key terms at the end of each chapter and in the glossary at the end of the book.

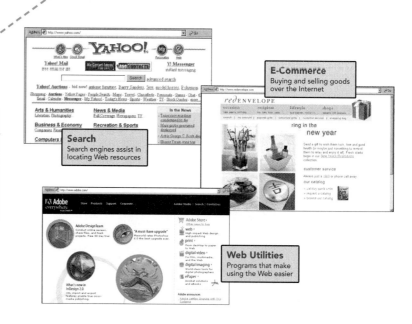

Browser Connect to sites and d Web pages

Search Search engines assist in locating Web resources

E-Commerce Buying and selling goods over the Internet

Web Utilities Programs that make using the Web easier

Concept Check

 What is a browser?

How do browsers locate/connect to other resources?

What are Web portals?

COMMUNICATION

As previously mentioned, communication is the most popular Internet activity. The impact of electronic communication cannot be overestimated. At a personal level, friends and family can stay in contact with one another even when separated by thousands of miles. At a business level, electronic communication has become a standard and many times preferred way to stay in touch with suppliers, employees, and customers.

> Communication by e-mail is the most common Internet activity. Discussion groups include mailing lists, newsgroups, chat groups, and instant messaging.

E-MAIL

You can communicate with anyone in the world who has an Internet address or e-mail account with a system connected to the Internet. All you need is access to the Internet and an e-mail program. Two of the most widely used e-mail programs are Microsoft's Outlook Express and Netscape's Navigator.

Suppose that you have a friend, Dan Coats, who is going to the University of Southern California. You and Dan have been calling back and forth at least once a week for the past month. Your telephone bill has skyrocketed. Fortunately, you both have Internet e-mail accounts through your schools. To save money, you and Dan agree to communicate via the Internet instead of the telephone. After exchanging e-mail addresses, you are ready to send your first Internet e-mail message to Dan.

A typical e-mail message has three basic elements: header, message, and signature. (See Figure 8-11.) The **header** appears first and typically includes the following information:

- **Addresses:** Addresses of the persons sending, receiving, and, optionally, anyone else who is to receive copies.
- **Subject:** A one-line description, used to present the topic of the message. Subject lines typically are displayed when a person checks his or her mailbox.
- **Attachments:** Many e-mail programs allow you to attach files such as documents and worksheets. If a message has an attachment, the file name appears on the attachment line.

On the Web Explorations

You can get e-mail service for free. To learn more about these free services, visit our site at:

http://www.mhhe.com/oleary

TIPS

You can go to e-mail address directories, also known as e-mail "white pages." These directories can be used much like you would use the telephone white pages. Here are three e-mail address directories you might try:

- www.bigfoot.com
- www.people.yahoo.com
- www.infospace.com

Company	Site	Cost of Course
Dell	www.educateu.com	$30 to $1300
Digital Think	www.digitalthink.com	$99 to $1000
EduPoint.com	www.edupoint.com	$10 to $1000
Hungry Minds	www.hungryminds.com	free to $1499
Learn2.com	www.learn2.com	$20 to $100

Figure 8-3 E-Learning sites

Communication   www.mhhe.com/oleary   **211**

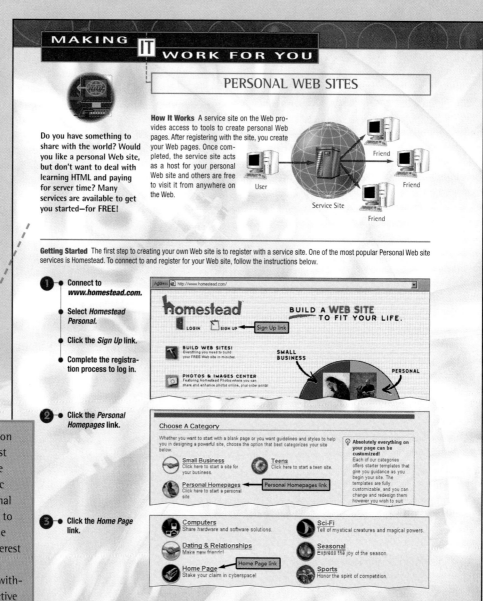

Making IT Work for You Based on student surveys, 12 special interest topics have been identified. These topics include downloading music from the Internet, creating personal Web sites, and using the Internet to place free long-distance telephone calls. Each of these 12 special interest topics is presented in a two-page Making IT Work for You section within the relevant chapter. The objective is to engage students by presenting high-interest topics that directly relate to concepts presented in the chapter.

Demonstration Videos Seven of the Making IT Work for You features have been exanded into video presentations available on CD and VHS tape. The objective of these videos is to motivate students by expanding and animating the material in the book.

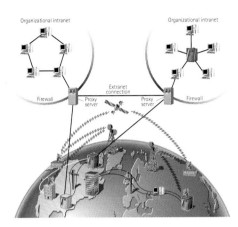

● **Figure 8-31** Intranets, extranets, firewalls, and proxy servers

A Look to the Future

Internet2 Will Be a Private High-Performance Internet

Have you ever been unable to connect to the Internet? Have you ever had a long wait before a Web page or a graphic appeared on your screen? Almost all of us have experienced busy servers and slow access. Unfortunately, Internet service is expected to get worse. For organizations that depend on the Internet to reach customers and conduct other business activities, this trend is very concerning.

To address this concern, a separate private Internet called Internet2 is being developed. It will be a high-speed network capable of dazzling feats that far exceed today's Internet capabilities. Expected to be fully operational by the end of next year, Internet2 will

have limited access to those willing to pay more to get more. Access to today's Internet will remain public and available for a nominal fee.

The primary beneficiaries of Internet2 will be federal agencies and major corporations. Each will pay an annual fee of $500,000 for access to this network that combines high performance with tightly controlled security. One of the first to take advantage of Internet2 will be online publishers of books, photographs, and original artwork. Advanced virtual reality interfaces, called "nanomanipulators," are expected to be available. Researchers from different parts of the world will be able to share devices such as atomic microscopes and to jointly study, experience, and move within realistic virtual subatomic environments.

Will moving power users to Internet2 increase the performance of the public Internet? Do you think Internet2 will have any effect on you? We will have to wait and see.

VISUAL SUMMARY
The Internet, the Web, and Electronic Commerce

ACCESS

Once connected to the Internet, your computer seemingly becomes an extension of a giant computer that branches all over the world.

Providers

The most common access is through a **provider** or **host computer.** Three widely used providers are:

* **National service providers**—like AOL, use standard telephone lines.
* **Regional service providers**—offer access within a specific geographic area.
* **Wireless service providers**—do not require any type of connecting lines to wireless devices.

Browsers

Browsers access the Web and provide Internet services. Some related terms are:

* **URLs**—addresses to Web resources.
* **Surfing**—moving from one Web site to another.
* **HTML**—commands that display Web pages.
* The **home page**—typically the first page at a Web site.
* **Hyperlinks**—connections to related sites and documents.
* **Java**—programming language for creating special programs called **applets**.
* **Web portals (horizontal and vertical)**—sites that provide a variety of services.

COMMUNICATION

Communication is the most popular Internet activity. Two categories are e-mail and discussion groups.

E-mail

An e-mail has three basic elements:

* **Header** including addresses, subject line, and attachments
* **Message** or text.
* **Signature line** providing sender information.

Discussion Groups

Discussion groups are ways to communicate electronically with one or more individuals. This type of communication includes:

* **Mailing lists**—use e-mail subscription and **list addresses.**
* **Newsgroups**—are organized by major topic areas and use the **UseNet** network.
* **Chat groups**—allow direct "live" communication.
* **Instant messaging**—provides greater flexibility than chat groups.

Terms associated with discussion groups include: **FAQ, flaming, lurking, RFD, saint, thread,** and **wizard.**

Visual Chapter Summaries appear in at least two pages at the end of each chapter. Like the chapter openers, the summaries use graphics to present the structure of the chapter and text to provide specifics. Using a columnar arrangement, major concepts are represented by graphics followed by detailed text summaries. The objective of the visual chapter summaries is to provide a detailed summary of key concepts and terms in an engaging and meaningful way.

CHAPTER REVIEW

MULTIPLE CHOICE

Circle the letter or fill in the correct answer.

1. The Internet was launched in 1969 when the U.S. funded a project to develop a national computer network called _____.
   a. ARPANET
   b. CERN
   c. WWW
   d. the Web
   e. IRC

2. _____ use telephone lines and service an area consisting of several states.
   a. Wireless service providers
   b. National service providers
   c. Local service providers
   d. Regional service providers
   e. Commercial ISPs

3. _____ present focused content to appeal to special-interest groups.
   a. Agents
   b. Horizontal portals
   c. Vertical portals
   d. Web portals
   e. UseNets

4. To participate in a chat group, select a _____ and communicate live with others.
   a. signal
   b. index
   c. engine
   d. list

5. Bots are also known as _____ an
   a. indexes, hits
   b. agents, spiders
   c. providers, hits

6. In a directory or _____ search, y
   a. packet
   b. keyword
   c. index

7. In _____ commerce, individuals
   a. C2C
   b. B2C
   c. B2B

8. _____ are programs that are aut
   a. Add-ins
   b. Plug-ins
   c. Helpers

9. _____ are independent programs
   a. Plug-ins
   b. Add-ons
   c. Providers

10. _____ are programs that automa and save them to your hard disk.
   a. Off-line browsers
   b. We
   c. Pu

MATCHING

Match each numbered item with the most closely related lettered item. Write your answers in the spaces provided.

a. Web portal
b. cyberspace
c. surfing
d. header
e. lurking
f. subscription address
g. Web auction
h. provider
i. metasearch engine
j. Web storefronts
k. commerce server
l. URLs
m. applets

sh
ature line
r. bots
s. e-commerce
t. carders

1. The space of electronic movement of ideas and information. ____
2. The most common way to access the Internet. ____
3. Addresses of Web resources. ____
4. Moving from one Web site to another. ____
5. Special programs written in Java. ____
6. Sites that offer a variety of services and are designed to act as a home base for users on the Web. ____
7. Part of an e-mail message that includes the subject, address, and attachments. ____
8. Typically includes the sender's name, address, and telephone number. ____
9. To participate in a mailing list, you must send a request to this address. ____
10. The most popular chat service. ____
11. Reading and observing discussions without participating. ____
12. Special programs that look for new information and update a search service database. ____
13. The list of sites that contain the keywords of a keyword search. ____
14. Program that automatically submits a search request to several search engines simultaneously. ____
15. Buying and selling goods over the Internet. ____
16. Program for creating Web sites for virtual stores. ____
17. Virtual stores where shoppers inspect goods and make purchases. ____
18. Similar to a traditional auction, but buyers and sellers interact only on the Web. ____
19. Criminals that specialize in stealing, trading, and using stolen credit cards over the Internet. ____
20. Internet equivalent to traditional cash. ____

OPEN-ENDED

On a separate sheet of paper, respond to each question or statement.

1. Discuss the uses of the Internet. Which activities have you participated in? Which one do you think is the most popular?
2. Explain the differences between the three types of providers.
3. What are the basic elements of an e-mail message?
4. What are the types of discussion groups? Describe any groups you participate in.
5. Describe the different types of search engine. What kinds of information does each return? Give an example of the type of search each engine is best for.

USING TECHNOLOGY

1 Instant Messaging

Do you enjoy chatting with your friends? Are you working on a project and need to collaborate with others in your group? Perhaps instant messaging is just what you're looking for. It's easy and free with an Internet connection and the right software. To learn more about instant messaging, review Making IT Work for You: Instant Messaging on pages 212 and 213. Then visit our Web site at http://www.mhhe.com/oleary, play the videos, and answer the following questions in a one-page paper: (a) What is the URL for creating a new AOL Instant Messenger account? (b) What users appear in the buddy list? (c) What users enter the newly created chat room?

2 Online Shopping

Shopping on the Internet can be a fast and convenient. Connect to our Web site at http://www.mhhe.com/oleary to link to a popular shopping site. Once there, try shopping for one or two products, and answer the following questions in a one-page paper: (a) What are the pros and cons of shopping online versus a traditional store? (b) What assurance does the site provide that personal information such as your credit card number will be secure when purchasing online? (c) What is this site's return policy? (d) Would you buy items from this site? Why or why not?

230   **CHAPTER 8**   The Internet, the Web, and Electronic Commerce

Using Technology appears in every chapter with two Web-related end-of-chapter exercises that direct students to explore current popular uses of technology. In most cases, the first question requires the student to view one of the Making IT Work for You Web-delivered demonstrations and to respond to a series of related questions. The other question requires Web research. One objective of the Using Technology feature is to provide support for instructors who want their students to view the demonstration on the Web rather than in class. The other objective is to provide a powerful tool to engage and motivate students by providing assignments related to technology that directly relates to them.

EXPANDING YOUR KNOWLEDGE

Interactive Companion CD-ROM 1

Complete the "Internet Overview" Lab located on your Interactive Companion CD-ROM, and then answer the following questions i n a one-page paper: (a) What types of Internet communications software are reviewed in the Lab? (b) What are **plug-ins**, and why are they useful? (c) In what ways is cable modem service different from DSL?

E-cash 2

Using e-cash is one way to add a level of security to online purchases. Research two or three companies that specialize in e-cash, and then answer the following questions in a one-page paper: (a) How is e-cash more secure than paying by cash, check, or credit card? (b) What does e-cash cost? Are there fees for the buyer? What about the seller? (c) How widely accepted is e-cash? Do all sites accept it? (d) Would you use e-cash for an online purchase today? Why or why not?

Expanding Your Knowledge appears in every chapter with two Web-related end-of-chapter exercises directing students to enhance their depth of knowledge on specific technologies introduced in the chapter. In most cases, the first question requires the students to use their free Interactive Companion CD-ROM and to respond to a series of related questions. The second question requires Web research into carefully selected topics. One objective of the Expanding Your Knowledge feature is to provide support for instructors who want their students to effectively use the free Interactive CD-ROM. The other objective is to support instructors who want their students to obtain greater in-depth understanding of key technologies.

1 Electronic Commerce

Electronic commerce is one of the most exciting Web applications. Write a two-page paper titled "Electronic Commerce" that addresses the following: (a) Define electronic commerce including B2C, C2C, and B2B. Provide examples. (b) What types of businesses and consumers are most affected by electronic commerce today? What types will be affected in the future? Discuss and justify your positions. (c) What are the greatest challenges to future developments in electronic commerce? Discuss and justify your conclusions.

2 Free Speech Online

Some feel that there is too much objectionable material allowed on the Internet, whereas others argue that the Internet should be completely uncensored. Consider these two viewpoints and answer the following questions in a two-page paper: (a) Should religious groups be allowed to distribute information over the Internet? What about groups that advocate hatred or oppression? (b) Is there any material you feel should not be freely available on the Web? What about child pornography? (c) If you think some regulation is required, who should determine what restrictions should be imposed? (d) The Internet is not "owned" by a particular group or country. What limitations does this impose on enforcement of restrictions?

Building Your Portfolio appears in every chapter with Web-related end-of-chapter exercises directing students to prepare and to write a one- or two-page paper on critical technology-related issues. The first question requires students to summarize and analyze select emerging technologies addressed in the chapter. The second question focuses on a critical chapter-related privacy, security, and/or ethical issue. Students are required to consider, evaluate, and formulate a position. One objective of the Building Your Portfolio feature is to support instructors who want their students to develop critical thinking and writing skills. Another objective is to provide support for instructors who want their students to create written document(s) recording their technology knowledge. A third objective is to provide support for instructors who want their students to recognize, understand, and analyze key privacy, security, and ethical issues relating to technology.

32 **CHAPTER 8** The Internet, the Web, and Electronic Commerce

Online Learning Center

Student Center

Instructor Center

Information Center

(P) preferences
(F) feedback
(H) help center

McGraw-Hill Irwin

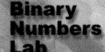

Computing Essentials 2002-2003, 14/e
Timothy J. O'Leary
Linda I. O'Leary

The Student Center content with testbank is available for WebCT, Blackboard, and McGraw-Hill's PageOut course management systems. For more information instructors should visit McGraw-Hill Digital Solutions.

2002 2003

Online Learning Center For each chapter, the student Online Learning Center offers both a review of the text material, and additional exercises organized around the following themes: Group/team projects, Internet/Web-related content, mini case studies of actual companies, and profiles of careers that are influenced by information technology. The content and activities for the exercises further establish O'Leary's three-level learning approach.

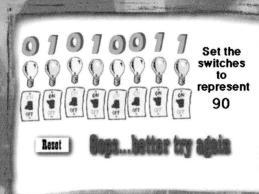

Binary Numbers Lab

Concept
Making numbers from binary
DIGI available!
Detail:
Places are bases.

0 1 0 1 0 0 1 1

Set the switches to represent 90

Reset   Oops...better try again

Finally, to round it out, each "place" is the base, raised to the place location, remember? So, in decimal, the ones place is 10^0, the tens is 10^1, hundreds is 10^2, thousands is 10^3. and so on.

Of course, it's the same in the binary:
ones is 2^0; twos is 2^1; fours is 2^2; 8 = 2^3; 16 = 2^4; 32 = 2^5; 64 = 2^6; 128 = 2^7.

Interactive Companion CD-ROM
Use this free CD-ROM to explore some of the most popular topics in information technology. Video, interactive exercises, animation and actual "labs" expand the reach and scope of the textbook.

Computing Essentials 2002-2003

INFORMATION TECHNOLOGY, THE INTERNET, AND YOU

After you have read this chapter, you should be able to:

1 Explain the five parts of an information system: people, procedures, software, hardware, and data.

2 Distinguish application software from system software.

3 Distinguish four kinds of computers—microcomputer, minicomputer, mainframe, and supercomputer—and describe hardware devices for input, processing, storage, and output.

4 Describe document, worksheet, database, and presentation files.

5 Explain computer connectivity, the Wireless Revolution, and the Internet.

Computer competency: This notion may not be familiar to you, but it's easy to understand. The purpose of this book is to help you become **competent** in computer-related skills. Specifically, we want to help you walk into a job and immediately be valuable to an employer. In this chapter, we first present an overview of what makes up an information system: people, procedures, software, hardware, and data. Competent end users need to understand these basic parts and how connectivity through the Internet and the Web expands the role of information technology (IT) in our lives. In subsequent chapters, we will describe these parts of information systems in detail.

Fifteen years ago, most people had little to do with computers, at least directly. Of course, they filled out computerized forms, took computerized tests, and paid computerized bills. But the real work with computers was handled by specialists—programmers, data entry clerks, and computer operators.

Then microcomputers came along and changed everything. Today it is easy for nearly everybody to use a computer. People who use microcomputers are called **end users.** Now:

- Microcomputers are common tools in all areas of life. Writers write, artists draw, engineers and scientists calculate—all on microcomputers. Students and businesspeople do all this, and more.

- New forms of learning have developed. People who are homebound, who work odd hours, or who travel frequently may take courses on the Web. A college course need not fit within the usual time of a quarter or a semester.

- New ways to communicate, to find people with similar interests, and to buy goods are available. All kinds of people are using electronic mail, electronic commerce, and the Internet to meet and to share ideas and products.

What about you? How can microcomputers enhance **your** life?

Chapter 1

Many interesting and practical uses for information technology have recently surfaced to make our personal lives richer and more entertaining. These applications range from recording video clips to creating personalized Web sites. (See Making IT Work for You below.) What about you? How can information technology and microcomputers enhance your life?

Competent end users need to know the five parts of an information system: people, procedures, software, hardware, and data. Additionally, they need to understand connectivity, the wireless revolution, the Internet, and the Web and to recognize the role of information technology in their professional and personal lives.

MAKING **IT** WORK FOR YOU

TV Tuner Cards and Video Clips
Want to watch your favorite television program while you work? Perhaps you would like to include a video clip from television in a class presentation. It's easy using a TV tuner card.

Voice Recognition Systems and Dictating a Paper
Tired of using your keyboard to type term papers and to control programs? Voice recognition may be just what you're looking for.

CD-R Drives and Music from the Internet
Did you know that you could use the Internet to locate music, download it to your computer, and create your own compact discs? All it takes is the right software, hardware, and a connection to the Internet.

Instant Messaging
Do you enjoy chatting with your friends? Are you working on a project and need to collaborate with others in your group? Perhaps instant messaging is just what you're looking for.

Personal Web Site
Do you have anything to share with the world? Would you like a personal Web site but don't want to deal with learning HTML and paying for server time? Many services are available to get you started for FREE!

INFORMATION SYSTEMS

> An information system has five parts: people, procedures, software, hardware, and data.

When you think of a microcomputer, perhaps you think of just the equipment itself. That is, you think of the monitor or the keyboard. There is more to it than that. The way to think about a microcomputer is as part of an information system. An **information system** has five parts: *people, procedures, software, hardware,* and *data.* (See Figure 1-1.)

- **People:** It is easy to overlook people as one of the five parts of a microcomputer system. Yet this is what microcomputers are all about— making **people,** end users like yourself, more productive.

- **Procedures:** The rules or guidelines people follow when using software, hardware, and data are **procedures.** Typically, these procedures are documented in manuals written by computer specialists. Software and hardware manufacturers provide manuals with their products.

- **Software:** A **program** consists of the step-by-step instructions that tell the computer how to do its work. **Software** is another name for a program or programs. The purpose of software is to convert *data* (unprocessed facts) into *information* (processed facts).

- **Hardware:** The equipment that processes the data to create information is called **hardware.** It includes the keyboard, mouse, monitor, system unit, and other devices. Hardware is controlled by software.

- **Data:** The raw, unprocessed facts, including text, numbers, images, and sounds are called **data.** Examples of raw facts are hours you worked and your pay rate. After data is processed through the computer, it is usually called **information.** An example of such information is the total wages owed you for a week's work.

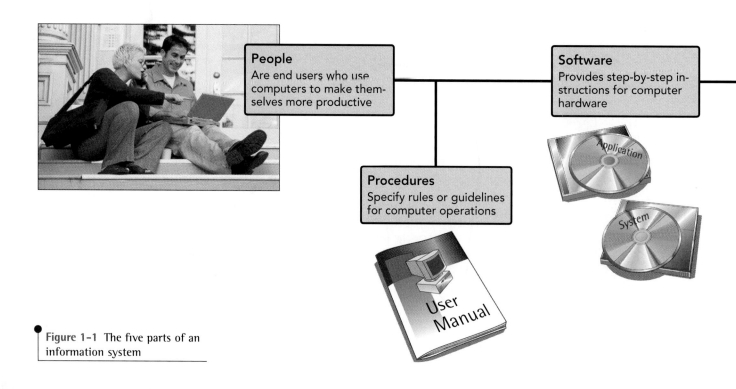

People
Are end users who use computers to make themselves more productive

Procedures
Specify rules or guidelines for computer operations

Software
Provides step-by-step instructions for computer hardware

Figure 1-1 The five parts of an information system

Almost all of today's computer systems add an additional part to the information system. This part, collected **connectivity,** allows computers to connect and to share information. These connections can be by telephone lines, cable, or through the air. Connectivity allows users to greatly expand the capability and usefulness of their information systems.

In large computer systems, there are specialists who deal with writing procedures, developing software, and capturing data. In microcomputer systems, however, end users often perform these operations. To be a competent end user, you must understand the essentials of **information technology (IT),** including software, hardware, and data.

Concept Check

✓ What are the five parts of an information system?

✓ What is required of a competent end user?

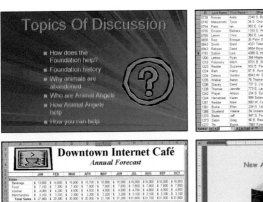

Data
Consists of unprocessed facts including text, numbers, images, and sounds

Hardware
Includes keyboard, mouse, monitor, system unit, and other devices

Connectivity
Allows computers to share information and to connect to the Internet

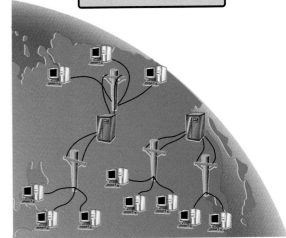

PEOPLE

People are the most important part of an information system. Examples include people in entertainment, medicine, education, and business.

Although easy to overlook, people are surely the most important part of any information system. Our lives are touched every day by computers and information systems. Many times the contact is direct and obvious such as when we create documents using a word processing program or when we connect to the Internet.

Other times, the contact is not as obvious. Nonetheless, computers and information systems touch our lives hundreds of times every day. Consider just the following four examples. (See Figure 1-2.)

People just like you are making information technology work for them every day. Throughout this book you will find a variety of features designed to make technology work for you. Three such features are Making IT Work for You topics, Tips, and On the Web Explorations. (See pages 7 and 8.)

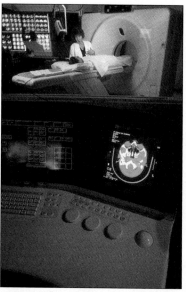

Figure 1-2 Computers in business, medicine, entertainment, and education

Information technology touches our lives every day in a personal way. Many interesting and practical uses of IT have recently surfaced to make our lives richer and more entertaining. In the following chapters, you will find these applications presented in detail.

INFORMATION TECHNOLOGY TOPICS

Web-based Applications Would you like access to free general-purpose applications from anywhere in the world? What about accessing your data files from any location? You can have it all with Web-based applications. See page 32.

Active Desktop Want to add some interest to your desktop? Would you like to see the most recent sports scores, news, or stock market updates? You can customize your desktop to provide that information and much more. See page 68.

TV Tuner Cards and Video Clips Want to watch your favorite television program while you work? Perhaps you would like to include a video clip from television in a class presentation. It's easy using a video TV card. See page 98.

Voice Recognition Systems and Dictating a Paper Tired of using your keyboard to type term papers and to control programs? Voice recognition may be just what you're looking for. See page 124.

Internet Telephones Want to make long distance calls for almost no cost using the Internet? It's easy and all you need is some software and an Internet connection to get started. See page 134.

CD-R Drives and Music from the Internet Did you know that you could use the Internet to locate music, download it to your computer, and create your own compact discs? All it takes is the right software, hardware, and a connection to the Internet. See page 156.

Home Networking Computer networks are not just for corporations and schools anymore. If you have more than one computer, you can use a home network to share files and printers, to allow multiple users access to the Internet at the same time, and to play interactive computer games. See page 186.

Personal Web Site Do you have anything to share with the world? Would you like a personal Web site but don't want to deal with learning HTML and paying for server time? Many services are available to get you started for FREE! See page 204.

Instant Messaging Do you enjoy chatting with your friends? Are you working on a project and need to collaborate with others in your group? Perhaps instant messaging is just what you're looking for. See page 212.

Virus Protection Has your computer ever been attacked by a computer virus? If not, chances are that it will in the near future. Fortunately, special software is available to protect you against computer viruses. See page 244.

Online Job Opportunities Did you know that you could use the Internet to find a job? You can browse through job openings, post your resume, and even use special programs that will search for the job that's just right for you.

TIPS AND WEB EXPLORATIONS

Two other features in this book that make technology work for you are a variety of Tips and On the Web Explorations.

We all can benefit from a few tips or suggestions. Throughout this book you'll find numerous tips ranging from the basics of cleaning a monitor to how to efficiently locate information on the Web. Just a few of these tips are listed below. For a more complete list go to: http://www.mhhe.com/oleary.

- **Inserting audio clips.** Want to add some interest and a personal touch to your correspondence? You can, by including an audio clip of your voice in a text document. See page 36.

- **Improving slow computer operations.** Does your computer seem to be getting slower and slower? Consider a few suggestions that might add a little zip to your current system. See page 97.

- **Cleaning your keyboard.** Is your keyboard looking tired and dirty? Are the keys sticking? Consider a few cleaning suggestions. See page 117.

- **Improving printed output.** Are your printouts blurry or smeared? It could be time to clean your printer. See page 129.

- **Playing music on your computer.** Do you like to listen to music while working on your computer? If you have a CD-ROM drive you can use it to play your favorite CDs while you work. See page 154.

- **Improving your e-mail.** Concerned your e-mail messages may be overlooked? Review some guidelines that will help insure your message gets across. See page 210.

- **Internet privacy.** Are you concerned about your privacy while on the Web? Consider some suggestions on protecting your identity online. See page 240.

There are numerous outstanding and informative Web sites. Throughout this book you will find several On the Web Explorations directing you to some of the best Web sites. Just a few of these are listed at the right. For a complete list, go to: http://www.mhhe.com/oleary.

On the Web Explorations

- Hotmail offers free e-mail service. See page 211.
- America Online provides an array of online services.
- Cosmo Software creates virtual reality applications on the Web. See *Complete* edition, page 274.
- Pretty Good Privacy develops encryption programs. See page 248.
- The Center for Democracy and Technology monitors privacy issues and legislation. See page 240.
- Macromedia, Inc., develops multimedia authoring programs. See *Complete* edition, page 269.
- Dragon Systems develops continuous-speech systems. See page 123.

SOFTWARE

Software, as we mentioned, is another name for programs. Programs are the instructions that tell the computer how to process data into the form you want. In most cases, the words *software* and *programs* are interchangeable.

> Software is of two kinds: system software and application software.

There are two major kinds of software—*system software* and *application software*. You can think of application software as the kind you use. Think of system software as the kind the computer uses.

SYSTEM SOFTWARE

The user interacts with application software. **System software** enables the application software to interact with the computer hardware. System software is "background" software that helps the computer manage its own internal resources.

The most important system software program is the **operating system,** which interacts with the application software and the computer. The operating system handles such details as running ("executing") programs, storing data and programs, and processing data. Windows XP is one of the best-known operating systems for today's microcomputer users. (See Figure 1-3.)

APPLICATION SOFTWARE

Application software might be described as "end-user" software. These programs are designed to address general-purpose and special-purpose applications.

General-purpose programs, or basic applications, are widely used in nearly all career areas. They are the kind of programs you *have* to know to be considered computer competent. One of these basic applications is a browser to navigate, explore, and find information on the Internet. (See Figure 1-4.) The two most widely used browsers are Microsoft's Internet Explorer and Netscape's Navigator. For a summary of the basic applications, see Figure 1-5.

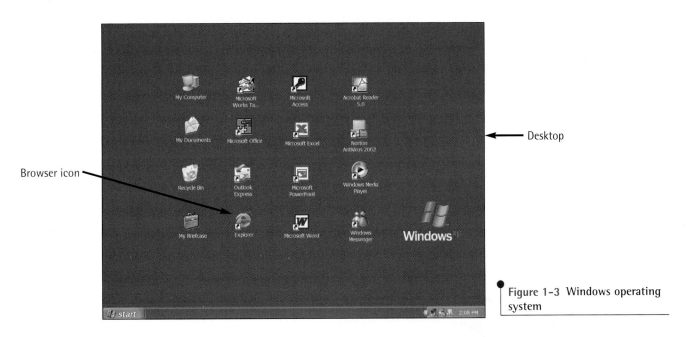

Desktop

Browser icon

Figure 1-3 Windows operating system

Location box

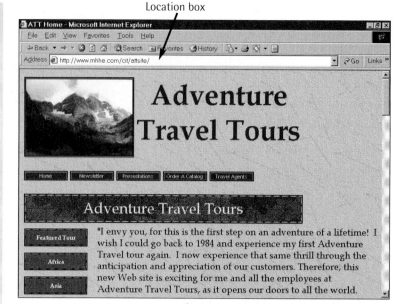

Figure 1-4 Browser (Internet Explorer)

Have you used the Internet? If so, then you probably already know how to use a browser. For those of you who do not, here are a few tips to get you started.

1 Start browser. Typically, all you need to do is double-click the browser's icon on the desktop.

2 Enter URL. In the browser's location box, type the URL (uniform resource locator, or address) of the Internet or Web location (site) that you want to visit.

3 Press ENTER. On your keyboard, press the ENTER key to connect to the site.

4 Read and explore. Once connected to the site, read the information displayed on your monitor. Using the mouse, move the pointer on the mointor. When the pointer changes from an arrow to a hand, click the mouse button to explore other locations.

5 Close browser. Once you are done exploring, click on your browser's CLOSE button.

Type	Description
Browser	Connect to Web sites and display Web pages
Word processor	Prepare written documents
Spreadsheet	Analyze and summarize numerical data
Database management system	Organize and manage data and information
Presentation graphics	Communicate a message or persuade other people

Figure 1-5 Basic applications

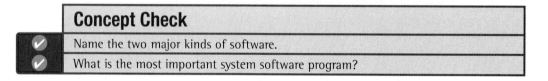

Concept Check

✓ Name the two major kinds of software.

✓ What is the most important system software program?

HARDWARE

Four types of computers are supercomputer, mainframe computer, minicomputer, and microcomputer. Microcomputer hardware consists of the system unit, input/output, secondary storage, and communications devices.

Computers are electronic devices that can follow instructions to accept input, process that input, and produce information. This book focuses principally on microcomputers. However, it is almost certain that you will come in contact, at least indirectly, with other types of computers.

TYPES OF COMPUTERS

There are four types of computers: supercomputers, mainframe computers, minicomputers, and microcomputers.

- **Supercomputers** are the most powerful type of computer. These machines are special high-capacity computers used by very large organizations. For example, NASA uses supercomputers to track and control space explorations.

- **Mainframe computers** occupy specially wired, air-conditioned rooms. Although not nearly as powerful as supercomputers, mainframe computers are capable of great processing speeds and data storage. (See Figure 1-6.) For example, insurance companies use mainframes to process information about millions of policyholders.

- **Minicomputers,** also known as **midrange computers,** are desk-sized machines. Medium-sized companies or departments of large companies typically use them for specific purposes. For example, production departments use minicomputers to monitor certain manufacturing processes and assembly line operations.

- **Microcomputers** are the least powerful, yet are the most widely used and fastest-growing type of computer. Categories of microcomputer include *desktop, notebook,* and *personal digital assistants.* (See Figure 1-7.) **Desktop computers** are small enough to fit on top of or alongside a desk yet are too big to carry around. **Notebook computers** are portable, weigh between 4 and 10 pounds, and fit into most briefcases. **Personal digital assistants (PDAs)** are also known as **palmtop computers** or **handheld computers.** They combine pen input, writing recognition, personal organizational tools, and communications capabilities in a very small package.

Figure 1-6 Mainframe computer

Colorful desktop computers from Apple (iMac)

Notebook computer

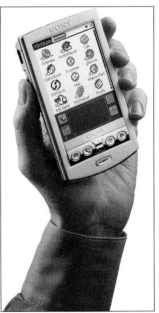

Personal digital assistant

Figure 1-7

Hardware

MICROCOMPUTER HARDWARE

Hardware for a microcomputer system consists of a variety of different devices. See Figure 1-8 for a typical desktop system. This physical equipment falls into three basic categories: system unit, input/output, and secondary storage. Because we discuss hardware in detail later in this book, we will present just a quick overview here.

- **System unit:** The **system unit,** also known as the **system cabinet** or **chassis,** is a container that houses most of the electronic components that make up a computer system. (See Figure 1-9.) Two important components

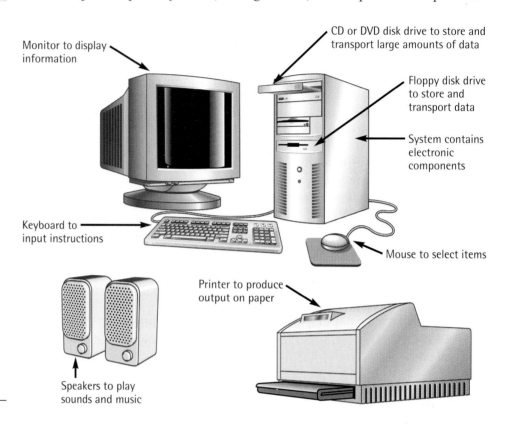

Monitor to display
information

CD or DVD disk drive to store and
transport large amounts of data

Floppy disk drive
to store and
transport data

System contains
electronic
components

Keyboard to
input instructions

Mouse to select items

Printer to produce
output on paper

Speakers to play
sounds and music

Figure 1-8 Microcomputer
system

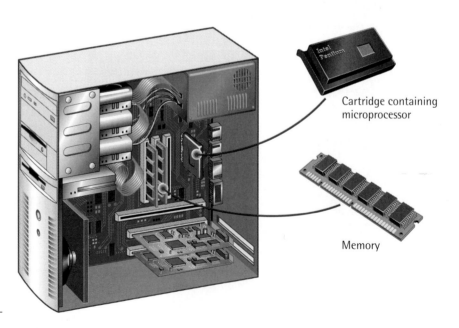

Cartridge containing
microprocessor

Memory

Figure 1-9 System unit

Figure 1–10 Keyboard and mouse

of the system unit are the *microprocessor* and *memory*. The **microprocessor** controls and manipulates data to produce information. Many times the microprocessor is contained with a protective cartridge. **Memory,** also known as **primary storage** or **random access memory (RAM),** holds data and program instructions for processing the data. It also holds the processed information before it is output. Memory is sometimes referred to as *temporary storage* because its contents will typically be lost if the electrical power to the computer is disrupted.

Figure 1–11 Monitor

- **Input/output devices: Input devices** translate data and programs that humans can understand into a form that the computer can process. The most common input devices are the **keyboard** and the **mouse.** (See Figure 1-10.) **Output devices** translate the processed information from the computer into a form that humans can understand. The most common output devices are **monitors** or **video display screens** (see Figure 1-11) and **printers.**

Figure 1–12 A 3½-inch floppy disk

- **Secondary storage devices:** Unlike memory, **secondary storage devices** hold data and programs even after electrical power to the computer system has been turned off. The most important kinds of secondary media are *floppy, hard,* and *optical disks.* **Floppy disks** are widely used to store and transport data from one computer to another. (See Figure 1-12.) They are called floppy because data is stored on a very thin flexible, or floppy, plastic disk. **Hard disks** are typically used to store programs and very large data files. Using a rigid metallic platter, hard disks have a much greater capacity and are able to access information much faster than floppy disks. **Optical disks** use laser technology and have the greatest capacity. (See Figure 1-13.) The two basic types of optical disks are **compact discs (CDs)** and **digital versatile (or video) discs (DVDs).**

Figure 1–13 An optical disk

Concept Check

 List the four types of computers.

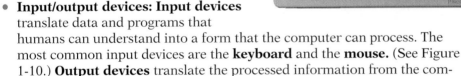 Describe the three categories of microcomputer hardware.

> Data is stored in document, worksheet, database, and presentation files.

Data is used to describe facts about something. When stored electronically in files, data can be used directly as input for the information system. Four common types of files (see Figure 1-14) are:

- **Document files,** created by word processors to save documents such as memos, term papers, and letters.
- **Worksheet files,** created by electronic spreadsheets to analyze things like budgets and to predict sales.
- **Database files,** typically created by database management programs to contain highly structured and organized data. For example, an employee database file might contain all the workers' names, social security numbers, job titles, and other related pieces of information.
- **Presentation files,** created by presentation graphics programs to save presentation materials. For example, a file might contain audience handouts, speaker notes, and electronic slides.

Concept Check

✓ How is data used?

✓ List four common types of files.

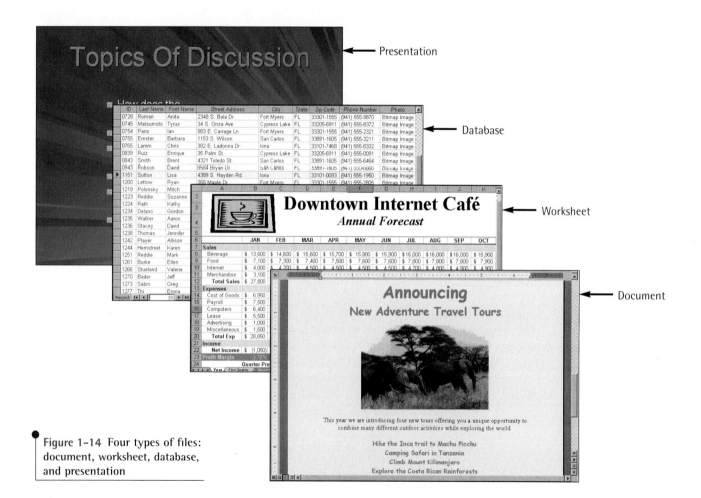

Figure 1-14 Four types of files: document, worksheet, database, and presentation

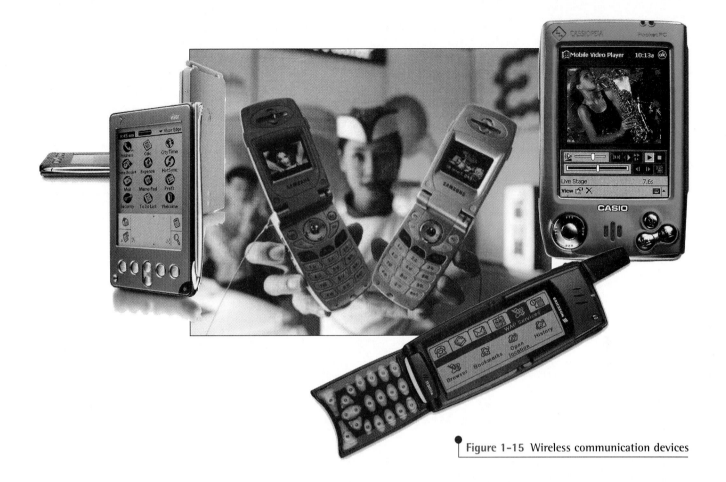

Figure 1-15 Wireless communication devices

CONNECTIVITY, THE WIRELESS REVOLUTION, AND THE INTERNET

Connectivity is the capability of your microcomputer to share information with other computers. Data and information can be sent over telephone lines or cable and through the air. Thus, your microcomputer can be *connected* to other computers. It can connect you to the Internet and to many computerized data banks and other sources of information that lie well beyond your desk.

> Connectivity is the microcomputer's ability to communicate with other computers and information sources. The Internet is the largest network in the world.

The single most dramatic change in connectivity in the past five years has been the widespread use of mobile or wireless communication devices. Once used exclusively for telephone communications, these devices are now widely used to connect people and computers located almost anywhere in the world. For just a few of these devices, see Figure 1-15. Many experts predict that these wireless applications are just the beginning of the **wireless revolution**, a revolution that is expected to dramatically affect the way we communicate and use computer technology.

Connectivity and the wireless revolution are significant developments, for they expand the uses of the microcomputer severalfold. Central to the concept of connectivity is the **computer network.** A network is a communications system connecting two or more computers. Networks connect people as close as the next office and as far away as halfway around the world.

The largest network in the world is the **Internet.** It is like a giant highway that connects you to millions of other people and organizations located throughout the world. (See Figure 1-16.) The Internet is a huge computer network available to nearly everyone with a microcomputer and a means to connect to it. The **Web,** also known as the **World Wide Web** or **WWW,** is an Internet service that provides a multimedia interface to numerous resources available on the Internet.

Concept Check

✔ Define connectivity.

✔ What is the Internet?

A Look to the Future

Establishing Computer Competency

Computer competency is understanding the rules and the power of micro-computers. Competency lets you take advantage of increasingly productive software, hardware, and the connectivity revolution that are expanding the microcomputer's capabilities.

The purpose of this book is to help you be computer competent not only in the present but also in the future. Having competency requires your having the knowledge and understanding of the rules and the power of the microcomputer. This will enable you to benefit from three important information technology developments: more powerful software, more powerful hardware, and connectivity to outside information resources. It will also help you remain computer competent and continue to learn in the future.

POWERFUL SOFTWARE

The software now available can do an extraordinary number of tasks and help you in an endless number of ways. More and more employers are expecting the people they hire to be able to use it. Basic application software and system software are discussed in Chapters 2 and 3.

POWERFUL HARDWARE

Microcomputers are now much more powerful than they used to be. Indeed, the newer models have the speed and power of room-size computers of only a few years ago. However, despite the rapid change of specific equipment, their essential features remain unchanged. Thus, the competent end user should focus on these features. Chapters 4 through 6 explain what you need to know about hardware: the central processing unit, input/output devices, and secondary storage. A Buyer's Guide and an Upgrader's Guide are presented at the end of this book for those considering the purchase or upgrade of a microcomputer system.

CONNECTIVITY, THE INTERNET, AND THE WEB

No longer are microcomputers and competent end users bound by the surface of the desk. Now they can reach past the desk and link with other computers to share data, programs, and information. The Internet and the Web are considered by most to be the two most important technologies for the 21st century.

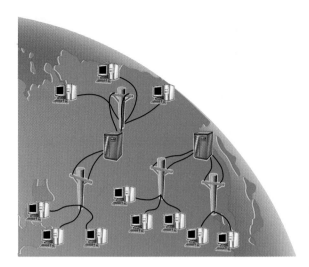

Figure 1-16 The Internet connects millions of people and computers worldwide

Accordingly, we devote Chapters 7 and 8 to discussing connectivity, the wireless revolution, communications, the Internet, and the Web.

SECURITY AND PRIVACY

What about people? Is there a downside to all these technological advances? Experts agree that we as a society must be careful about the potential of technology to negatively impact our personal privacy and security. Additionally, we need to be aware of potential physical and mental health risks associated with using technology. Finally, we need to be aware of negative effects on our environment caused by the manufacture of computer-related products. Thus, Chapter 9 explores each of these critical issues in detail.

CHANGING TIMES

Are the times changing any faster now than they ever have? Most people think so. Those who were alive when radios, cars, and airplanes were being introduced certainly lived through some dramatic changes. Has technology made our own times even more dynamic? Whatever the answer, it is clear we live in a fast-paced age. The Evolution of the Computer Age section presented at the end of this book tracks the major developments since computers were first introduced.

Most businesses have become aware that they must adapt to changing technology or be left behind. Many organizations are now making formal plans to keep track of technology and implement it in their competitive strategies. Nearly every corporation in the world has a presence on the Internet. Delivery services such as Federal Express and UPS provide customers with the ability to personally track the delivery of their packages. Retail stores such as JCPenney and Wal-Mart provide catalog support and sales. Banks such as Wells Fargo and Citibank support home banking and electronic commerce. You can even purchase tickets to music, theater, and sporting events on the Internet.

Clearly, such changes do away with some jobs—those of many bank tellers and cashiers, for example. However, they create opportunities for other people. New technology requires people who are truly capable of working with it. These are not the people who think every piece of equipment is so simple they can just turn it on and use it. Nor are they those who think each new machine is a potential disaster. In other words, new technology needs people who are not afraid to learn it and are able to manage it. The real issue, then, is not how to make technology better. Rather, it is how to integrate the technology with people.

After reading this book, you will be in a very favorable position compared with many other people in industry today. You will learn not only the basics of hardware, software, connectivity, the Internet, and the Web. You will also learn the most current technology. You will therefore be able to use these tools to your advantage—to be a winner.

A Look to the Future

INFORMATION SYSTEMS

The way to think about a microcomputer is to realize that it is one part of an **information system.** Five parts of an information system:

1. **People** are obviously the essential part of the system! The purpose of information systems is to make people, or end users like you, more productive.

2. **Procedures** are rules or guidelines to follow when using software, hardware, and data. They are typically documented in manuals written by computer professionals.

3. **Software** (**programs**) provides step-by-step instructions to control the computer to convert **data** into **information.**

4. **Hardware** consists of the physical equipment. It is controlled by software and processes data to create information.

5. **Data** consists of unprocessed facts including text, numbers, images, and sound. **Information** is data that has been processed by the computer.

PEOPLE

People are the most important part of an information system. People are touched hundreds of times daily by computers.

Some examples of how information technology can work for you:

Entertainment

Business

PROCEDURES

Procedures are the rules or guidelines people follow when using software, hardware, and data. These procedures are usually documented in manuals provided by manufacturers with their products.

To prepare for your future as a competent end user, you need to understand the basic parts of an information system: people, procedures, software, hardware, and data. Also you need to understand connectivity through the Internet and the Web and to recognize the role of technology in our professional and personal lives.

SOFTWARE

Software or **programs** consist of system and application software.

System Software

System software—*background* software that manages internal resources. An example is an operating system such as Windows XP.

Application Software

Application software—software that performs useful work on general-purpose problems. Basic applications include:

- **Browser** to connect to Web sites and display Web pages.
- **Word processor** to prepare written documents.
- **Spreadsheet** to analyze and summarize numerical data.
- **Database management system** to organize and manage data.
- **Presentation graphics** to communicate or persuade.

HARDWARE

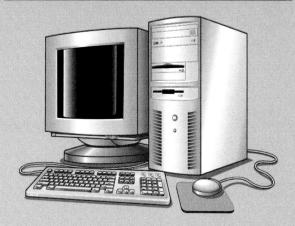

Hardware is the physical equipment in an information system.

Types of Computers

There are four types of computers:

- **Supercomputers**—the most powerful.
- **Mainframe**—used by large companies.
- **Minicomputers**—also known as **midrange computers.**
- **Microcomputers**—the fastest growing type. Categories include **desktop, notebook,** and **personal digital assistant.**

Microcomputer Hardware

The three categories of devices are:

- The **system unit** contains the electronic circuitry, including the CPU and memory.
- **Input/output devices** are translators between humans and computers.
- **Secondary storage devices** store data and programs. Typical media include **floppy, hard,** and **optical disks.**

Visual Summary

DATA

Data describes something and is typically stored electronically in a file.

Common types of files are:

Document

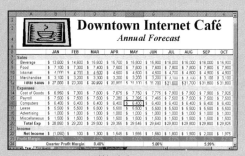

Worksheet

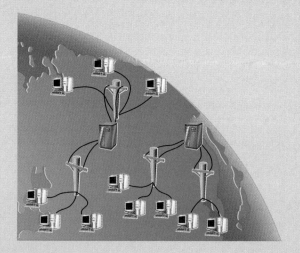

Database

Presentation

CONNECTIVITY AND THE INTERNET

Connectivity

Connectivity is a concept describing the ability of end users to tap into resources well beyond their desktops. Computer **networks** are connected computers that share data and resources.

The Wireless Revolution

The wireless revolution is the widespread and increasing use of mobile (wireless) communication devices.

Internet

The **Internet** is the world's largest computer network. The **Web,** also known as the **World Wide Web (WWW),** is an Internet service that provides a multimedia interface to resources available on the Internet.

application software (9)
chassis (12)
compact disc (CD) (13)
computer competency (2)
computer network (15)
connectivity (5, 15)
data (4)
database file (14)
desktop computer (11)
digital versatile (or video) disc (DVD) (13)
document file (14)
end user (2)
floppy disk (13)
handheld computer (11)
hard disk (13)
hardware (4)
information (4)
information system (18)
information technology (IT) (5)
input device (13)
Internet (16)
keyboard (13)
mainframe computer (11)
memory (13)
microcomputer (11)
microprocessor (13)
midrange computer (11)

minicomputer (11)
monitor (13)
mouse (13)
notebook computer (11)
operating system (9)
optical disk (13)
output device (13)
palmtop computer (11)
people (4)
personal digital assistant (PDA) (11)
presentation file (14)
primary storage (13)
printer (13)
procedures (4)
program (4)
random access memory (RAM) (13)
secondary storage device (13)
software (4)
supercomputer (11)
system cabinet (12)
system software (9)
system unit (12)
video display screen (13)
Web (16)
wireless revolution (15)
worksheet file (14)
World Wide Web (WWW) (16)

CHAPTER REVIEW

MULTIPLE CHOICE

Circle the letter or fill in the correct answer.

1. The _____ consists of the equipment: keyboard, mouse, monitor, system unit, and other devices.
   a. people
   b. procedures
   c. hardware
   d. system unit
   e. information

2. The most important system software program is the _____.
   a. word processor
   b. database management system
   c. operating system
   d. application software
   e. information system

3. A production department might use a _____ to monitor manufacturing processes and assembly line operations.
   a. system unit
   b. mainframe
   c. microcomputer
   d. midrange computer
   e. supercomputer

4. _____ holds data and program instructions for processing data.
   a. Memory
   b. Primary storage
   c. RAM
   d. a and b
   e. a, b, and c

5. The most common input devices are the _____ and the _____.
   a. keyboard, printer
   b. mouse, monitor
   c. printer, monitor
   d. keyboard, microphone
   e. mouse, keyboard

6. _____ are widely used to store and transport data from one computer to another.
   a. Hard disks
   b. Wireless connections
   c. Floppy disks
   d. CD-ROMs
   e. DVD-ROMs

7. A(n) _____ file might contain audience handouts, speaker notes, and electronic slides.
   a. document
   b. database
   c. worksheet
   d. presentation
   e. floppy disk

8. The largest network in the world is called the _____.
   a. Internet
   b. WWW
   c. World Wide Web
   d. Web
   e. all of the above

9. _____ is understanding the rules and the power of microcomputers.
   a. Computer competency
   b. Wireless Revolution
   c. Connectivity
   d. Reactivity
   e. Proactivity

10. The term _____ refers to the widespread use of mobile communication devices.
   a. IT
   b. Wireless Revolution
   c. PDA
   d. RAM
   e. WWW

Match each numbered item with the most closely related lettered item. Write your answers in the spaces provided.

a. application software

b. secondary storage device

c. procedures

d. hard disks

e. database files

f. optical disks

g. connectivity

h. information

i. mainframe computer

j. output device

k. input device

l. computer network

m. document files

n. primary storage

o. supercomputers

p. the Internet

q. microcomputers

r. system unit

s. program

t. system software

1. Guidelines for people to follow when using software, hardware, and data. __c__

2. Consists of the step-by-step instructions that tell the computer how to do its work. __s__

3. Data that has been processed through the computer. __h__

4. Part of an information system that allows computers to connect and share information. __g__

5. Software that enables the application software to interact with the computer hardware. __t__

6. End user software. __a__

7. High-capacity computers used by very large organizations. __o__

8. Capable of great processing speeds and data storage. __i__

9. The least powerful and most widely used type of computer. __q__

10. Container that houses most of the electronic components that make up a computer system. __r__

11. Translates data and programs that humans can understand into a form that the computer can process. __k__

12. Translates processed information from the computer into a form that humans can understand. __j__

13. Holds data and program instructions for processing data. __n__

14. Holds data and programs even after electrical power to the system has been turned off. __d__

15. Typically used to store programs and very large data files. __b__

16. Use laser technology and have the greatest capacity of all secondary storage. __f__

17. Created by word processors to save documents. __m__

18. Typically created by database management programs. __e__

19. Communications system connecting two or more computers. __l__

20. The largest network in the world. __p__

On a separate sheet of paper, respond to each question or statement.

1. Explain the five parts of an information system. What part do people play in this system?

2. What is connectivity? How are the wireless revolution and connectivity related? How are you a part of this revolution?

3. Describe the different types of computers. What is the most common type? How is it used? What is the difference between a mainframe and a supercomputer?

4. What is the difference between input and output? What are the most common input devices?

5. What is system software? What is the most important type of system software? What is the difference between system software and application software? What are the most common basic applications?

USING TECHNOLOGY

Making a habit of keeping current with technology trends is a key to your success with information technology. In the following chapters, the Using Technology feature will ask you to examine some specific applications of current technologies to gain a better understanding of how technology is used today. Some of those technologies are listed below. Select the two that you find the most interesting and describe why they are of interest to you.

- **Desktop and Notebook Computers.** Thinking of buying a new computer? Are you considering a desktop or a notebook? Each has advantages and disadvantages. See page 110.

- **Digital Video Editing.** Digital photography is very popular today. Taking pictures is one thing. Editing the pictures to create interesting effects is another. Digital video editing software, like Adobe Premiere, can turn your computer into an editing studio. See page 142.

- **Ricochet Internet Access.** One of the hottest technologies today is mobile, wireless Internet access. Ricochet is an innovative new technology that provides high-speed Internet access to mobile computer users. See page 196.

- **Virus Protection.** Worried about computer viruses? Concerned about protecting your credit card numbers and other personal information while surfing the Web? Internet security suites are designed to help protect you against viruses and the theft of personal information. See page 261.

- **Instant Messaging.** Are you working on a project and need to collaborate with your group? Instant messaging may fit the bill. It's easy and free. See page 230.

- **Active Desktop.** Would you like sports, weather, or stock updates to appear on your desktop? Desktop customization is easy over the Web. See page 85.

- **Personal Web Sites.** Do you have anything to share with the world? Would you like a personal Web site, but don't want to deal with learning HTML and paying for server time? Many services are available to get you started—for FREE! See **Complete** edition, page 284.

- **Jobs Online.** Did you know that you can use the Internet to find a job? You can browse job listings and post your resume online. See **Complete** edition, page 407, or **Introductory** edition, page 283.

A deeper knowledge of select topics can enhance your understanding of information technology. In the following chapters, the Expanding Your Knowledge feature will direct you to examine some specific technical topics introduced in the chapter. Many of these will direct you to your Interactive Companion CD-ROM. Some of these topics are listed below. Select the two that you believe to be the most important and describe why you selected them.

- **File Organization.** Your computer uses system and user files. What are the differences? What are "hidden" files and how are they used? See page 86.

- **Binary Numbers.** While people use letters and numbers to communicate, computers are only able to understand and process 0s and 1s. How is this accomplished? What are binary numbers and how are they used? See page 111.

- **Computer Anatomy.** Data and programs are stored on secondary storage devices including floppy disks, hard disks, CDs, and magnetic tape. What are the differences between these devices? How much more can be stored on a CD-ROM than on a floppy disk? See page 168.

- **Disk Fragmentation.** Data and programs are stored on disks using sectors and tracks. What is disk fragmentation? What problems can it cause and what precautions should be taken to minimize these problems? See page 168.

- **Network Communications.** Information to be sent over a network is often broken down into smaller parts called packets. These packets are formed, sent, and assembled following protocols. What are packets and protocols? How do they work? See page 197.

- **Online Backup.** A good way to safequard data is to use an online backup service. What are the general features of such services? How can they aid companies in an emergency or natural disaster? See page 262.

- **Handwriting Recognition.** Handwriting recognition is a valuable type of input. What types of devices use handwriting recognition? See page 143.

BUILDING YOUR PORTFOLIO

A portfolio can be used to demonstrate your knowledge of relevant IT topics to a potential employer or recruiter. In the following chapters, the Building Your Portfolio feature will ask you to compose short papers on topics relating to key emerging technologies and technology related security, privacy, and ethical issues. Some of these topics are listed below. Select the two that you would consider to be the most effective to include in your portfolio and describe why you selected them.

- **Linux.** Linux is a powerful operating system used by many computer professionals. What is Linux and why is it receiving so much attention recently? How is Linux being used today? How will it likely be used in the future? See page 87.

- **DVD.** CD technology is being replaced by DVD technology. Compare these two types of technology and define the following terms: **DVD-ROM, DVD-R,** and **DVD-RW.** See page 169.

- **Artificial Intelligence.** Simulating human senses, thought processes, and actions with an eye toward productivity is the goal of Artificial Intelligence. How is it currently used? How can software exhibit Artificial Intelligence? See **Complete** edition, page 286.

- **Antitrust.** Microsoft's legal battles over antitrust issues are well known. What are the key issues in this case? Do you believe that Microsoft has acted unethically? Will the final outcome of this case significantly affect consumers. See page 87.

- **CD-R and Music Files.** Downloading music from the Internet and creating custom CDs is a common activity. Many artists complain that their work is being illegally copied and distributed over the Internet. Do you see a moral, ethical, and/or legal issue related to copying copyrighted music from the Internet? Discuss your position. See page 169.

- **Free Speech Online.** Some people feel there is too much objectionable material allowed on the Internet. Others feel there should be no limits to online content. Should regulations limit available material? See page 232.

APPLICATION SOFTWARE

After you have read this chapter, you should be able to:

1 Discuss common features of most software applications.

2 Describe browsers.

3 Discuss word processors.

4 Describe spreadsheets.

5 Discuss database management systems.

6 Describe presentation graphics.

7 Discuss software suites and integrated software.

Browsers
Connect to Web sites and display Web pages

Word Processing Software
Create text-based documents

Not long ago, trained specialists were required to perform many of the operations you can now perform with a microcomputer. Computer scientists used the Internet. Secretaries used typewriters to create professional-looking business correspondence. Market analysts used calculators to project sales. Graphic artists drew by hand. Data processing clerks created electronic files to be stored on large computers. Now you can do all these tasks—and many others—with a microcomputer and the appropriate application software.

Think of the microcomputer as an electronic tool. You may not consider yourself very good at typing, calculating, organizing, presenting, or managing information. A microcomputer, however, can help you to do all these things—and much more. All it takes is the right kinds of software.

While most end users today own and run their own application software, an emerging trend is to use Web-based applications. These are programs you access from the Internet and run on your microcomputer.

Competent end users need to understand the capabilities of basic application software, which includes browsers, word processors, spreadsheets, database management systems, and presentation programs.

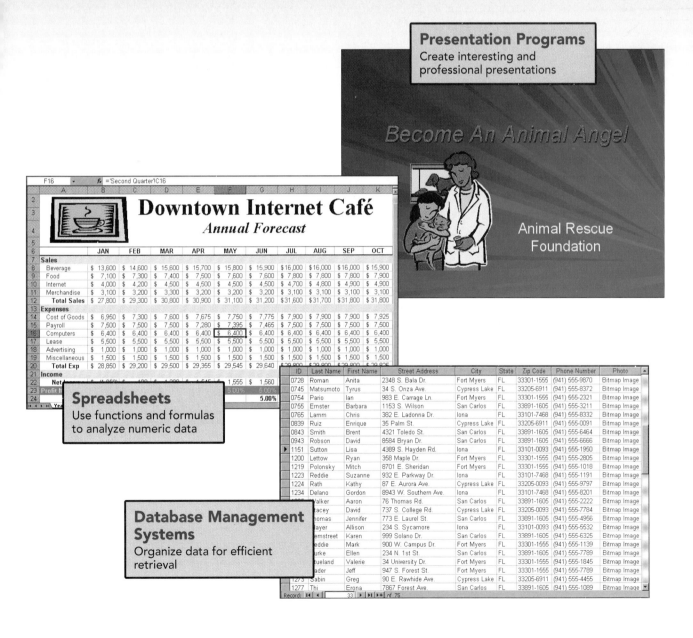

Presentation Programs
Create interesting and professional presentations

Spreadsheets
Use functions and formulas to analyze numeric data

Database Management Systems
Organize data for efficient retrieval

General-purpose and special-purpose are the two categories of software applications. Common features include windows, menus, help, and toolbars.

Software applications, or programs, can be divided into two categories. One category, **general-purpose applications,** is the focus of this chapter. These programs, also known as **basic applications,** are widely used in nearly every discipline and occupation. They include browsers, word processors, spreadsheets, database management systems, and presentation graphics. The other category, **special-purpose applications,** also known as **advanced applications,** includes thousands of other programs that are more narrowly focused on specific disciplines and occupations. Some of the best known are multimedia, Web authoring, graphics, virtual reality, and artificial intelligence programs.

COMMON FEATURES

A **window** is simply a rectangular area that can contain a document, program, or message. (Do not confuse the term *window* with the various versions of Microsoft's Windows operating systems, which are programs.) Many operating systems and application programs use windows to display information and request input. More than one window can be opened and displayed on the computer screen at one time. For example, one window might contain a browser, another a word processing program, and another a graphic image. Windows can generally be resized, moved, and closed.

Almost all software packages have **menus** to present commands. Typically, menus are displayed in a **menu bar** at the top of the screen. When one of the menu items is selected, a pull-down menu appears. This is a list of options or commands associated with the selected menu.

For most application packages, one of the commands on the menu bar is **Help.** The Help menu options typically provide access to a variety of Help features. The first option commonly allows access to a table of contents, a keyword index and a search feature to help you locate the information you need.

Toolbars typically are below the menu bar. They contain buttons and menus that provide quick access to commonly used commands. The **standard toolbar** and the **formatting toolbar** are common to most applications.

To learn more about the common features of most software applications, study Figure 2-1.

Typically, application programs are owned by users and stored on their hard disk drive. An emerging trend, however, is to free users from owning and storing applications by using Web-based applications. (See Making IT Work for You: Web-based Applications on pages 32–33.)

TIPS Have you ever been working on a document when the power goes off? Your original document and all your recent changes are gone. Fortunately, most applications automatically save your work every few minutes to a temporary recovery or backup file. Here are a few tips that might help you to quickly get back under way again.

1 **Restart your computer.**

2 **Restart the application.**

3 **Open the recovery file.** If the recovery file is not automatically opened, select the option to open it.

4 **Verify recovery file contents.** The recovery file should contain the document current up to the last automatic save. Compare the contents of the recovery file to the contents of the original file (if you have one).

5 **Save the recovery file.** If the recovery file contains the information you want, save it using the original file name or some other appropriate name.

Concept Check

- ✔ What are general-purpose applications?
- ✔ What are special-purpose applications?
- ✔ Describe four common software features.

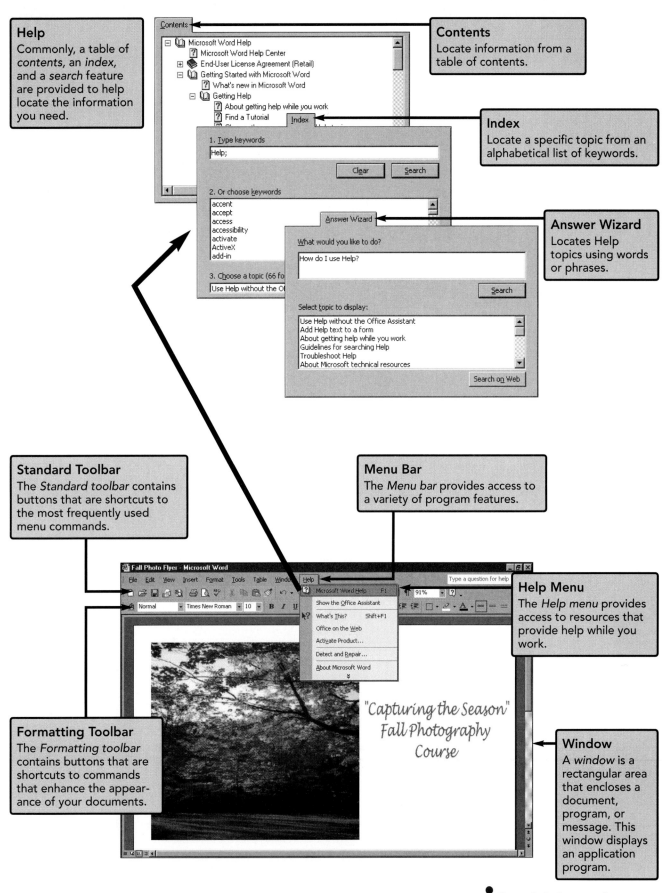

Help
Commonly, a table of *contents,* an *index,* and a *search* feature are provided to help locate the information you need.

Contents
Locate information from a table of contents.

Index
Locate a specific topic from an alphabetical list of keywords.

Answer Wizard
Locates Help topics using words or phrases.

Standard Toolbar
The *Standard toolbar* contains buttons that are shortcuts to the most frequently used menu commands.

Menu Bar
The *Menu bar* provides access to a variety of program features.

Help Menu
The *Help menu* provides access to resources that provide help while you work.

Formatting Toolbar
The *Formatting toolbar* contains buttons that are shortcuts to commands that enhance the appearance of your documents.

Window
A *window* is a rectangular area that encloses a document, program, or message. This window displays an application program.

Figure 2-1 Common features

WEB-BASED APPLICATIONS

Would you like access to free general-purpose applications from anywhere in the world? What about accessing your data files from any location? You can have it all with Web-based applications.

How It Works A server on the Web, known as an Application Service Provider (ASP), provides access to programs such as word processors, spreadsheets, and more. After registering with an ASP, you can use the Web to access these applications and store data files at the ASP rather than on your hard disk. You can run programs and access data using the Web from any location in the world.

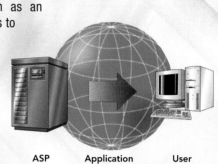

ASP   Application   User

Registering Several ASP sites exist on the Web and some of them offer free services. One of the best-known sites is WebOS. Their only requirement is that you register for their service.

1 ● Connect to *www.WebOS.com*.

● Click the *sign up* link.

● Follow the instructions to register for your account.

2 ● Once you've signed up for your account, return to the WebOS home page.

● Scroll the page to the Login area.

● Enter your Username and Password.

● Select *WebOS Desktop*.

● Click *Login*.

The Web-based desktop appears, similar to the figure to the right.

Accessing Applications Each time you connect to the WebOS site and log in, your Web-based desktop will appear. It will display numerous icons that can be used to access Web-based applications. These include a word processor, spreadsheet, personal information manager, and a variety of games.

Word Processor

Spreadsheet

Personal Information Manager

Games

Web-based Desktop The Web-based desktop looks and operates like the traditional Windows desktop. It contains a variety of icons that are used to load and run applications.

Some suggest that Web-based applications may replace traditional application software some time in the future. They point out that Web-based applications offer advantages beyond universal access to software and to data. One advantage is that users may no longer need to upgrade software on their hard disk when a new version becomes available. Of course, there are some potential disadvantages or challenges of Web-based applications. One challenge relates to privacy and security of personal data stored at an ASP.

The Web is continually changing and some of the specifics presented in this Making IT Work for You may have changed. See our Web site at http://www.mhhe.com/oleary for possible changes and to learn more about this application of technology.

Browsers connect to Web sites and display Web pages.

The Web is accessed through your computer using special software known as a **browser.** This software helps you connect to remote computers, open and transfer files, and display text and images, and provides in one tool an uncomplicated interface to the Internet and the Web. The two most widely used browser programs are Microsoft's Internet Explorer and Netscape's Navigator.

FEATURES

In order to connect to other resources with a browser, the location, or address, of the resources must be specified. These addresses are called **uniform resource locators (URLs)** or simply **Web site addresses.**

Once the browser has connected to a Web site, a document file is sent to your computer. This document contains **Hypertext Markup Language (HTML)** commands. The browser interprets the HTML commands and displays the document as a **Web page.** Typically, the first page of a Web site is referred to as its **home page.** It presents information about the site along with references and **hyperlinks,** or connections to other documents that contain related information. These hypertext links typically appear as colored and/or underlined text, buttons, or other graphic images. (A thorough and detailed discussion of the Internet and the Web is presented in Chapter 8.)

CASE

Assume that you have accepted a job as advertising coordinator for Adventure Travel Tours, a travel agency specializing in active adventure vacations. Carol, your supervisor, has asked you to review the company Web site, to locate travel information on Peru, and to communicate your findings to her. To learn more about browsers and how they could assist you to navigate, search, and communicate, study Figures 2-2 through 2-4.

Web Page
An HTML document sent to your computer and displayed by a browser is a *Web page.*

Web Site Address
Each Web page has its own *Web site address,* called the Uniform Resource Locator (URL), which provides location information used to navigate through the Internet to access a page.

Hypertext Links
A *hypertext link,* also called a hyperlink or simply a link, is a connection to another Web page or to another location on the current page.

CASE: After your browser connects to the Web, you begin navigating by entering the *Web address* for Adventure Travel Tours and connecting to that site. The company's *Web page* appears on your display. You begin your evaluation by exploring the site and its *hypertext links.*

Figure 2-2 Navigating

Keyword Search

A *keyword search* is conducted by entering a specific word or words into a text box, then searching through a list of resulting Web sites that contain the word or words.

Topic Search

A *topic search* is conducted by selecting a category and then continuing to select subcategories until your search has been narrowed and a list of relevant documents appears.

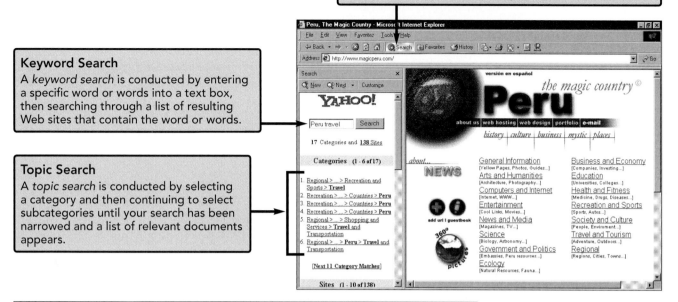

CASE: After reviewing the company site, you begin your search for information on Peru. Using the Search button, you connect to Yahoo!, a well-known *search service*. After conducting a *topic search* and a *keyword search*, you locate a site that provides just the information you are looking for.

Figure 2-3 Searching

E-Mail Address

On the Internet, each person has a unique *e-mail address* or means of identification.

Attachment

An *attachment* is a file that is included with an e-mail message.

New Message Window

The *new message window* is a part of Microsoft Outlook Express and is used to create e-mail messages.

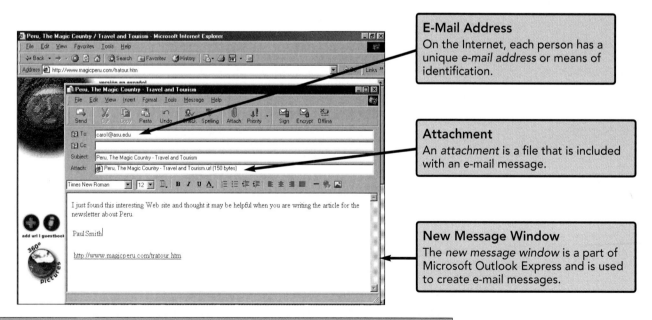

CASE: To share the Peru site with your supervisor, you choose File/Send/Link By E-Mail from the browser's menu bar. An e-mail *new message window* opens with a hyperlink to the Peru site and an *attachment* containing the HTML document. All you need to do is enter your supervisor's *e-mail address*, type your note, and send it.

Figure 2-4 Communicating

> Word processing software is used to create text-based documents.

Word **processing** software creates text-based **documents** such as reports, letters, and memos. Word processors are one of the most flexible and widely used software tools. Students and researchers use word processors to create reports. Organizations of all types create newsletters to communicate with their members. Businesses create form letters to reach new and current customers. All types of people and organizations use word processors to create personalized Web pages.

The three most widely used word processing programs are Microsoft Word, Corel WordPerfect, and Lotus Word Pro.

FEATURES

Most word processors include features to help you write better. For example, as you enter text, spelling errors are identified. They can be quickly corrected by selecting from a list of suggested alternative spellings. In a similar manner, grammar errors, such as capitalization, punctuation and subject-verb agreement problems are identified and can be corrected by selecting from a list of proposed grammar corrections. Another feature that helps you write better is the thesaurus which provides synonyms, antonyms, and related words for a word you look up.

You can quickly locate any character, word, or phrase in your document using the **search** or **find** commands. In addition, you can replace the located text with other text you specify using the **replace** command. For example, you could quickly locate each occurrence of the word *Chicago* and replace it with the word *Denver*.

One basic word processing feature is **word wrap.** A word processor automatically moves the insertion point to the next line once the current line is full. As you type, the words "wrap around" to the next line. To begin a new paragraph or leave a blank line, you press the Enter key.

CASE

Your primary responsibilities as the advertising coordinator for Adventure Travel Tours are to create and coordinate the company's promotional materials, including flyers, form letters, and travel reports. To learn more about word processor features and how they could assist you, see Figures 2-5 through 2-7.

 TIPS Want to add some interest and a personal touch to your correspondence? You can by including an audio clip of your voice in the text document. If you are using Word 97, 2000, or 2002:

1 **Position cursor.** Place the cursor where you want the voice attachment to appear.

2 **Start recording.** From the menu bar, choose Insert/Object/Wave/ Sound OK/Record.

3 **Start talking.** Dictate a short message into the microphone.

4 **Stop recording.** Choose Stop/File/Exit & Return.

A speaker icon appears in your document. To hear the audio clip, double-click the icon.

Concept Check
✔ What do browsers do?
✔ Describe how a browser displays a Web page.
✔ What do word processors do?
✔ Describe three basic word processor features.

Font and Font Size
A *font,* also commonly referred to as a typeface, is a set of characters with a specific design. *Font size* refers to a character's height and width commonly measured in points.

Graphics
A *graphic* is a nontext element or object, such as a drawing or picture that can be added to a document.

Word Wrap
Word Wrap automatically begins a new line of text once the current line is full.

Alignment
Alignment is how text is positioned on a line between the margins or indents. There are four types of paragraph alignment: left, center, right, and justified.

Automatic Features
Automatic features include:
- Spelling Check identifies misspelled words and proposes corrections.
- Grammar Check identifies incorrect grammar and proposes corrections.
- AutoText and AutoComplete anticipate commonly used phrases and insert them upon request.
- AutoCorrect identifies basic typing errors and automatically corrects them.

Announcing
New Adventure Travel Trips

Attend an Adventure Travel presentation to learn about some of the earth's greatest unspoiled habitats and find out how you can experience the adventure of a lifetime. This year we are introducing four new tours and offering you a unique opportunity to combine many different outdoor activities while exploring the world.

Hike the Inca trail to Machu Picchu
Camp on safari in Tanzania
Climb Mt. Kilimanjaro
Explore the Costa Rican rain forests

Presentation dates and times are January 5 at 7 PM, February 3 at 7:30 PM, and March 8 at 7 PM. All presentations are held at convenient hotel locations. The hotels are located in downtown Los Angeles, Santa Clara and at the airport.

Call 1-800-777-0004 for presentation locations, a full color brochure, and itinerary information, costs, and trip dates.

CASE: You have been asked to create an advertising flyer for upcoming promotional presentations. After discussing the flyer's contents and basic structure with your supervisor, you enter the flyer's text. As you type, the text word wraps to the next line. You also notice several helpful *automatic features.* To maximize the flyer's visual impact, you experiment with different character and paragraph formats including *fonts, font sizes,* colors, and *alignments.* Finally, you add an interesting *graphic.*

Figure 2-5 Flyers

Page Margins

A *page margin* is the blank space around the edge of the page. Standard single-sized documents have four margins: top, bottom, left, and right.

Thesaurus

A *Thesaurus* is a reference tool that provides synonyms, antonyms, and related words for a selected word or phrase.

Indents

To help your reader find information quickly, you can *indent* paragraphs from the margins. Indenting paragraphs sets them off from the rest of the document.

Find and Replace

To make editing easier, you can use the *Find and Replace* feature to find text in a document and replace it with other text as directed.

Bulleted and Numbered Lists

Whenever possible, use *bulleted* or *numbered lists* to organize information and make your writing clear and easy to read.

Move and Copy

Text and graphic selections can be *moved* or *copied* to new locations in a document or between documents.

October 30, 2001

Dear Adventure Traveler,

Imagine hiking and paddling your way through the rain forests of Costa Rica, camping under the stars in Africa, or following in the footsteps of the ancient Inca as you backpack along the Inca trail to Machu Picchu. Turn these dreams of adventure into memories you will cherish forever by joining Adventure Travel Tours on one of our four new adventure tours.

To tell you more about these exciting new adventures, we are offering several presentations in your area. These presentations will focus on the features and cultures of the region. We will also show you pictures of the places you will visit and activities you can participate in, as well as a detailed agenda and package costs. Plan on attending one of the following presentations:

Date	Time	Location	Room
January 5	7:00 PM	Town Center Hotel	Room 284B
February 3	7:30 PM	Airport Manor	Conference Room A
March 8	7:00 PM	Country Inn	Mountainside Room

In appreciation of your past patronage, we are pleased to offer you a 10% discount on the price of any of the new tour packages. You must book the trip at least 60 days prior to the departure date. Please turn in this letter to qualify for the discount.

Our vacation tours are professionally developed solely for your enjoyment. We include almost everything in the price of your tour while giving you the best possible value for your dollar. All trips include:

- Professional tour manager and local guides
- All accommodations and meals
- All entrance fees, excursions, transfers and tips

We hope you will join us this year on another special Adventure Travel Tours journey. Your memories of fascinating places and challenging physical adventures should linger for a long, long time. For reservations, please see your travel agent, or contact Adventure Travel Tours directly at 1-800-777-0004. You can also visit our new Web site at AdventureTravelTours.com

Best regards,

Student Name

CASE: After creating the brochure, you draft a letter to accompany it and submit the draft to your supervisor. She reviews the draft and makes several editing suggestions. One is to increase name recognition by repeating the name of the company several times. You quickly accomplish this request by *copying* the name and inserting it in several places. To improve the logical flow of the text, you reorder or *move* several paragraphs. To improve wording, you use the *Thesaurus* to identify alternative word choices and the *find and replace* feature to locate and replace selected words. To improve the format, you adjust *page margins* and add paragraph *indents*. Finally, you use the *numbered and bulleted list* feature to improve the clarity.

Figure 2-6 Letters

Style
A *style* is a set of formats that is assigned a name and can be quickly applied to a selected text.

Text Wrapping
You can control how text appears around a graphic object by specifying the *text wrapping* style.

Footnote and Endnote
A *footnote* is a source reference or explanatory text offering that is placed at the bottom of a page. An *endnote* is a source reference or a long comment that typically appears at the end of a document.

Peru

Geography and Climate

Peru, located in South America, borders the Pacific Ocean on its west and shares common borders with the countries of Ecuador, Colombia, Brazil, and Bolivia. Peru is subdivided into three regions – La Costa, La Sierra, and La Selva – based on differing climate and geographical features. Though entirely within the tropics, Peru's climate varies from region to region, ranging from tropical to arctic. Its varied climate corresponds to the sharply contrasting geographical features of seafront, mountains, and rainforests.

La Costa

Occupying the slender area along Peru's western coastline, La Costa, provides a division between the mountains and sea. Although some of this area is fertile, mostly it is extremely dry and arid. The Andes Mountains prevent greater annual precipitation coming from the east. Some areas in the south are considered drier than the Sahara. Conversely, there are a few areas in this region where mountain rivers meet the ocean that are green with life and do not give the impression of being in a desert at all.

La Sierra

Inland and to the east is the mountainous region called La Sierra, encompassing Peru's share of the Andes mountain range. The southern portion of this region is prone to volcanic activity, and some volcanoes are active today. La Sierra is subject to a dry season from May to September, which is winter in that part of the world. The weather is typically sunny, with moderate annual precipitation. The former Incan capital Cuzco is in this region, as well as the Sacred Valley of the Incas. This region also contains Lake Titicaca, the world's highest navigable lake.[1]

Figure 1-Sacred Valley

La Selva

La Selva, a region of tropical rainforest, is the easternmost region in Peru. This region, with the eastern foot of the Andes Mountains, forms the Amazon Basin, into which numerous rivers flow. La Selva is extremely wet, with some areas exceeding an annual precipitation of 137 inches. Its wettest season occurs from November to April. The weather here is humid and extremely hot.

Region	Annual Rainfall (Inches)	Average Temperature (Fahrenheit)
La Costa	2	68
La Sierra	35	54
La Selva	137	80

[1] Lake Titicaca is 12,507 feet above sea level.

Captions and Cross References
A *caption* is a title or explanation for a table, picture, or graph. A *cross reference* is a reference from one part of a document to related information in another part.

Table
A *table* is used to organize information into an easy-to-read format of rows and columns.

Figure 2-7 Reports

Spreadsheet programs organize, analyze, and graph numeric data such as budgets and financial reports. Spreadsheets are widely used by people in nearly every profession. Students and teachers record grades and calculate grade point averages. Marketing professionals analyze sales trends. Financial analysts evaluate and graph stock market trends.

The three most widely used spreadsheet programs are Microsoft Excel, Corel Quattro Pro, and Lotus 1-2-3.

FEATURES

Data and information are stored in a **workbook,** which can contain one or more related worksheets. A **worksheet,** also known as a **spreadsheet** or **sheet,** is a rectangular grid of **rows** and **columns.** The columns are identified by letters and the rows are identified by numbers. The intersection of a row and column creates a **cell.** For example the cell A1 is formed by the intersection of column A and row 1.

Information is entered into cells. **Text entries** are typically used to identify or label information while **numeric entries** include numbers and formulas.

Formulas are instructions for calculations. They calculate results using the number or numbers in referenced cells. For example, the formula B9–B18

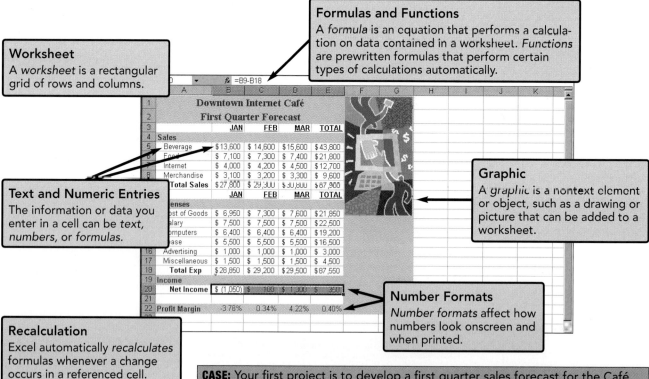

Formulas and Functions
A *formula* is an equation that performs a calculation on data contained in a worksheet. *Functions* are prewritten formulas that perform certain types of calculations automatically.

Worksheet
A *worksheet* is a rectangular grid of rows and columns.

Text and Numeric Entries
The information or data you enter in a cell can be *text, numbers,* or *formulas.*

Graphic
A *graphic* is a nontext element or object, such as a drawing or picture that can be added to a worksheet.

Recalculation
Excel automatically *recalculates* formulas whenever a change occurs in a referenced cell.

Number Formats
Number formats affect how numbers look onscreen and when printed.

Figure 2-8 Worksheets

CASE: Your first project is to develop a first quarter sales forecast for the Café. After planning the basic structure of the *worksheet,* you enter descriptive *text* labels to identify the row and column headings. Then you enter *numeric* data and *formulas* and *functions* to perform calculations. To test the accuracy of the worksheet, you enter different numeric data and compare the *recalculated* spreadsheet results with hand calculations. Finally, you focus on the appearance of the worksheet by applying *number formats,* including currency ($) and percent (%) symbols to selected *cells* and by inserting a *graphic.*

means to subtract the value in cell B18 from the value in cell B9. **Functions** are prewritten formulas that perform calculations automatically. For example, the function @SUM(B5:B8) adds all the values in the **range** of cells B5 to B8.

If you change one or more numbers in your spreadsheet, all related formulas will recalculate automatically. Thus, you can substitute one value for another in a cell and observe the effect on other related cells in the worksheet. This is called **what-if analysis.**

To help visualize the data in your worksheets, you can create **analytical graphs** or **charts.** For example, you could display the numerical data in a worksheet as a pie chart, bar chart, or line graph. When the data changes, the graphs are automatically updated.

CASE

Assume that you have just accepted a job as manager of the Downtown Internet Café. This Café provides a variety of flavored coffees as well as Internet access. One of your responsibilities is to create a financial plan for the next year. To learn more about spreadsheet features and how they could assist you as manager of an Internet café, see Figures 2-8 through 2-10.

Chart
A *chart* is a visual representation of worksheet data that is used to convey information in an easy-to-understand and attractive manner. Different types of charts are used to represent data in different ways.

Chart Wizard
The *Chart Wizard* is an interactive program accessed from the Formatting toolbar that guides you through the steps to create a variety of different types of charts.

Textbox
A *textbox* is a rectangular object in which text is entered.

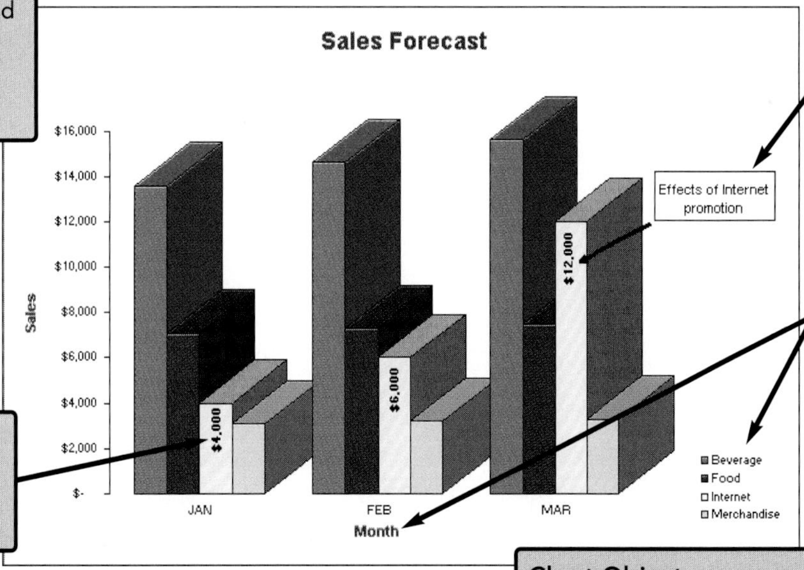

Chart Elements
Chart elements consist of a number of parts that are used to graphically display the worksheet data.

Data Label
Data labels provide additional information about a data marker.

Chart Object
A *chart object* is a graphic object that is created using charting features included in Excel. It can be inserted directly into the worksheet.

CASE: After completing the First Quarter Forecast for the Café, you decide to *chart* the sales data to make it easier to see the trends and growth patterns. Using the *Chart Wizard* you define *chart elements* such as the chart title, labels for the axes, and the legend. You insert the chart as a *chart object* into the worksheet. Finally, you decide to add *data labels* and a *text box* to clarify the meaning of the chart data and to add color to different chart elements to enhance the appearance of the chart.

Figure 2-9 Charts

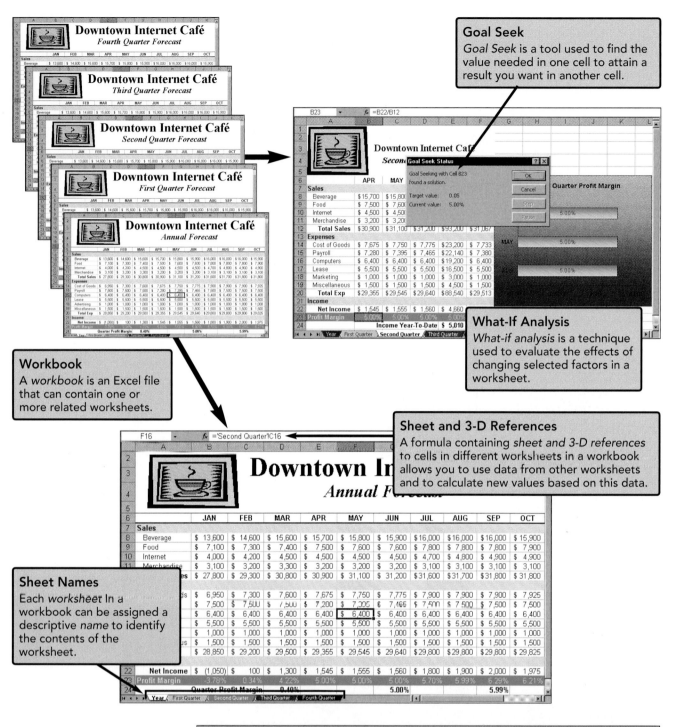

Goal Seek
Goal Seek is a tool used to find the value needed in one cell to attain a result you want in another cell.

What-If Analysis
What-if analysis is a technique used to evaluate the effects of changing selected factors in a worksheet.

Sheet and 3-D References
A formula containing *sheet and 3-D references* to cells in different worksheets in a workbook allows you to use data from other worksheets and to calculate new values based on this data.

Workbook
A *workbook* is an Excel file that can contain one or more related worksheets.

Sheet Names
Each *worksheet* in a workbook can be assigned a descriptive *name* to identify the contents of the worksheet.

CASE: After presenting the First Quarter Forecast to the owner, you revise the format and expand the *workbook* to include worksheets for each quarter and an annual forecast summary. Each worksheet is given a descriptive *sheet name*. This annual forecast uses *sheet and 3-D references* to calculate and display values from the other sheets. At the request of the owner, you perform a *what-if analysis* to test the effect of different estimates for payroll and you use *Goal Seek* to determine how much payroll would have to be decreased to produce a profit margin of 5.00 percent.

Figure 2-10 Workbooks

DATABASE MANAGEMENT SYSTEMS

A database is a collection of related data. A **database management system (DBMS)** or **database manager** is a program that sets up, or structures, a database, such as an inventory of supplies or a list of employees. It also provides tools to enter, edit, and retrieve data from the database. Database managers are used by all kinds of people, from teachers to police officers.

> A database manager organizes a related collection of data so that information can be retrieved easily.

The **relational database** is the most widely used database structure. Data is organized into related **tables.** Each table is made up of rows called **records** and columns called **fields.** Each record contains fields of data about some specific item. For example, in a table containing information on employees, a record would contain fields of data such as a person's last name, first name, and street address.

Three of the most widely used database management systems are Microsoft Access, Corel Paradox, and Lotus Approach.

FEATURES

A basic feature of all database programs is the capability to **locate** and **display** just the information you want from the tables of data. For example, you could ask or *query* a database of employees to locate only those who work in a specific department and display just their name and job title. Then, you could print a *report* of the information in **sorted** alphabetical order by last name.

Further, you can **analyze** the data using built-in math formulas. For example, in a database of sales information, you could calculate the total and average sales during a specified time period.

Most database management programs include a **programming control language** for advanced users to create sophisticated applications. In addition, they allow direct communication to larger, more specialized mainframe databases through languages like **structured query language (SQL).**

CASE

Assume that you have accepted a job as employment administrator for the Lifestyle Fitness Club. One of your responsibilities is to create a database management system to replace the club's manual system for recording employee information. To learn more about database management system features and how they could assist you as an employee administrator at the Lifestyle Fitness Club, see Figure 2-11 and Figure 2-12.

Concept Check
✔ What is a workbook?
✔ What is a worksheet?
✔ What is a database?
✔ What is a database management system (DBMS)?
✔ What are the three most common database management systems?

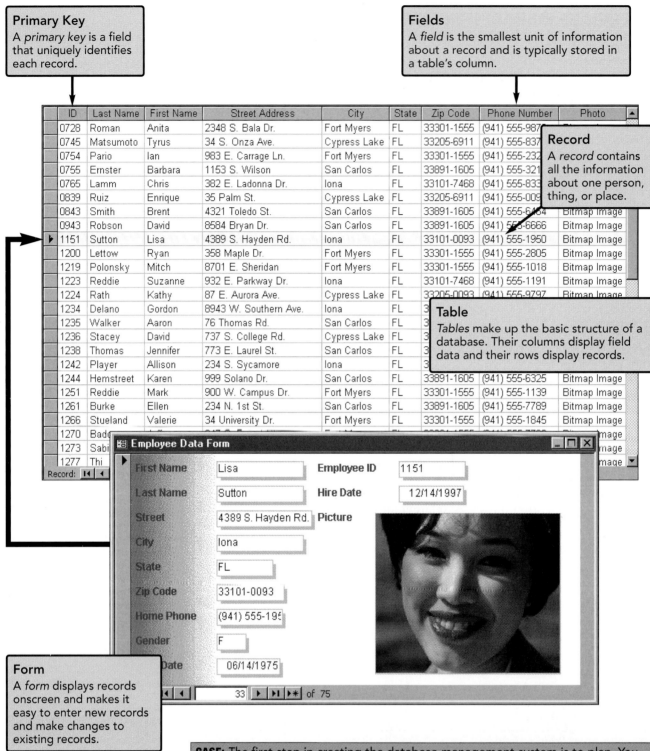

Primary Key
A *primary key* is a field that uniquely identifies each record.

Fields
A *field* is the smallest unit of information about a record and is typically stored in a table's column.

Record
A *record* contains all the information about one person, thing, or place.

	ID	Last Name	First Name	Street Address	City	State	Zip Code	Phone Number	Photo
	0728	Roman	Anita	2348 S. Bala Dr.	Fort Myers	FL	33301-1555	(941) 555-987	
	0745	Matsumoto	Tyrus	34 S. Onza Ave.	Cypress Lake	FL	33205-6911	(941) 555-837	
	0754	Pario	Ian	983 E. Carrage Ln.	Fort Myers	FL	33301-1555	(941) 555-232	
	0755	Ernster	Barbara	1153 S. Wilson	San Carlos	FL	33891-1605	(941) 555-321	
	0765	Lamm	Chris	382 E. Ladonna Dr.	Iona	FL	33101-7468	(941) 555-833	
	0839	Ruiz	Enrique	35 Palm St.	Cypress Lake	FL	33205-6911	(941) 555-009	
	0843	Smith	Brent	4321 Toledo St.	San Carlos	FL	33891-1605	(941) 555-6464	Bitmap Image
	0943	Robson	David	8584 Bryan Dr.	San Carlos	FL	33891-1605	(941) 555-6666	Bitmap Image
▶	1151	Sutton	Lisa	4389 S. Hayden Rd.	Iona	FL	33101-0093	(941) 555-1950	Bitmap Image
	1200	Lettow	Ryan	358 Maple Dr.	Fort Myers	FL	33301-1555	(941) 555-2805	Bitmap Image
	1219	Polonsky	Mitch	8701 E. Sheridan	Fort Myers	FL	33301-1555	(941) 555-1018	Bitmap Image
	1223	Reddie	Suzanne	932 E. Parkway Dr.	Iona	FL	33101-7468	(941) 555-1191	Bitmap Image
	1224	Rath	Kathy	87 E. Aurora Ave.	Cypress Lake	FL	33205-0093	(941) 555-9797	Bitmap Image
	1234	Delano	Gordon	8943 W. Southern Ave.	Iona	FL	3		
	1235	Walker	Aaron	76 Thomas Rd.	San Carlos	FL	3		
	1236	Stacey	David	737 S. College Rd.	Cypress Lake	FL	3		
	1238	Thomas	Jennifer	773 E. Laurel St.	San Carlos	FL	3		
	1242	Player	Allison	234 S. Sycamore	Iona	FL	3		
	1244	Hemstreet	Karen	999 Solano Dr.	San Carlos	FL	33891-1605	(941) 555-6325	Bitmap Image
	1251	Reddie	Mark	900 W. Campus Dr.	Fort Myers	FL	33301-1555	(941) 555-1139	Bitmap Image
	1261	Burke	Ellen	234 N. 1st St.	San Carlos	FL	33891-1605	(941) 555-7789	Bitmap Image
	1266	Stueland	Valerie	34 University Dr.	Fort Myers	FL	33301-1555	(941) 555-1845	Bitmap Image
	1270	Bad...							mage
	1273	Sabi...							mage
	1277	Thi...							mage

Record: ▐◀ ◀

Table
Tables make up the basic structure of a database. Their columns display field data and their rows display records.

Employee Data Form _ □ ×

First Name	Lisa
Last Name	Sutton
Street	4389 S. Hayden Rd.
City	Iona
State	FL
Zip Code	33101-0093
Home Phone	(941) 555-195
Gender	F
Date	06/14/1975

Employee ID 1151
Hire Date 12/14/1997
Picture

◀ ◀ 33 ▶ ▶▐ ▶* of 75

Form
A *form* displays records onscreen and makes it easy to enter new records and make changes to existing records.

CASE: The first step in creating the database management system is to plan. You study the existing manual system focusing on how and what data is collected and how it is used. Next, you design the basic structure or organization of the new database system to have two related *tables*, which will make entering data and using the database more efficient. Focusing on the first table, Employees, you create the table structure by specifying the *fields*, data types, and the *primary key field*. You then enter the data for each employee as a *record* in the table. To make the process faster and more accurate you create a *form*.

Figure 2-11 Tables and Forms

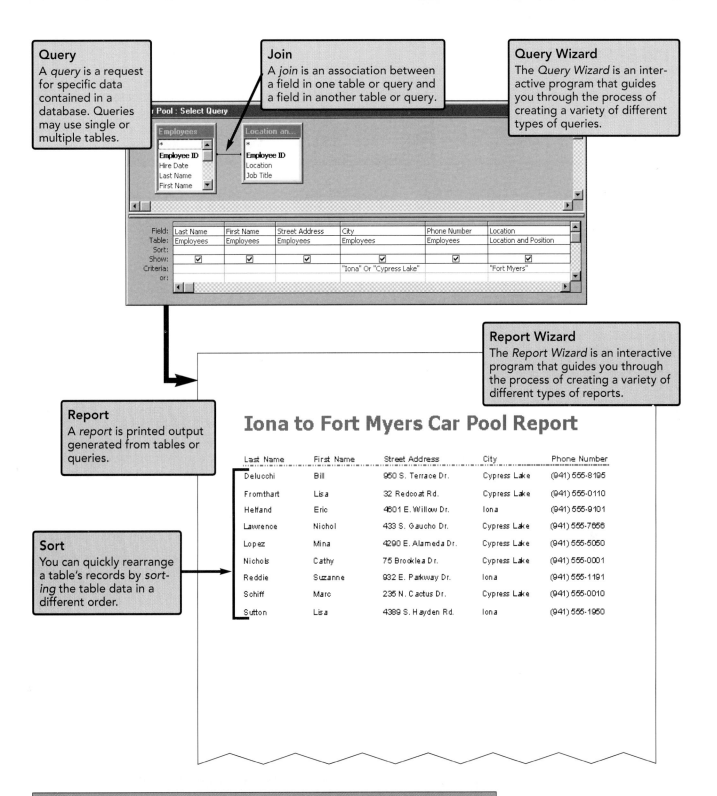

Query
A *query* is a request for specific data contained in a database. Queries may use single or multiple tables.

Join
A *join* is an association between a field in one table or query and a field in another table or query.

Query Wizard
The *Query Wizard* is an interactive program that guides you through the process of creating a variety of different types of queries.

Report Wizard
The *Report Wizard* is an interactive program that guides you through the process of creating a variety of different types of reports.

Report
A *report* is printed output generated from tables or queries.

Sort
You can quickly rearrange a table's records by *sorting* the table data in a different order.

Iona to Fort Myers Car Pool Report

Last Name	First Name	Street Address	City	Phone Number
Delucchi	Bill	950 S. Terrace Dr.	Cypress Lake	(941) 555-8195
Fromthart	Lisa	32 Redcoat Rd.	Cypress Lake	(941) 555-0110
Helfand	Eric	4601 E. Willow Dr.	Iona	(941) 555-9101
Lawrence	Nichol	433 S. Gaucho Dr.	Cypress Lake	(941) 555-7656
Lopez	Mina	4290 E. Alameda Dr.	Cypress Lake	(941) 555-5050
Nichols	Cathy	75 Brooklea Dr.	Cypress Lake	(941) 555-0001
Reddie	Suzanne	932 E. Parkway Dr.	Iona	(941) 555-1191
Schiff	Marc	235 N. Cactus Dr.	Cypress Lake	(941) 555-0010
Sutton	Lisa	4389 S. Hayden Rd.	Iona	(941) 555-1950

CASE: You have continued to build the database by creating a second table containing information about the employee's work location and job title. Now you want to create a *report* to help employees form car pools. To do this you use the *Query Wizard* to create a *query* using information from both tables. The tables are *joined* on the primary keys and the query specifies the information to display from both tables. Then you use the *Report Wizard* to quickly create a professional report of the query results *sorted* alphabetically by the employee's last name.

Figure 2-12 Reports

Presentation graphics create interesting and professional presentations.

Research shows that people learn better when information is presented visually. A picture is indeed worth a thousand words or numbers. **Presentation graphics** are used to combine a variety of visual objects to create attractive, visually interesting presentations. They are excellent tools to help you communicate a message or persuade people.

People in a variety of settings and situations use presentation graphic programs to make their presentations more interesting and professional. For example, a marketing manager may present information to a group on marketing strategy and a salesperson may make a presentation to persuade you to purchase a product. Students use presentation graphics programs to create high-quality class presentations that effectively convey their message.

Three of the most widely used presentation graphics programs are Microsoft PowerPoint, Corel Presentations, and Lotus Freelance Graphics.

FEATURES

Most presentation programs include features that help you organize the content of your presentation. Commonly, an outline feature is included that helps you enter and organize the topics of your talk. Most programs also provide presentation **layout files** that include sample text for many different types of presentations—from delivering a report to selling a product.

Professionally designed **templates** or model presentations are provided. These can help take the worry out of the design and layout decisions. They include selected combinations of text layouts with features such as title placement and size. Additionally, various bullet styles, background colors, patterns, borders, and other enhancements are provided.

Animations include special visual and sound effects. These effects include moving pictures and transitions between topics. You can insert audio and video clips that play automatically or when selected. You can even record your own voice to provide a narration to accompany a slide show.

CASE

Assume that you have volunteered for the Animal Rescue Foundation, a local animal rescue agency. You have been asked to create a powerful and persuasive presentation to encourage other members from your community to volunteer. To learn more about presentation software features and how they could assist you to create a presentation for the Animal Rescue Foundation, see Figure 2-13.

TIPS Planning a presentation for school or work? Here are a few tips from professionals to make it the best ever:

1 **Be prepared.** Know your audience, equipment, and presentation room. Practice out loud in the room.

2 **Begin and end well.** Begin with a joke or story. End with a summary.

3 **Know when to move.** Move around to focus attention on you. Remain still to focus attention on your slides.

4 **Relax.** Prior to a presentation, take a short walk, stretch, or just take a few quiet moments to breathe deeply.

Concept Check

✓ What do presentation graphics software do?

✓ What are the three most widely used presentation graphics programs?

✓ Describe three basic presentation graphics features.

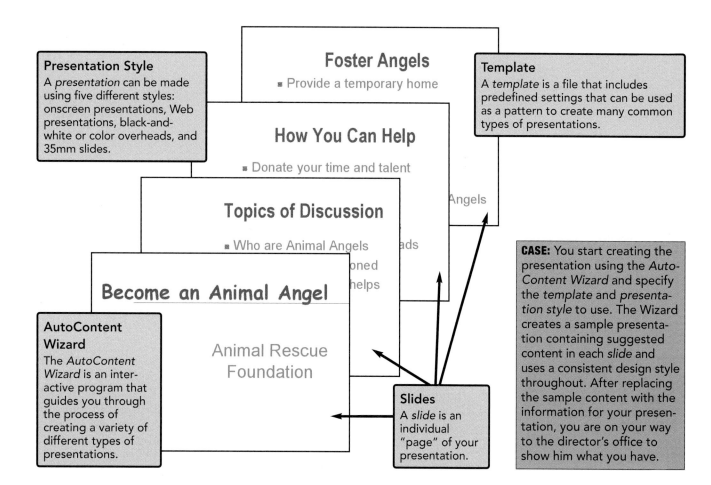

Presentation Style
A *presentation* can be made using five different styles: onscreen presentations, Web presentations, black-and-white or color overheads, and 35mm slides.

Foster Angels
- Provide a temporary home

Template
A *template* is a file that includes predefined settings that can be used as a pattern to create many common types of presentations.

How You Can Help
- Donate your time and talent

Topics of Discussion
- Who are Animal Angels

Become an Animal Angel

Animal Rescue Foundation

AutoContent Wizard
The *AutoContent Wizard* is an interactive program that guides you through the process of creating a variety of different types of presentations.

Slides
A *slide* is an individual "page" of your presentation.

CASE: You start creating the presentation using the *Auto-Content Wizard* and specify the *template* and *presentation style* to use. The Wizard creates a sample presentation containing suggested content in each *slide* and uses a consistent design style throughout. After replacing the sample content with the information for your presentation, you are on your way to the director's office to show him what you have.

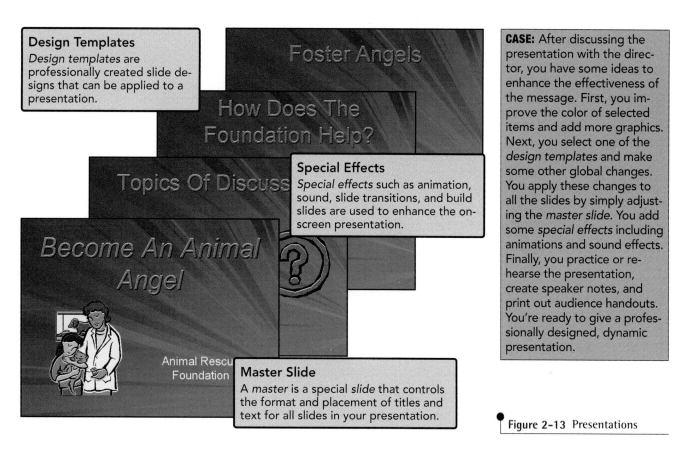

Design Templates
Design templates are professionally created slide designs that can be applied to a presentation.

Foster Angels

How Does The Foundation Help?

Topics Of Discuss

Special Effects
Special effects such as animation, sound, slide transitions, and build slides are used to enhance the on-screen presentation.

Become An Animal Angel

Animal Rescu Foundation

Master Slide
A *master* is a special *slide* that controls the format and placement of titles and text for all slides in your presentation.

CASE: After discussing the presentation with the director, you have some ideas to enhance the effectiveness of the message. First, you improve the color of selected items and add more graphics. Next, you select one of the *design templates* and make some other global changes. You apply these changes to all the slides by simply adjusting the *master slide*. You add some *special effects* including animations and sound effects. Finally, you practice or rehearse the presentation, create speaker notes, and print out audience handouts. You're ready to give a professionally designed, dynamic presentation.

Figure 2-13 Presentations

Presentation Graphics

A software suite is a group of application programs. OLE allows you to share information between applications.

A **software suite** is a collection of separate applications bundled together and sold as a group. While the applications function *exactly* the same whether purchased in a suite or separately, it is significantly less expensive to buy a suite of applications than to buy each application separately.

Microsoft Office is the most popular software suite. It comes in several different versions. One of the most recent is Microsoft Office XP Professional Edition, which includes Word, Excel, Access, and PowerPoint. (See Figure 2-14.) Other popular software suites are Corel WordPerfect Office and Lotus SmartSuite.

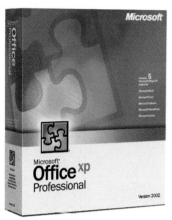

Figure 2-14 Microsoft Office XP Professional Edition

OBJECT LINKING AND EMBEDDING

Object linking and embedding (OLE) is a powerful feature of many application programs. Using OLE, you can share information or objects between files created in different applications. For example, you could create a chart in Excel and then use it in a Word document.

With **object linking,** a copy of the object from the **source file** (the file in which it was created) is inserted in the **destination file** (the file receiving the object) and a *link* or connection between the two files is established. If the source file changes, the object in the destination file is updated automatically.

For example, if a chart (an **object**) in an Excel workbook file (the source file) is *linked* to a Word document (the destination file), the chart appears in the Word document. Later, if the Excel worksheet changes the chart, the Word document will be automatically updated. Object linking is useful if you want the destination document to always contain the most up-to-date information.

With **object embedding,** the object from the source file is *embedded* or added to the destination document and becomes part of the destination document. The embedded object can be opened and edited from within the destination document using the source application. However, changes you make to the embedded object are not reflected in the source file.

For example, if a presentation (an object) created in PowerPoint is embedded in a Word document (the destination file), the presentation can be run from the Word document. Object embedding is useful for providing activity and flexibility to a document.

CASE

Assume that as manager and financial planner for the Internet Café, you have been working on a presentation for the annual sales meeting. You have analyzed recent sales trends using Excel and have drafted a presentation using PowerPoint. To present your work to Evan, the owner, you have just completed a Word document. To learn more about OLE and how you could use it, see Figure 2-15.

Concept Check

 What is a software suite?

 Describe object-linking and embedding.

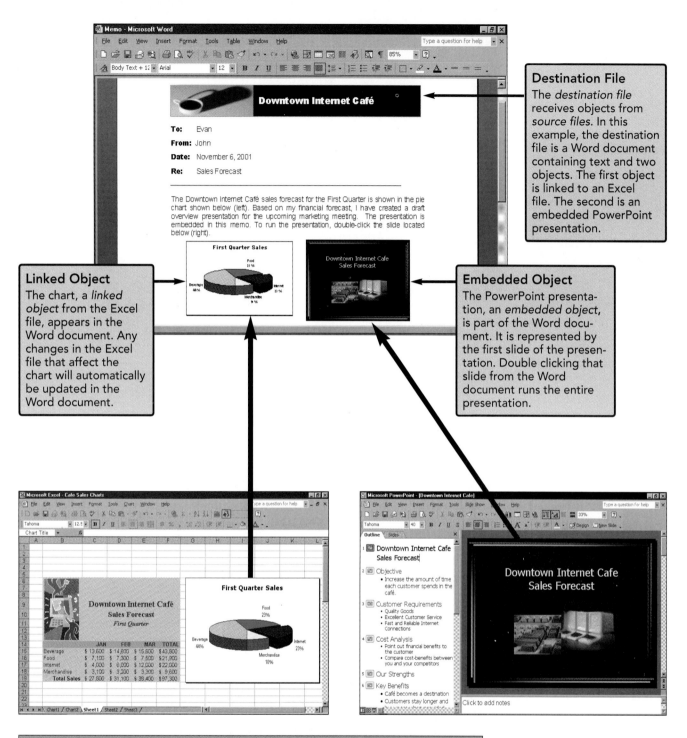

Destination File

The *destination file* receives objects from *source files*. In this example, the destination file is a Word document containing text and two objects. The first object is linked to an Excel file. The second is an embedded PowerPoint presentation.

Linked Object

The chart, a *linked object* from the Excel file, appears in the Word document. Any changes in the Excel file that affect the chart will automatically be updated in the Word document.

Embedded Object

The PowerPoint presentation, an *embedded object*, is part of the Word document. It is represented by the first slide of the presentation. Double clicking that slide from the Word document runs the entire presentation.

CASE: Your supervisor, Evan, has requested an update on your work, which includes an ongoing analysis of sales data using Excel and a PowerPoint presentation. You create a memo to Evan using Word. This *destination file* includes a chart as an *object linked* to your Excel spreadsheet and a PowerPoint presentation as an *embedded object*. By linking your spreadsheet, you can continue with your analysis with Excel and any changes in the chart will automatically be reflected in the memo. By embedding your presentation, Evan will be able to run the entire presentation directly from the memo.

Figure 2-15 Object linking and embedding

Integrated software is an all-in-one application program.

An **integrated package** is a single program that provides the functionality of a word processor, spreadsheet, database manager, and more. For example, to create a report on the growth of sales for a sporting goods store, you could use all parts of an integrated package. You could use the database to search and retrieve yearly sales data. The spreadsheet could be used to analyze the data and graphics to visually present the data. You could use the word processor to write the report that includes data and a chart from the spreadsheet program. (See Figure 2-16.)

The primary disadvantage of an integrated package is that the capabilities of each function (such as word processing) are not as extensive as in the specialized programs (such as Microsoft Word). The primary advantage is that the cost of an integrated package is much less than the cost of purchasing a software suite or the individual application. The most widely used integrated packages are Microsoft Works (see Figure 2-17) and AppleWorks.

For a summary of the basic application software, see Figure 2-18.

Figure 2-16 Microsoft Works

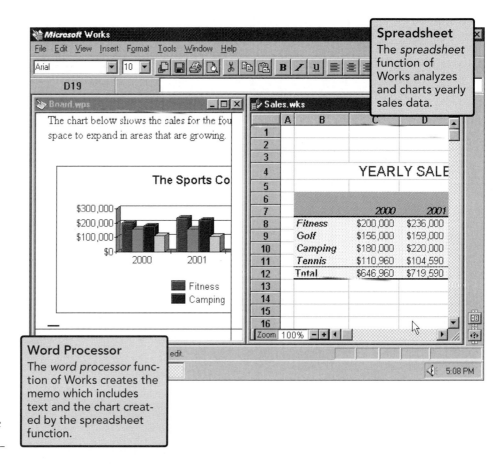

Figure 2-17 Integrated package (Microsoft Works)

Concept Check

✔ What is an integrated package?

✔ Describe the advantages and disadvantages of an integrated package.

Browsers	Microsoft Internet Explorer, Netscape Navigator
Word processors	Microsoft Word, Corel WordPerfect, Lotus Word Pro
Spreadsheets	Microsoft Excel, Corel Quattro Pro, Lotus 1-2-3
Database management systems	Microsoft Access, Corel Paradox, Lotus Approach
Presentation graphics	Microsoft PowerPoint, Corel Presentations, Lotus Freelance Graphics
Software suites	Microsoft Office, Corel Office, Lotus SmartSuite
Integrated packages	Microsoft Works, AppleWorks

Figure 2-18 Software programs

A Look to the Future

Web-based Application Software Updates Ease Maintenance

New software versions will offer more capabilities, freeing your creativity and enhancing the quality and quantity of your work.

New versions of basic application software are being released all the time. One way these programs change is in the way you interact with them. Another way is in the software's capabilities.

Interacting with them may not be as difficult as you might think. That's because almost all new software today has a similar command and menu structure. When a new version comes out, it looks and feels quite similar to the previous version. This frees you to focus on the new capabilities.

Basic applications will continue to become more and more powerful by adding breadth to their capabilities. They are no longer limited by the machines that they were designed to replace. Word processors, for example, do much more than typewriters ever could. Recent versions have added desktop publishing and Web page design capabilities.

Some experts predict that our days of buying, installing, and upgrading software will some day be a thing of the past. These activities will be done by specialized Web sites that provide Web-based applications. When you want to run the most recent and powerful applications, you will connect to the appropriate site, pay a fee, and run the application.

What does all this mean to you? You will have access to more powerful applications, which will free your creativity and enhance the quality and quantity of your work. Additionally, you will be challenged to learn how and when to use these more powerful tools.

BROWSERS

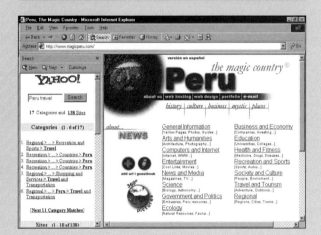

Browsers connect to remote computers, open and transfer files, display text and images, and provide an uncomplicated interface to the Internet and the Web.

Features

Principal browser features include the following:

- **Uniform resource locators (URLs)**—in order to connect to other resources with a browser the address, or URL, must be specified.
- **Hypertext Markup Language (HTML)**—browsers interpret HTML documents to display **Web pages.**
- **Home page**—typically the first page of a Web site is referred to as its home page.
- **Hyperlinks**—these create connections between information references within a document or between documents.

WORD PROCESSORS

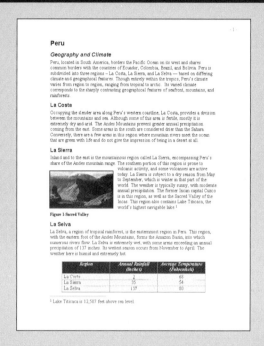

Word processors allow you to create, edit, save, and print text-based **documents** including flyers, letters, and reports.

Features

Principal word processing features include the following:

- **Word wrap**—automatically moves the insertion point to the next line.
- **Search**—quickly locates characters, words, or phrases.
- **Replace**—replaces the located text with new text.

Common Software Application Features	
Windows	Rectangular display areas for documents, programs, or messages
Menu Bar	List of commands that display a pull-down menu of selectable commands
Help	Command on menu bar providing access to a variety of help features
Toolbars	Contain buttons and menu, such as standard and formatting

To be a competent end user, you need to understand the capabilities of basic application software, which includes browsers, word processors, spreadsheets, database management systems, and presentation programs.

SPREADSHEETS

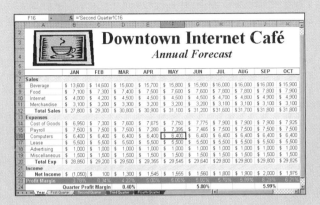

Spreadsheet programs are used to organize, analyze, and graph numeric data. Data and information are stored in **workbooks** containing **worksheets.** Also known as a **worksheet,** a spreadsheet consists of **rows** and **columns** forming **cells.** Individual cells are identified by their **cell address.**

Features

Principal spreadsheet features include the following:

- **Spreadsheets,** also known as worksheets and **sheets,** are rectangular grids.
- **Rows** are identified by numbers.
- **Columns** are identified by letters.
- **Cells** hold data and are formed by the intersection of rows and columns.
- **Text entries** and **numeric entries** are entered in cells.
- **Formulas** are instructions for calculations.
- **Functions** are prewritten formulas.
- **What-if analysis** is the result of changing one or more values and observing the effect on related cells in the spreadsheet.
- **Analytical graphs** or **charts** are used to help visualize data in a spreadsheet.

DATABASE MANAGEMENT SYSTEMS

Database management systems are used to create and use databases. A **relational database** organizes data into related **tables.** Tables are organized by rows called **records** and columns called **fields.**

Features

Principal database management system features include the following:

- **Locate**—find specific information by querying the database.
- **Display**—present selected information on computer monitor or printed in a report.
- **Sort**—arrange records in alphabetical order.
- **Analyze**—use built-in math formulas to manipulate and analyze data.
- **Program control languages**—like SQL (Structured Query Language) are programming languages for advanced users to create sophisticated database applications.

Visual Summary

PRESENTATION GRAPHICS

Presentation graphics are used to create professional and exciting presentations.

Features

Principal presentation graphics features include the following:

- **Outline**—most programs allow users to enter and organize their presentations in outline form.
- **Layout files**—these files present sample text for many different types of presentations.
- **Design templates**—these templates provide selected combinations of text layouts, bullet styles, background colors, patterns, borders, and other enhancements.
- **Animations** include special visual and sound effects including moving graphics and transitions between topics. Additionally, audio and video clips can be inserted. These features add interest and keep the audience's attention.

SOFTWARE SUITES

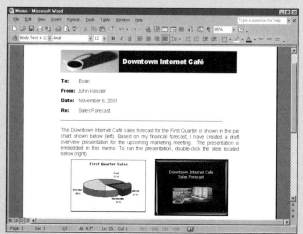

A **software suite** is a collection of individual application packages sold together. While functionally identical, application packages purchased in a suite are significantly less expensive than those purchased separately.

OLE

OLE, or **object linking and embedding,** allows sharing of information (objects) between applications.

- **Source file**—these files provide the objects that can be linked or embedded.
- **Destination file**—these files receive the objects from other (source) files.
- **Object linking**—linked objects are automatically updated whenever a change occurs in the source file.
- **Object embedding**—embedded objects become part of the destination file and can be run from the destination file.

INTEGRATED PACKAGES

An **integrated package** is a single program providing the functionality of a word processor, spreadsheet, database manager, and more. Although not as powerful, integrated packages are much less expensive than software suites or individual applications.

KEY TERMS

advanced application (30)
analytical graph (41)
analyze (43)
animations (46)
basic application (30)
browser (34)
cell (40)
chart (41)
column (40)
database (43)
database management system (DBMS) (43)
database manager (43)
destination file (48)
display (43)
document (36)
field (43)
find (36)
formatting toolbar (30)
formula (40)
function (41)
general-purpose application (30)
Help (30)
home page (34)
hyperlink (34)
Hypertext Markup Language (HTML) (34)
integrated package (50)
layout files (46)
locate (43)
menu (30)
menu bar (30)
numeric entry (40)
object embedding (48)

object linking (48)
object linking and embedding (OLE) (48)
outline (46)
presentation graphics (46)
programming control lanugage (43)
range (41)
record (43)
relational database (43)
replace (36)
row (40)
search (36)
sheet (40)
software suite (48)
sorting (43)
source file (48)
special-purpose application (30)
spreadsheet (40)
standard toolbar (30)
structured query language (SQL) (43)
table (43)
template (46)
text entry (40)
toolbar (30)
uniform resource locator (URL) (34)
Web page (34)
Web site address (34)
what-if analysis (41)
window (30)
word processing (36)
word wrap (36)
workbook (40)
worksheet (40)

CHAPTER REVIEW

Circle the letter or fill in the correct answer.

1. General-purpose applications are also known as _____.
    a. software suites
    b. advanced applications
    c. basic applications
    d. special-purpose applications
    e. none of the above

2. Multimedia, Web authoring, graphics, and virtual reality programs are examples of _____.
    a. special-purpose applications
    b. general-purpose applications
    c. basic applications
    d. occupational applications
    e. b and c

3. Web site addresses are also called _____.
    a. HTML
    b. home pages
    c. URLs
    d. hyperlinks
    e. none of the above

4. _____ are prewritten formulas that perform calculations automatically.
    a. Functions
    b. Macros
    c. Templates
    d. Calculators
    e. none of the above

5. In a relational database, data is organized into _____.
    a. fields
    b. columns
    c. records
    d. tables
    e. rows

6. Database management systems are comprised of tables that are made up of rows called _____ and columns called _____.
    a. fields, records
    b. records, fields
    c. addresses, fields
    d. ranges, sheets
    e. records, ranges

7. Most presentation graphics programs provide _____ that include sample text for many different types of presentations.
    a. layout files
    b. templates
    c. samples
    d. records
    e. formatting

8. The file an object is linked from is called the _____.
    a. destination file
    b. origin file
    c. layout file
    d. support file
    e. source file

9. To have an object automatically updated in a destination file when a change is made to the source file, the object must be _____.
    a. embedded
    b. linked
    c. replaced
    d. resolved
    e. amended

10. A(n) _____ is a single program that provides the functionality of a word processor, spreadsheet, database manager, and more.
    a. general-purpose application
    b. software suite
    c. integrated package
    d. program manager
    e. none of the above

Match each numbered item with the most closely related lettered item. Write your answers in the spaces provided.

a. browser
b. cell
c. word processor
d. general-purpose applications
e. HTML
f. find
g. range
h. formulas
i. toolbar
j. template
k. window
l. what-if analysis
m. spelling checker
n. relational database
o. URL
p. sorting
q. home page
r. presentation graphics
s. software suite
t. OLE

1. Word processors, spreadsheets, database management systems, and presentation graphics. _d_
2. Rectangular area that can contain a document, program, or message. _k_
3. A feature that contains buttons and menus to provide access to commonly used commands. _h_
4. Software that connects to and displays Web resources. _a_
5. Addresses of resources on the Web. _o_
6. Programming language for the document files that are used to display Web pages. _e_
7. Opening page of a Web site. _q_
8. Software that creates text-based documents such as reports, letters, and memos. _c_
9. Identifies incorrectly spelled words and suggests alternatives. _m_
10. Tool that quickly locates any character, word, or phrase in a document. _f_
11. The intersection of a row and column in a spreadsheet. _b_
12. A collection of two or more cells in a spreadsheet. _g_
13. Instructions for calculations. _h_
14. Spreadsheet feature in which changing one or more numbers results in the automatic recalculation of all related fields. _l_
15. A widely used database structure, in which data is organized into related tables. _n_
16. Arranging objects numerically or alphabetically. _p_
17. Graphics used to communicate a message or to persuade. _r_
18. Professionally designed model presentations provided in a presentation graphics program. _j_
19. Individual application programs that are sold together as a group. _s_
20. Powerful feature of many application programs that allows sharing of information. _t_

On a separate sheet of paper, respond to each question or statement.

1. Explain the difference between general-purpose and special-purpose applications.
2. What is the difference between a function and a formula? How is a formula related to what-if analysis?
3. What are presentation graphics programs? How are they used?
4. Explain the difference between a linked object and an embedded object? What are the advantages of OLE?
5. What is the difference between an integrated package and a software suite? What are the advantages and disadvantages of each?

1 Online Personal Information Managers

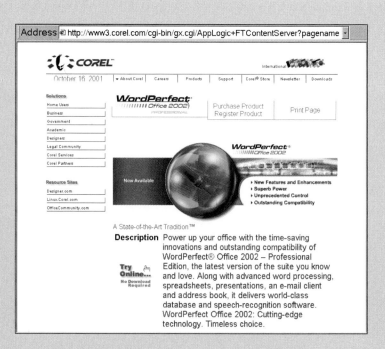

Online Personal Information Managers, or PIMs, are among the most popular Web-based applications. Visit our Making IT Work for You page at http://www.mhhe.com/oleary and link to some online PIMs. Explore each, and then answer the following questions: (a) Describe the common features of online PIMs. (b) What is the advantage of using an online PIM versus one that is stored on your system's hard disk? (c) What are the disadvantages? (d) Which would you choose? Why?

2 Corel Office Suite

Microsoft's major competitor in the office suite market is Corel. Visit our site at http://www.mhhe.com/oleary to connect to Corel's Web site. Review the site, and then write a one-page paper that answers the following questions: (a) What applications are provided in Corel's WordPerfect Office Suite? (b) What are the similarities and differences between the Microsoft and Corel office suites? (c) Which suite would you choose? Why?

Interactive Companion CD-ROM 1

Complete the "Word Processing and Spreadsheets Lab" located on your Interactive Companion CD-ROM, and then answer the following questions in a one-page paper: (a) What was the first really successful microcomputer, and why did people buy it? (b) What advantages of word processors are described in the Lab? (c) What is the sample spreadsheet in the Lab used to calculate?

Application Service Providers 2

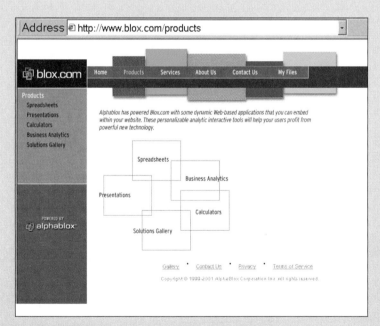

Application Service Providers (ASPs) offer access to basic applications from anywhere in the world. Visit the Making IT Work for You page from our site at http://www.mhhe.com/oleary to link to some ASPs. Explore each, then answer the following questions in a one-page paper: (a) List common applications provided by ASPs. (b) What are some advantages to users of ASPs beyond universal access to software and data? (c) What concerns might a user have about personal data stored at an ASP? (d) Would you use an ASP? If so, how? If not, explain why.

1 Software Suites

Software suites offer both end users and businesses some unique advantages. In a two-page paper titled "Software Suites," address the following items: (a) Define software suites. (b) Which ones are the most popular today? Why? (c) New versions of software suites are coming out all the time. As a user, how can you know when it's time to upgrade?

2 Acquiring Software

There are three common ways to obtain new software (use public domain software, use shareware, buy commercial software). In addition to these three ways, two others are to copy programs from a friend or purchase unauthorized copies of programs. Investigate each option, and then answer the following questions in a two-page paper: (a) Define and discuss each option. Be sure to discuss both the advantages and disadvantages of each. (b) Which seems like the best method to

you? Why? (c) Do you think there is anything wrong with obtaining and using unauthorized software in this manner? Identify and explore the key issues.

SYSTEM SOFTWARE

After you have read this chapter, you should be able to:

1 Describe the differences between system software and application software.

2 Discuss the three basic functions of any operating system.

3 Describe the three categories of operating systems.

4 Discuss the purpose of utilities and utility suites.

5 Identify the five most essential utilities.

6 Define device drivers.

7 Discuss language translators.

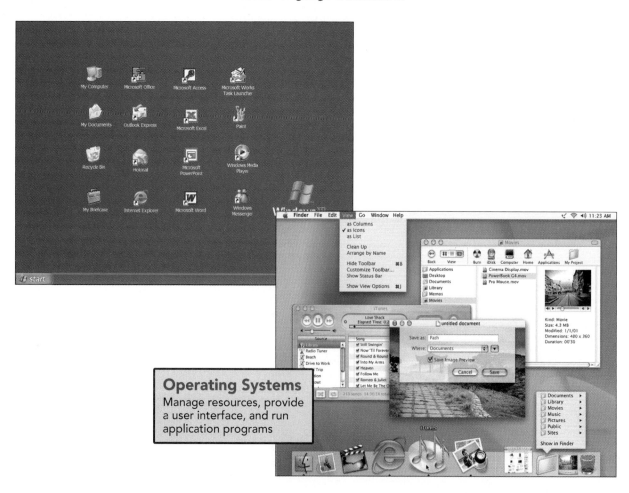

Operating Systems
Manage resources, provide a user interface, and run application programs

Chapter 3

When most people think about computers, they think about surfing the Web, creating reports, analyzing data, storing information, making presentations, and any number of other valuable applications. Most of us think about using the technology. We think about applications and application software. Computers and computer applications have become a fabric in our everyday lives. Most of us agree that they are great . . . as long as they are working.

We don't think about the more mundane and behind-the-scenes computer activities: loading and running programs, coordinating networks that share resources, organizing files, protecting our computers from viruses, performing periodic maintenance to avoid problems, and controlling hardware devices so that they can communicate with one another.

That's the way it should be and the way it is as long as everything is working perfectly. What if new application programs are not compatible and will not run on our current computer system? What if we get a computer virus? What if our hard disk fails? What if we buy a new digital video camera and can't store and edit the images on our computer system? What if our computer starts to run slower and slower?

These are mundane, but critical, issues. This chapter covers these vital issues. System software is designed to handle these and many other concerns. A little knowledge about these programs can go a long way to making your computing life easier. To effectively use computers, competent end users need to understand the functionality of systems software including operating systems, utility programs, device drivers, and language translators.

Utilities
Make computing easier by providing tools to correct problems and to avoid problems

SYSTEM SOFTWARE

System software consists of operating systems, utilities, device drivers, and language translators.

End users like you and me focus on applying computer technology to accomplish specific tasks. We focus on application software. For example, we use word processors to create brochures, letters, and reports. **System software** works with application software to handle the majority of technical details. For example, system software controls where a word processing program is stored in memory, how commands are converted so that the system unit can process them, where a completed document or file is saved, and how the output is printed. (See Figure 3-1.)

System software is not a single program. Rather it is a collection or a system of programs that handle hundreds of technical details with little or no user intervention. System software consists of four kinds of programs:

- **Operating systems** are programs that coordinate computer resources, provide an interface between users and the computer, and run applications.
- **Utilities,** also known as **service programs,** perform specific tasks related to managing computer resources.
- **Device drivers** are specialized programs designed to allow particular input or output devices to communicate with the rest of the computer system.
- **Language translators** convert the programming instructions written by programmers into a language that computers understand and process.

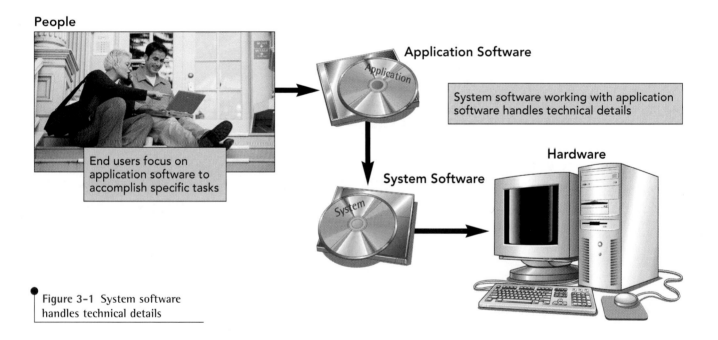

People

End users focus on application software to accomplish specific tasks

Application Software

System software working with application software handles technical details

System Software

Hardware

Figure 3-1 System software handles technical details

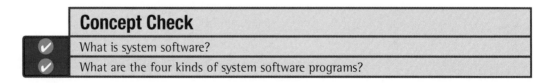

Concept Check

✓ What is system software?

✓ What are the four kinds of system software programs?

OPERATING SYSTEMS

Every computer has an operating system and every operating system performs three basic functions: managing resources, providing a user interface, and running applications.

> Operating systems manage resources, provide a user interface, and run applications.

- **Resources:** These programs coordinate all the computer's **resources** including keyboard, mouse, printer, monitor, storage devices, and memory.

- **User interface:** Users interact with application programs and computer hardware through a **user interface.** Almost all operating systems today provide a windows-like **graphical user interface** (**GUI**) in which graphic objects called **icons** are used to represent commonly used features.

- **Applications:** These programs load and run **applications** such as word processors and spreadsheets. Most operating systems support **multitasking,** or the ability to run more than one application at a time.

CATEGORIES

While there are hundreds of different operating systems, there are only three basic categories: embedded, network, or stand-alone.

- **Embedded operating systems** are used for handheld computers and smaller devices like PDAs. (See Figure 3-2.) These operating systems are called embedded because they are completely stored within the device in its ROM memory. Popular embedded operating systems include Windows CE and Palm OS.

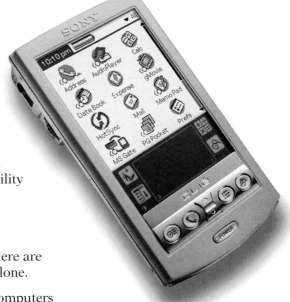

Figure 3-2 PDAs have embedded operating systems

- **Network operating systems** (**NOS**) are used to control and coordinate computers that are linked together. (See Figure 3-3.) The operating system typically is located on one of the connected computers' hard disks. Called the **network server**, this computer coordinates all communication between the other computers. Popular network operating systems include NetWare, Windows NT Server, Windows XP Server, and UNIX.

- **Stand-alone operating systems**, also called **desktop operating systems**, control a single desktop or notebook computer. These operating systems are located on the computer's hard disk. Often desktop computers and notebooks are part of a network. In these cases, the desktop operating system works with the network's NOS to share and coordinate resources. In these situations, the desktop operating system is referred to as the **client operating system**. Popular desktop operating systems include Windows, Mac OS, and some versions of UNIX. For most end users, these are the most important operating systems.

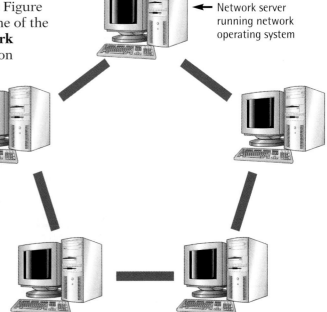

Network server running network operating system

Figure 3-3 Network operating systems run on one computer and control all network communications

Name	Description
DOS	Microsoft's first operating system provided a character-based interface in which commands are typed or selected from menus
Windows 95	Microsoft's first true multitasking and GUI operating system
Windows NT Workstation	Client operating system designed to work with the Windows NT Server
Windows 98	Upgrade to Windows 95
Windows 2000 Professional	Upgrade to Windows NT Workstation
Windows Millennium Edition	Also known as Windows ME, upgrade to Windows 98 specifically designed for home users
Windows XP	Microsoft's newest and most powerful desktop operating system

Figure 3-4 Microsoft Desktop Operating Systems

WINDOWS

By far the most popular microcomputer operating system today is Microsoft's **Windows** with over 80 percent of the market. Windows is designed to run with Intel and Intel-compatible microprocessors such as the Pentium IV. It comes in a variety of different versions. For a summary of Microsoft's desktop operating systems, see Figure 3-4.

Windows gets its name from its use of rectangular boxes called windows. These boxes are extensively used to display information and run programs. Multiple windows can be open at the same time, making it easy to multitask, or work with different programs simultaneously.

Windows provides a user interface called the **desktop.** (See Figure 3-5.) Windows has the look and feel of the Internet Explorer browser. In the

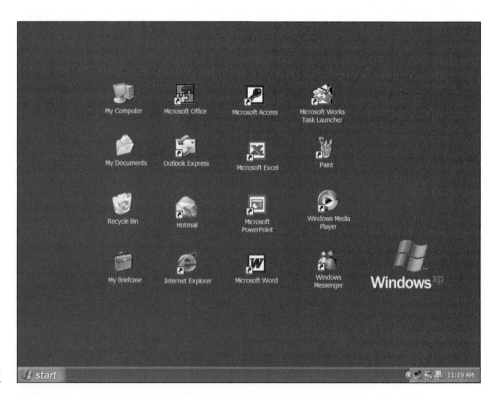

Figure 3-5 Windows XP desktop

Web-style view, you can even use Microsoft's **Active Desktop** to display "active content" from Web pages on your desktop. For example, you could have constantly updating news, weather, sports, and stock prices. (See Making IT Work for You: Active Desktop on pages 68–69.)

Like a traditional filing cabinet, Windows and many other operating systems store information in a system of **files** and **folders**. Unlike the traditional filing cabinet, the information is stored on a secondary storage device such as your hard disk. Files are used to store data and programs. Related files are stored within a folder, and for organization purposes, a folder can contain other folders. For example, to organize your electronic files including those you have created (or will create) for this class, you might use the *My Documents* folder on your hard disk. This folder could contain other folders, each named to indicate their contents. One might be "Computers" and could contain all the files you have created (or will create) for this course.

One of the most common ways for users to interact with the Windows operating system is by selecting icons. For example, you could use icons to list the contents of your *My Documents* folder by taking the steps shown in Figure 3-6.

Figure 3-6 Using icons with Windows XP

1 ● Click the *My Computer* icon on the desktop to open a window providing access to information about your computer system.

2 ● Click the *My Documents* folder in the *Other Places* section in the Web View panel.

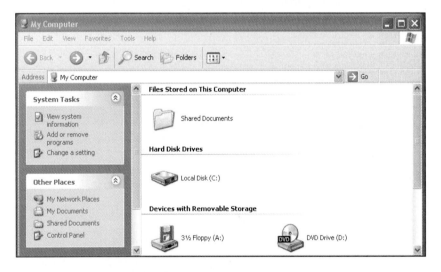

My Documents folder opens displaying your subfolders.

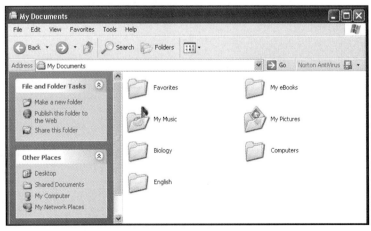

ACTIVE DESKTOP

Want to add some interest to your desktop? Would you like to see the most recent sports scores, news, or stock market updates? Using the Web, you can customize your desktop to provide that information and much more.

How It Works Specialized Web sites called channels provide access to their continually updated or active content. For example, a sports channel would continually update the scores of ongoing baseball games. Using the Web, you select or add active content to your desktop. Throughout the day, your active desktop automatically connects to the channel site, receives updated information, and displays that information on your desktop.

Channel   Active Content   User

Adding Active Content While you can have any Web page displayed on your desktop, Web pages from specialized channel sites provide the most current information. For example, you can add a dynamic weather map to your desktop using Microsoft's Active Desktop Gallery:

 1 • **While connected to the Internet, right-click in any open area of the Desktop.**

• **Click** *Properties.*

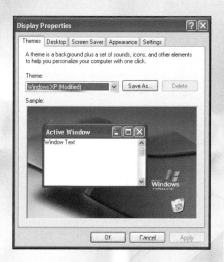

 2 • **Open the** *Desktop* **tab and choose** *Customize Desktop.*

• **Open the** *Web* **tab and click** *New.*

• **Click** *Visit Gallery* **and click the** *Add to Active Desktop* **button for the MSNBC weather map.**

• **Click** *Yes* **to add the item to your desktop, and click** *OK* **to complete the process.**

Refreshing Content The content of your active desktop is updated or refreshed automatically by periodically connecting to the channel site and downloading the current information from that site. You can specify how frequently this should occur:

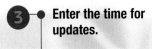 **Move the pointer toward the top of the map until bar appears.**

Open the drop-down menu.

Click *Properties.*

Open the *Schedule* **tab.**

Click *Add.*

Enter the time for updates.

Click *OK.*

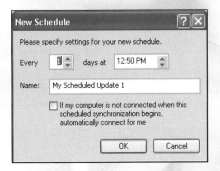

Customizing Your Desktop You can customize the appearance of your active desktop in a variety of ways. For example, you can resize and reposition the weather map and lock its new setting:

 Move pointer toward top of map until bar appears.

Click and drag window to relocate map on the desktop.

Resize window.

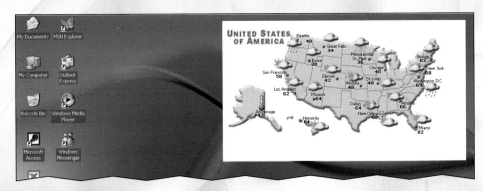

The Web is continually changing and some of the specifics presented in this Making IT Work for You may have changed. See our Web site at http://www.mhhe.com/oleary for possible changes and to learn more about this application of technology.

The **Start menu** displays a list of commands that can be used to gain access to information, change hardware settings, find information, get online help, run programs, log off a network, and shut down your computer system. For example, you could use the Start menu to run the Internet Explorer program as shown in Figure 3-7.

1 Click *Start* on the task bar to open the Start Menu.

2 Click the *Internet Explorer* icon to open your homepage.

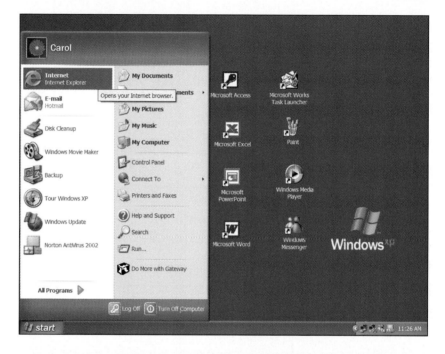

Internet Explorer opens to the address chosen as your homepage.

Figure 3-7 Using the Start menu with Windows XP

MAC OS

The **Mac OS** is designed to run on Macintosh computers. (See Figure 3-8.) While its market share is much less than that of Windows, it is a very powerful and easy-to-use operating system. The latest version of the Macintosh operating system is OS X. This operating system provides a number of unique features:

- **Aqua** is an intuitive user interface.
- **Dock** provides a flexible tool for organizing files.
- **Sherlock** locates information on the Web as well as on the user's computer system.

UNIX

The **Unix** network operating system was originally designed to run on minicomputers in network environments. Now, it is also used by powerful microcomputers and by servers on the Web. There are a large number of different versions of UNIX. One receiving a great deal of attention today is **Linux.**

Figure 3-8 Mac OS

While Windows, the Mac OS, and many versions of UNIX are **proprietary operating systems** (that is, they are owned and licensed by a company), Linux is not. It is free and available from many sources, including the Web. As a graduate student at the University of Helsinki, Linus Torvalds developed Linux in 1991. He has provided the operating system free to others and has encouraged further development. (See Figure 3-9.)

Concept Check

✓ List the three basic functions of an operating system.

✓ What are the three basic categories of operating systems?

✓ Name three common operating systems for microcomputers.

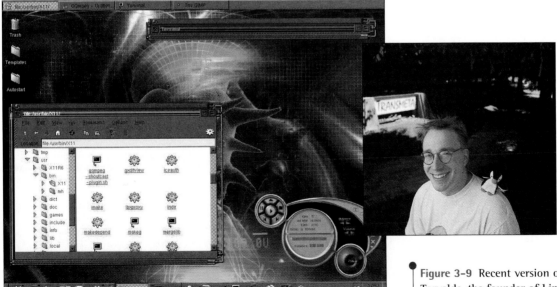

Figure 3-9 Recent version of Linux and Linus Torvalds, the founder of Linux

Utilities are programs that make computing easier. Operating systems often include utility programs. Norton SystemWorks and McAfee Office are utility suites.

Ideally, microcomputers should run and run and run without problems. However, that simply is not the case. All kinds of things can happen—internal hard disks can crash, destructive programs called viruses can invade a system, computers can freeze up, operations can slow down, and so on. These events can make computing very frustrating. That's where utilities come in. Utilities are specialized programs designed to make computing easier.

There are hundreds of different utility programs. The five most essential utilities are:

- **Troubleshooting programs** that recognize and correct problems, ideally before they become serious problems.
- **Antivirus programs** that guard your computer system against viruses or other damaging programs that can invade your computer system.
- **Uninstall programs** that allow you to safely and completely remove unneeded programs and related files from your hard disk.
- **Backup programs** that make copies of files to be used in case the originals are lost or damaged.
- **File compression programs** that reduce the size of files so they require less storage space and can be sent more efficiently over the Internet.

Most operating system programs provide some utility programs. Even more powerful utility programs can be purchased separately or in utility suites.

1 ● Click *Start.*

2 ● Click *All Programs.*

● Click *Accessories.*

● Choose *System Tools.*

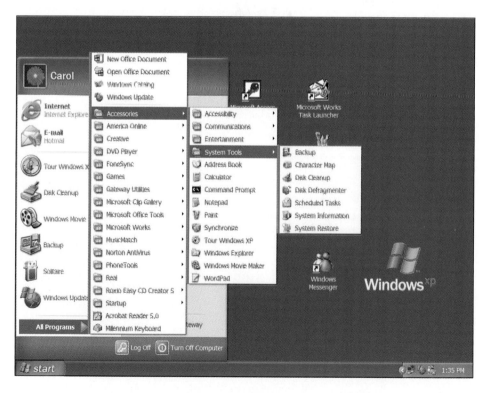

Figure 3-10 Windows utilities

WINDOWS UTILITIES

The Windows operating systems are accompanied with several utility programs, including Backup, Disk Cleanup, and Disk Defragmenter. These utilities can be accessed from the Systems Tools menu. (See Figure 3-10.)

Backup is a utility program that makes a copy of selected or all files that have been saved onto a disk. It helps to protect you from the effects of a disk failure. For example by selecting *Backup* from the Windows XP System Tools menu, you can create a backup for your hard disk as shown in Figure 3-11.

When you surf the Web, a variety of programs and files are saved on your hard disk. Many of these and other files are not essential. **Disk Cleanup** is a trouble-shooting utility that identifies and eliminates nonessential files. This frees up valuable disk space and improves system performance.

1 • Click *Start.*

• Select *Accessories* from the *All Programs* menu.

• Select *Backup* from the *System Tools* menu.

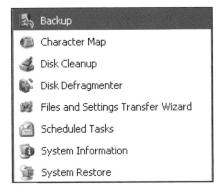

2 • Run the Wizard and specify your settings.

• Choose *Backup* and choose the files you want to include.

• Choose the destination for the backup.

3 • Finish the Wizard to back up the selected drive.

• Close the *Progress Window* or view the report.

Figure 3-11 Backup utility

For example, by selecting *Disk Cleanup* from the Windows XP System Tools menu, you can eliminate unneeded files on your hard disk as shown in Figure 3-12.

Typically, after a hard disk has been used for a while, a large file cannot be stored in one location. Rather, the file has to be broken up, or **fragmented**, into small parts and the parts are stored wherever space is available. After a period of time, the hard disk becomes highly fragmented, slowing operations.

1 Click *Start.*

Select *Accessories* from the *All Programs* menu.

Select *Disk Cleanup* from the *System Tools* menu.

2 Verify the files suggested for cleanup.

Click *OK.*

Click *Yes* to begin disk cleanup.

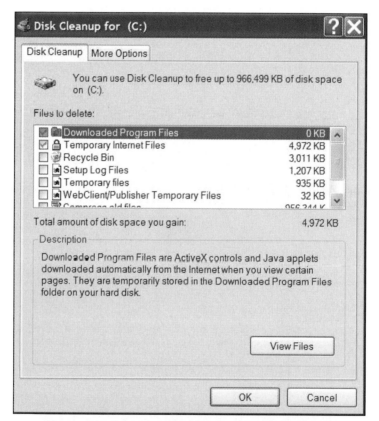

3 The utility cleans the selected files.

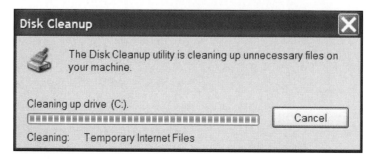

Figure 3-12 Disk cleanup utility

Disk Defragmenter is a utility program that locates and eliminates unnecessary fragments and rearranges files and unused disk space to optimize operations. For example, by selecting *Disk Defragmenter* from the Windows XP Systems Tool menu, you can defrag your hard disk as shown in Figure 3-13.

While these and other utility programs included with Windows are effective, specialty programs offer a wider variety and higher level of support. These programs can be purchased separately or in suites.

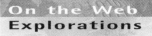
1 ● Click *Start.*

● Select *Accessories* from the *All Programs* menu.

● Select *Disk Defragmenter* from the *System Tools* menu.

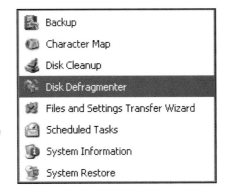

2 ● If necessary, choose the drive you want to analyze and defragment.

● Click the *Analyze* button to determine whether defragging is needed.

● View the report or, if necessary, defragment the drive.

● Click the *Defragment* button to begin defragging.

● When defragmentation is complete for the selected drive, view the report or close the window.

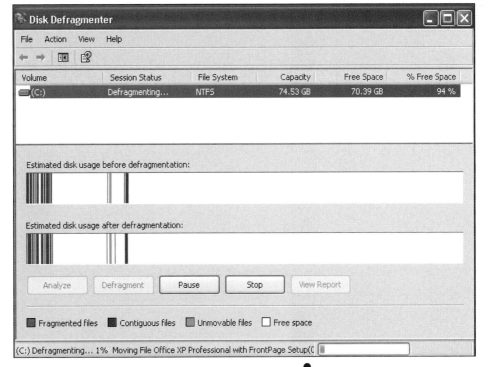

Figure 3-13 Disk defragmenter utility

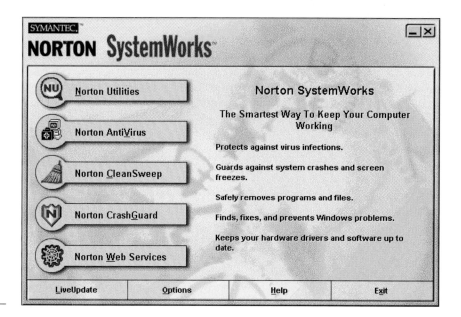

Figure 3-14 Norton
SystemWorks

UTILITY SUITES

Like application software suites, utility suites combine several programs into one package. Buying the package is less expensive than buying the programs separately. The two best-known utility suites are McAfee Office and Norton SystemWorks.

Norton SystemWorks includes a suite of five separate program groups. Each group can be purchased separately or as part of the suite. (See Figure 3-14.)

- **Norton Utilities** is a collection of several separate troubleshooting utilities. These programs can be used to find and fix problems, improve system performance, prevent problems from occurring, and troubleshoot a variety of other problems.
- **Norton AntiVirus** is a collection of antivirus programs that can protect your system from over 21,000 different viruses, quarantine or delete existing viruses, and automatically update its virus list to check for the newest viruses. (See Figure 3-15.)

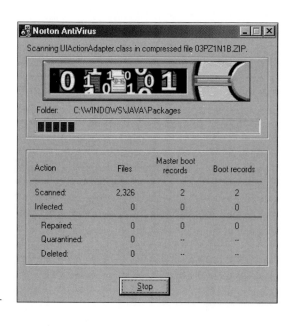

Figure 3-15 Norton AntiVirus

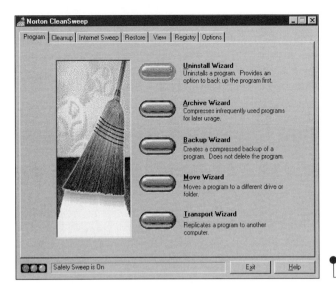

Figure 3-16 Norton CleanSweep

- **Norton CleanSweep** is a collection of programs that guide you through the process of safely removing programs and files you no longer need. (See Figure 3-16.) Additionally, they will archive, move, and make backups of programs as well as clean up your hard disk. They can also protect your existing files from damage when you install new programs.
- **Norton CrashGuard** is a collection of troubleshooting utilities. These programs can automatically protect you against programs that crash or freeze the display screen. Before an event causes your system to crash or freeze, CrashGuard intervenes, providing you with options to recover your current work.
- **Norton Web Services** monitors your system for out-of-date software and notifies you of available software updates that can be installed automatically from the Internet.

Concept Check

- ✓ What are utilities?
- ✓ List some common utilities.
- ✓ Name some of the utility suites currently available.

DEVICE DRIVERS

Every device, such as a mouse or printer, that is connected to a computer system has a special program associated with it. This program, called a **device driver** or simply a **driver,** works with the operating system to allow communication between the device and the rest of the computer system. Each time the computer system is started, the operating system loads all of the device drivers into memory.

> Device drivers are specialized programs that allow devices such as a mouse or keyboard to communicate with the rest of the computer system.

Whenever a new device is added to a computer system, a new device driver must be installed before the device can be used. Windows supplies hundreds of different device drivers with its system software. If a particular device drive is not included, the product's manufacturer will supply one. Many times these drivers are available directly from the manufacturer's Web site.

To assist in the installation and removal of device drivers, Windows provides an Add/Remove Hardware Wizard that offers step-by-step guidance. To access this wizard, follow the steps presented in Figure 3-17.

Concept Check

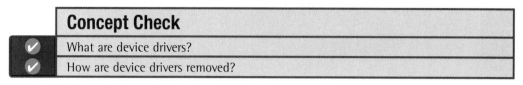

What are device drivers?

How are device drivers removed?

Click *Start.*

Select *Control Panel.*

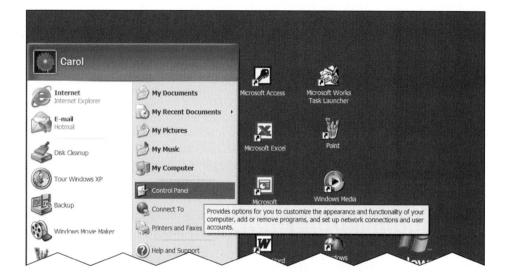

Choose *Add or Remove Programs.*

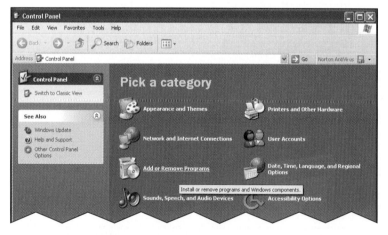

Select the files to add or remove.

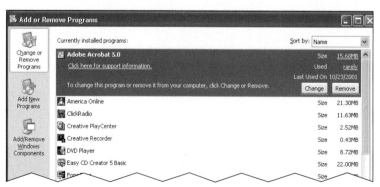

Figure 3–17 Add/Remove Programs

LANGUAGE TRANSLATORS

Computers only understand a language consisting of 0's and 1's called **machine language,** as we will discuss in the next chapter. At one time programmers and computer scientists had to program entirely in 0's and 1's. As you might expect, this communication was very tedious and difficult. To ease this burden, special programming languages were developed that more closely approximate human language. **Language translators** convert these programming statements into the zeros and ones that the computer is able to process. These translators are indispensable tools for developing new software applications and for maintaining existing applications.

> Language translators convert human-oriented programming languages to machine language.

Concept Check

✔ What is machine language?

✔ What do language translators do?

A Look to the Future

IBM Commits to Autonomic Computing with eLiza Project

Wouldn't it be nice if computers could fix themselves? What if you never had to worry about installing or updating software? What if your computer could continually finetune its operations to maintain peak performance? For many people, this all sounds too good to be true; such maintenance tasks can be time-consuming and confusing. Now imagine you run a business and unless these tasks are performed, you will lose valuable time and money. It is not a pleasant daydream and it quickly becomes a nightmare without properly trained systems administrators to keep servers running smoothly. Add to the problem the predicted shortage of trained systems administrators and you have the makings of a real disaster. Yet recent news from IBM makes the dream of a self-repairing, self-updating, and self-protecting server seem ever closer.

IBM has announced plans to concentrate research efforts on developing just such a server. The project, called eLiza, aims to allow businesses to free themselves from time-consuming maintenance and to create a more complex business infrastructure. The company is dedicating almost 25 percent of its research and development budget to the project, meaning that the project could cost billions. The foundation of this new project lies in the idea of autonomic computing. Such a system is analogous to the human body's ability to regulate systems, such as breathing, on its own. IBM hopes this new system will be similarly self-regulating and invisible. Such a system would revolutionize the way that businesses run.

Given the potential for self-maintaining servers, the question of such a system for microcomputers seems like a natural consequence. What do you think—will microcomputers someday care for themselves?

VISUAL SUMMARY
System Software

OPERATING SYSTEMS

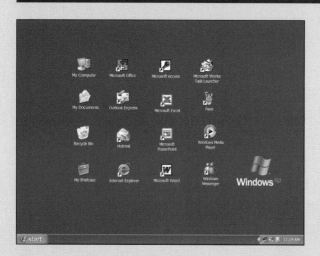

System software consists of operating systems, utilities, device drivers, and language translators.

Operating systems perform three basic functions: manage resources, provide a user interface, and run application programs.

Categories

Three basic categories of operating systems are:

- **Embedded** for handheld computers and smaller devices.
- **NOS** for networked computers.
- **Stand-alone** for desktop and notebook computers.

Windows

Windows is the most widely used operating system. The name Windows comes from the rectangular boxes (windows) used to display information and run applications.

Multiple windows can be open to **multitask**, or work with different programs simultaneously. The **desktop** is the user interface provided by Windows. Windows stores information in **files** and **folders**.

Icons are often used to interact with the Windows operating system. Another common way is to use the **Start menu**.

Mac OS

Apple's **Mac OS** is a powerful easy-to-use operating system designed to run on Macintosh computers. The latest version is OS X, which includes the following features:

- **Aqua**—an intuitive user interface.
- **Dock**—a flexible tool for organizing files.
- **Sherlock**—a search tool for locating information on the Web and on the user's computer system.

UNIX

UNIX was originally designed to run on minicomputers in network environments. Now it is also used on powerful microcomputers and servers on the Web. There are many different versions of UNIX.

One version, **Linux**, is receiving a great deal of attention today. While Windows and Mac OS are proprietary **operating systems** (owned and licensed), Linux is free and available from many sources including the Web. Linus Torvalds originally developed Linux in 1991.

To manage time effectively, competent end users need to understand the functionality of system software including operating systems, utility programs, device drivers, and language translators.

UTILITIES

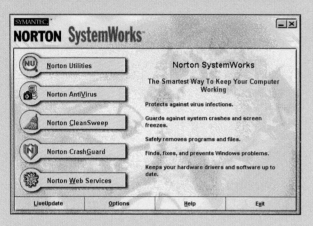

Utilities are specialized programs designed to make computing easier. The most essential are **troubleshooting**, **antivirus**, **uninstall**, **backup**, and **file compression programs**.

Windows Utilities

The Windows operating systems come with several utility programs accessible from the Systems Tools menu. Three such utilities are:

- **Backup**—for backing up files.
- **Disk Cleanup**—a troubleshooting utility for monitoring storage capacity.
- **Disk Defragmenter**—for locating and eliminating unnecessary fragments and rearranging files and unused disk space.

Utility Suites

Utility suites combine several programs into one package. The two best known are McAfee Office and Norton SystemWorks.

Norton SystemWorks has five program groups:

- **Norton Utilities**
- **Norton AntiVirus**
- **Norton CleanSweep**
- **Norton CrashGuard**
- **Norton Web Services**

DEVICE DRIVERS

Device Drivers are specialized programs that work with the operating system to allow communication between hardware devices and the rest of the computer system.

Many device drivers are included with Windows. Alternatively, they can be downloaded from the manufacture's Web site. Windows provides a wizard to assist in device driver installation and removal.

LANGUAGE TRANSLATORS

Computers understand the 0's and 1's of **machine language**. At one time all programs were written in machine language, which made programming tedious and difficult. To relieve the burden of writing programs in machine language, special programming languages were developed. These languages consisted of statements that more closely approximated human language. **Language translators** convert these statements into the 0's and 1's that computers are able to process.

KEY TERMS

Active Desktop (67)
antivirus program (72)
applications (65)
backup (73)
backup program (72)
client operating system (65)
desktop (66)
desktop operating systems (65)
device drivers (64, 77)
Disk Cleanup (73)
Disk Defragmenter (75)
driver (77)
embedded operating system (65)
file compression program (72)
files (67)
folders (67)
fragmented (74)
graphical user interface (GUI) (65)
icons (65)
language translators (64, 79)

Linux (71)
Mac OS (71)
machine language (79)
multitasking (65)
network operating systems (NOS) (65)
network server (65)
operating systems (64)
proprietary operating system (71)
resources (65)
service programs (64)
stand-alone operating systems (65)
Start menu (70)
system software (64)
troubleshooting program (72)
uninstall program (72)
UNIX (71)
user interface (65)
utilities (64)
Windows (66)

CHAPTER REVIEW

MULTIPLE CHOICE

Circle the letter or fill in the correct answer.

1. Service programs are another name for _____.
   a. operating systems
   b. utilities
   c. device drivers
   d. language translators
   e. interfaces

2. _____ are specialized programs designed to allow input and output devices to communicate with a computer system.
   a. Utilities
   b. Resources
   c. Device drivers
   d. GUIs
   e. Windows

3. Language translators convert human language into _____.
   a. machine language
   b. UNIX
   c. service programs
   d. operating systems
   e. none of the above

4. Desktop operating systems are also called _____.
   a. network operating systems
   b. embedded operating systems
   c. client operating systems
   d. Mac operating systems
   e. stand-alone operating systems

5. The _____ operating system is designed to run on Intel and Intel-compatible micro-processors.
   a. Windows
   b. Mac OS
   c. Linux
   d. Sherlock
   e. Norton

6. The _____ operating system was originally designed to run on minicomputers in network environments.
   a. Windows
   b. Mac OS
   c. UNIX
   d. Sherlock
   e. Norton

7. To remove unneeded programs and related files from a hard disk you would use a _____.
   a. backup program
   b. trouble-shooting program
   c. file compression program
   d. antivirus program
   e. uninstall program

8. Files that are broken into small parts and stored wherever space is available are said to be _____.
   a. compressed
   b. fragmented
   c. lost
   d. uninstalled
   e. none of the above

9. _____ is a Windows program that locates and eliminates unnecessary fragments and rearranges files and unused disk space to optimize operations.
   a. Disk Cleanup
   b. Active Desktop
   c. Sherlock
   d. Disk Defragmenter
   e. Resource Locator

10. Norton SystemWorks is a _____.
   a. Web service
   b. troubleshooting program
   c. utility
   d. utility suite
   e. none of the above

Match each numbered item with the most closely related lettered item. Write your answers in the spaces provided.

a. network operating system (NOS)

b. operating systems

c. icons

d. utilities

e. resources

f. desktop operating system

g. graphical user interface (GUI)

h. system software

i. multitasking

j. embedded operating system

k. desktop

l. network server

m. folders

n. proprietary operating system

o. Mac OS

p. backup program

q. antivirus program

r. file compression program

s. Linux

t. Disk Cleanup

1. Software that deals with the complexities of computer hardware. _____

2. Programs that coordinate computer resources. _b_

3. Programs that perform specific tasks related to managing computer resources. _____

4. Keyboard, mouse, printer, monitor, storage devices, and memory. _e_

5. Interface that allows user to interact with the operating system graphically. _g_

6. Graphic elements that represent commonly used features. _c_

7. A computer's ability to run more than one application at a time. _i_

8. Operating systems completely stored within ROM memory. _j_

9. Operating system used to control and coordinate computers that are linked together. _a_

10. A computer that coordinates all communication between other computers. _l_

11. An operating system located on a single stand-alone hard disk. _____

12. User interface provided by Windows. _____

13. Operating system used by Macintosh computers. _____

14. Along with files, a component of the system that Windows stores information in. _____

15. One popular, and free, version of the UNIX operating system. _____

16. Operating system owned and operated by a company. _____

17. Program that guards your computer system against damaging and invasive programs. _____

18. Program that makes copies of files to be used if originals are lost or damaged. _____

19. Program that reduces the size of files for efficient storage. _____

20. Trouble-shooting utility that identifies and eliminates nonessential files. _____

On a separate piece of paper, respond to each question or statement.

1. Describe system software. What does it consist of?

2. Explain the differences between the three basic categories of operating system.

3. Describe the five most essential utilities.

4. Explain the differences and similarities between Windows, Mac OS, and Linux.

5. Explain the role that language translators play in the relationship between machine and human language.

Active Desktop **1**

Want to add some interest to your desktop? Would you like to see the most recent sports scores, news, or stock market updates? Using the Web, you can customize your desktop to provide that information and much more. To learn more about this technology, review Making IT Work for You: Active Desktop on pages 68 and 69. Then visit our Web site at http://www.mhhe.com/oleary. Once at that site, play the videos and answer the following questions in a one-page paper: (a) How is a new Active Desktop item added? (b) How are the properties for the Active Desktop item displayed? (c) What is the procedure to lock in the position of an Active Desktop item on the Windows Desktop?

McAfee Utility Suite **2**

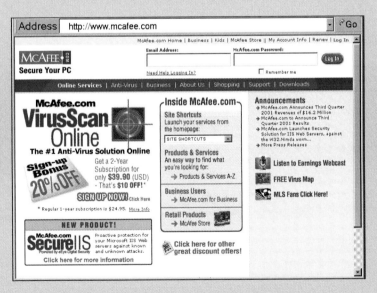

McAfee and Symantec are producers of some of the most widely used utility software. Visit our site at http://www.mhhe.com/oleary to link to their Web sites. Research their latest utility suites, and then write a one-page paper that answers the following questions: (a) What utilities are included in McAfee's suite? (b) What are the similarities and differences between McAfee's and the Symantec suite? (c) Which suite would you purchase? Why?

EXPANDING YOUR KNOWLEDGE

1 Interactive Companion CD-ROM

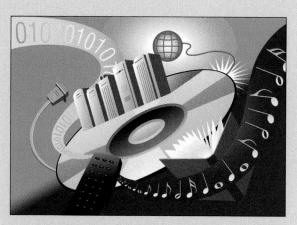

Complete the "File Organization" Lab located on your Interactive Companion CD-ROM and then answer the following questions in a one-page paper: (a) What necessary disk operations does a file system "hide" from the user? (b) What does the term "slack" refer to? (c) What is the difference between a system file and a user file?

2 Customized Desktop

There are several ways to customize your computer's desktop to make it more interesting, informative, or efficient. To learn about customizations, connect to the Yahoo site at http://www.yahoo.com and look at the subject area "Computers and Internet: Desktop Customization" or search the Web using the keywords "desktop customization."

Explore several options and then write a one-page paper that addresses the following: (a) Summarize some of the customizations you found. (b) Briefly explain how these customizations are added to a user's computer. (c) Explain how you could use these customizations to make your computing experience more enjoyable or productive.

Address	http://dir.yahoo.com/Computers_and_Internet/Software/Desktop_Customization ▾	⟲Go

More Yahoo!

Site Listings

Most Popular

- EZskins.com - includes desktop themes, screensavers, and skins.
- Stardock - offers The Object Desktop Network, a component based environment that integrates into your existing OS.
- Celebrity Desktop - related desktop themes, wallpaper backgrounds, screen savers, winamp skins, and more.
- Desktops Unlimited - offers startup and shutdown screens, ICQ and WinAmp skins, screen savers, themes, icons, cursors and more.
- Lighttek Software - makers of Talisman, which replaces the standard Windows desktop interface.

Alphabetical

- 3DTop - uses the icons that are present on your normal desktop and represents them in 3 dimensions instead.
- Awaken Software - offering freeware for desktop customization and Internet browsing.

Featured Category: Information Warfare

News: Digital Music

News: Hackers and Internet Attacks

News: Microsoft Windows

Linux 1

Linux is a powerful operating system used by many computer profession-als. Research Linux and then write a two-page paper titled "Linux" that covers the following points: (a) What is Linux? (b) How was it originally developed? (c) How is Linux currently used? (d) How might it be used in the future? (e) Why is Linux receiving so much attention recently?

Antitrust 2

Much attention has been focused on Microsoft's legal bat-tles over antitrust issues. It has been argued that Microsoft has an unfair marketing advantage because their Windows operating system has been tailored to use Microsoft applica-tions. Write a two-page paper responding to the following questions: (a) Do you think Microsoft has an unfair advan-tage in the software market? (b) How can the outcomes of decisions on the Microsoft case affect the software available for consumers to buy? (c) What ethical obligations do you think Microsoft has to other software devel-opers? What ethical obligations do they have to the consumer? Explain your answer.

THE SYSTEM UNIT

After you have read this chapter, you should be able to:

1

Describe how a computer uses binary codes to represent data in electrical form.

2

Discuss each of the major system unit components.

3

Explain the differences among the three types of memory.

4

Discuss the four principal types of bus lines.

5

Discuss four types of ports.

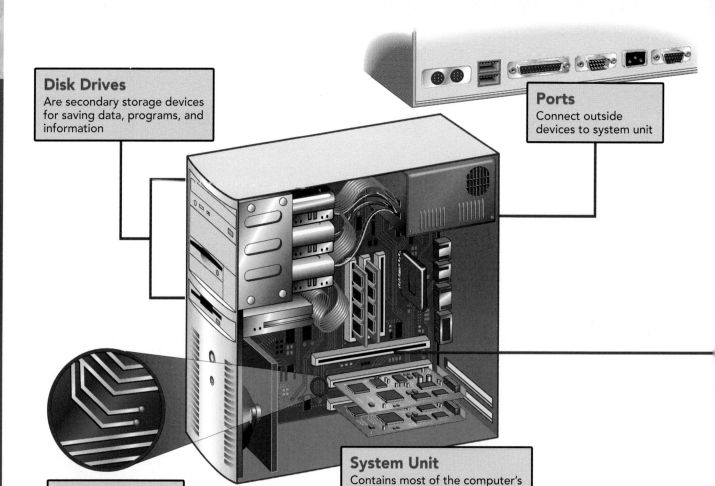

Disk Drives
Are secondary storage devices for saving data, programs, and information

Ports
Connect outside devices to system unit

Bus Lines
Provide data pathways that connect various system components

System Unit
Contains most of the computer's electronic components

How does the system unit work? This chapter explains the workings of the system unit. Why are some microcomputers more powerful than others? The answer lies in three words: **speed, capacity,** and **flexibility.** After reading this chapter, you will be able to judge how fast, powerful, and versatile a particular microcomputer is. As you might expect, this knowledge is valuable if you are planning to buy a new microcomputer system or to upgrade an existing system. (The Buyer's Guide and the Upgrader's Guide at the end of this book provide additional information.) It will also help you to evaluate whether or not an existing microcomputer system is powerful enough for today's new and exciting applications. For example, with the right hardware, you can use your computer to watch TV while you work and to capture video clips for class presentations.

Sometime you may get the chance to watch when a technician opens up a microcomputer. You will see that it is basically a collection of electronic circuitry. While there is no need to understand how all these components work, it is important to understand the principles. Once you do, you will then be able to determine how powerful a particular microcomputer is. This will help you judge whether it can run particular kinds of programs and can meet your needs as a user.

Competent end users need to understand the functionality of the basic components in the system unit, including the system board, microprocessor, memory, system clock, expansion slots and cards, bus lines, ports, and cables.

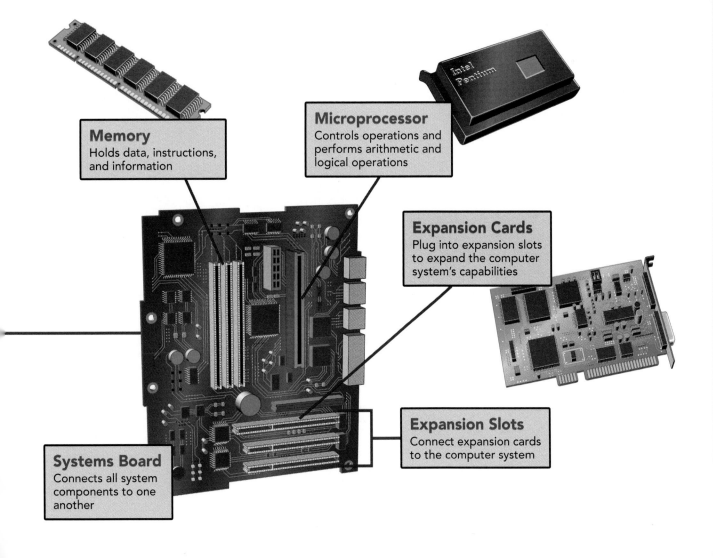

Memory
Holds data, instructions, and information

Microprocessor
Controls operations and performs arithmetic and logical operations

Expansion Cards
Plug into expansion slots to expand the computer system's capabilities

Expansion Slots
Connect expansion cards to the computer system

Systems Board
Connects all system components to one another

System components are housed within the system unit or system cabinet.

The **system unit**, also known as the **system cabinet** or **chassis**, is a container that houses most of the electronic components that make up a computer system. All computer systems have a system unit. For microcomputers, there are three basic types. (See Figure 4-1.)

- **Desktop system units** typically contain the system's electronic components and selected secondary storage devices. Input and output devices, such as a mouse, keyboard, and monitor are located outside the system unit.

- **Notebook system units** are portable and much smaller. These units contain the electronic components, selected secondary storage devices, and input devices (keyboard and pointing device). Located outside the system unit, the monitor is attached by hinges.

- **Personal digital assistant (PDA) system units** are the smallest and contain an entire computer system including the electronic components, secondary storage, and input and output devices.

While the actual size may vary, each type of system unit has the same basic system components including system board, microprocessor, and memory. Before considering these components, however, a more basic issue must be addressed. How do we as human beings communicate with and control all this electronic circuitry?

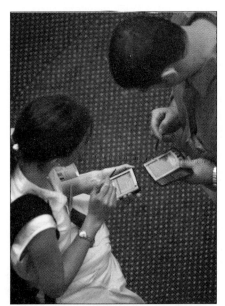

PDA

Desktop system unit

Notebook system unit

Figure 4–1 Basic types of system units

Have you ever wondered why it is said that we live in a digital world? (See Figure 4-2.) It's because computers cannot recognize information the same way you and I can. People follow instructions and process data using letters, numbers, and special characters. For example, if we wanted someone to add the numbers 3 and 5 together and record the answer, we might say "please add 3 and 5 and write the sum on a piece of paper." The system unit, however, is electronic circuitry and cannot directly process such a request. Before any processing can occur within the system unit, a conversion must occur from what we understand to what the system unit can electronically process.

What is the most fundamental statement you can make about electricity? It is simply this: It can be either *on* or *off*. Indeed, there are many forms of technology that can make use of this **two-state** on/off, yes/no, present/absent arrangement. For instance, a light switch may be on or off, or an electric circuit open or closed. A magnetized spot on a tape or disk may have a positive charge or a negative charge. This is the reason, then, that a two-state or binary system is used to represent data and instructions.

The decimal system that we are all familiar with has 10 digits (0, 1, 2, 3, 4, 5, 6, 7, 8, 9). The **binary system,** however, consists of only two digits—0 and 1. Each 0 or 1 is called a **bit**—short for *bi*nary digi*t*. In the system unit, the 0 can be represented by electricity being off, and the 1 by electricity being on. In order to represent numbers, letters, and special characters, bits are combined into groups of eight bits called **bytes.** Each byte typically represents one character.

> Data and instructions are represented electronically with a binary, or two-state, numbering system.

Figure 4-2 The digital world

BINARY CODING SCHEMES

Now let us consider an important question. How are characters represented as 0s and 1s ("off" and "on" electrical states) in the computer? The answer is in the use of **binary coding schemes.** (See Figure 4-3.)

Two of the most popular binary coding schemes use eight bits to form each byte. These two codes are *ASCII* and *EBCDIC*. (See Figure 4-4.) A recently developed code, *unicode,* uses sixteen bits.

- **ASCII,** pronounced *"as*-key," stands for *A*merican *S*tandard *C*ode for *I*nformation *I*nterchange. This is the most widely used binary code for microcomputers.

- **EBCDIC,** pronounced *"eb*-see-dick," stands for *E*xtended *B*inary *C*oded *D*ecimal *I*nterchange *C*ode. It was developed by IBM and is used primarily for large computers.

- **Unicode** is a 16-bit code designed to support international languages like Chinese and Japanese. These languages have too many characters to be represented by the eight-bit ASCII and EBCDIC codes. Unicode was developed by Unicode, Inc., with support from Apple, IBM, and Microsoft.

Code	Uses
ASCII	Microcomputers
EBCDIC	Larger computers
Unicode	International languages

Figure 4-3 Binary codes

When you press a key on the keyboard, a character is automatically converted into a series of electronic pulses that the system can recognize. For example, pressing the number 3 on a keyboard causes an electronic signal to be sent to the microcomputer's system unit where it is converted to the ASCII code of 0011 0011.

Symbol	ASCII	EBCDIC	Symbol	ASCII	EBCDIC
A	0100 0001	1100 0001	X	0101 1000	1110 0111
B	0100 0010	1100 0010	Y	0101 1001	1110 1000
C	0100 0011	1100 0011	Z	0101 1010	1110 1001
D	0100 0100	1100 0100	!	0010 0001	0101 1010
E	0100 0101	1100 0101	"	0010 0010	0111 1111
F	0100 0110	1100 0110	#	0010 0011	0111 1011
G	0100 0111	1100 0111	$	0010 0100	0101 1011
H	0100 1000	1100 1000	%	0010 0101	0110 1100
I	0100 1001	1100 1001	&	0010 0110	0101 0000
J	0100 1010	1101 0001	(	0010 1000	0100 1101
K	0100 1011	1101 0010	)	0010 1001	0101 1101
L	0100 1100	1101 0011	*	0010 1010	0101 1100
M	0100 1101	1101 0100	+	0010 1011	0100 1110
N	0100 1110	1101 0101	0	0011 0000	1111 0000
O	0100 1111	1101 0110	1	0011 0001	1111 0001
P	0101 0000	1101 0111	2	0011 0010	1111 0010
Q	0101 0001	1101 1000	3	0011 0011	1111 0011
R	0101 0010	1101 1001	4	0011 0100	1111 0100
S	0101 0011	1110 0010	5	0011 0101	1111 0101
T	0101 0100	1110 0011	6	0011 0110	1111 0110
U	0101 0101	1110 0100	7	0011 0111	1111 0111
V	0101 0110	1110 0101	8	0011 1000	1111 1000
W	0101 0111	1110 0110	9	0011 1001	1111 1001

ASCII code for + ← 0010 1011

ASCII code for 3 ← 0011 0011

ASCII code for 5 ← 0011 0101

Figure 4-4 ASCII and EBCDIC binary coding schemes

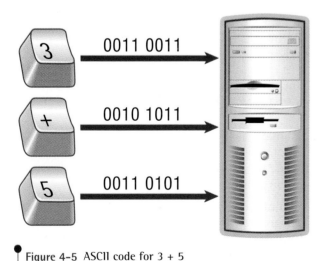

Figure 4-5 ASCII code for 3 + 5

All instructions and data have to be converted into binary data before they can be executed. For example, the instructions 3 + 5 requires 24 bits using the ASCII coding scheme. (See Figure 4-5.)

Why are coding schemes important? Whenever files are used or shared by different computers or applications, the same coding scheme must be used. Generally, this is not a problem if both computers are microcomputers since both would most likely use ASCII code. And most microcomputer applications store files using this code. However, problems occur when files are shared between microcomputers and larger computers that use EBCDIC code. The files must be translated from one coding scheme to the other before processing can begin. Fortunately, special conversion programs are available to help with this translation.

SYSTEM BOARD

The **system board** is also known as the **main board** or **motherboard.** (See Figure 4-6.) The system board is the communications web for the entire computer system. Every component of the system unit connects directly to the system board. It acts as a data path allowing the various components to communicate with one another. External devices such as keyboard, mouse, and monitor could not communicate with the system unit without the system board.

> The system board connects all system components and allows input and output devices to communicate with the system unit.

On a desktop computer, the system board is located at the bottom of the systems unit. It is a large flat circuit board covered with sockets and other electronic parts, including a variety of chips. A **chip** consists of a tiny circuit-board etched on a postage-stamp-sized square of sandlike material called silicon. (See Figure 4-7.) A chip is also called a **silicon chip, semiconductor,** or **integrated circuit.** Chips are mounted on carrier packages, which then plug into sockets on the system board.

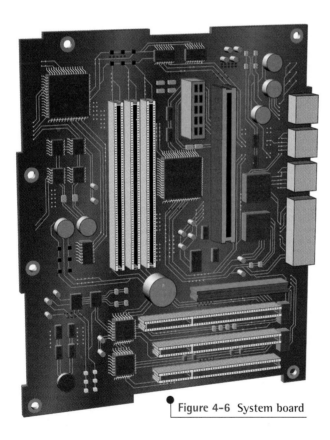

Figure 4-6 System board

Figure 4-7 Chip

Concept Check

✔	What is the system unit? Name and describe the three basic types of system units.
✔	What are bits and bytes?
✔	Name and describe the three most popular binary coding schemes.
✔	What is the system board and what does it do?

The CPU is located on the microprocessor chip and has two components—the control unit and the arithmetic-logic unit.

In a microcomputer system, the **central processing unit (CPU)** or **processor** is contained on a single chip called the **microprocessor.** The microprocessor is often contained within a cartridge that plugs in to the system board. (See Figure 4-8.) The microprocessor is the "brains" of the system. It has two basic components: the control unit and the arithmetic-logic unit.

CONTROL UNIT

The **control unit** tells the rest of the computer system how to carry out a program's instructions. It directs the movement of electronic signals between memory—which temporarily holds data, instructions, and processed information—and the arithmetic-logic unit. It also directs these control signals between the CPU and input and output devices.

Figure 4–8 Microprocessor cartridge

ARITHMETIC-LOGIC UNIT

The **arithmetic-logic unit,** usually called the **ALU,** performs two types of operations—arithmetic and logical. **Arithmetic operations** are, as you might expect, the fundamental math operations: addition, subtraction, multiplication, and division. **Logical operations** consist of comparisons. That is, two pieces of data are compared to see whether one is equal to (=), less than (<), or greater than (>) the other.

MICROPROCESSOR CHIPS

Chip capacities are often expressed in word sizes. A **word** is the number of bits (such as 16, 32, or 64) that can be accessed at one time by the CPU. The more bits in a word, the more powerful—and the faster—the computer is. As mentioned previously, eight bits group together to form a byte. A 32-bit-word computer can access 4 bytes at a time. A 64-bit-word computer can access 8 bytes at a time. Therefore, the 64-bit computer is faster.

Most microcomputers process data and instructions in millionths of a second, or **microseconds.** Supercomputers, by contrast, operate at speeds measured in nanoseconds and even picoseconds—1,000 to 1 million times as fast as microcomputers. (See Figure 4-9.)

There are two types of microprocessor chips.

- **CISC chips:** The most common type of microprocessor is the **complex instruction set computer (CISC)** chip. This design was popularized by Intel and is the basis for their line of microprocessors. It is the most widely used chip design with thousands of programs written specifically for it. Intel's Pentium III and Pentium IV are CISC chips. AMD, another manufacturer of CISC chips, produces the Athlon chip.

- **RISC chips: reduced instruction set computer (RISC)** chips use fewer instructions. This design is simpler and less costly than CISC chips. The PowerPC is a chip produced by Motorola with IBM and Apple. Two other recent RISC chips are Digital Equipment Corporation's (DEC) Alpha chip and Silicon Graph's MIPS

Unit	Speed
Millisecond	Thousandth of a second
Microsecond	Millionth of a second
Nanosecond	Billionth of a second
Picosecond	Trillionth of a second

Figure 4–9 Processing speeds

chip. These chips are used in many of today's most powerful microcomputers. See Figure 4-10 for a table of popular microprocessors.

Some specialized processor chips are available. One example is the chip used in smart cards. A **smart card** is essentially a plastic card the size of a regular credit card that has an embedded chip. While most current smart cards can store 80 times the information stored on the magnetic strip of a regular credit card, larger capacity cards are expected soon. A single smart card can replace many of the items we carry in our wallets including personal identification cards, credit cards, debit cards, and phone cards. They can be used to record personal financial and medical information. Since the information contained on the chip can be encrypted or coded and protected by a password or pin number, they offer strong security and privacy.

Visa, MasterCard, and American Express have introduced their smart cards to millions of users. (See Figure 4-11.) Many colleges and universities are distributing smart cards to their students for identification. The University of Michigan, for example, provides its students with a smart card called the Mcard.

Microprocessor	Type	Typical Use
Pentium	CISC	Microcomputers
Athlon	CISC	Microcomputers
PowerPC	RISC	Apple Computers
ALPHA	RISC	Supercomputers, workstations
MIPS	RISC	Workstations, video games

Figure 4-10 Popular microprocessors

Figure 4-11 Smart card

MEMORY

Memory is a holding area for data, instructions, and information. Like microprocessors, **memory** is contained on chips connected to the system board. There are three well-known types of memory chips: random-access memory (RAM), read-only memory (ROM), and complementary metal-oxide semiconductor (CMOS).

> Memory holds data, instructions, and information.

RAM

Random-access memory (RAM) chips hold the program and data that the CPU is presently processing. (See Figure 4-12.) That is, it is temporary or volatile storage. (Secondary storage, which we shall describe in Chapter 6, is permanent storage, such as the data stored on diskettes. Data from this kind of storage must be loaded into RAM before it can be used.)

RAM is called temporary because as soon as the microcomputer is turned off, everything in RAM is lost. It is also lost if there is a power failure that disrupts the electric current going to the microcomputer. For this reason, as we mentioned earlier, it is a good idea to save your work in progress. That is, if you are working on a document or a spreadsheet, every few minutes you should save, or store, the material.

There is a relatively new type of RAM, however, that is not temporary. **Flash RAM** or **flash memory** chips can retain data even if power is disrupted. This

Figure 4-12 RAM chips mounted on circuit board

Unit	Capacity
Kilobyte (KB)	1,000 bytes
Megabyte (MB)	1 million bytes
Gigabyte (GB)	1 billion bytes
Terabyte (TB)	1 trillion bytes

Figure 4-13 Memory capacity

type of memory is more expensive and used primarily in high-end portable computers.

Having enough RAM is important! Some programs may require more memory than a particular microcomputer offers. For instance, Excel 2000 requires 20MB of RAM. Additional RAM is needed to hold any data or other applications. However, many microcomputers—particularly older ones—may not have enough memory to hold the program or to run the program. The capacity or amount of RAM is expressed in bytes. There are four commonly used units of measurement to describe memory capacity. (See Figure 4-13.)

Even if your computer does not have enough RAM to hold a program, it might be able to run the program using **virtual memory.** Most of today's operating systems support virtual memory. With virtual memory, large programs are divided into parts and the parts stored on a secondary device, usually a hard disk. Each part is then read into RAM only when needed. In this way, computer systems are able to run very large programs.

Another term you are apt to hear about in conjunction with RAM is **cache memory** or **RAM cache.** Cache (pronounced "cash") memory is used to store the most frequently accessed information stored in RAM. The cache acts as a temporary high-speed holding area between the memory and the CPU. In a computer with a cache (not all machines have one), the computer detects which information in RAM is most frequently used. It then copies that information into the cache. When needed, the CPU can quickly access the information from the cache. Most newer microprocessors have cache memory built in.

ROM

Read-only memory (ROM) chips have programs built into them at the factory. Unlike RAM chips, ROM chips are not volatile and cannot be changed by the user. "Read only" means that the CPU can read, or retrieve, the programs written on the ROM chip. However, the computer cannot write—encode or change—the information or instructions in ROM.

ROM chips typically contain special instructions for detailed computer operations. For example, ROM instructions may start the computer, give keyboard keys their special control capabilities, and put characters on the screen. ROMs are also called **firmware.**

Type	Use
RAM	Programs and data
ROM	Fixed startup instructions
CMOS	Flexible startup instructions

Figure 4-14 Memory

CMOS

A **complementary metal-oxide semiconductor (CMOS)** chip provides flexibility and expandability for a computer system. It contains essential information that is required every time the computer system is turned on. The chip supplies such information as the amount of RAM, type of keyboard, mouse, monitor, and disk drives. Unlike RAM, it is powered by a battery and does not lose its contents when the power is turned off. Unlike ROM, its contents can be changed to reflect changes in the computer system such as increased RAM and new hardware devices.

See Figure 4-14 for a summary of the three types of memory.

Concept Check

✔ Which two basic components make up the CPU?

✔ Name two types of microprocessor chips.

✔ What are the three well-known types of memory chips?

✔ What makes RAM different from ROM?

SYSTEM CLOCK

The **system clock** is located on a small specialized chip that produces precisely timed electrical beats or impulses. The microprocessor uses these beats as a timing mechanism to coordinate and synchronize all computer operations. The clock speed for powerful microcomputers is measured in **gigahertz** or billions of beats per second. The faster the clock speed, the faster the computer can process information.

> Speed of computer operations is measured in gigahertz, or billionths of a second.

EXPANSION SLOTS AND CARDS

Computers are known for having different kinds of "architectures." Machines that have **closed architecture** are manufactured in such a way that users cannot easily add new devices. Most microcomputers have **open architecture.** They allow users to expand their systems by providing **slots** on the system board. Users can insert optional devices known as **expansion cards** into these slots. (See Figure 4-15.) Expansion cards are also called **plug-in boards, controller cards, adapter cards,** and **interface cards.**

> Expansion slots provide an open architecture. Expansion cards provide network connections, TV tuner cards, and more.

Expansion cards plug into slots located on the system board. Ports on the cards allow cables to be connected from the expansion cards to devices outside the system unit. Among the kinds of expansion cards available are:

Figure 4-15 Expansion card

- **Network adapter cards:** These cards are used to connect a computer to one or more other computers. This forms a communication network whereby users can share data, programs, and hardware. The network adapter card typically connects the system unit to a cable that connects to the other devices on the network. The network adapter card plugs into a slot inside the system unit.

- **Modem cards:** Most computers today have modem cards, also known as **internal modems.** These cards allow distant computers to communicate with one another by converting electronic signals from within the system unit into electronic signals that can travel over telephone lines and other types of connections.

- **TV tuner cards:** Now you can watch television, capture video, and surf the Internet at the same time. TV tuner cards, also known as **television boards** and **personal video recorder cards,** contain a TV tuner and a video converter that changes the TV signal into one that can be displayed on your monitor. (See Making IT Work for You: TV Tuner Cards and Video Clips, on pages 98–99.)

TIPS

Does your computer seem to be getting slower and slower? Perhaps it's so slow you are thinking about buying a new one. Before doing that, consider the following suggestions that might add a little zip to your current system.

1 **Uninstall programs you no longer need.** Explore the contents of your hard disk and identify programs that you no longer need. If you have Windows XP, use Start/Control Panel/Add/Remove Programs (for Windows 2000 use Start/Settings/Control Panel/Add/Remove Programs) to access the Uninstall feature.

2 **Remove unneeded fonts.** If you have Windows XP use Start/Control Panel/Fonts in the classic view (for Windows 2000 use Start/Settings/Control Panel/Fonts) to determine the different font types stored on your system. To see a sample of any font type, double-click it. Review the fonts and delete those you will not need.

3 **Empty the Recycle Bin.** If you have either Windows 2000 or Windows XP, files are not removed from your hard disk when you delete them. Rather, they are moved to the Recycle Bin. To empty or remove files from the Recycle Bin, open the Recycle Bin and use File/Empty Recycle Bin.

TV TUNER CARDS AND VIDEO CLIPS

Want to watch your favorite television program while you work? Perhaps you would like to include a video clip from television and include it in a class presentation. It's easy using a video TV card.

How It Works A video capture card converts analog signals from a television or VCR into digital signals that your computer can process. Once the card has been installed, you can view, capture, and use television video clips in a variety of ways.

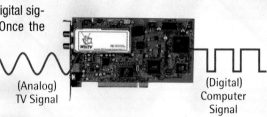

(Analog) TV Signal

(Digital) Computer Signal

Viewing You can be running an application such as Excel and view your favorite TV shows, by taking the steps shown here.

1
- Click the *TV icon* on the desktop.

- Size and move the television window and control box window.

- Select the channel.

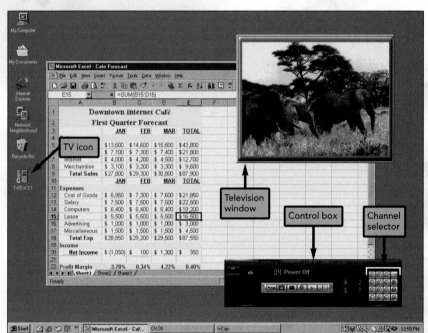

TV icon

Television window

Control box

Channel selector

Capturing You can capture the video playing in the TV window into a digital file by taking the steps shown here.

1
- Specify where to save the video clip on your computer by clicking the *Properties* button.

- Click the *Record* button to start recording.

- Click the *Stop* button to stop recording.

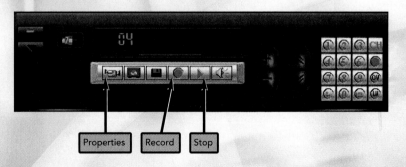

Properties

Record

Stop

Using Once captured in a file, a video can be used in any number of ways. It can be added to a Web page, attached to an e-mail, or added to a class presentation.

For example, you could include a video clip into a PowerPoint presentation by taking the steps shown here.

1 ● Insert the video clip into a page in the presentation by clicking *Insert/Picture/ From File.*

2 ● Click on the image of the inserted video clip anytime during your presentation to play it.

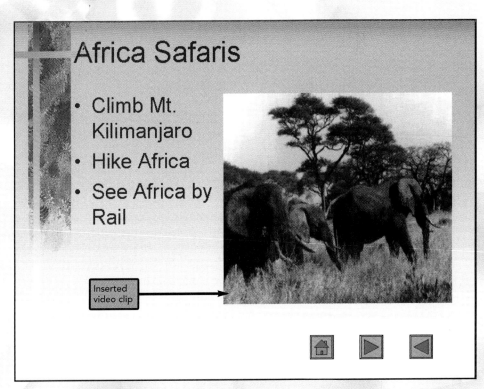

TV tuner cards are relatively inexpensive and easy to install. Some factors limiting their performance on your computer are the speed of your processor, the amount of memory and secondary storage capacity.

TV tuner cards are continually changing and some of the specifics presented in this Making IT Work for You may have changed. See our Web site at http://www.mhhe.com/oleary for possible changes and to learn more about this application of technology.

Figure 4-16 A PC card

- **PC cards:** To meet the size and constraints of portable computers, credit card–sized expansion boards have been developed. These cards can be easily inserted and replaced from the outside of a portable computer. They are called **PC cards** or **Personal Computer Memory Card International Association (PCMCIA) cards.** These cards can be used for a variety of purposes, including increasing memory and connecting to the Internet. (See Figure 4-16.)

A wide variety of other expansion boards exist. Some of the most widely used are the following: Video adapter cards are used to adapt a variety of color video display monitors to a computer. CD-ROM cards connect optical disk drives (which we discuss in Chapter 6), and sound boards can record and play back digital sound.

To access the capabilities of an expansion board, the board must be inserted into a slot on the system board and the system reconfigured to recognize the new board. Reconfiguration typically involves installing device drivers as discussed in Chapter 3.

Plug and Play is a set of hardware and software standards developed by Intel, Microsoft, and others. It is an effort by hardware and software vendors to create operating systems, processing units, and expansion boards, as well as other devices, that are able to configure themselves. Ideally, to install a new expansion board all you have to do is insert the board and turn on the computer. As the computer starts up, it will search for these Plug and Play devices and automatically configure the devices and the computer system. Plug and Play is an evolving capability. A limited number of completely Plug and Play–ready systems exist today. However, observers predict that within the next few years this will become a widely adopted standard, and adding expansion boards will be a simple task.

 TIPS Having problems or want to upgrade your system and would like professional help? Here are a few suggestions.

1. **Select a reputable computer store.** Consider local as well as national chain stores. Check them out with the Better Business Bureau.

2. **Visit the store with your computer.** Ideally, have a knowledgeable friend accompany you. Describe the problem and get a written estimate. Ask about the company's warranty.

3. **Tag your system.** If you leave the system, attach a tag with your name, address, and telephone number.

4. **Pay by credit card.** If a dispute occurs, many credit card companies will intervene on your side.

Concept Check

✓	What is the relationship between the microprocessor and the system clock?
✓	What is the difference between a computer with closed architecture and one with open architecture?
✓	What is the difference between a card and a slot?
✓	What is Plug and Play?

A bus line—also known as **data bus** or simply **bus**—connects the parts of the CPU to each other. It also links the CPU to various other components on the system board. A bus is a data roadway along which bits travel. (See Figure 4-17.) Such data pathways resemble a multilane highway. The more lanes there are, the faster traffic can go through. Similarly, the greater the capacity of a bus, the more powerful and faster the operation. A 64-bit bus has greater capacity than a 32-bit bus, for example.

> Bus lines provide data pathways that connect various system components.

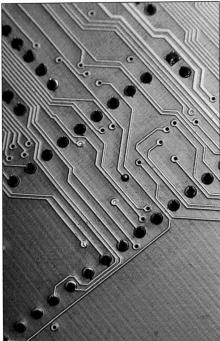

Figure 4–17 Bus lines

Why should you even have to care about what a bus line is? The answer is that, as microprocessor chips have changed, so have bus lines. Many devices, such as expansion boards, will work with only one type of bus line.

A system unit has more than one type of bus line. The four principal bus lines (or "architectures") are:

- **Industry standard architecture (ISA)** was developed for the IBM Personal Computer. First it was an 8-bit-wide data path; then it was 16 bits wide. Although too slow for many of today's applications, the ISA bus is still widely used.
- **Peripheral component interconnect (PCI)** was originally developed to meet the video demands of graphical user interfaces. PCI is a high-speed 32-bit or 64-bit bus that is over 20 times faster than ISA buses. The PCI is expected to replace the ISA bus in the near future. PCI buses are widely used to connect the CPU, memory, and expansion boards.
- **Accelerated graphics port (AGP)** is the newest bus and over twice as fast as the PCI bus. While the PCI bus is used for a variety of purposes, the AGP bus is dedicated to the acceleration of graphics performance. Widely used for graphics and 3-D animations, the AGP is replacing the PCI bus for the transfer of video data.
- **Universal serial bus (USB)** combines with a PCI bus on the system board to support several external devices without inserting cards for each device. The external USB devices are connected from one to another and then on to the USB bus. The USB bus then connects to the PCI bus on the motherboard. USB buses are widely used to support high-speed scanners, printers, and video-capturing devices.

Concept Check

- ✓ What is a bus and what is its function?
- ✓ Describe the four principle buses.
- ✓ Identify the types of devices supported by each architecture.

Ports are connecting sockets. Cables connect input and output devices to ports.

A **port** is a connecting socket on the outside of the system unit. (See Figure 4-18.) Some ports, like the mouse, keyboard, and video ports, are for specific devices. Others, like those listed below, can be used for a variety of different devices.

- **Serial ports** are used for a wide variety of purposes. They are used to connect a mouse, keyboard, modem, and many other devices to the system unit. Serial ports send data one bit at a time and are very good for sending information over a long distance.
- **Parallel ports** are used to connect external devices that need to send or receive a lot of data over a short distance. These ports typically send eight bits of data simultaneously across eight parallel wires. Parallel ports are mostly used to connect printers to the system unit.
- **Universal serial bus (USB) ports** are gradually replacing serial and parallel ports. They are faster, and one USB port can be used to connect several devices to the system unit.
- **High perfomance serial bus (HPSB),** also know as **FireWire ports,** are the newest type. They are 33 times faster than USB ports and are used to connect high-speed printers and even video cameras to the system unit.

Cables are used to connect input and output devices to the system unit via the ports.

Figure 4-18 Ports

Concept Check

- ✓ What is a port and what is its function?
- ✓ Describe four different ports other than the keyboard, mouse, and video ports.
- ✓ What is FireWire?

A Look to the Future

Dallas Semiconductor: Leading the Way to Widespread Use of Wearable Computers

Wouldn't it be nice if you could conveniently access the Internet, send and receive e-mail, maintain your personal schedule book, play interactive games, and surf the Web from anywhere? Of course you can do all that, and more, using wireless technologies and PDAs. What's the next step? Will computers keep getting smaller and more portable? Will people be wearing computers rather than carrying them?

Have you seen photos of prototype wearable computers? Many show people wearing computers like a wristwatch or wearing special eyeglasses with miniature monitors mounted in each lens. A keyboard hangs from their belt or attached to their wrist and a portable system unit is attached to their waist or their arms. Can you see yourself wearing one of these outfits?

Today many people are wearing specialized computers and you can't even tell that they are. Dallas Semiconductor has an entire line of devices including watches, wallets, badge holders, key fobs, and rings. The ring looks just like a high school ring, but is actually a tiny computer capable of downloading information from another computer. The ring acts as a digital identification card, a smart card, and a homing device all in one. The ring can even protect the wearer's privacy by encrypting sensitive information.

Many futurists see people routinely wearing tiny computers that will monitor their health, help them work smarter, and generally enrich their lives. Researchers at George Washington University recently released a list of the top 10 technologies they expect will impact the first 10 years of this century. Included in this list are virtual assistants or computers that will automatically file digital documents, screen calls and e-mail, and even write letters for people. They expect that computers and microchips will literally be everywhere.

Will we be wearing computers soon? Some of us already are and most experts think that the majority of us will be before the end of the decade. What do you think?

VISUAL SUMMARY
The System Unit

SYSTEM UNIT

System unit components are housed within the **system unit** or **system cabinet.**

Three types are:

- **Desktop**—contains electronic components and selected storage devices.
- **Notebook**—portable, monitor attached by hinges.
- **PDA (personal digital assistant)**—smallest, most portable, contains entire system.

ELECTRONIC REPRESENTATION

Data and instructions are represented **electronically** with a two-state **binary system** of numbers (0 and 1). Each 0 or 1 is called a **bit**. A **byte** consists of eight bits and represents one character.

Binary Coding Schemes

Binary coding schemes convert binary data into characters. Three such schemes are:

- **ASCII**—the most widely used for microcomputers.
- **EBCDIC**—developed by IBM and used primarily by large computers.
- **Unicode**—16-bit code to support international languages like Chinese and Japanese.

SYSTEM BOARD

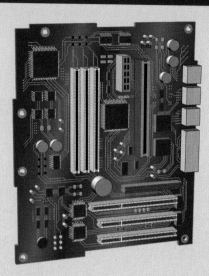

The **system board**, also known as the **main board** or the **motherboard**, connects all system components. It is a flat circuit board covered with sockets and other electronic parts, including a variety of chips.

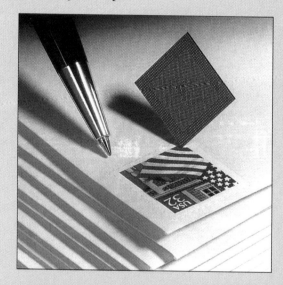

A **chip**, also known as a **silicon chip, semiconductor,** or **integrated circuit,** is a postage stamp–sized circuitboard.

To be a competent end user, you need to understand how data and programs are represented electronically. Additionally, you need to understand the functionality of the basic components in the system unit: system board, microprocessor, memory, system clock, expansion slots and cards, bus lines, and ports and cables.

MICROPROCESSOR

Unit	Speed
Millisecond	Thousandth of a second
Microsecond	Millionth of a second
Nanosecond	Billionth of a second
Picosecond	Trillionth of a second

The **microprocessor** plugs into the system board, contains the **CPU,** and is the "brains" of the system unit. Two basic components of the microprocessor are the *control unit* and the *arithmetic-logic* unit.

Control Unit

The **control unit** executes programs by directing the other system components. It directs electronic signals between memory, the arithmetic-logic unit, and input/output devices.

Arithmetic-Logic Unit

The **arithmetic-logic unit,** commonly referred to as the **ALU,** performs **arithmetic** (math) and **logical** (comparisons) **operations.**

Microprocessor Chips

A **word** is the number of bits (such as 16, 32, or 64) that can be accessed by the microprocessor at one time. The more bits in a word, the more powerful the microprocessor. Microprocessors process data and instructions in **microseconds.**

Two types of microprocessor chips are:

- **Complex instruction set computer (CISC) chips**—the basis for Intel's Pentium III and Pentium IV microprocessors.
- **Reduced instruction set computer (RISC) chips**—fewer instructions. They are the basis for IBM and Motorola's PowerPC microprocessor.

Smart cards contain built-in microprocessor chips.

MEMORY

There are three types of **memory** chips: RAM, ROM, and CMOS.

RAM

RAM (random access memory) chips are called temporary or volatile because their contents are lost if power is disrupted.

- **Flash RAM** or **flash RAM memory** is a special type of RAM that does not lose its contents when power is disrupted.
- **Virtual memory** uses the hard disk to run large programs on systems with limited memory.
- **Memory cache** or **RAM cache** is a high-speed holding area for frequently used data and information.

ROM

ROM (read only memory) chips, also called **firmware,** are permanent and control essential system operations.

CMOS

CMOS (complementary metal-oxide semiconductor) chips provide flexibility and expandability to computer systems.

Unit	Capacity
Kilobyte (KB)	1,000 bytes
Megabyte (MB)	1 million bytes
Gigabyte (GB)	1 billion bytes
Terabyte (TB)	1 trillion bytes

SYSTEM CLOCK

The **system clock** controls the speed of computer operations. It is measured in **gigahertz (GHz).**

EXPANSION SLOTS AND CARDS

Computers with **closed architecture** are not easily expanded. **Open architecture** computers typically have slots on their system boards to accept **expansion cards.**

Example of expansion cards are:

- **Network adapter cards**—connect to a network.
- **Modem cards**—connect over a telephone line.
- **Television boards**—contain TV tuner and video capture capabilities, also known as **personal video recorder cards.**
- **PC cards**—credit card–size expansion cards for portable computers, also known as **PCMCIA (Personal Computer Memory Card International Association)** cards.

Plug and Play is an evolving set of hardware standards designed to assist with the installation of expansion cards.

BUS LINES

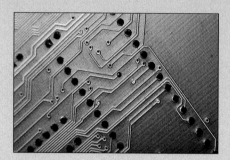

Bus lines, also known as **data buses** and **buses,** provide data pathways that connect various system components. Four principal types are:

- **ISA (Industry Standard Architecture)**—older and slower but still widely used.
- **PCI (Peripheral Component Interconnect)**—high-speed; used to connect CPU, memory, and expansion boards.
- **AGP (Accelerated Graphics Port)**—faster than PCI; used for video data.
- **USB (Universal Serial Bus)**—fastest; used to support high-speed devices.

PORTS AND CABLES

Ports and **cables** allow external devices to connect to the system unit.

Ports

Ports are connecting sockets on the outside of the system unit. They are used to connect keyboards, mouse, monitors, modems, printers, and video cameras. The five most common types are **serial, parallel, USB,** and **HPSB,** which is also known as **FireWire.**

Cables

Cables are used to connect external devices to the system unit via ports.

KEY TERMS

accelerated graphics port (AGP) (101)
adapter cards (97)
arithmetic operations (94)
arithmetic-logic unit (ALU) (94)
ASCII (91)
binary coding schemes (91)
binary system (91)
bit (91)
bus (101)
bus line (101)
byte (91)
cables (102)
cache memory (96)
central processing unit (CPU) (94)
chassis (90)
chip (93)
closed architecture (97)
complementary metal-oxide semiconductor
    (CMOS) (96)
complex instruction set computer (CISC) chip
    (94)
control unit (94)
controller cards (97)
data bus (101)
desktop system unit (90)
EBCDIC (91)
expansion cards (97)
FireWire port (102)
firmware (96)
flash RAM (95)
flash memory (95)
gigahertz (97)
high performance serial bus (HPSB) (102)
industry standard architecture (ISA) (101)
integrated circuit (93)
interface cards (97)
internal modem (97)
logical operations (94)
main board (93)
memory (95)

microprocessor (94)
microseconds (94)
modem card (97)
motherboard (93)
network adapter card (97)
notebook system unit (90)
open architecture (97)
parallel ports (102)
PC card (100)
peripheral component interconnect (PCI) (101)
Personal Computer Memory Card International
    Association (PCMCIA) (100)
personal digital assistant (PDA) system unit (90)
personal video recorder card (97)
Plug and Play (100)
plug-in boards (97)
port (102)
processor (94)
RAM cache (96)
random-access memory (RAM) (95)
read-only memory (ROM) (96)
reduced instruction set computer (RISC) chip (94)
semiconductor (93)
serial ports (102)
silicon chip (93)
slots (97)
smart card (95)
system board (93)
system cabinet (90)
system clock (97)
system unit (90)
television boards (97)
TV tuner card (97)
two-state system (91)
unicode (91)
universal serial bus (USB) (101)
universal serial bus (USB) port (102)
virtual memory (96)
word (94)

CHAPTER REVIEW

MULTIPLE CHOICE

Circle the letter or fill in the correct answer.

1. The system unit is also called the _____.
   a. system cabinet
   b. chassis
   c. system board
   d. system cabinet and chassis
   e. chassis and system board

2. A chip is also called a _____.
   a. silicon chip, processor, or system clock
   b. semiconductor, silicon chip, or expansion card
   c. processor, smart card, or integrated circuit
   d. semiconductor, main board, or processor
   e. silicon chip, semiconductor, or integrated circuit

3. ASCII, EBCDIC, and Unicode are examples of _____.
   a. two-state systems
   b. integrated circuits
   c. binary coding schemes
   d. adapter cards
   e. none of the above

4. Microcomputers process data and instructions in _____.
   a. milliseconds
   b. microseconds
   c. nonseconds
   d. picoseconds
   e. all of the above

5. Random-access memory (RAM) is a kind of _____ storage.
   a. permanent
   b. temporary
   c. flash
   d. smart
   e. expansion

6. Type of RAM that is NOT temporary is _____.
   a. virtual memory
   b. Flash RAM
   c. cache memory
   d. virtual and cache memory
   e. none of the above

7. ROM is a type of _____.
   a. semiconductor
   b. slot
   c. adapter
   d. network
   e. firmware

8. _____ is a set of hardware and software standards that allows expansion boards and other devices to install themselves.
   a. Plug and Play
   b. Unicode
   c. System Unit
   d. Industry Standard Architecture
   e. none of the above

9. A(n) _____, also called a data bus, connects the parts of the CPU together.
   a. adapter card
   b. parallel port
   c. serial port
   d. ISA
   e. bus line

10. A(n) _____ chip provides flexibility and expandability for a computer system; it contains essential information that is required every time the computer system is turned on.
    a. ROM
    b. RAM
    c. TCP/IP
    d. CMOS
    e. ALU

Match each numbered item with the most closely related lettered item. Write your answers in the spaces provided.

a. CISC chip
b. binary system
c. closed architecture
d. cache memory
e. data bus
f. expansion card
g. chip
h. PC card
i. control unit
j. arithmetic-logic unit
k. system unit
l. system board
m. smart card
n. cables
o. FireWire port
p. system clock
q. modem card
r. port
s. parallel port
t. RAM

1. The container that houses most of the electronic components that make up a computer system. _k_
2. Numbering system in which all numbers consist of only two digits—0 and 1. _b_
3. The communications web for the entire computer system. _____
4. Consists of a tiny circuitboard etched on a stamp-sized square of silicon. _l_
5. Tells the rest of the computer system how to carry out a program's instructions. _____
6. Performs arithmetic operations and logical operations. _j_
7. The most common type of microprocessor. _a_
8. A plastic card, the size of a regular credit card, with an embedded chip. _m_
9. Volatile storage that holds the program and the data the CPU is currently processing. _t_
10. Temporary high-speed holding area between the memory and the CPU. _____
11. Produces precisely timed electrical beats used as a timing mechanism. _p_
12. Machines manufactured so that users cannot easily add new devices. _c_
13. Also called plug-in boards, controller cards, adapter cards, and interface cards. _f_
14. Card that allows distant computers to communicate, via converted electronic signals, over telephone lines. _q_
15. Credit card–sized expansion boards used by portable computers. _m_
16. Connects the parts of the CPU to each other. _____
17. Connecting socket on the outside of the system unit. _r_
18. Connects external devices that need to send or receive a lot of data over a short distance. _s_
19. 33 times faster than USB ports and used to connect high-speed printers and other devices. _o_
20. Connects input and output devices to the system unit via the ports. _n_

OPEN-ENDED

On a separate sheet of paper, respond to each question or statement.

1. Describe the basic components of the CPU.
2. Describe the three basic types of system unit.
3. What are the differences and similarities between the three types of memory?
4. Name four expansion cards and describe the function of each.
5. Name and describe four ports.

1 TV Tuner Cards and Video Clips

Want to watch your favorite television program while you work? Perhaps you would like to include a video clip in a class presentation. It's easy using a video TV card. To learn more about this technology, review Making IT Work for You: TV Tuner Cards and Video Clips on pages 98 and 99. Then visit our Web site at http://www.mhhe.com/oleary. Once at that site, play the videos and answer the following questions in a one-page paper: (a) Describe the two windows that open when the TV icon is selected. (b) What are the basic functions of the control box? (c) What is the command sequence to insert a video clip into a PowerPoint presentation?

2 Desktop and Notebook Computers

Have you recently purchased a new computer? Are you thinking about purchasing one? The Web is an excellent source for reviewing, comparing, and purchasing computers. Visit our site at http://www.mhhe.com/oleary to link to several sites that present information about the newest desktop and notebook computers. Connect to these sites to check out different desktop and note-

book models, and then answer the following questions in a one-page paper: (a) If you were to purchase a desktop computer, which one would you select? Describe how it would fit your needs and print out its specifications. (b) If you were to purchase a notebook computer, which one would you select? Describe how it would fit your needs and print out its specifications. (c) If you had to choose between the desktop and notebook, which one would you choose? Defend your selection in one paragraph by discussing the relative advantages and disadvantages of each type.

Interactive Companion CD-ROM 1

Complete the "Binary Numbers" Lab located on your Interactive Companion CD-ROM, and then answer the following questions in a one-page paper: (a) Represent the number 30 as a binary number. (b) What is the result of the OR operation on the binary numbers 1101 and 0101? (c) What is the largest base-10 number that can be represented by one byte?

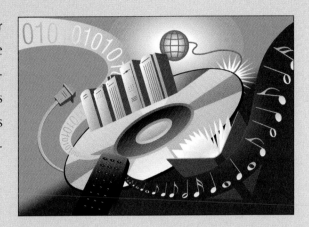

Expansion Cards 2

New or enhanced computer functionality can often be obtained with a simple hardware solution. Open architecture and Plug and Play standards make expanding microcomputer systems a much simpler task now than in the past. Expansion cards such as network adapter, modem, TV tuner and PC cards allow you to add new features easily. Select one of these categories of expansion cards and locate

a specific manufacturer's card. Write a one-page paper to answer the following: (a) Describe the specific card. (b) What are the requirements for the system unit in order to use this card? (c) How would this card add new or enhanced functionality?

1 Microprocessors

The microprocessor is the "brains" of the system unit. It has two basic components: control unit and arithmetic-logic unit. Microprocessors approximately double their speed once every year and a half. New technologies make for faster chips and faster PCs. Research the latest microprocessors from industry leaders Intel, AMD, and Cyrix. Then write a two-page paper titled "Current Microprocessors" that addresses the following points: (a) Describe the chips you located. (b) How does each of these chips differ from their last generation? What improvements have been made? (c) Describe any special features that these chips offer and explain each.

2 Processor Serial Numbers

When the Intel Pentium III microprocessor was released, each unit originally contained a unique Processor Serial Number, or PSN. This PSN could be used by online e-commerce sites to identify and to track individuals by the computer they used. This tracking would be similar to keeping track of car owners by their license plate numbers. Write a two-page paper that addresses the following items: (a) What are the benefits of a PSN for a computer user? For society? Explain your answers. (b) What privacy issues does a PSN raise for a computer user? (c) Describe how a PSN could be misused.

INPUT AND OUTPUT

COMPETENCIES

After you have read this chapter, you should be able to:

1

Describe input.

2

Describe keyboard entry, pointing devices, and scanning devices.

3

Discuss image capture, digitizing, and audio-input devices.

4

Discuss output.

5

Describe monitors, printers, and audio output.

6

Discuss combination input and output devices.

Input Devices

Translate words, sounds, images, and actions that people understand into symbols that the system unit can process; input devices include keyboards, digital cameras, and light pens

Light Pen

Digital Camera

Keyboard

How do you get data to the CPU? How do you get information out? Here we describe the two most important places where the computer interfaces with people. The first half of the chapter covers input devices and the second half covers output devices.

People understand language, which is constructed of letters, numbers, and punctuation marks. However, computers can understand only the binary machine language of 0s and 1s. Input and output devices are essentially translators. Input devices translate numbers, letters, and actions that people understand into symbols that computers can process. Output devices do the reverse: They translate machine output to output people can comprehend.

How would you like talking to your computer and having it respond to you? You can! You can create e-mail, dictate term papers, and control computer operations with the appropriate input and output devices.

How would you like talking long distance to friends and family over the Internet at no or very low cost? You can do that too. All you need are the right kinds of input and output devices and a connection to the input.

Competent end users need to know about the most commonly used input devices, including keyboards, mice, scanners, digital cameras, digitizing tablets, and voice recognition devices. Additionally, they need to know about the most commonly used output devices, including monitors, printers, and audio output devices. And end users need to know about combination devices including multifunctional devices, terminals, and Internet telephones.

Output Devices
Translate symbols processed by the system unit into words, sounds, images, and actions that people understand; output devices include monitors, printers, and music players

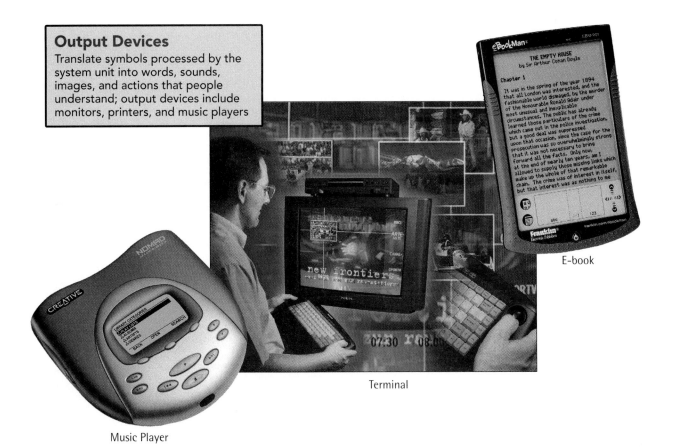

E-book

Terminal

Music Player

WHAT IS INPUT?

Input consists of data and instructions. Input devices translate what language people understand into a form that computers can process.

Input is any data or instructions that are used by a computer. It can come directly from you or from other sources. You provide input whenever you use system or application programs. For example, when using a word processing program, you enter data in the form of numbers and letters and issue commands such as to save and to print documents. You can also enter data and issue commands using your voice, by pointing to items, and by writing on special devices. Other sources of input include data from scanned or photographed images.

Input devices are hardware used to provide input to the computer. For example when using a word processor, you typically use a keyboard to enter text and a mouse to issue commands. In addition to keyboards and mice, widely used input devices include scanning, image capturing, digitizing, and audio-input devices. These devices are effectively translators from what people can understand to what the computer can process.

KEYBOARD ENTRY

Keyboards translate numbers, letters and special characters. Traditional, ergonomic, and folding are types of keyboards.

One of the most common ways to input data is by keyboard. As mentioned in Chapter 4, keyboards convert numbers, letters, and special characters that people understand into electrical signals. These signals are sent to and processed by the system unit.

There are a wide variety of different keyboard designs. They range from the traditional keyboards to ergonomic keyboards to space-saving folding keyboards. (See Figure 5-1.)

Traditional keyboard

Folding keyboard

Ergonomic keyboard

Figure 5-1 Three types of keyboard

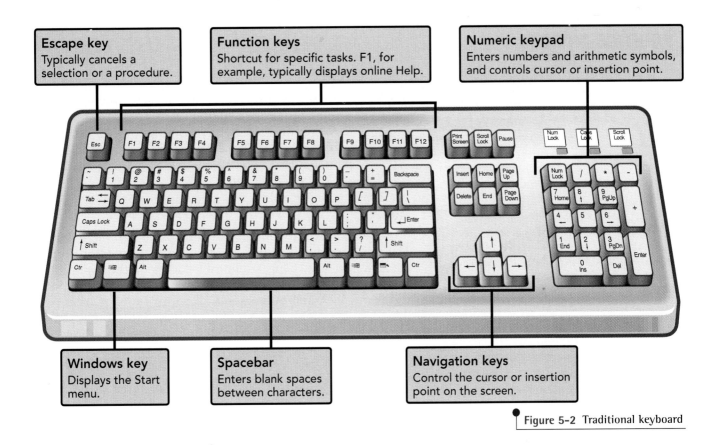

Escape key
Typically cancels a selection or a procedure.

Function keys
Shortcut for specific tasks. F1, for example, typically displays online Help.

Numeric keypad
Enters numbers and arithmetic symbols, and controls cursor or insertion point.

Windows key
Displays the Start menu.

Spacebar
Enters blank spaces between characters.

Navigation keys
Control the cursor or insertion point on the screen.

Figure 5-2 Traditional keyboard

A computer keyboard combines a typewriter keyboard with a numeric keypad. Additionally, it has many special-purpose keys. Some keys such as the *Caps Lock* key are **toggle keys.** These keys turn a feature on or off. Others such as the *Ctrl* key are **combination keys** that perform an action when held down in combination with another key. To learn more about keyboard features, see Figure 5-2.

Concept Check

✓ What are input devices?

✓ What are some common keyboard features?

Is your keyboard looking tired and dirty? Are the keys sticking? Then it may be time to clean your keyboard. Follow the guidelines below to make it shine again.

TIPS

1 Disconnect. Turn off the computer and disconnect the keyboard.

2 Vacuum. Use a vacuum or a blow-dryer to remove dust and particles from the keyboard.

3 Clean keys. Using a soft cloth moistened with 90 percent isopropyl alcohol, gently clean the key surfaces. Carefully dry with another soft cloth.

4 Clean case. Using a soft cloth moistened with liquid cleaning solution, clean the keyboard case. Dry with another soft cloth.

5 Reconnect. When the keys and case are completely dry, plug in the keyboard and turn on the computer.

> A mouse controls a pointer on the monitor. Joysticks are used primarily for games. Touch screens are pressure-sensitive monitors. Light pens close circuits on special monitors.

Pointing, of course, is one of the most natural of all human gestures. Pointing devices provide a comfortable interface with the system unit, by accepting point gestures and converting them into machine-readable input. There are a wide variety of different pointing devices including the mouse, joystick, touch screen, and light pen.

MOUSE

A **mouse** controls a pointer that is displayed on the monitor. The **pointer** usually appears in the shape of an arrow. It frequently, however, changes shape depending on the application. A mouse can have one, two, or more buttons, which are used to select command options and to control information presented on the monitor. Some have a wheel button that can be rotated to scroll through information presented on the monitor. Although there are several different mouse types, there are three basic designs:

- **Mechanical mouse** is generally considered the traditional type and is currently the most widely used. It has a ball on the bottom and is attached with a cord to the system unit. As you move the mouse across a smooth surface, the roller rotates and controls the pointer on the screen. (See Figure 5-3.)
- **Optical mouse** has no moving parts. It emits and senses light to detect mouse movement. This newer type of mouse has some advantages compared to the mechanical mouse: It can be used on any surface, is more precise, and does not require periodic cleaning.
- **Cordless** or **wireless mouse** is a battery-powered device that typically uses radio waves or infrared light waves to communicate with the system unit. These devices eliminate the mouse cord and free up desk space.

TIPS Does your mouse pointer move smoothly across your screen? Or does it jerk, start, and stop occasionally? If it does, then it may be time for a cleaning. To clean a standard mouse, follow these steps:

1 **Disconnect.** Turn off the computer and disconnect the mouse from the computer.

2 **Take out ball.** Turn the mouse upside down, gently unscrew the cover to the compartment containing the mouse ball with your thumbs, and allow the ball to drop into your hand.

3 **Clean ball.** Clean the ball with a mild detergent or alcohol and a soft cloth; then dry it with a clean, lint-free cloth.

4 **Clean compartment.** Blow into the ball compartment to remove any dust or lint from the inside. Remove any oil on the rollers in the compartment by cleaning with a cotton swab and tape-head cleaner.

5 **Reassemble.** Put the ball back into the compartment and replace the cover.

6 **Reconnect.** Connect the mouse and you're ready to go.

If you do not have a standard mouse, consult the manufacturer's Web page for cleaning instructions.

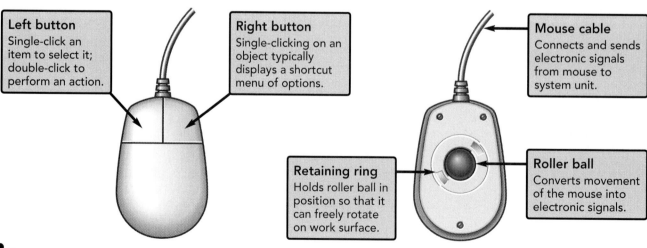

Left button Single-click an item to select it; double-click to perform an action.

Right button Single-clicking on an object typically displays a shortcut menu of options.

Mouse cable Connects and sends electronic signals from mouse to system unit.

Retaining ring Holds roller ball in position so that it can freely rotate on work surface.

Roller ball Converts movement of the mouse into electronic signals.

Figure 5-3 Standard mouse

Three devices similar to a mouse are trackballs, touch surfaces, and pointing sticks. You can use the **trackball,** also known as the **roller ball,** to control the pointer by rotating a ball with your thumb. You can use **touch surfaces** (see Figure 5-4) to control the pointer by moving and tapping your finger on the surface of a pad. You can use a **pointing stick,** located in the middle of the keyboard, to control the pointer by directing the stick with your finger.

JOYSTICK

A **joystick** is the most popular input device for computer games. You control game actions by varying the pressure, speed, and direction of the joystick. Additional controls such as buttons and triggers are used to specify commands or initiate specific actions. (See Figure 5-5.)

TOUCH SCREEN

A **touch screen** is a particular kind of monitor screen covered with a plastic layer. Behind this layer are crisscrossed invisible beams of infrared light. This arrangement enables someone to select actions or commands by touching the screen with a finger. Touch screens are easy to use, especially when people need information quickly. They are commonly used at restaurants, automated teller machines (ATMs), and information centers. (See Figure 5-6.)

LIGHT PEN

A **light pen** is a light-sensitive penlike device. The light pen is placed against the monitor. This closes a photoelectric circuit and identifies the spot for entering or modifying data. For example, light pens are used to edit digital images. (See Figure 5-7.)

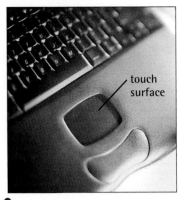

Figure 5-4 A touch surface: typically part of a portable computer

Figure 5-5 A joystick: used for computer games

Figure 5-6 A touch screen: a consumer application

Figure 5-7 A light pen: a home application

Optical scanners copy or reproduce text and images. Bar code readers identify and price products. Character and mark recognition devices recognize special characters and marks.

Scanners read data or information from a source. This source could be a written document, an inventory tag, a price tag, a graphic image, or even a photograph. A scanner device reads the data or information and then converts it into a form that the system unit can process. There are three types of scanning devices: optical scanners, bar code readers, and character and mark recognition devices.

OPTICAL SCANNERS

An **optical scanner**, also known simply as a **scanner**, copies or reproduces text as well as images. These devices record the light and dark areas as well as color of the scanned document. After the image has been scanned, it can be displayed, printed on paper, and stored for later uses. There are two basic types of scanners: flatbed and portable. (See Figure 5-8.)

- **Flatbed scanner** is much like a copy machine. The image to be scanned is placed on a glass surface and the scanner records the image from below.
- **Portable scanner** is typically a handheld device that slides across the image, making direct contact.

Optical scanners are powerful tools for a wide variety of end users including graphics and advertising professionals who scan images and combine them with text. Lawyers and students use portable scanners as a valuable research tool to record information.

BAR CODE READERS

You are probably familiar with **bar code readers** from grocery stores. (See Figure 5-9.) **Wand readers** or **platform scanners** are photoelectric scanners that read the **bar codes,** or vertical zebra-striped marks, printed on product containers. Supermarkets use electronic cash registers and a bar code system called

Figure 5-8 Two types of scanners

Flatbed scanner

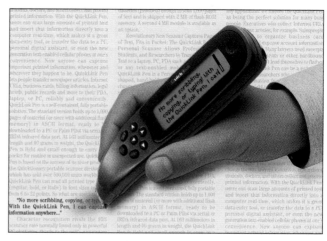

Portable scanner

the Universal Product Code (UPC). The bar code identifies the product to the supermarket's computer, which has a description and the latest price for the product. The computer automatically tells the electronic cash register the price. These devices are so easy to use that many retail companies are offering their customers self-checkout stations.

Figure 5-9 A bar code reader: recording product codes

CHARACTER AND MARK RECOGNITION DEVICES

Character and mark recognition devices are scanners that are able to recognize special characters and marks. They are specialty devices that are essential tools for certain applications. Three types are:

- **Magnetic-ink character recognition (MICR)**—used by banks to automatically read those unusual numbers on the bottom of checks. A special-purpose machine known as a **reader/sorter** reads characters made of ink containing magnetized particles.
- **Optical-character recognition (OCR)**—uses special preprinted characters that can be read by a light source and changed into machine-readable code. A common OCR device is the handheld wand reader discussed above. (See Figure 5-10.) These are used in department stores to read retail price tags by reflecting light on the printed characters.
- **Optical-mark recognition (OMR)** is also called **mark sensing.** An OMR device senses the presence or absence of a mark, such as a pencil mark. OMR is often used to score multiple-choice tests such as the College Board's Scholastic Aptitude Test and the Graduate Record Examination.

Figure 5-10 A wand reader: recording product codes

Concept Check

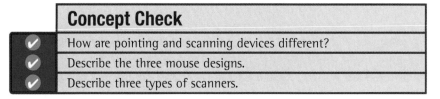

✓ How are pointing and scanning devices different?

✓ Describe the three mouse designs.

✓ Describe three types of scanners.

IMAGE CAPTURING DEVICES

Optical scanners like traditional copy machines can make a copy from an original. For example, an optical scanner can make a digital copy of a photograph. **Image capturing devices**, on the other hand, create or capture original images. These devices include digital cameras and digital video cameras.

> Digital cameras capture still images. Digital video cameras capture motion. Webcams are specialized digital video cameras.

- **Digital cameras** are similar to traditional cameras except that images are recorded digitally on a disk or in the camera's memory rather than on film. (See Figure 5-11.) You can take a picture, view it immediately, and even place it on your own Web page, within minutes.
- Unlike traditional video cameras, **digital video cameras** record motion digitally on a disk or in the camera's memory. (See Figure 5-12.) **Webcams** are specialized digital video cameras that capture images and send them to a computer for broadcast over the Internet. (See Figure 5-13.)

Image Capturing Devices

Figure 5-11 A digital camera

Figure 5-12 A digital video camera

Figure 5-13 A Webcam

DIGITIZING DEVICES

Graphic tablets record sketches and tracings of maps and other drawings. Digital notebooks record handwritten notes.

Digitizing devices convert a sketch or figure into a form that can be processed by a computer. Typically, these devices have some type of flat surface and a writing device. As the user moves the writing device across the surface, the digitizing device records the movement as a series of points and sends this information to the computer. Two widely used digitizing devices are graphic tablets and digital notebooks.

- **Graphic tablets** use a special graphics surface or tablet and a special stylus or pen-like device. Either the user directly sketches on the tablet or traces images that have been placed on the tablet. Graphics tables are used by artists for creating illustrations, by mapmakers to record or trace maps, and by engineers to digitally save mechanical drawings.
- **Digital notebooks** typically use a regular notepad positioned on top of an electronic pad or tablet. Using a regular pen, the user takes notes and creates drawings on the notepad. The underlying electronic pad records the movements. Students and business people frequently use these devices to record class or meeting notes. (See Figure 5-14.) These notes can later be processed, edited, and used with a word processing program.

Figure 5-14 A digital notebook: a student application

AUDIO-INPUT DEVICES

Audio-input devices convert sounds into a form that can be processed by a computer. These sounds can be from a wide variety of sources. By far the most widely used audio-input device is the microphone. This input device is an essential part of a voice recognition system.

> Audio-input devices convert sounds for processing. Voice recognition systems accept voice commands to control computer operations and to create documents.

VOICE RECOGNITION SYSTEMS

Voice recognition systems use a microphone, sound card, and special software. (See Making IT Work for You: Voice Recognition Systems and Dictating a Paper on pages 124–125.) These systems allow users to operate computers and to create documents using voice commands. (See Figure 5-15.) Portable voice recognition systems are widely used by doctors, lawyers, and others to record dictation. (See Figure 5-16.) These devices are able to record for several hours before connecting to a computer system to edit, store, and print the dictated information. Some systems are even able to translate dictation from one language to another, such as from English to Japanese.

On the Web Explorations

Dragon Systems Inc. is a leader in developing continuous-speech systems. To learn more about the company, visit our Web site at

http://www.mhhe.com/oleary

There are two types of voice recognition systems: discrete-speech recognition systems and continuous-speech recognition systems.

- **Discrete-speech recognition systems** are able to recognize individual words based on their sound. They cannot, however, distinguish between same-sound words such as *there*, *their*, and *they're*. This limitation requires users to review captured dictation and make corrections.

  - **Continuous-speech recognition systems** are able to distinguish between same-sounding words by evaluating the context within which individual words are used. These systems are considered to be one of the key technologies for the twenty-first century. Two well-known systems are NaturallySpeaking from Dragon Systems and ViaVoice from IBM.

Figure 5-15 A voice recognition system: a business application

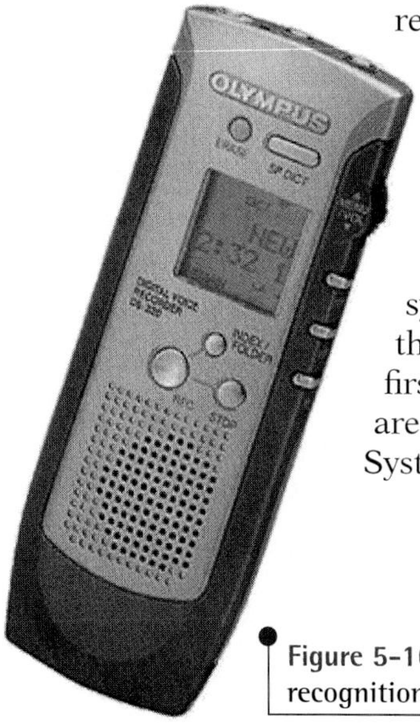

Figure 5-16 A portable voice recognition system

Concept Check

✔ Describe two image capturing devices.

✔ What are digital notebooks?

✔ Describe a voice recognition system.

VOICE RECOGNITION SYSTEMS AND DICTATING A PAPER

Tired of using your keyboard to type term papers and to control programs? Perhaps voice recognition is just what you're looking for. It's easy with the right software and hardware.

How It Works A voice recognition system consists of a combination of standard hardware components and some specialized software like NaturallySpeaking from Dragon Systems, Inc. Once the software has been trained, you can dictate papers and surf the Web using only voice commands.

Training the Software The first step is to train your system to recognize your voice. For example, you can train NaturallySpeaking.

1
- **Create your personal user profile, which will store your speech patterns.**
- **Read prearranged standard text to teach the software your unique speech patterns.**
- **Refine your profile to include specialized vocabulary.**

The wizard provided with the NaturallySpeaking software guides you through the training process.

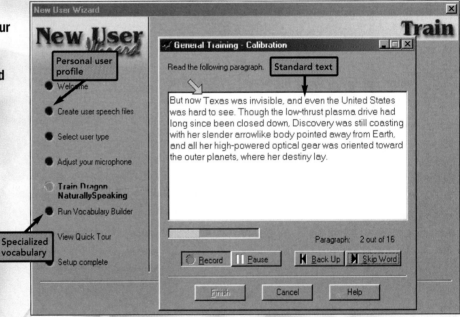

Dictating Once your system has been trained, you can use it to interact with a variety of applications.

For example, you can create a text document using voice recognition software and Word. As you speak into the microphone, your words will appear on your monitor and in the word processing document.

1 • **Using a microphone, dictate the text you want to appear in the Word document.**

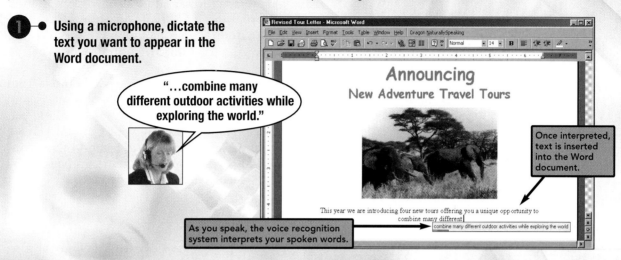

"...combine many different outdoor activities while exploring the world."

Once interpreted, text is inserted into the Word document.

As you speak, the voice recognition system interprets your spoken words.

Surfing You can control many computer operations with just your voice. You can load, run, and interact with programs without using your mouse or keyboard.

For example, you could connect to the Web through your browser, enter Web addresses, and use hyperlinks.

1 • **From the desktop, instruct your computer to load your browser.**

"Start Internet Explorer."

• **Instruct your computer to go to the *Address box,* dictate the Web address, and instruct your computer to connect to that Web address.**

"Go to address www.yahoo.com. Go there."

• **Surf by selecting and connecting to hyperlinks.**

"Click Auctions."

The selected hyperlink is displayed.

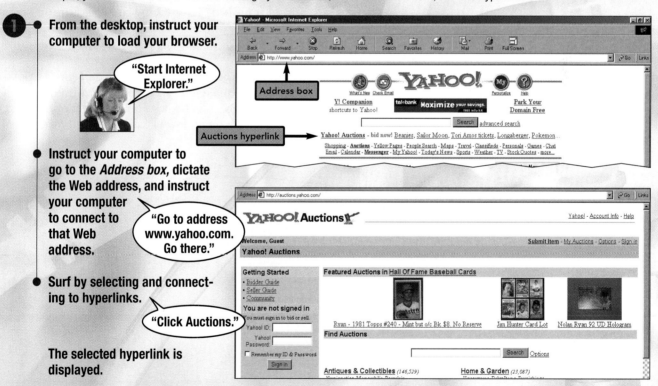

Many voice recognition programs are reasonably priced and relatively easy to install. For effective utilization, however, you must carefully train your system to recognize your speech patterns and vocabulary.

Voice dictation systems are continually changing and some of the specifics presented in this Making IT Work for You may have changed. See our Web site at http://www.mhhe.com/oleary for possible changes and to learn more about this application of technology.

WHAT IS OUTPUT?

Output is processed data or information. Output devices provide output for people by translating what the computer has processed into a form that people can use and understand.

Output is processed data or information from a computer. Output typically takes the form of text, graphics, photos, audio, and/or video. For example, when you create a presentation using a presentation graphics program, you typically input text and graphics. You could also include photographs and even add voice narration. The output would be the completed presentation.

Output devices are any hardware used to provide or to create output from the computer. The most widely used output devices are monitors, printers, and audio-output devices. For example, after you have created a presentation, you typically use your monitor to practice the presentation, your printer to create audience handouts, and your computer's audio system to listen to the narrations. These devices are effectively translators from information processed by the computer into something that people can understand and use.

MONITORS

Monitor standards indicate screen quality. Some monitors are used on the desktop; others to display book content, presentations, and television.

The most frequently used output device is the **monitor.** Two important characteristics of monitors are **size** and **clarity.** A monitor's size is indicated by the diagonal length of its viewing area. Common sizes are 15, 17, 19, and 21 inches. Larger monitors have the advantage of displaying more information at one time; however, they are more expensive.

A monitor's clarity is indicated by its **resolution,** which is measured in pixels. **Pixels** are individual dots or "picture elements" that form images on a monitor. For a given size monitor, the greater the resolution (the more pixels), the better the clarity of the image. For a given level of clarity, larger monitors require a higher resolution (more pixels). (See Figure 5-17.)

Pixel

Figure 5-17 Monitor resolution

STANDARDS

To indicate a monitor's resolution capabilities, several standards have evolved. The four most common today are SVGA, XGA, SXGA, and UXGA. (See Figure 5-18.)

Standard	Pixels
SVGA	800 × 600
XGA	1,024 × 768
SXGA	1,280 × 1,024
UXGA	1,600 × 1,200

Figure 5-18 Resolution standards

- **SVGA** stands for Super Video Graphics Array. It has a minimum resolution of 800 by 600 pixels. A few years ago, SVGA was the most popular standard. Today, it is used primarily with 15-inch monitors.
- **XGA** stands for Extended Graphics Array. It has a resolution of up to 1,024 by 768 pixels. It is a popular standard today, especially with 17- and 19-inch monitors.
- **SXGA** stands for Super Extended Graphics Array. This standard has a resolution of 1,280 by 1,024 pixels. It is popular with 19- and 21-inch monitors.
- **UXGA** stands for Ultra Extended Graphics Array. UXGA is the newest and highest standard. Although not as widely used as the XGA and SXGA monitors, its popularity is expected to increase dramatically as 21-inch monitors become more widely used. UXGA monitors are primarily used for high-end engineering design and graphic arts.

CATHODE-RAY TUBES

The most common type of monitor for the office and the home is the **cathode-ray tube (CRT).** (See Figure 5-19.) These monitors are typically placed directly on the system unit or on the desktop. CRTs are similar in size and technology to televisions. Compared to other types of monitors, their primary advantages are low cost and excellent resolution. Their primary disadvantage is size.

Figure 5-19 CRT monitor

FLAT-PANEL MONITORS

Because CRTs are too bulky to be transported, portable monitors known as **flat-panel monitors** or **liquid crystal display (LCD) monitors** were developed. Unlike the technology used in CRTs, the technology for portable monitors involves liquid crystals. Flat-panel monitors are much thinner than CRTs. Once used exclusively for portable computers, flat-panel monitors are used for desktop systems as well. (See Figure 5-20.)

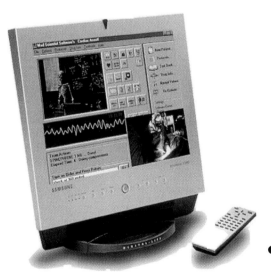

Figure 5-20 A flat-panel monitor

There are two basic types of flat-panel monitors: **passive-matrix** and **active-matrix.** Passive-matrix or **dual-scan monitors** create images by scanning the entire screen. This type requires very little power, but the clarity of the images is not as sharp. Active-matrix or **thin film transistor (TFT) monitors** do not scan down the screen; instead, each pixel is independently activated. More colors with better clarity can be displayed. Active-matrix monitors are more expensive and require more power.

OTHER MONITORS

There are several other types of monitors. These monitors are used for more specialized applications such as reading books, making presentations, and watching television. Three of these specialized devices are e-books, data projectors, and high-definition television.

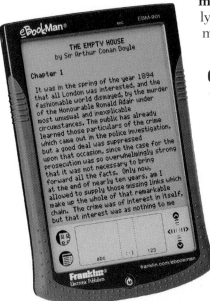

Figure 5–21 E-book

- **E-books,** also known as **e-book readers,** are handheld, book-sized devices that display text and graphics. Using content downloaded from the Web or from special cartridges, these devices are used to read newspapers, magazines, and entire books. The cost of producing and distributing e-book content is less than publishing and delivering traditional print media. Additionally, the time to create and distribute the content is much less. For these reasons and others, many experts predict that e-books will soon become as commonplace as today's traditional books. (See Figure 5-21.)

- **Data projectors** are specialized devices similar to slide projectors. These devices, however, connect to microcomputers and project computer output just as it would appear on a traditional monitor. (See Figure 5-22.) Marketing people, educators, and students frequently use presentation graphics programs like Power-Point to create presentations and then deliver the presentation using data projectors. Data projectors are commonly used for presentations almost anywhere including the classroom and the boardroom.

- **High-definition television (HDTV)** is a recent development in the merger of microcomputers and television called PC/TV. HDTV delivers a much clearer and more detailed wide-screen picture than regular television. Because the output is digital, users can readily freeze video sequences to create high-quality still images. The video and still images can then be digitized, edited, and stored on disk for later use. This technology is very useful to graphic artists, designers, and publishers.

Figure 5–22 Data projector

Concept Check

✔ What do output devices do?

✔ How is monitor clarity measured?

✔ List the four standards of monitor resolution.

The images output on a monitor are often referred to as **soft copy.** Information output on paper— whether by a printer or by a plotter—is called **hard copy.** Three popular kinds of printers used with microcomputers are ink-jet, laser, and thermal.

> There are three types of printers: ink-jet, laser, and thermal.

INK-JET PRINTER

An **ink-jet printer** sprays small droplets of ink at high speed onto the surface of the paper. This process not only produces a letter-quality image but also permits printing to be done in a variety of colors. (See Figure 5-23.) Most **photo printers** are special-purpose ink-jet printers designed to print photo-quality images from digital cameras. (See Figure 5-24.) Ink-jet printers are the most widely used printer. They are reliable, quiet, and inexpensive. Ink-jet printers are used wherever color and appearance are important, as in advertising and public relations.

LASER PRINTER

The **laser printer** uses a technology similar to that used in a photocopying machine. (See Figure 5-25.) It uses a laser beam to produce images with excellent letter and graphics quality. More expensive than ink-jet printers, laser printers are used in applications requiring high-quality output.

There are two categories of laser printers. **Personal laser printers** are inexpensive and used by many single users. They typically can print four to six pages a minute. **Shared laser printers** are more expensive and are used (shared) by a group of users. Shared laser printers typically print over 30 pages a minute.

THERMAL PRINTER

A **thermal printer** uses heat elements to produce images on heat-sensitive paper. Originally these printers were used in scientific labs to record data. More recently, color thermal printers have been widely used to produce very high-quality color artwork and text.

TIPS

Is your ink-jet printer producing smeared pages? Are the characters looking blurry? Then it could be time to give it a cleaning. Here are a few cleaning suggestions:

1 **Disconnect.** Turn off the printer and unplug the electricity.

2 **Open.** Open the printer and locate the spray nozzles.

3 **Clean.** Wipe the nozzles with a dry lint-free cloth or a swab moistened with distilled water.

4 **Reconnect.** When completely dry, plug in the printer and turn it on.

To prevent clogging in the future, always allow your printer to finish printing the current page and to return the print head to its resting position before removing the page or turning off the power.

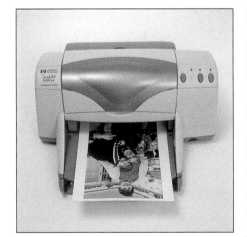

Figure 5-23 An ink-jet printer

Figure 5-24 A photo printer

Figure 5-25 A laser printer

Printer	Characteristics	Typical Use
Ink-jet	High color quality; inexpensive; sprays drops of ink on paper	Internal and external communications, advertising pieces
Laser	Very high quality; uses photocopying process	Desktop publishing, external documents
Thermal	Very high quality; uses heat elements on special paper	Art and design work

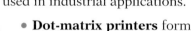

Figure 5-26 Three types of printers

Color thermal printers are not as popular because of their cost and the requirement of specially treated paper. They are a more special-use printer that produces near-photographic output. They are widely used in professional art and design work where very high-quality color is essential.

Some of the important characteristics of the three most widely used microcomputer printers are summarized in Figure 5-26.

OTHER PRINTERS

There are several other types of printers. These printers are primarily used for specialized printing jobs where print quality is the key consideration. Dot-matrix printers are primarily used when large quantities of material must be printed quickly and high quality is not required. Chain printers and plotters are both special-purpose printers primarily used in industrial applications.

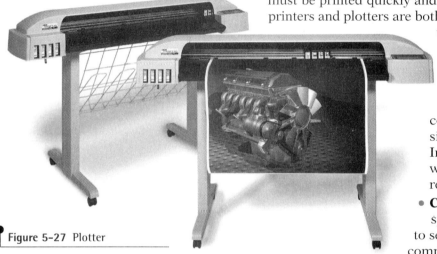

Figure 5-27 Plotter

- **Dot-matrix printers** form characters and images using a series of small pins on a print head. Once a widely used microcomputer printer, they are inexpensive and reliable but quite noisy. In general, they are used for tasks where high-quality output is not required.

- **Chain printers** are expensive high-speed machines. You are not likely to see one connected to a single microcomputer. They are typically used within organizations to serve several computers connected by a network or a mainframe computer requiring large quantities of printed output.

- **Plotters** are special-purpose printers for producing a wide range of specialized output. Using output from digitizing tables and other graphics input devices, plotters can create maps, images, and architectural and engineering drawings. They can produce high-quality, multicolor documents and also documents that are larger than most printers can handle. (See Figure 5-27.) Plotters are widely used by graphic artists, engineers, and architects to print out designs, sketches, and drawings.

Concept Check

✔ What are the three printer types commonly used with microcomputers?

✔ What type of printer is typically used for professional art and design work?

AUDIO-OUTPUT DEVICES

Audio-output devices translate audio information from the computer into sounds that people can recognize and understand. The most widely used audio-output devices are speakers and headphones. (See Figures 5-28 and 5-29.) These devices are connected to a sound card in the system unit. The sound card is used to capture as well as play back recorded sounds. Audio-output devices are used to play music (see Figure 5-30), vocalize translations from one language to another, and communicate information from the computer system to users.

Creating voice output is not anywhere near as difficult as recognizing and interpreting voice input. In fact, voice output is quite common. It is used with many soft-drink machines, telephones, and in cars. It is used as a reinforcement tool for learning, such as to help students study a foreign language. It is also used in many supermarkets at the checkout counter to confirm purchases. One of its most powerful capabilities is to assist the physically challenged.

> Audio-output devices produce sounds for people. Voice output is common and simpler than voice recognition.

Figure 5-28 Speakers

Figure 5-29 Headphones

Figure 5-30 Music player

COMBINATION INPUT AND OUTPUT DEVICES

Many devices combine input and output devices. Sometimes this is done to save space. Other times it is done for very specialized applications. Common combination devices include fax machines, multifunction devices, Internet telephones, and terminals.

> Fax machines send and receive images over telephone lines. Multifunction devices have input and output capabilities. Internet telephones use telephony to connect people. Terminals connect to the host computer or server.

FAX MACHINES

A **fax machine**, also known as a facsimile transmission machine, is a standard tool in nearly every office. At one time, all fax machines were separate stand-alone devices for sending and receiving images over telephone lines. Now, most computer systems have that capability with the simple addition of a fax/modem board, which also operates as a modem. To send a fax, these devices scan the image of a document converting the light and dark areas into a format that can be sent electronically over standard telephone lines. To receive a fax, these devices reverse the process and print the document (or display the document on your monitor) using signals received from the telephone line.

Combination Input and Output Devices

Figure 5-31 Multifunction device

MULTIFUNCTION DEVICES

Multifunctional devices typically combine the capabilities of a scanner, printer, fax, and copying machine. (See Figure 5-31.) These multifunctional devices offer a cost and space advantage. They cost about the same as a good printer or copy machine but require much less space than the single-function devices they replace. Their disadvantage is that the quality and functionality are not quite as good as those of the separate single-purpose devices. Even so, multifunctional devices are widely used in home and small business offices.

INTERNET TELEPHONE

Telephony, also known as **Internet telephony**, uses the Internet rather than traditional communication lines to connect two or more people via telephone. This communication requires an Internet telephone (or other appropriate audio input and output devices), the Internet, a special service provider, a sound card, and special software. (See Making IT Work for You: Internet Telephony on pages 134–135.) With this combination, users can make long-distance telephone calls very inexpensively. Although not currently available to all locations worldwide and although connection quality may vary, Internet telephone connections are rapidly gaining popularity.

TERMINALS

A **terminal** is an input and output device that connects you to a mainframe or other type of computer called a **host computer** or **server.** There are four kinds of terminals:

- A **dumb terminal** can be used to input and receive data, but it cannot process data independently. It is used only to gain access to information from a computer. Such a terminal may be used by an airline reservations clerk to access a mainframe computer for flight information.
- An **intelligent terminal** includes a processing unit, memory, and secondary storage such as a magnetic disk. Essentially, an intelligent terminal is a microcomputer with communications software and a telephone hookup (modem) or other communications link. These connect the terminal to the larger computer or to the Internet. An increasingly popular type is the **Net PC,** also known as the **Net Personal Computer.** These low-cost and limited microcomputers typically have only one type of secondary storage (an internal hard disk drive), a sealed system unit, and no expansion slots.
- A **network terminal,** also known as a **thin client** or **network computer,** is a low-cost alternative to an intelligent terminal. Most network terminals do not have a hard-disk drive and must rely on a host computer or server for application and system software. These devices are becoming increasingly popular in many organizations.
- An **Internet terminal,** also known as a **Web terminal** or **Web appliance,** provides access to the Internet and typically displays Web pages on a standard television set. (See Figure 5-32.) These special-purpose terminals offer Internet access without a microcomputer. Unlike the other types of terminals, Internet terminals are used almost exclusively in the home.

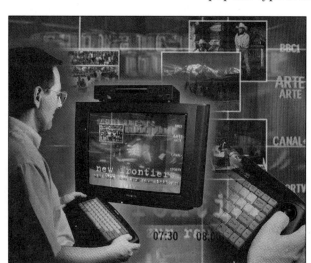

Figure 5-32 Web terminal

A Look to the Future

Microsoft Investment Could Lead to the Merger of Digital Television and Microcomputers

Have you been hearing a lot about digital TV? It promises to combine the power and flexibility of a microcomputer with the entertainment capabilities of a large-screen TV. You and a whole group of friends could play computer games, interact with life-sized figures, surf the Web, capture video, edit it, and paste into electronic presentations.

Of course, that's what PC/TV is all about. These systems contain special devices that convert analog signals required for today's television sets to digital signals required for microcomputers. Unfortunately, this conversion greatly constrains the speed, flexibility, and quality of these systems. But all that's going to change in the next few years.

All-digital television broadcasting is just getting started and promises greater image and sound quality. The Federal Communications Commission is leading the way. Every major network is required to offer digital signals to their top 30 markets this year.

Microsoft, a leader in software technology, has recently taken steps to position itself for this change. One step has been the recent investment of nearly a half billion dollars in WebTV, a company that manufactures Internet terminals for television sets. Another step is the introduction of Broadcast Technology in Microsoft's Windows operating systems. This technology presents a cable TV interface that lets you choose content on screen from the Internet, local TV, cable TV, and other sources.

Will your current television set become useless? It will not be able to display the new digital signals; by the year 2006, all analog broadcasts are expected to be eliminated. However, the transition to digital will occur gradually over the next few years.

INTERNET TELEPHONY

Do you need a cheaper way to stay in touch with friends and family? Did you know you can use your computer and the Internet to make long distance calls to regular phones? All you need is some software and an Internet connection to get started.

How It Works Internet telephony calls use a protocol known as *Voice over Internet Protocol*, or VoIP. To make a call, you use special software on your computer to connect to a VoIP service provider, who maintains servers in several calling areas. The server nearest your call's destination makes a local phone call to your destination number and relays your conversation digitally over the Internet. A microphone and headset or speakers connected to your computer are used like a telephone receiver to conduct the conversation.

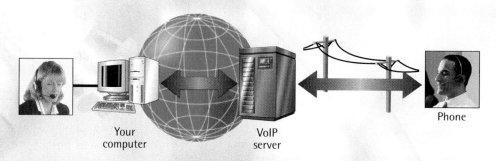

Your computer

VoIP server

Phone

Creating an Account The first step is to connect to an Internet Phone service provider and set up an account. You will also need to download custom software from the provider you choose. For example, follow these steps to get started with the service provider iConnectHere.com:

①
- Connect your browser to www.iConnectHere.com.

- Click on the *Sign Up Now* link.

- Follow the on-screen instructions to select an account that meets your needs.

- Continue to follow the on-screen instructions to download the *PC-to-Phone* software.

Sign up link

Configuring the Software When making an Internet call, you will use a regular microphone to speak and your computer's speakers or headphones to hear the conversation. Before making your first call, you will need to configure the software to work with these items as well as check your connection to the Internet. To configure the PC-to-Phone software:

- If necessary, turn on your speakers or plug in your headphones and connect your microphone to your computer.

- Double-click the file you downloaded in the Creating an Account step to start the setup wizard.

- Follow the wizard's instructions to select the correct input and output devices from the drop-down lists.

- Adjust the sliders to comfortable volume levels for your microphone input and pre-recorded sample output.

- Use the option to test your Internet connection and take the recommended steps to resolve any detected errors.

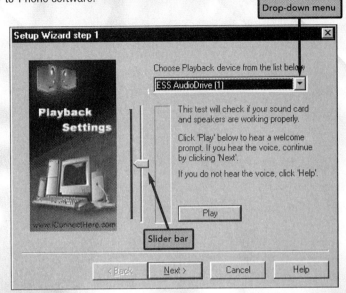

Making a Call To make an Internet call, use the specialized software like a regular phone. For example, to make a call with the PC-to-Phone software:

- Start the PC-to-Phone software.

- Click the buttons on the on-screen keypad to input the phone number you wish to dial:

  [country code] + [area code] + [number]

  for example:

  14805555555

- Click the call button to begin the call.

- Use the microphone and speaker sliders to make adjustments to these levels during the call.

- Click the Hang Up button to end the call.

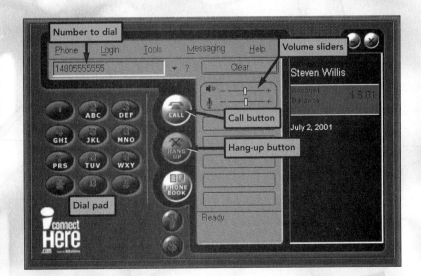

Internet telephones are continually changing and some of the specifics presented in this Making IT Work may have changed. See our Web site at http://www.mhhe.com/oleary for possible changes and to learn more about this application of technology.

INPUT

Input is any data or instructions that are used by a computer. Input devices translate words, images, and actions that people understand into a form a computer can process.

Keyboards

Traditional, natural, and folding keyboards have various types of keys including toggle and combination keys.

Pointing

The most common pointing device is the mouse. The three basic mouse designs include mechanical mouse, optical mouse, and cordless or wireless mouse. Devices similar to the mouse include trackballs, touch surface, and pointing sticks.

Other pointing devices include:

- Joysticks—control game action by varying pressure, speed, and direction.
- Touch screens—touching finger to screen to control operations.
- Light pens—directed at screen to control operations.

INPUT

Scanning

Scanners convert images to digital data. There are two basic types of scanners:

- Flatbed scanner—like a copy machine.
- Portable scanner—handheld device that slides directly across the image.

Other common scanning devices include bar code readers, MIRC, OCR, and OMR devices.

Image Capturing

Image capturing devices create or capture original images. These devices include:

- Digital cameras—similar to traditional cameras except that images are recorded digitally on a disk or in the camera's memory rather than on film.
- Digital video cameras—record motion digitally on a disk or in the camera's memory. Webcams are specialized digital video cameras that capture images and send them to a computer for broadcast over the Internet.

To be a competent end user you need to be aware of the most commonly used input and output devices. These devices are translators for information into and out of the system unit. Input devices translate words, sounds, images, and actions into symbols the system unit can process. Output devices translate symbols from the system unit into words, images, and sounds that people can understand.

INPUT

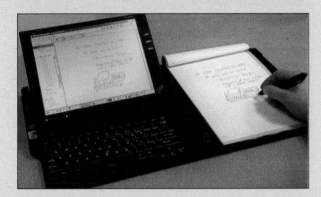

Digitizing Devices

Digitizing devices convert a sketch or a figure into a form that can be processed by a computer. These devices include:

- **Graphic tablet**—uses a special surface and pen-like device to directly capture or trace images on the tablet.
- **Digital notebook**—uses a regular notebook placed over an electronic pad. The underlying pad records the movements of the pen as the user takes notes.

Audio-Input Devices

These devices convert a person's spoken words into digital data. **Voice recognition systems** are a combination of hardware and software that allows users to control operations and create documents using voice commands.

Two types of voice recognition systems include:

- **Discrete-speech recognition system**—recognizes only individual words.
- **Continuous-speech recognition system**—recognizes individual words and phrases in context, a key technology for the twenty-first century.

OUTPUT

Output is processed data or information from a computer. **Output devices** are hardware used to provide or create output from a computer.

Monitors

A monitor's **size** is indicated by its diagonal length. **Clarity** is indicated by its **resolution** measured in **pixels**. The standards are:

- **SVGA** has a resolution of 800×600 pixels.
- **XGA** has a resolution of $1,024 \times 768$ pixels.
- **SXGA** has a resolution of $1,280 \times 1,024$ pixels.
- **UXGA** has a resolution of $1,600 \times 1,200$ pixels.

There are several types of monitors including:

- **CRTs**—placed on a system unit or directly on a desk. Primary advantages are low cost and high resolution.
- **Flat-panel monitors**—used for portable computers and desktop systems. Also known as **liquid crystal display (LCD)** monitors. Two basic types are: **passive-matrix (dual-scan)** and **active-matrix** or **thin film transistor (TFT).**
- **Other monitors**—other, more specialized, monitors include **e-books** or **e-book readers, data projectors,** and **high-definition television (HDTV).**

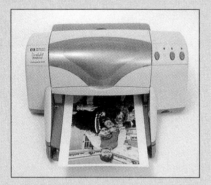

Printers

The images displayed on a monitor are referred to as **soft copy**; information output on paper is referred to as **hard copy.** There are several types of printers including:

- **Ink-jet printer**—sprays small droplets of ink onto paper.
- **Laser**—uses a laser beam to produce images. Two types of laser printer are **personal laser printer** and **shared laser printer.**
- **Thermal**—uses heat elements to produce images on heat-sensitive paper.
- **Other printers**—there are many specialized printers including **dot-matrix, chain printer,** and **plotters.**

Audio-Output Devices

Audio-output devices translate audio information from the computer into sounds people understand. The most widely used examples are speakers, headphones, and music players.

Combination Input and Output

Many devices combine input and output functions. Common types of combination devices include:

- **Fax machines**—send and receive images via standard telephone lines.
- **Multifunctional devices**—combine the capabilities of a scanner, printer, fax, and copy machine.
- **Terminals**—are input and output devices that connect to a **host computer** or **server.**
- **Internet telephony**—uses the Internet rather than traditional phone lines to connect people over the phone.

Terminals

There are four types of terminal:

- **Dumb**—sends and receives, but does no processing.
- **Intelligent**—sends, receives, and processes; one popular type is **Net PC.**
- **Network**—low-cost alternative to intelligent terminal; also known as **thin client** or **network computer.**
- **Internet**—accesses the Internet without a microcomputer; also known as **Web terminal** or **Web appliance.**

KEY TERMS

active-matrix (128)
audio-output device (131)
bar code (120)
bar code readers (120)
cathode-ray tube (CRT) (127)
chain printer (130)
character and mark recognition device (121)
clarity (126)
combination key (117)
continuous-speech recognition system (123)
cordless or wireless mouse (118)
data projector (128)
digital cameras (121)
digital notebook (122)
digital video camera (121)
discrete-speech recognition system (123)
dot-matrix printer (130)
dual-scan monitor (128)
dumb terminal (132)
e-book (128)
e-book reader (128)
fax machine (131)
flatbed scanner (120)
flat-panel monitor (127)
graphic tablet (122)
hard copy (129)
high-definition television (HDTV) (128)
host computer (132)
image capturing device (121)
ink-jet printer (129)
input (116)
input device (116)
intelligent terminal (132)
Internet telephony (132)
Internet terminal (132)
joystick (119)
laser printer (129)
light pen (119)
liquid crystal display monitor (LCD) (127)
magnetic-ink character recognition (MICR) (121)
mark sensing (121)
mechanical mouse (118)
monitor (126)
mouse (118)

multifunctional device (132)
Net PC (132)
Net Personal Computer (132)
network computer (132)
network terminal (132)
optical mouse (118)
optical scanner (120)
optical-character recognition (OCR) (121)
optical-mark recognition (OMR) (121)
output (126)
output device (126)
passive-matrix (128)
personal laser printer (129)
photo printer (129)
pixel (126)
platform scanner (120)
plotter (130)
pointer (118)
pointing stick (119)
portable scanner (120)
resolution (126)
roller ball (119)
scanner (120)
server (132)
shared laser printer (129)
size (126)
soft copy (129)
SVGA (127)
SXGA (127)
telephony (132)
terminal (132)
thermal printer (129)
thin client (132)
thin film transistor monitor (TFT) (128)
toggle key (117)
touch screen (119)
touch surface (119)
trackball (119)
UXGA (127)
voice recognition system (123)
wand reader (120)
Web appliance (132)
Web terminal (132)
Webcam (121)
XGA (127)

CHAPTER REVIEW

MULTIPLE CHOICE

Circle the letter or fill in the correct answer.

1. _____ perform an operation when held down with another key.
   a. Toggle keys
   b. Combination keys
   c. Wand readers
   d. Monitors
   e. Touch screens

2. A(n) _____ mouse emits and senses light to detect movement.
   a. mechanical
   b. cordless
   c. wireless
   d. pointer
   e. optical

3. A(n) _____ is an input device similar to a copy machine.
   a. flatbed scanner
   b. printer
   c. digital camera
   d. graphic tablet
   e. portable scanner

4. A wand reader is a type of _____ recognition device.
   a. MICR
   b. OCR
   c. OMR
   d. touch surface
   e. scanner

5. A handheld, book-sized device used to read downloaded content is a _____.
   a. wand reader
   b. e-book
   c. light pen
   d. graphic tablet
   e. digital notebook

6. A special-purpose output device for producing bar charts, maps, architectural drawings, and three-dimensional illustrations is a _____.
   a. chain printer
   b. portable scanner
   c. ink-jet printer
   d. plotter
   e. thermal printer

7. Speakers and headphones are the most widely used _____ devices.
   a. audio-input
   b. audio
   c. audio-output
   d. multifunctional
   e. personal

8. A(n) _____ typically combines the capabilities of a scanner, printer, fax, and copying machine.
   a. multifunctional device
   b. output device
   c. input device
   d. MICR
   e. dumb terminal

9. _____ uses the Internet rather than traditional communication lines to connect two or more people via telephone.
   a. A multifunctional device
   b. A fax machine
   c. A dumb terminal
   d. Telephony
   e. An output device

10. A network computer is also known as a(n) _____.
    a. thin client
    b. intelligent terminal
    c. dumb terminal
    d. Net PC
    e. Web terminal

Match each numbered item with the most closely related lettered item. Write your answers in the spaces provided.

a. clarity

b. image capturing device

c. optical scanner

d. output

e. input

f. CRT

g. digital notebook

h. thermal

i. discrete-speech recognition system

j. toggle

k. thin client

l. SXGA

m. plotter

n. passive-matrix

o. data projector

p. Internet terminal

q. OMR device

r. ink-jet

s. dumb terminal

t. wand reader

1. Data or instructions used by a computer. _____
2. These keys turn features on or off. __j__
3. Copies or reproduces text and images. __c__
4. Photoelectric scanners that read bar codes. _____
5. Device that senses the presence or absence of a pencil mark. _____
6. Creates or captures original images. _____
7. An input device that records and stores pen movements. _____
8. Voice recognition system that recognizes individual words based on their sound. _____
9. Processed data or information from a computer. _____
10. Indicated by resolution and measured in pixels. _____
11. Super Extended Graphics Array. _____
12. Type of desktop monitor built like a television set. _____
13. Monitor that creates images by scanning the entire screen. _____
14. Device that connects to a microcomputer and projects output to a screen as it would appear on the monitor. _____
15. Printer that sprays small droplets of ink at high speed onto the surface of the paper. _____
16. Printer that uses heat elements to produce images on heat sensitive paper. _____
17. Printer used to create maps, images, and architectural and engineering drawings. _____
18. Can be used to input and receive data, but cannot process data independently. _____
19. Terminal that relies on host computer or server for software. _____
20. Terminal that provides Web access without a microcomputer. _____

On a separate sheet of paper, respond to each question or statement.

1. What are the differences between keyboards, pointing, scanning, image capturing, digitizing, and audio-input devices?
2. Discuss the advantages and disadvantages of the three basic designs for the mouse.
3. Explain the differences between discrete-speech and continuous-speech recognition systems.
4. Describe the three categories of output devices.
5. What are combination input and output devices? Describe four such devices.

1 Digital Video Editing

Adobe Premiere is a popular video editing software package that can turn your computer into an editing studio. To learn more about Premiere, connect to our Web site at http://www.mhhe.com/oleary to link to Adobe's Web site. Once there, read about this product and write a one-page paper that answers the following questions: (a) What features does Premiere offer? (b) How is Premiere similar to Windows Movie Maker? How is it different? (c) Who would likely use this product? (d) Describe a way that you would use video editing software. Which software would you choose? Why?

2 Web TV

Web TV provides Internet access without the need for a traditional computer. Visit our Web site at http://www.mhhe.com/ oleary to connect to the WebTV homepage. Once connected, read about this product and answer the following questions in a one-page paper: (a) What is WebTV? (b) What is required to use WebTV? (c) What type of user might use this product? (d) Consider your own Internet and general computing needs. Is WebTV a product for you? Why or why not?

EXPANDING YOUR KNOWLEDGE

Interactive Companion CD-ROM 1

Complete the "Computer Anatomy" Lab located on your Interactive Companion CD-ROM, and then answer the following questions in a one-page paper: (a) Which output devices were discussed in this Lab? (b) How many floppy disks would be necessary to store the same amount of data as a CD-ROM? (c) According to the Lab, in what ways are floppy and hard disks similar to a cassette tapes? How are they dissimilar?

Handwriting Recognition 2

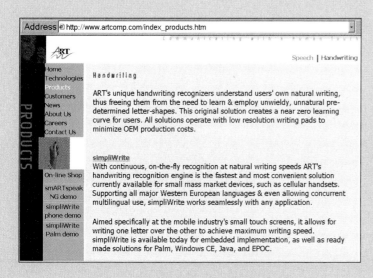

Address http://www.artcomp.com/index_products.htm

Communicating with a Human Touch

ART

Speech | Handwriting

Home
Technologies
Products
Customers
News
About Us
Careers
Contact Us

On-line Shop
smARTspeak NG demo
simpliWrite phone demo
simpliWrite Palm demo

Handwriting

ART's unique handwriting recognizers understand users' own natural writing, thus freeing them from the need to learn & employ unwieldy, unnatural pre-determined letter-shapes. This original solution creates a near zero learning curve for users. All solutions operate with low resolution writing pads to minimize OEM production costs.

simpliWrite

With continuous, on-the-fly recognition at natural writing speeds ART's handwriting recognition engine is the fastest and most convenient solution currently available for small mass market devices, such as cellular handsets. Supporting all major Western European languages & even allowing concurrent multilingual use, simpliWrite works seamlessly with any application.

Aimed specifically at the mobile industry's small touch screens, it allows for writing one letter over the other to achieve maximum writing speed. simpliWrite is available today for embedded implementation, as well as ready made solutions for Palm, Windows CE, Java, and EPOC.

Handwriting recognition is a developing technology for direct input. Conduct a Web search with the keywords "handwriting recognition" to learn more about this technology. Then write a one-page paper that addresses the following: (a) What types of devices and applications use handwriting recognition now? (b) What are some applications where handwriting recognition is the best choice for input. Why is this the case? (c) What are current limitations of handwriting recognition?

BUILDING YOUR PORTFOLIO

1 Digital Input

Digitizing devices convert sketches, figures, or images into a form that can be processed by a computer. These devices typically record the movement of a writing device as a series of points and send this information to the computer. Write a two-page paper titled "Digital Input" that answers the following questions: (a) Define **digitizer, digital camera, digital video camera,** and **digital notebook.** (b) Give examples of ways that you would use the devices above. (c) Give examples of ways that individuals in corporations use the devices above.

2 Electronic Security

Electronic monitoring equipment is becoming more widely used in stores, the workplace, and in public. Consider the following questions and discuss your answers. Write a two-page summary of your analysis: (a) What common applications of electronic monitoring or surveillance equipment have you noticed recently? (b) Does knowing that an electronic security device is in place make you feel more secure? (c) Have you ever felt that electronic surveillance equipment

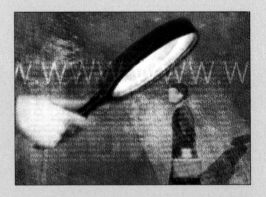

was an invasion of your privacy? (d) Consider the trade-off between security and privacy. In what cases is one more important than the other? Are these cases the same for everyone? Explain your answer.

SECONDARY STORAGE

COMPETENCIES

After you have read this chapter, you should be able to:

1

Describe today's standard floppy disk and compare it to Zip disks, SuperDisks, and HiFD disks.

2

Describe the following kinds of disks: internal hard disks, hard-disk cartridges, and hard-disk packs.

3

Describe ways to improve hard-disk operations: disk caching, redundant arrays of inexpensive disks, and data compression.

4

Compare the CD and DVD formats.

5

Describe the different types of optical disks.

6

Describe other kinds of secondary storage: magnetic tape, Internet drives, and solid state storage.

Optical Disks

Use reflected light to record data and have very large storage capacities

Hard Disks

Use magnetic charges to record data; have large storage capacities and fast retrieval times

Floppy Disks

Use magnetic charges to record data and are an inexpensive, removable storage media

An essential feature of every computer is the ability to save, or store, information. Computers can save information permanently after you turn them off. This way, you can save your work for future use, share information with others, or modify information already available. Secondary storage holds information external from the CPU. Secondary storage allows you to store programs, such as Word and Excel. It also allows you to store the data processed by programs, such as text or the numbers in a spreadsheet.

We described random-access memory (RAM) in Chapter 4. This is the internal and temporary storage of data and programs in the computer's memory. Once the power is turned off or interrupted, everything in internal storage disappears. Such stor-

age is therefore said to be **volatile storage.** This volatility results in a need for more permanent, or **nonvolatile storage,** for data and programs. We also need external storage, because users need much more capacity than is possessed by a computer's primary memory.

CDs, for example, store data that can be used over and over again. You can download music from the Internet, play it on your computer, and create custom CDs with the right hardware and software.

Competent end users need to be aware of the different types of secondary storage. They need to know the capabilities, limitations, and uses of floppy disks, hard disks, optical disks, and other types of secondary storage.

Solid State Storage
Has no moving parts and data is stored and retrieved electronically

Internet Hard Drives
Provide Web-based, low cost storage

Floppy disks are removable storage media. Today's standard is 1.44 MB. Tomorrow's standard might be a Zip, SuperDisk, or HiFD. Data is recorded on tracks and sectors.

loppy disks, often called **diskettes** or simply **disks,** are a portable or removable storage media. They are used to store and to transport word processing, spreadsheet, and other types of files. They use flat circular pieces of Mylar plastic that rotate within a jacket. Data is stored as electromagnetic charges on a metal oxide film coating the Mylar plastic. Data and programs are represented by the presence or absence of these charges, using the ASCII or EBCDIC data representation codes.

Floppy disks are also called **flexible disks** and **floppies.** This is because the plastic disk inside the diskette covers is flexible, not rigid. Although there are several different types of floppy disks, there is just one standard and several others that are competing to become the next standard.

TODAY'S STANDARD

The most widely used floppy disk is the **1.44 MB 3½-inch disk.** (See Figure 6-1.) These disks are typically labeled **2HD,** which means "two-sided, high-density." This disk can store 1.44 megabytes—the equivalent of 400 typewritten pages. It has a thin exterior jacket made of hard plastic to protect the flexible disk inside. When the disk is inserted into a floppy disk drive, the shutter slides open to expose the 3½-inch flexible disk. A read-write head from the disk drive moves across the exposed disk to store and retrieve data.

These disks also have a **write-protect notch.** When the notch is open, data cannot be added on the disk. This is to provide protection against accidentally writing over information on the disk that you want to keep.

Figure 6-1 A 3½-inch floppy disk

TOMORROW'S STANDARD FLOPPY DISK

Today's standard floppy disk is very reliable and widely used to store data. Its major limitation is its capacity. While 1.44 MB is fine for many text and spreadsheet files, it is not sufficient to hold larger files. For example, many presentations far exceed 1.44 MB. Most multimedia applications require greater capacity.

Several other floppy disks, known as **floppy-disk cartridges,** are competing to become the next higher-capacity floppy disk standard. These contenders are also 3½-inch; however, they are thicker and require special disk drives. The three best known are Zip disks, SuperDisks, and HiFD disks.

- **Zip disks** are produced by Iomega and typically have a 100 MB or 250 MB capacity—over 170 times as much as today's standard floppy disk. Internal Zip drives are a standard feature on many of today's system units. External Zip drives are generally connected to the system unit in parallel and USB ports. (See Figure 6-2.) Zip disks are widely used to store multimedia, database, large text, and spreadsheet files. Many observers predict that Zip disks will become the next floppy disk standard.

- **SuperDisks** are produced by Imation and have a 120 MB capacity. They have one major advantage over Zip disks. SuperDisk drives are able to read and store data on today's 1.44 MB standard disk. Zip disk drives cannot. For this reason, SuperDisks are popular for use with notebook computers.

Figure 6-2 Zip disk and drive

Description	Capacity
2HD	1.44 MB
Zip	100 MB/250 MB
SuperDisk	120/240 MB
HiFD	200 MB

Figure 6-3 Typical floppy-disk capacities

- **HiFD disks** from the Sony Corporation are the newest challenger. They have a capacity of 200 MB and, like SuperDisk drives, HiFD disk drives are able to use today's 1.44 MB standard disks.

Each of these will likely improve its capacity and speed in the near future. Will one of them become the next standard floppy disk? While most observers believe one *will* become the next standard, they are less certain *when* this will occur. For a summary of floppy disks, see Figure 6-3.

THE PARTS OF A FLOPPY DISK

Data is recorded on a disk in rings called **tracks.** (See Figure 6-4.) These tracks are closed concentric circles, not a single spiral as on a phonograph record. Unlike on a phonograph record, these tracks have no visible grooves. Looking at an exposed floppy disk, you would see just a smooth surface. Each track is divided into invisible wedge-shaped sections known as **sectors.**

Some disks are manufactured without tracks and sectors in place. They must be adapted to the type of microcomputer and disk drive you are using. You do this using a process called **formatting,** or **initializing.**

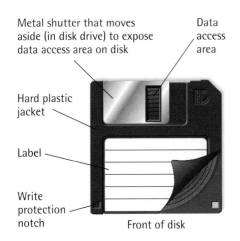

Metal shutter that moves aside (in disk drive) to expose data access area on disk

Data access area

Hard plastic jacket

Label

Write protection notch

Front of disk

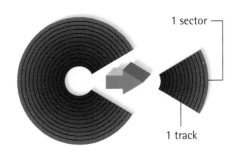

1 sector

1 track

Figure 6-4 The parts of a 3½-inch floppy disk

Concept Check

✔ How do floppy disks store information?

✔ What is today's standard floppy disk?

✔ What are likely to be tomorrow's standard floppy disks?

Hard disks are of three types: internal hard disk, hard-disk cartridge, and hard-disk pack.

While floppy disks use thin flexible plastic disks, **hard disks** use thicker, rigid metallic platters. (See Figure 6-5.) Hard disks are able to store and retrieve information much faster and have a greater capacity. They are sensitive instruments. The read-write head rides on a cushion of air about 0.000001 inch thick. It is so thin that a smoke particle, fingerprint, dust, or human hair could cause what is known as a head crash. (See Figure 6-6.)

A **head crash** happens when the surface of the read-write head or particles on its surface contact the magnetic disk surface. A head crash is a disaster for a hard disk. It means that some or all of the data on the disk is destroyed.

There are three types of hard disks: internal hard disk, hard-disk cartridge, and hard-disk pack.

INTERNAL HARD DISK

An **internal hard disk** is also known as a **fixed disk** because it is located inside the system unit. It is used to store programs and large data files. For example, nearly every microcomputer uses its internal hard disk to store its operating system and major applications like Word and Excel.

An internal hard disk consists of one or more metallic platters sealed inside a container. The container includes the motor for rotating the disks. It also contains an access arm and read-write heads for writing data to and reading data from the disks. From the outside of a microcomputer, an internal hard disk looks like part of a front panel on the system cabinet. Typically, inside are four 3½-inch metallic platters with access arms that move back and forth. (See Figure 6-7.)

Internal hard disks have two advantages over floppy disks: capacity and speed. An 80-gigabyte internal hard disk, for instance, can hold almost as much information as 56,000 standard floppy disks. Moreover, access is faster. For these reasons, almost all of today's powerful applications are designed to be stored on and run from an internal hard disk. Adequate capacity or size of a microcomputer's internal hard disk is essential.

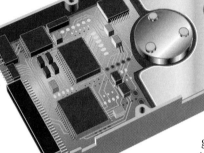

Figure 6-5 Hard disk

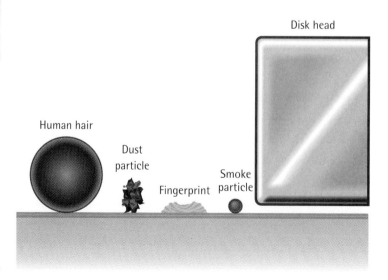

Disk head

Human hair

Dust particle

Fingerprint

Smoke particle

Figure 6-6 Materials that can cause a head crash

Figure 6-7 Inside of an internal hard-disk drive

HARD-DISK CARTRIDGES

While internal hard disks provide fast access, they have a fixed amount of storage and cannot be easily removed. **Hard-disk cartridges** are as easy to remove as a cassette from a videocassette recorder. The amount of storage available to a computer system is limited only by the number of cartridges.

Hard disk cartridges are used primarily to complement an internal hard disk. Because the cartridges are easily removed, they are particularly useful to protect or secure sensitive information. For example, personnel administrators need to have access to highly confidential employee information. When information is stored on a hard-disk cartridge, it is readily available, yet can be easily locked up when not in use. Other uses for hard-disk cartridges include backing up the contents of the internal hard disk and providing additional hard disk capacity.

Hard-disk cartridges for desktop computers have typical capacities up to 2 gigabytes. Two well-known desktop hard-disk cartridges are Jaz from Iomega and SparQ from SyQuest. Hard-disk cartridges for notebook computers are called **PC Card hard disks** and have typical capacities up to 1 gigabyte. Two well-known PC Card hard disks are IBM's Microdrive and Hitachi's PC Card hard drive. (See Figure 6-8.)

HARD-DISK PACKS

Hard-disk packs are removable storage devices used to store massive amounts of information. (See Figure 6-9.) Their capacity far exceeds the other types of hard disks. Although you may never have seen one, it is almost certain that you have used them. Microcomputers that have access to the Internet, minicomputers, or mainframes often have access to external hard-disk packs through communication lines. Banks and credit card companies use them to record financial information.

Figure 6-8 Hard-disk cartridges

Figure 6-9 Hard-disk packs

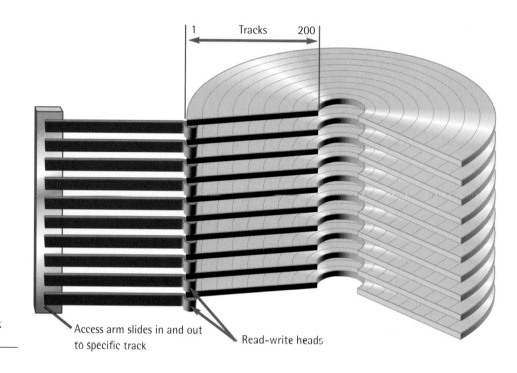

1   Tracks   200

Figure 6-10 How a hard-disk
pack works

Access arm slides in and out
to specific track

Read-write heads

Hard-disk packs consist of several platters aligned one above the other. They resemble a stack of phonograph records. The difference is that there is space between the disks to allow the access arms to move in and out. (See Figure 6-10.) Each access arm has two read-write heads. One reads the disk surface above it; the other reads the disk surface below it. A disk pack with 11 disks provides 20 recording surfaces. This is because the top and bottom outside surfaces of the pack are not used.

All the access arms move in and out together. However, only one of the read-write heads is activated at a given moment. **Access time** is the time between the computer's request for data from secondary storage and the completion of the data transfer.

You may well use your microcomputer to gain access to information over a telephone or other communications line. (We show this in the next chapter.) Such information is apt to be stored on disk packs. For example, one large information service, named Dialog, has over 300 databases. These databases cover all areas of science, technology, business, medicine, social science, current affairs, and humanities. All of these are available through a telephone

Type	Description
Internal	Fast access to applications, fixed
Cartridge	Complement to internal hard disk, removable
Disk pack	Massive storage capacity, removable

Figure 6-11 Types of hard disks

link with your desktop computer. There are more than 100 million items of information, including references to books, patents, directories, journals, and newspaper articles. Such an information resource may be of great value to you in your work.

For a summary of the different types of hard disks, see Figure 6-11.

PERFORMANCE ENHANCEMENTS

Three ways to improve the performance of hard disks are disk caching, redundant arrays of inexpensive disks, and file compression/decompression.

Disk caching improves hard-disk performance by anticipating data needs. It requires a combination of hardware and software. During idle processing time, frequently used data is read from the hard disk into memory (cache). When needed, the data is then accessed directly from memory. The transfer rate from memory is much faster than from hard disk. As a result, overall system performance is often increased by as much as 30 percent.

Redundant arrays of inexpensive disks (RAIDs) improve performance by expanding external storage. Groups of inexpensive hard-disk drives are related or grouped together using networks and special software. These grouped disks are treated as a single large-capacity hard disk. They can outperform single disks of comparable capacities.

File compression and **file decompression** increase storage capacity by reducing the amount of space required to store data and programs. File compression is not limited to hard-disk systems. It is frequently used to compress files on floppy disks as well. File compression also helps to speed up transmission of files from one computer system to another. Sending and receiving compressed files across the Internet is a common activity.

Special file compression programs scan files for ways to reduce the amount of required storage. One way is to search for repeating patterns. The repeating patterns are replaced with a token, leaving enough so that the original can be rebuilt or decompressed.

File compression programs typically can shrink files to a quarter of their original size. Two well-known file compression programs are WinZip from Nico Mak Computing and PKZip from PKWare.

Are you running short of hard-disk storage space? Want to send a large file or several files at once over the Internet? You can save both space and valuable connection time by compressing the files first. Here's how, using WinZip, a popular compression program:

1 Start. Start the WinZip program.

2 Create file. Click the *New* button on the toolbar to create and name a zip file.

3 Select. Locate and select the file(s) you want to compress.

4 Compress. Click the *Add* button to compress and add the selected file(s) to the zip file.

You can now replace the selected file(s) with the much smaller zip file. To access the original files at any time, use the *WinZip Extract* button.

Concept Check

✓ What are the three types of hard disks?

✓ What are the advantages of hard disks over floppy disks?

✓ List three ways to improve the performance of hard disks.

Optical disks use laser technology. Today's standard is CD. Tomorrow's will be DVD. DataPlay is a new format for digital photography and music.

Today's optical disks can hold over 17 gigabytes of data. (See Figure 6-12.) That is the equivalent of over several million typewritten pages or a medium-sized library all on a single disk. Optical disks are having a great impact on storage today, but we are probably only beginning to see their effects.

In optical-disk technology, a laser beam alters the surface of a plastic or metallic disk to represent data. Unlike floppy and hard disks, which use magnetic charges to represent 1s and 0s, optical disks use reflected light. The 1s and 0s are represented by flat areas called **lands** and bumpy areas called **pits** on the disk surface. The disk is read by a laser that projects a tiny beam of light on these areas. The amount of reflected light determines whether the area represents a 1 or a 0. (See Figure 6-13.)

Optical disks come in many different sizes including $3^1/_2$, $4^3/_4$, $5^1/_4$, 8, 12, and 14 inches. The most common size is $4^3/_4$-inch. Data is stored on these disks in different ways or different formats. The two most common are CD and DVD.

TODAY'S STANDARD

Compact disc, or as it is better known, **CD,** format is the most widely used today. (See Figure 6-14.) CD drives are standard on many microcomputer systems. Typically, CD drives can store 650 megabytes of data on one side of a CD. One important characteristic of CD drives is their speed. The rotational speed is important because it determines how fast data can be transferred from the CD. For example, a 24X or 24-speed CD drive can transfer 3.6 MB per second, while a 32X drive can transfer 4.8 MB per second. The faster the drive, the faster data can be read from the CD and used by the computer system.

There are three basic types of CDs: CD-ROM, CD-R, and CD-RW:

- **CD-ROM,** which stands for **compact disc-read only memory,** is similar to a commercial music CD. **Read-only** means it cannot be written on or erased by the user. Thus, you as a user have access only to the data imprinted by the publisher. CD-ROMs are used to distribute large databases and references. They are also used to distribute large software appli-

Figure 6-12 Optical disk

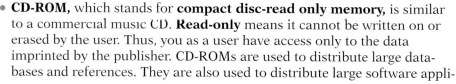

TIPS Do you like to listen to music while working on your computer? If you have a CD-ROM drive you can use it to play your favorite CDs while you work. Just follow these simple steps:

1 **Insert headphones.** Insert your headphone jack (commonly located on the front of the CD-ROM drive or on the back of your computer) or turn on your speakers.

2 **Insert CD.** Insert the music CD into the drive.

3 **Start player.** If the CD does not play automatically and you use either Windows 95, 98, or 2000, choose Start/Programs/Accessories/ Entertainment/CD Player to start the Windows CD player.

4 **Adjust volume.** Adjust the volume by clicking the speaker icon on the taskbar.

Although you can use the CD-ROM drive on your computer to play music CDs, do not use your audio CD player to play CDs intended for computers—this could damage your audio CD player's speakers.

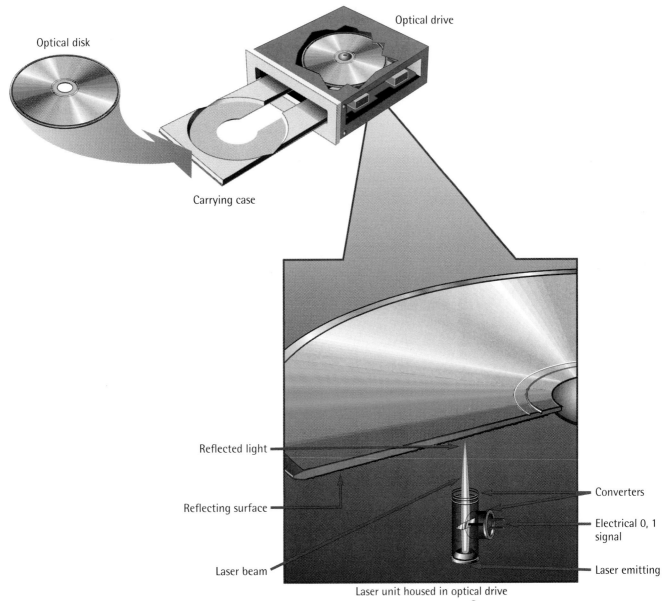

Optical disk

Optical drive

Carrying case

Reflected light

Reflecting surface

Converters

Electrical 0, 1 signal

Laser beam

Laser emitting

Laser unit housed in optical drive

Figure 6-13 How optical disks work

cation packages. For example, Microsoft Office is available on a single CD-ROM or on 38 floppy disks.

- **CD-R** stands for **CD-recordable.** Also known as **WORM,** or **write once, read many,** CD-Rs can be written to once. After that they can be read many times without deterioration but cannot be written on or erased. CD-Rs are used to create custom music CDs (see Making IT Work for You: CD-R Drives and Music from the Internet on pages 156–157) and to archive data.

- **CD-RW** stands for **compact disc rewritable.** Also known as **erasable optical disks,** these disks are very similar to other CD-Rs except that the disk surface is not permanently altered when data is recorded. Because they can be changed, CD-RWs are often used to create and edit multimedia presentations.

Figure 6-14 CD in drive

Optical Disks

CD-R DRIVES AND MUSIC FROM THE INTERNET

Did you know that you can use the Internet to locate music, download it to your computer, and create your own compact discs? All it takes is the right software, hardware, and a connection to the Internet.

How It Works Music is available on the Internet in special compressed music files called MP3s. You can download these music files to your system via your Internet connection. Using your system and some specialized software, you can store and play these files. You can even create a custom CD using a CD-R drive.

Internet → Your System → CD

Downloading Music There are several sites on the Web that offer free music that you can download to your system. Some Web sites are set up to offer a convenient way to browse and select these files, such as www.mp3.com.

For example, you can download files to your system:

1 • **Connect your browser to *mp3.com*.**

• **Select a featured artist.**

2 • **Select a song to download.**

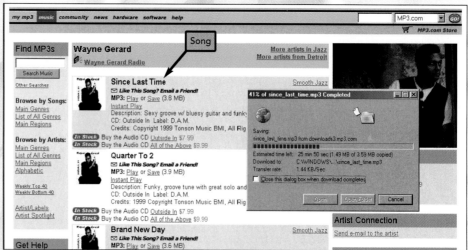
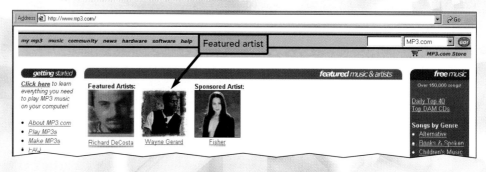

Playing Music To arrange and play downloaded music files, you need specialized software called a player. WinAmp from Nullsoft (www.winamp.com) is one of the best known.

For example, using WinAmp, you can play music files:

• **Click the *Add* button to select the music files to play.**

• **Click the *Play* button to play the music.**

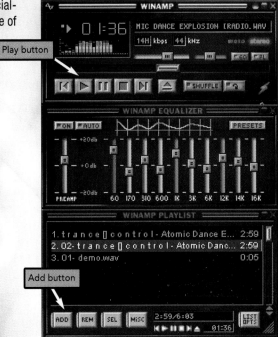

Creating a Custom CD If your computer is equipped with a CD-R or CD-RW drive, you can create your own music CDs. You'll need a blank recordable compact disc and special CD-creation software, such as Easy CD Creator by Adaptec. You use this software to organize and save the music files onto your CD.

For example, using Easy CD Creator, you can create a custom CD:

• **Select music files.**

• **Click *Create* to start recording the CD.**

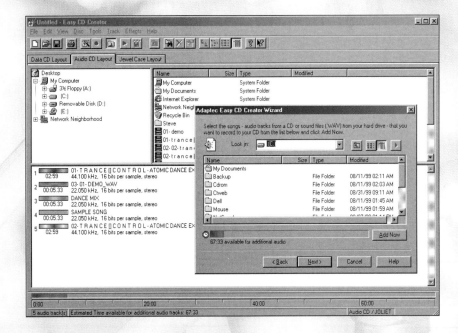

Not all MP3 files can be legally copied. To protect yourself, only download music files from reputable sites.

The Web is continually changing and some of the specifics presented in this Making IT Work for You may have changed. See our Web site at http://www.mhhe.com/oleary for possible changes and to learn more about this application of technology.

TOMORROW'S STANDARD

DVD stands for **digital versatile disc** or **digital video disc.** This is a newer format that is rapidly replacing CDs as the standard optical disk. DVD and DVD drives are very similar to CDs except that more data can be packed into the same amount of space. The DVD drives can store 17 gigabytes—more than 30 times the capacity of a CD.

While CDs may be the standard optical disk format today, DVDs are quickly replacing them. Many of today's more powerful microcomputer systems come with DVD drives. Like CDs, there are three basic types of DVDs:

- **DVD-ROM** stands for **digital versatile disc-read only memory.** DVD-ROMs are having a major impact on the video market. While CD-ROMs can store just over an hour of fair-quality video, DVD-ROMs can provide over two hours of very high-quality video and sound comparable to that found in motion picture theaters.

- **DVD-R** stands for **DVD-recordable.** DVD-Rs and DVD-R drives are starting to be used to create permanent archives for large amounts of data. Currently, they are not as widely used as CD-Rs because of their higher costs. This is expected to change as the costs for DVD-R become lower.

- **DVD-RAM** (**DVD-random-access memory**) and **DVD-RW** (**DVD-rewritable**) are two different types of reusable DVD disks. Like CD-RW, they can be used over and over again. They will be used for a wide variety of applications including the creation and editing of large-scale multimedia presentations.

DataPlay is a new optical write-once format similar to CD-R. This format is designed for optical disks the size of a quarter with the capacity of 500 MB or enough to hold 5 hours of CD-quality sound. (Scc Figure 6-15.) Users will be able to record data, such as music files, and to play pre-recorded music. Although more specialized than the other formats, DataPlay appears likely to become widely used for specialized applications, including storing digital photographs and music for portable players. The music industry is supporting this format, in part, because pre-recorded music in the DataPlay format is more difficult to copy than with music stored on traditional CDs.

For a summary of optical disk storage capacities, see Figure 6-16.

Figure 6-15 DataPlay disks

Concept Check

✓ How do optical disks record 1s and 0s?

✓ How much data can DVD drives store on one side of a DVD? What is the difference between CD and DVD discs?

✓ What are DataPlay disks used for?

Format	Typical Capacity	Type	Description
CD	650MB	CD-ROM	Fixed content, used to distribute databases, reference books, and software
		CD-R	Written-to one time only, used to archive large amounts of data
		CD-RW	Reusable, used to create and edit large multimedia presentations
DVD	17GB	DVD-ROM	Fixed content, distribute theater-quality video and sound presentations
		DVD-R	Written-to one time only, used to archive very large amounts of data
		DVD-RAM	Reusable, used to create and edit large-scale multimedia presentations
		(DVD-RW)	
DataPlay	500MB		New specialized format for digital photography and music.

Figure 6-16 Types of optical disks

OTHER TYPES OF SECONDARY STORAGE

For the typical microcomputer user, the three basic storage options—floppy disk, hard disk, and optical disk—are complementary, not competing. Almost all microcomputers today have at least one floppy-disk drive, one hard disk drive, and one optical drive. For many users, these secondary storage devices are further complemented with more specialized devices such as magnetic tape devices, Internet drives, and solid-state storage devices.

> Magnetic tape is sequential access for backup. Internet drives use the Internet to store data and information. Solid-state storage does not have moving parts.

MAGNETIC TAPE

To find a particular song on an audiotape, you may have to play several inches of tape. Finding a song on an audio compact disc, in contrast, can be much faster. You select the song, and the disc player moves directly to it. That, in brief, represents the two different approaches to external storage. The two approaches are called **direct access** and **sequential access.**

Disks provide fast direct access. Tapes provide sequential access. With tape, information is stored in sequence, such as alphabetically. You may have to search a tape past all the information from *A* to *P*, say, before you get to *Q*. This may involve searching several inches or feet, which takes time.

Although tape may be slower to access specific information, it is an effective and commonly used tool for backing up data. Microcomputers typically use **magnetic tape streamers** or **backup tape cartridge units.** Data is stored on cassette tapes with a typical capacity of 4 gigabytes. Mainframe computers use **magnetic tape reels**. The tape is typically ½-inch wide and ½-mile long and has massive storage capacity. (See Figure 6-17.)

Figure 6-17 Magnetic tape reels

Figure 6-18 An Internet hard drive

INTERNET HARD DRIVES

Special service sites on the Web provide users with free or low-cost storage. This storage is called an **Internet hard drive**, also known as **i-drive** or **online storage**. (See Figure 6-18.)

Advantages of Internet hard drives compared to other types of secondary storage is low (or no) cost and the flexibility to access information from any location using any computer that is connected to the Internet. Because all information must travel across the Internet, however, access time is greater. Another consideration is that users are dependent on the availability and security procedures of the service site. Because of these limitations, Internet hard drives are typically used as a specialized secondary storage device and not for storing highly personalized or sensitive information. For a list of sites that provide Internet hard drive services, see Figure 6-19.

SOLID-STATE STORAGE

Each of the secondary storage devices discussed thus far has moving parts. For example, hard disks rotate and read-write heads move in and out. Unlike these devices, **solid-state storage** devices have no moving parts. Data and information are stored and retrieved electronically directly from these devices much as they would be from conventional computer memory. While this type

Company	Location
Apple	http://itools.mac.com
Freedrive	http://www.freedrive.com
MSN	http://www.msn.com
Xdrive	http://www.xdrive.com
Yahoo	http://briefcase.yahoo.com

Figure 6-19 Internet Drive Sites

of storage is more expensive than the others, it is more reliable and requires less power. For these reasons, this technology is becoming widely used for specialized secondary storage.

Flash memory cards are solid-state storage devices widely used in notebook computers. (See Figure 6-20.) **Flash memory** is also used in a variety of specialized input devices to capture and transfer data to desktop computers. For example, flash memory is used to store images captured from digital cameras and then to transfer the images to desktop and other computers. Flash memory is also used to record MP3 music files and to transfer those files to computers and other devices.

Figure 6-20 Flash memory cards

A Look to the Future

Near-Field Recording Devices and Holographic Storage Systems Offer Increased Storage Capacity

Have you ever wondered why we need such large-capacity secondary storage devices? As we mentioned earlier, DVD drives have a 17-gigabyte capacity. Soon we can expect 140-gigabyte FMD-ROM 3D (Fluorescent Multilayer Disk) from Constellation 3D. When will this trend of increasing capacity end? Probably not in the near future.

As we use more graphical interfaces like Windows XP, store images from the Web, and work with more advanced applications like multimedia and virtual reality, the demand for larger and faster secondary storage devices will continue to grow. Fortunately, several new technologies promise to meet this demand.

One is called near-field recording. These devices use a revolutionary new drive head that utilizes lasers and a special focusing lens called a solid immersion lens. This lens precisely directs the laser's path, thereby allowing more information to be stored on a disk. Near-field recording devices are expected to cost the same as today's hard disk systems yet provide ten times more storage capacity.

A bit further on the horizon is holographic storage. Holograms, as you may know, are those shimmering, three-dimensional images often seen on credit cards. Holographic systems can store data equivalent to thousands of books inside a container the size of a sugar cube.

When will we be able to purchase systems using these new technologies? Prototypes have been created and we can expect to see near-field recording devices and holographic systems in the next few years

A Look to the Future

FLOPPY DISKS

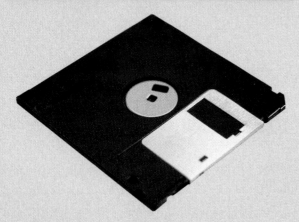

Floppy disks are also known as **diskettes** or simply as **disks.** They are inexpensive removable storage media. Floppy disks are primarily used to save and transport documents.

Today's Standard

Today's standard floppy disk is the **1.44 MB 3½-inch disk, or 2HD.** It is by far the most widely used floppy disk today. Due to its relatively low storage capacity, however, it is expected to be replaced by higher-capacity floppy disks.

Tomorrow's Standard

Three types of **floppy-disk cartridges** are competing to become the next standard:

- **Zip disks**—considered by many to be the leading contender to replace today's standard; storage capacity 100 MB and 250 MB.
- **SuperDisks**—120 MB capacity; SuperDisk drives are able to read today's standard disks.
- **HiFD**—200 MB capacity; like SuperDisk drives, HiFD drives are able to read today's standard disks.

Parts of a Floppy Disk

Data is recorded in rings called **tracks.** Each track is divided into wedge-shaped sections known as **sectors.** The process of preparing a disk with tracks and sectors is called **formatting** or **initializing.**

HARD DISKS

Compared to floppy disks, **hard disks** are rigid, faster, and provide much greater storage. A **head crash** damages the surface of a hard disk.

Internal Hard Disk

An **internal hard disk** or **fixed disk** is located inside the system unit.

Hard-Disk Cartridge

Unlike internal hard disks, **hard-disk cartridges** are removable and only the number of cartridges limits the amount of storage capacity. **PC Card hard disks** are for notebooks.

Hard-Disk Pack

Hard-disk packs consist of several platters and have a capacity that greatly exceeds both internal and hard-disk cartridges.

Performance Enhancements

Three ways to improve hard disk performance are:

- **Disk caching**—reduces time to access data by anticipating data needs.
- **RAIDs**—expand storage capacity by grouping inexpensive hard disk drives.
- **File compression and decompression**—increases storage capacity by reducing the space required to store data and programs.

CHAPTER REVIEW

MULTIPLE CHOICE

Circle the letter or fill in the correct answer.

1. ____C____ is permanent storage used to preserve data and programs.
   a. Internal storage
   b. Volatile storage
   c. Nonvolatile storage
   d. File compression
   e. Read-only memory

2. Another name for floppy disks is _____.
   a. diskettes
   b. disks
   c. flexible disks
   d. floppies
   e. all of the above

3. The most widely used floppy disk is the _____.
   a. 1.44 MB 3½-inch disk, 2HD
   b. 100 MB 3½-inch disk, 2HD
   c. 120 MB 3½-inch disk, 2HD
   d. 250 MB 3½-inch disk, 2HD
   e. 200 MB 3½-inch disk, 2HD

4. Before a disk without tracks and sectors can be used for storage, it must be _____.
   a. opened
   b. compressed
   c. expanded
   d. initialized
   e. scanned

5. An internal hard disk is also known as a _____ because it is located inside the system unit.
   a. hard-disk pack
   b. PC Card hard disk
   c. fixed disk
   d. removable disk
   e. hard disk cartridge

6. Groups of inexpensive hard-disk drives grouped together and treated as a single large-capacity hard disk are called _____.
   a. disk caches
   b. versatile disks
   c. RAIDs
   d. DVDs
   e. hard-disk packs

7. _____ is exclusively a sequential-access storage media.
   a. A floppy disk
   b. A hard disk
   c. Magnetic tape
   d. CD-ROM
   e. WORM

8. The disk with the largest capacity is _____.
   a. Zip
   b. 3½-inch 2HD
   c. SuperDisk
   d. CD-ROM
   e. DVD-ROM

9. _____ is a type of optical disk widely used to distribute large software application packages.
   a. CD-ROM
   b. CD-R
   c. CD-RW
   d. DVD
   e. DVD-RW

10. _____ can provide over two hours of high quality video and sound comparable to that found in theaters.
    a. CD-RW
    b. CD
    c. CD-ROM
    d. DVD-R
    e. DVD-ROM

Match each numbered item with the most closely related lettered item. Write your answers in the spaces provided.

a. hard disk

b. lands and pits

c. write-protect notch

d. disk caching

e. track

f. head crash

g. hard-disk pack

h. floppy disk

i. flash memory card

j. compact disc (CD)

k. magnetic tape streamer

l. access time

m. floppy-disk cartridge

n. erasable optical disk

o. online storage

p. sector

q. file compression

r. WORM

s. solid-state storage

t. read-only

1. Also known as a diskette. _h_

2. Zip disks, SuperDisks, HiFD disks. _m_

3. Used to prevent the computer from destroying data on a disk. _c_

4. Closed concentric ring on a disk on which data is recorded. _e_

5. Invisible wedge-shaped sections of a floppy disk. _p_

6. Enclosed disk drive that contains one or more metallic disks. _a_

7. Happens when the read-write heads contact the surface of a hard disk. _f_

8. Several platters aligned one above the other, allowing greater storage capacity. _g_

9. Time between the computer's request for data from secondary storage and the completion of the data transfer. _l_

10. A combination of hardware and software that improves hard-disk performance by anticipating data needs. _d_

11. Helps increase storage capacity by reducing the amount of space required to store data and programs. _q_

12. Flat and bumpy areas that represent 1s and 0s on the optical disk surface to be read by laser. _b_

13. Widely used optical disk format. _r_

14. Cannot be written on or erased by the user. _t_

15. Write once, read many. _j_

16. Similar to CD-Rs except the disk surface is not permanently altered when data is recorded. _n_

17. Cassette tapes with a typical capacity of 4 gigabytes that are an effective, yet slow, tool for backing up data. _k_

18. Device that stores and retrieves data and information electronically and has no moving parts. _s_

19. Free or low-cost storage available at special service Web sites. _o_

20. Solid-state storage device widely used in notebook computers. _i_

On a separate sheet of paper, respond to each question or statement.

1. Discuss the three most likely successors to the 1.44 MB 3½-inch floppy.

2. What are the three types of hard disk? What is so disastrous about a head crash?

3. Describe the three ways to improve hard disk performance.

4. What are the two types of optical disks? What are the advantages and disadvantages of each?

5. Explain the concept of Internet storage. What are the advantages and disadvantages of this system?

CD-R Drives and Music from the Internet 1

Did you know that you could use the Internet to locate music, download it to your computer, and create your own compact discs? All it takes is the right software, hardware, and a connection to the Internet. To learn more about creating your own CDs, review Making IT Work for You: CD-R Drives and Music from the Internet on pages 156 and 157. Then visit our Web site at http://www.mhhe.com/oleary, play the videos, and answer the following questions: (a) What

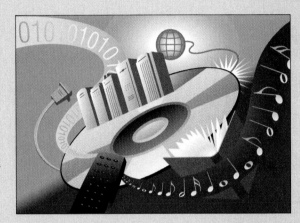

is the title of the song that was selected for download from the Internet? (b) Describe the procedure for adding music files to the WinAmp Playlist. (c) Describe the windows that popped up after the Create CD button was clicked in the Adaptec Easy CD Creator program.

TiVo 2

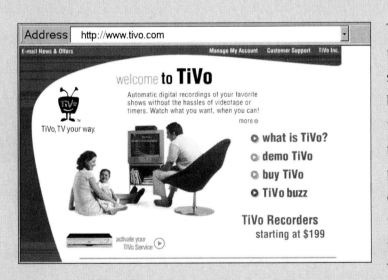

TiVo is a device that, among other features, allows users to pause live television. Connect to our Web site at http://www.mhhe.com/oleary to connect to TiVo's Web site. Once connected, explore the TiVo product and write a one-page paper that answers the following questions: (a) What are the basic functions of TiVo? (b) How could TiVo be an improvement on the traditional VCR? (c) What type of secondary storage does TiVo use? (d) How does TiVo receive updated television program information? (e) Would you use TiVo? Why or why not?

1 Interactive Companion CD-ROM

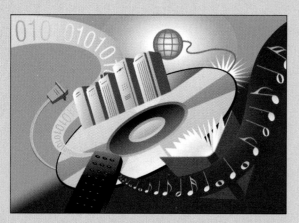

Complete the "Disk Fragmentation" Lab located on your Interactive Companion CD-ROM, and then answer the following questions in a one-page paper: (a) Why is data stored in sectors, instead of a continuous "stream"? (b) Define fragment, and explain why they occur. (c) What causes fragmentation? What precautions should you take before using software to defragment your hard disk?

2 High Capacity Floppy Disks

Several manufacturers are producing high capacity floppy disks including Iomega, Imation, and Sony Corporation. Conduct a Web search to learn more about high capacity floppy disks. Then write a one-page pager that addresses the following: (a) What are the most widely used high capacity floppy disks? (b) Compare their capacities and costs. (c) Discuss their relative advantages and

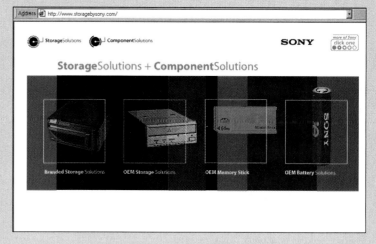

disadvantages. (d) If you were to use a high capacity floppy disk, which one would you select? Discuss and justify your choice.

DVD 1

DVD is a newer optical format that is rapidly replacing CDs as the standard in optical disks. DVDs can store 17 gigabytes, more than 30 times the capacity of a CD. Many of today's microcomputers come with DVD drives. Write a two-page paper titled "DVD Technology" that answers the following questions: (a) Define DVD-ROM, DVD-R, and DVD-RW. (b) Compare DVD technology to other types of secondary storage in terms of speed, portability, and capacity. (c) Give examples of applications where DVD would be the best choice for storage. What are some applications where DVD would not be the best choice? Explain your answers.

CD-R and Music Files 2

Burning a custom CD of your favorite music is a popular use of secondary storage. Many sites on the Web offer free music that you can download. However, not all music files that are available on the Internet are freely distributable. Consider the following points and write a two-page paper addressing the following issues: (a) Is it fair to make a copy of a CD you have purchased on your computer? (b) Would it be fair to give a burned copy of a CD to a friend? What if the friend would not have otherwise purchased that CD? (c) People have been making illegal copies of music cassette tapes for some time. How is using the Internet different?

CONNECTIVITY, THE WIRELESS REVOLUTION, AND COMMUNICATIONS

Connectivity
Provides incredible power to you while at and away from your desk

Microwave Dish

Wireless Revolution
Extends wireless voice communication to computer communication to free users from their desks

Satellite

The telephone has extended our uses for the microcomputer enormously. The mobile telephone and other wireless technologies are revolutionizing how we use computers today. You can connect your microcomputer to the microcomputers of other people, to the Internet, and to other, larger computers located throughout the world. As we've mentioned earlier, this connectivity puts incredible power on your desk. The result is increased productivity—for you as an individual and for the groups and organizations of which you are a member. Connectivity has become particularly important in business, where individuals now find themselves connected in networks to other individuals and departments.

Communication systems are the electronic systems that transmit data over communications lines from one location to another. You might use a wearable computer and a satellite communication system to access the Internet from almost anywhere. You might work for an organization whose computer system is spread throughout a building, or even throughout the country or world. Or you might use telecommunications lines—telephone lines—to tap into information located in an outside data bank. You could then transmit it to your microcomputer for your own reworking and analysis.

You can even set up a network in your home or apartment using existing telephone lines. Then you can share files, use one Internet connection, and play interactive games with others in your home.

Competent end users need to understand the concept of connectivity and the impact of the wireless revolution. Additionally, they need to know the elements of a communications system, including channels, connections, transmission, network architectures, and network types.

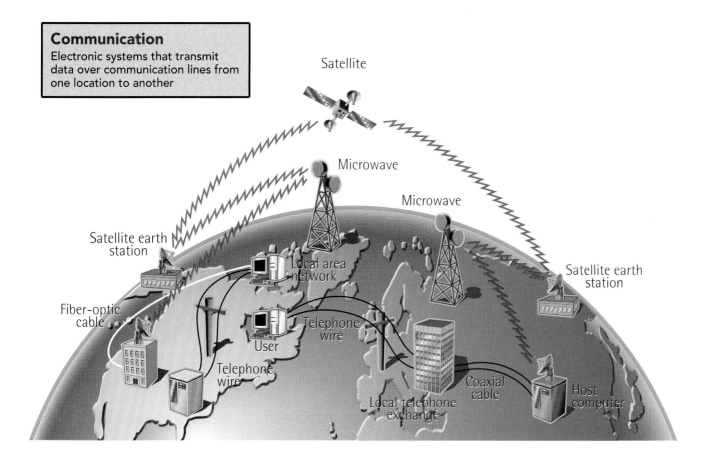

Communication
Electronic systems that transmit data over communication lines from one location to another

Satellite

Microwave

Microwave

Satellite earth station

Satellite earth station

Fiber-optic cable

Local area network

Telephone wire

User

Telephone wire

Local telephone exchange

Coaxial cable

Host computer

Connectivity is a concept related to using computer networks to link people and resources. Mobile telephone and Bluetooth are technologies of The Wireless Revolution.

You may have a microcomputer connected to the Internet using a telephone line. Perhaps you have a portable computer that is connected to a mobile phone. Or, you may have a microcomputer that is directly connected to other computers without using telephone lines. (See Figure 7-1.) Whatever the case, these situations allow you to connect to other people and resources, perhaps using wireless technologies that form a communication system. Connectivity, the wireless revolution, and communications are key concepts and technologies for the twenty-first century.

Figure 7–1 Communications

CONNECTIVITY

Connectivity is a concept related to using computer networks to link people and resources. For example, connectivity means that you can connect your microcomputer by telephone or other telecommunications links to other computers and information sources almost anywhere. With this connection, you are linked to the world of larger computers and the Internet. This includes minicomputers and mainframes and their large storage devices, such as disk packs, and their enormous volumes of information. Thus computer competence becomes a matter of knowing, not only about connectivity through networks to microcomputers, but also about larger computer systems and their information resources.

THE WIRELESS REVOLUTION

Figure 7–2 Connectivity options

The single most dramatic change in connectivity and communications in the past five years has been the widespread use of mobile or wireless telephones.

Students, parents, teachers, business people, and others routinely talk and communicate with these devices. It is estimated that over 600 million mobile telephones are in use worldwide. This wireless technology allows individuals to stay connected with one another from almost anywhere at any time.

So what's the revolution? While this wireless technology was originally intended for voice communication, it is now becoming widely used to support all kinds of communication, especially computer communication. (See Figure 7-2.) In addition, recently released technology call **Bluetooth** promises to allow a wide variety of nearby devices to communicate with one other without any physical connection. You can share a high-speed printer, share data files, and collaborate on working documents with a nearby co-worker without having your computers connected by cables or telephone—wireless communication. But is it a revolution? Most expects say yes and the revolution is in its infancy.

COMMUNICATION SYSTEMS

Communication systems are electronic systems that transmit data from one location to another. Whether wired or wireless, every communication system has four basic elements. (See Figure 7-3.)

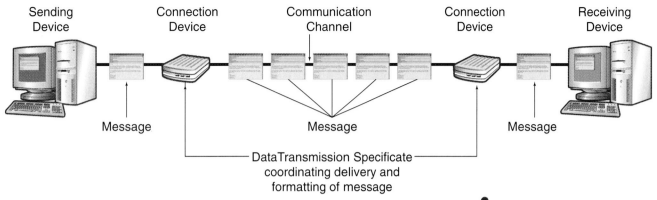

Figure 7-3 Basic elements of a communications system

- **Sending and receiving devices**. These are often a computer or specialized communication device. They originate (send) as well as accept (receive) messages in the form of data, information, and/or instructions.
- **Communication channel**. This is the actual connecting medium that carries the message. This medium can be a physical wire or cable or it can be a wireless connection.
- **Connection devices**. These devices act as an interface between the sending and receiving devices and the communication channel. They convert outgoing messages into a form and format so that they can travel across the communication channel. They also reverse the process for incoming messages.
- **Data transmission specifications**. These are rules and procedures that coordinate the sending and receiving devices by precisely defining how the message will be sent across the communication channel.

For example, if you wanted to send an e-mail to a friend, you could create and send the message using your computer, the *sending device*. Your modem, a *connection device,* would modify and format the message so that it could travel efficiently across *communication channels* such as telephone lines. The specifics describing how the message is modified, reformatted, and sent would be described in the *data transmission specifications*. After traveling across the channel, the receiver's modem, a *connection device,* would reform the message so that it could be displayed on your friend's computer, the *receiving device.* (Note: This example presents the basic communication system elements involved in sending e-mail. It does not and is not intended to demonstrate all the specific steps and equipment involved in an e-mail delivery system.)

Concept Check

✓ What is The Wireless Revolution?

✓ Describe the four elements of every communication system?

Communication channels carry data. Telephone lines, coaxial, and cable are physical connections. Microwave signals and satellites support wireless connections.

Communication channels are an essential element of every communication system. These channels actually carry the data from one computer to another. There are two categories of communications channels. One category connects sending and receiving devices by providing physical connection such as a wire or cable. The other category is wireless.

PHYSICAL CONNECTIONS

Physical connections use a solid medium to connect sending and receiving devices. These connections include telephone lines (twisted pair), coaxial cable, and fiber-optic cable.

Figure 7-4 Twisted pair cable

- **Telephone lines** you see strung on poles consist of **twisted pair** cable, which is made up of hundreds of copper wires. A single twisted pair culminates in a wall jack into which you can plug your phone and computer. (See Figure 7-4.) Telephone lines have been the standard transmission medium for years for both voice and data. However, they are now being phased out by more technically advanced and reliable media.

- **Coaxial cable,** a high-frequency transmission cable, replaces the multiple wires of telephone lines with a single solid-copper core. (See Figure 7-5.) In terms of number of telephone connections, a coaxial cable has over 80 times the transmission capacity of twisted pair. Coaxial cable is used to deliver television signals as well as to connect computers in a network.

Figure 7-5 Coaxial cable

- **Fiber-optic cable** transmits data as pulses of light through tiny tubes of glass. (See Figure 7-6.) In terms of number of telephone connections, fiber-optic cable has over 26,000 times the transmission capacity of twisted pair. However, it is significantly smaller. Indeed, a fiber-optic tube can be half the diameter of a human hair. Although limited in the distance they can carry information, fiber-optic cables have several advantages. Such cables are immune to electronic interference, which makes them more secure. They are also lighter and less expensive than coaxial cable and are more reliable at transmitting data. They transmit information using beams of light at light speeds instead of pulses of electricity, making them far faster than copper cable. Fiber-optic cable is rapidly replacing twisted pair telephone lines.

Figure 7-6 Fiber-optic cable

WIRELESS CONNECTIONS

Wireless connections do not use a solid substance to connect sending and receiving devices. Rather, they use the air itself. Two primary technologies used for wireless connections are microwave and satellite.

- **Microwave** communication uses high-frequency radio waves. This technology is sometimes referred to as **line of sight communication** because the radio waves travel in a straight line. Because the waves cannot bend with the curvature of the earth, they can be transmitted only over short distances. Thus, microwave is a good medium for sending data between buildings in a city or on a large college campus. For longer distances, the waves must be relayed by means of "dishes," or antennas.

These can be installed on towers, high buildings, and mountaintops, for example. (See Figure 7-7.) Bluetooth, a technology mentioned earlier, uses microwaves to transmit data over short distances of up to approximately 33 feet. It is anticipated that within the next few years, this technology will be widely used to connect a variety of different communication devices.

- **Satellite** communication uses satellites orbiting about 22,000 miles above the earth as microwave relay stations. (See Figure 7-8.) Many of these are offered by Intelsat, the *International Tele*communications *Sat*ellite Consortium, which is owned by 114 governments and forms a worldwide communications system. Satellites rotate at a precise point and speed above the earth. This makes them appear stationary, so they can amplify and relay microwave signals from one transmitter on the ground to another. Thus, satellites can be used to send large volumes of data. Their major drawback is that bad weather can sometimes interrupt the flow of data.

For a summary of communications channels, see Figure 7-9.

Figure 7-7 Microwave dish

Figure 7-8 Satellite

Channel	Description
Twisted pair	Copper wire, standard voice telephone line
Coaxial cable	Solid copper core, more than 80 times capacity of twisted pair
Fiber-optic	Light carries data, more than 26,000 times capacity of twisted pair
Microwave	High-frequency radio waves carry data, travels in straight line through the air
Satellite	Microwave relay station in the sky, rotates at fixed point above the earth

Figure 7-9 Types of communications channels

Concept Check

✓ Discuss the types of communications channels.

✓ Which is the fastest form of cable communications channels?

✓ What is one limitation of microwave communications?

Conventional modems convert analog and digital signals. Other user connections are T1, DSL, cable modems, and satellite.

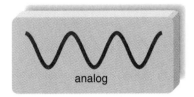

Figure 7-10 Analog versus digital signals

Unit	Speed
bps	bit per second
kbps	thousand bits per second
mbps	million bits per second
gbps	billion bits per second

Figure 7-11 Communication speeds

A great deal of computer communications, especially connecting to the Internet, take place over telephone lines. However, because the telephone was originally designed for voice transmission, telephones typically send and receive **analog signals**, which are continuous electronic waves. Computers, in contrast, send and receive **digital signals.** (See Figure 7-10.) These represent the presence or absence of an electronic pulse—the on/off binary signals we mentioned in Chapter 4. To convert the digital signals of your microcomputer to analog and vice versa, you need a modem.

MODEMS

The word **modem** is short for "*mo*dulator-*dem*odulator." **Modulation** is the name of the process of converting from digital to analog. **Demodulation** is the process of converting from analog to digital. The modem enables digital microcomputers to communicate across analog telephone lines. Both voice communications and data communications can be carried over the same telephone line.

The speed with which modems transmit data varies. Communications speed is typically measured in *bits per second (bps)*. (See Figure 7-11.) The higher the speed, the faster you can send and receive information. For example, transferring an image like Figure 7-10, might take 75 seconds with a 33.6 kbps modem and only 45 seconds with a 56 kbps modem.

TYPES OF MODEMS

There are four basic types of modems: external, internal, PC Card, and wireless.

- The **external modem** stands apart from the computer and typically is connected by a cable to the computer's serial port. Another cable connects the modem to the telephone wall jack.

- The **internal modem** consists of a plug-in circuitboard inside the system unit. A telephone cable connects the modem to the telephone wall jack. (See Figure 7-12.)

- The **PC Card modem** is a credit card–size expansion board that is inserted into portable computers. A telephone cable connects the modem to the telephone wall jack.

- The **wireless modem** is very similar to the external modem. Typically, it connects to the computer's serial port. Unlike an external modem, it does not connect with a cable. Rather, wireless modems send and receive through the air.

TYPES OF CONNECTIONS

Standard telephone lines and conventional modems provide what is called a **dial-up service.** Although still the most popular type of connection service, dial-up service is quite slow, and many users find it inadequate to meet their communication needs.

For years, large corporations have been leasing special high-speed lines from telephone companies. These lines—known as **T1, T2, T3,** and **T4 lines**—support all digital communications, do not require conventional modems, and provide very high capacity. Unfortunately, this type of connection is very expensive. For example, T1 lines provide a speed of 1.5 mbps (over 26 times as fast as a conventional modem) and cost several thousands of dollars.

While the special high-speed lines are too costly for most individuals, there are affordable connections that provide significantly higher capacity than standard dial-up service. These include DSL, cable modems, and satellite.

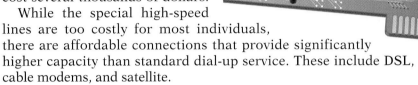

Figure 7-12 Internal modem

- **Digital subscriber line (DSL)** uses existing telephone lines to provide high-speed connections. This technology is widely available in most areas.
- **Cable modems** use existing television cables to provide high-speed connections as fast as a T1 or DSL connection, at a lower cost. Although cable connections reach 90 percent of the homes in America, all cable companies do not support cable modems. Industry observers, however, predict 100 percent availability within the next few years.
- **Satellite/air connection services** use satellites and the air to download or send data to users at a rate seven times faster than dial-up connections. While older satellite services could not upload or send data to satellites and had to rely on slow dial-up connection, newer two-way satellite connections are now available. While slower than DSL and cable modems, satellite/air connections are available almost anywhere that a satellite-receiving disk can be aimed at the southern skies.

For a comparison of typical user connection costs and speeds, see Figure 7-13.

Type	Cost/Year	Speed	Seconds to Receive Image
Dial-up	$250	56 kbps	45.0 seconds
DSL	750	1.5 mbps	1.7 seconds
Cable modem	750	1.5 mbps	1.7 seconds
Satellite/air	1,050	900 kbps	2.8 seconds

Figure 7-13 Typical user connection costs and speeds to download information

(Cost/Year includes equipment and connection charges.)

Concept Check

✓ Discuss the four basic types of modems.

✓ Describe the high-speed internet options available to most users.

> Several technical matters affect data communications. They are bandwidth, serial versus parallel transmission, direction of flow, modes of transmission, and protocols.

Several factors affect how data is transmitted. They include bandwidth, serial or parallel transmission, direction of data flow, and protocols.

BANDWIDTH

Bandwidth is a measurement of the capacity of the communication channel. Effectively, it means how much information can move across the communication channel in a given amount of time. For example, to transmit text documents, a slow bandwidth would be acceptable. However, to effectively transmit video and audio, a wider bandwidth is required. There are three categories of bandwidth.

- **Voiceband**, also known as **low bandwidth**, is used for standard telephone communication. Microcomputers with standard modems and dial-up service use this bandwidth. While effective for transmitting text documents, it is too slow for many types of transmission including high-quality video. Typical speeds are 56 to 96 kbps.
- **Medium band** is the bandwidth used in special leased lines to connect minicomputers and mainframes as well as to transmit data over long distances. Unlike voice band and broadband, medium band is not typically used by individuals.
- **Broadband** is the bandwidth used for high-capacity transmissions. Microcomputers with DSL, cable, and satellite connections as well as other more specialized high-speed devices use this bandwidth. It is capable of effectively transmitting high-quality video and most of today's communication needs. Speeds are typically 1.5 mbps although much higher speeds are possible.

SERIAL AND PARALLEL TRANSMISSION

Data travels in two ways: serially and in parallel. (See Figure 7-14.)

- In **serial data transmission,** bits flow in a series or continuous stream, like cars crossing a one-lane bridge. Serial transmission is the way most data is sent over telephone lines. For this reason, external modems typically connect to a microcomputer through a serial port. More technical names for the serial port are **RS-232C connector** and **asynchronous communications port.**
- With **parallel data transmission,** bits flow through separate lines simultaneously. In other words, they resemble cars moving together at the same speed on a multilane freeway. Parallel transmission is typically limited to communications over short distances and typically is not used over telephone lines. It is, however, a standard method of sending data from the system unit to a printer.

DIRECTION OF DATA TRANSMISSION

There are three directions or modes of data flow in a data communications system. (See Figure 7-15.)

- **Simplex communication** resembles the movement of cars on a one-way street. Data travels in one direction only. The simplex mode is not frequently used in data communications systems today. One instance

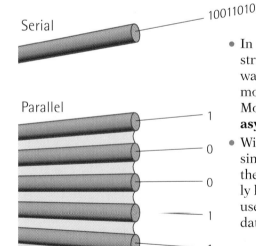

Serial
10011010

Parallel
1
0
0
1
1
0
1
0

Figure 7-14 Serial versus parallel transmission

in which it is used may be in point-of-sale (POS) terminals in which data is being entered only.

- In **half-duplex communication,** data flows in both directions, but not simultaneously. That is, data flows in only one direction at any one time. This resembles traffic on a one-lane bridge. Half-duplex is very common and frequently used for linking microcomputers by telephone lines to other microcomputers.

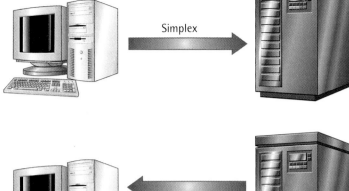

- In **full-duplex communication,** data is transmitted back and forth at the same time, like traffic on a two-way street. It is clearly the fastest and most efficient form of two-way communication. Full-duplex has been widely used for mainframe communications for years. Now, it is becoming the standard mode for microcomputers as well.

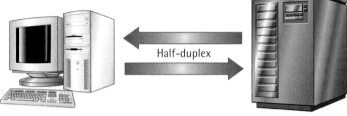

PROTOCOLS

For data transmission to be successful, sender and receiver must follow a set of communication rules for the exchange of information. These rules for exchanging data between computers are known as **protocols.**

The standard protocol for the Internet is **TCP/IP (transmission control protocol/Internet protocol)**. The essential features of this protocol involve (1) identifying sending and receiving devices and (2) reformatting information for transmission across the Internet.

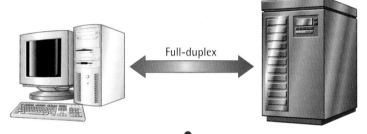

Figure 7-15 Simplex, half-duplex, and full-duplex communication

- **Identification:** Every computer on the Internet has a unique numeric address called an **IP address (Internet Protocol address)**. Similar to the way a postal service uses addresses to deliver mail, the Internet uses IP addresses to deliver e-mail and to locate Web sites. Because these numeric addresses are difficult for people to remember and use, a system was developed to automatically convert text-based addresses to numeric IP addresses. This system is called the **domain name system (DNS)** and will be discussed in the next chapter.

- **Reformatting:** Information sent or transmitted across the Internet usually travels through numerous interconnected networks. Before the message is sent, it is reformattted or broken down into small parts called **packets.** Each packet is then sent separately over the Internet, possibly traveling different routes to one common destination. At the receiving end, the packets are reassembled into the correct order.

Concept Check

✓ What are the three categories of bandwidth?

✓ What are the three directions of data flow?

✓ What is the standard protocol for the Internet?

> **Network architecture describes how a computer network is configured and what strategies are used.**

Communications channels can be connected in different arrangements, or **networks,** to suit different users' needs. A **computer network** is a communications system connecting two or more computers that work together to exchange information and share resources. **Network architecture** describes how the network is arranged and how the resources are coordinated and shared.

TERMS

There are a number of specialized terms that describe computer networks. Some terms often used with networks are:

- **Node**—any device that is connected to a network. It could be a computer, printer, or data storage device.
- **Client**—a node that requests and uses resources available from other nodes. Typically, a client is a user's microcomputer.
- **Server**—a node that shares resources with other nodes. Depending on the resources shared, it may be called a file server, printer server, communication server, Web server, or database server.
- **Network operating systems (NOS)**—controls and coordinates the activities of all computers and other devices on a network. These activities include electronic communication and the sharing of information and resources.
- **Distributed processing**—a system in which computing power is located and shared at different locations. This type of system is common in decentralized organizations where divisional offices have their own computer systems. The computer systems in the divisional offices are networked to the organization's main or centralized computer.
- **Host computer**—a large centralized computer, usually a minicomputer or a mainframe.

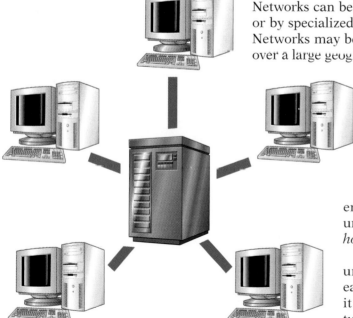

Figure 7-16 Star network

A network may consist only of microcomputers, or it may integrate microcomputers or other devices with larger computers. Networks can be controlled by all nodes working together equally or by specialized nodes coordinating and supplying all resources. Networks may be simple or complex, self-contained or dispersed over a large geographical area.

CONFIGURATIONS

A network can be arranged or configured in several different ways. This arrangement is called the network's **topology.** The four principal network topologies are star, bus, ring, and hierarchical.

In a **star network,** a number of small computers or peripheral devices are linked to a central unit. (See Figure 7-16.) This central unit may be a *host computer* or a *file server.*

All communications pass through this central unit. Control is maintained by **polling.** That is, each connecting device is asked ("polled") whether it has a message to send. Each device is then in turn allowed to send its message.

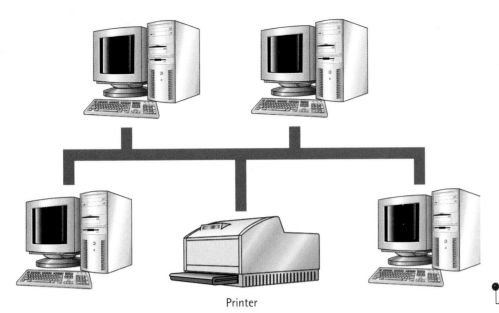

Printer

Figure 7-17 Bus network

One particular advantage of the star form of network is that it can be used to provide a **time-sharing system.** That is, several users can share resources ("time") on a central computer. The star is a common arrangement for linking several microcomputers to a mainframe that allows access to an organization's database.

In a **bus network,** each device in the network handles its own communications control. There is no host computer. All communications travel along a common connecting cable called a **bus.** (See Figure 7-17.) As the information passes along the bus, it is examined by each device to see if the information is intended for it.

The bus network is typically used when only a few microcomputers are to be linked together. This arrangement is common for sharing data stored on different microcomputers. The bus network is not as efficient as the star network for sharing common resources. (This is because the bus network is not a direct link to the resource.) However, a bus network is less expensive and is in very common use.

In a **ring network,** each device is connected to two other devices, forming a ring. (See Figure 7-18.) There is no central file server or computer. Messages are passed around the ring until they reach the correct destination. With microcomputers, the ring arrangement is the least frequently used of the four networks. However, it often is used to link mainframes, especially over wide geographical areas. These mainframes tend to operate fairly autonomously. They perform most or all of their own processing and only occasionally share data and programs with other mainframes.

A ring network is useful in a decentralized organization because it makes possible a **distributed data processing system.** That is, computers can perform processing tasks at their own dispersed locations. However, they can also share programs, data, and other resources with each other.

Figure 7-18 Ring network

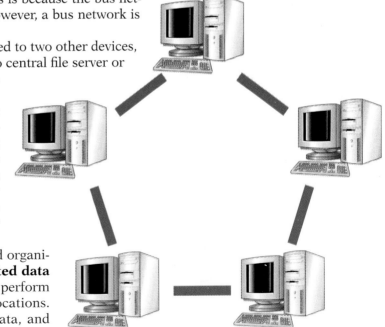

Network Architecture

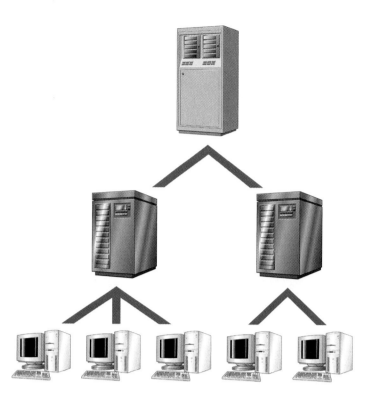

Figure 7-19 Hierarchical network

The **hierarchical network**—also called a **hybrid network**—consists of several computers linked to a central host computer, just like a star network. However, these other computers are also hosts to other, smaller computers or to peripheral devices. (See Figure 7-19.)

Thus, the host at the top of the hierarchy could be a mainframe. The computers below the mainframe could be minicomputers, and those below, microcomputers. The hierarchical network allows various computers to share databases, processing power, and different output devices.

A hierarchical network is useful in centralized organizations. For example, different departments within an organization may have individual microcomputers connected to departmental minicomputers. The minicomputers in turn may be connected to the corporation's mainframe, which contains data and programs accessible to all.

For a summary of the network configurations, see Figure 7-20.

Figure 7-20 Principal network configurations

Type	Description
Star	Several computers connected to a central server or host; all communications travel through central server; good for sharing common resources
Bus	Computers connected by a common line; communication travels along this common line; less expensive than star
Ring	Each computer connected to two others forming a ring; communications travel around ring; often used to link mainframe computers in decentralized organizations
Hierarchical	One top-level host computer connected to next-level computers, which are connected to third-level computers; often used in centralized organizations

Concept Check

✔ What is a network topology? List the four principal network topologies.

✔ What is one advantage of the star network topology?

✔ Where might you find a hierarchical network?

STRATEGIES

Every network has a **strategy,** or way of coordinating the sharing of information and resources. The most common network strategies are terminal, peer-to-peer, and client/server systems.

In a **terminal network system,** processing power is centralized in one large computer, usually a mainframe. The nodes connected to this host computer are either terminals, with little or no processing capabilities, or microcomputers running special software that allows them to act as terminals. (See Figure 7-21.) The star and hierarchical networks are typical configurations with UNIX as the operating system.

Many airline reservation systems are terminal systems. A large central computer maintains all the airline schedules, rates, seat availability, and so on. Travel agents use terminals to connect to the central computer and use it to schedule reservations. Although the tickets may be printed along with travel itineraries at the agent's desk, nearly all processing is done at the central computer.

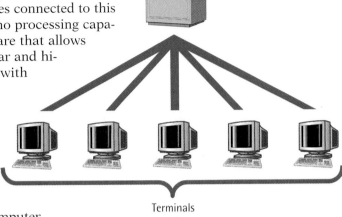

Figure 7-21 Terminal network system

One advantage of terminal network systems is the centralized location and control of technical personnel, software, and data. One disadvantage is the lack of control and flexibility for the end user. Another disadvantage is that terminal systems do not use the full processing power available with microcomputers. Though the terminal strategy was once very popular, most new systems do not use it.

In a **peer-to-peer network system,** nodes have equal authority and can act as both servers and clients. For example, one microcomputer can *obtain* files located on another microcomputer and can also *provide* files to other microcomputers. (See Figure 7-22.) A typical configuration for a peer-to-peer system is the bus network. Commonly used network operating systems are Novell's NetWare Lite, Microsoft's Windows NT, and Apple's Macintosh Peer-to-Peer LANs.

There are several advantages to using this type of strategy. The networks are inexpensive and easy to install, and they usually work well for smaller systems with fewer than ten nodes. As the number of nodes increases, however,

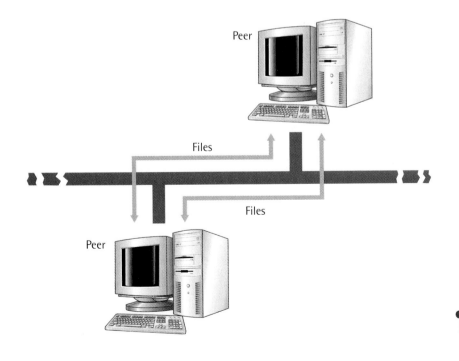

Figure 7-22 Peer-to-peer network system

Network Architecture

Client

Server

Client   Client

Figure 7-23 Client/server network system

Figure 7-24 Network strategies

the performance of the network declines. Another disadvantage is the lack of powerful management software to effectively monitor a large network's activities. For these reasons, peer-to-peer networks are typically used by small networks.

Client/server network systems use one computer to coordinate and supply services to other nodes on the network. The server provides access to resources such as Web pages, databases, application software, and hardware. (See Figure 7-23.) This strategy is based on specialization. Server nodes coordinate and supply specialized services, and client nodes request the services. Commonly used network operating systems are Novell's NetWare, Microsoft's Windows NT, IBM's LAN Server, and Banyan Vines.

One advantage of client/server network systems is their ability to handle very large networks efficiently. This strategy is extensively used on the Internet. For example, when you connect to a Web site, you are the client and the Web site's computer is the server. Another advantage of client/server networks is the powerful network management software that monitors and controls the network's activities. The major disadvantages are the cost of installation and maintenance.

For a summary of the network strategies, see Figure 7-24.

Computer networks in organizations have evolved over time. Most large organizations have a wide range of different network configurations, operating systems, and strategies. These organizations are moving toward integrating or connecting all of these networks together. That way, a user on one network can access resources available throughout the company. This is called **enterprise computing.**

Type	Description
Terminal	One large computer provides all processing, strong central control, limited flexibility, and control for users
Peer-to-peer	Computers act as both servers and clients, inexpensive and easy to install, works well in small networks
Client/server	Several clients or computers depend upon one server or computer to coordinate and supply services

Concept Check

✔ What are the most common network strategies?

✔ What are the advantages of each network strategy?

NETWORK TYPES

Clearly, different types of channels—cable or air— allow different kinds of networks to be formed. Telephone lines, for instance, may connect communications equipment within the same building. You can even create your own network in your home or apartment. (See Making IT Work for You: Home Networking on pages 186–187.)

Networks may also be citywide and even international, using both cable and air connections. Here let us distinguish among three types: *local area networks, metropolitan area networks,* and *wide area networks.*

> Communications networks differ in geographical size. Three important types are LANs, MANs, and WANs.

LOCAL AREA NETWORKS

Networks with computers and peripheral devices in close physical proximity—within the same building, for instance—are called **local area networks (LANs).** Linked by cable—telephone, coaxial, or fiber-optic—LANs often use a bus form of organization.

Our illustration shows an example of a LAN. (See Figure 7-25.) This typical arrangement has two benefits. People can share different equipment, which lowers the cost of equipment. For instance, here the four microcomputers share the laser printer and the file server, which are expensive pieces of hardware. (Individual microcomputers also often have their own less expensive printers, such as the ink-jet printer shown in our illustration.) Other equipment may also be added to the LAN—for instance, mini- or mainframe computers or optical-disk storage devices.

Note that the LAN shown in our illustration also features a **network gateway.** A LAN may be linked to other LANs or to larger networks in this manner. For example, the LAN of one office group may be connected to the LAN of another office group. It may also be connected to others in the wider world, even if their configurations are different. Alternatively, a **network bridge** would be used to connect networks with the same configurations.

On the Web Explorations

What about LANs for the home? Intelogis and ShareWave are leaders in developing wireless home networks. To learn more about these companies, visit our Web site at

http://www.mhhe.com/oleary

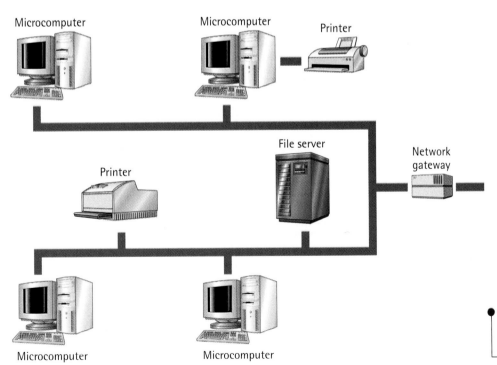

Figure 7-25 A local area network that includes a file server and network gateway

MAKING IT WORK FOR YOU

HOME NETWORKING

Computer networks are not just for corporations and schools anymore. If you have more than one computer, you can use a home network to share files and printers, to allow multiple users access to the Internet at the same time, and to play interactive computer games.

How It Works Computers can be connected using a variety of ways including electrical wiring, special cables, and radio frequencies. One of the simplest ways, however, is to use your home's existing telephone wiring system. Using this approach, telephone network adapter cards are installed in each computer. The adapter cards are connected to the telephone wiring system using standard telephone connections. Without affecting normal telephone use, your computers are connected and can share resources.

Installing the Network Various telephone home networking kits are available. These kits typically include adapter card(s), standard telephone extension lines, and installation software. Once the adapter cards have been installed and connected to the telephone wiring system, you need to run the installation software.

For example, using Intel's AnyPoint Home Network installation software, you could set up your home network as shown here.

① **Type unique name for your computer. This is how others on the network will identify your computer.**

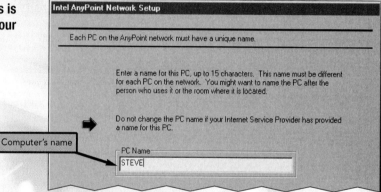

② **Specify resources you are willing to share.**

③ **Select resources from other computers you would like to access.**

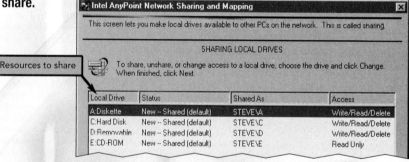

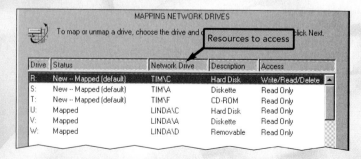

Using the Network Now your computers are ready to share their resources. The four most common uses of a home network are to share files, printers, and Internet access, and to run multiplayer computer games.

Sharing printers: Any computer can print files using any printer that is connected to a computer on the network. This is handy if you have only one printer, or would like to use separate printers for different tasks. For example, you might have one inexpensive black and white printer for written materials and a more expensive color printer for graphics.

Sharing files: You are able to access files stored on other computers on your network. For example, the computer identified as TIM can access files stored on LINDA's and STEVE's hard disk drives.

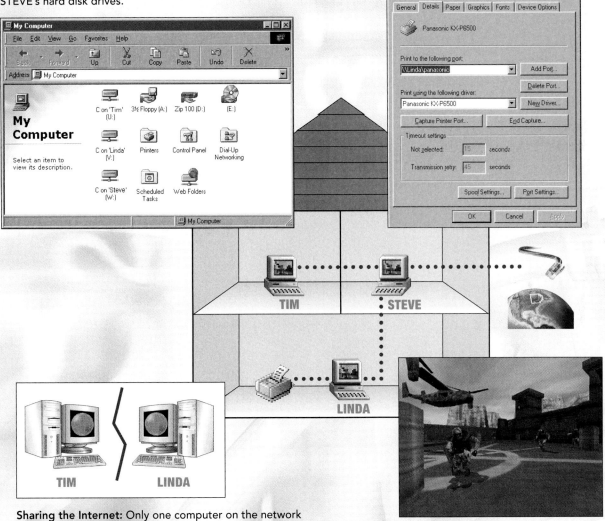

Sharing the Internet: Only one computer on the network connects directly to the Internet. It is known as the *server*. Whenever the server is connected to the Internet, each computer can surf the Internet independently at the same time. For example, the computer identified as STEVE is the server connected to the Internet. You could be researching a paper on the Web using TIM while someone else is using LINDA to send and receive e-mail.

Multiplayer computer games: Several computer games have options to play against other people. Players interact using different computers on the network. For example, you could be using TIM while two friends are using LINDA and STEVE.

Home networks are continually changing and some of the specifics presented in this Making IT Work for You may have changed. See our Web site at http://www.mhhe.com/oleary for possible changes and to learn more about this application of technology.

METROPOLITAN AREA NETWORKS

The next step up from the LAN might be the **MAN**—the **metropolitan area network.** These networks are used as links between office buildings in a city. Cellular phone systems expand the flexibility of MANs by allowing links to car phones and portable phones.

WIDE AREA NETWORKS

Wide area networks (WANs) are countrywide and worldwide networks. Among other kinds of channels, they use microwave relays and satellites to reach users over long distances—for example, from Los Angeles to Paris. (See Figure 7-26.) Of course, the widest of all WANs is the Internet, which spans the entire globe.

The primary difference between a LAN, MAN, and WAN is the geographical range. Each may have various combinations of hardware, such as microcomputers, minicomputers, mainframes, and various peripheral devices.

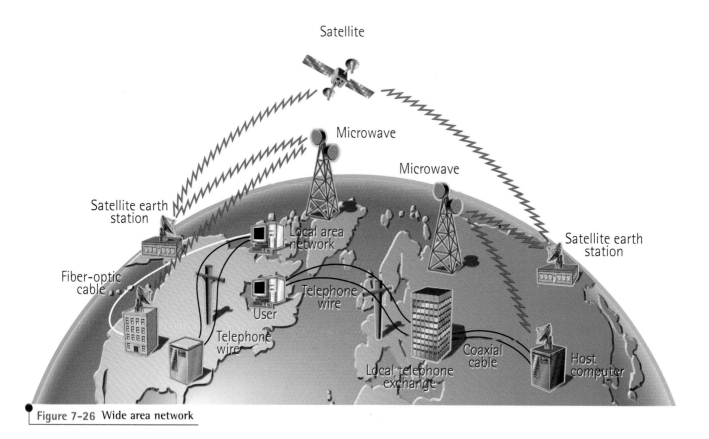

Figure 7-26 Wide area network

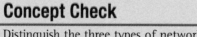

Concept Check

 Distinguish the three types of networks described here.

 What is the primary difference between network types?

A Look to the Future

Teledisc Corporation Creates Airborne Internet

Can you imagine what it would be like if all of the world's people could directly communicate with one another? If you wanted to know more about life in a remote African village, you could directly connect to members of that village to share experiences and explore the future. Medical researchers from every corner of the world could meet daily to coordinate and share their work. The world community could quickly react to and unite to face global crises.

Of course, these connections are what the Internet is all about. All the major cities in North America and Europe are wired for fast, efficient Internet access. Most of the rest of the world, however, is not. While satellites can be used to connect these other areas, most satellites orbit at such high altitudes that Internet connections are not effective. But that may be changing.

Bill Gates from Microsoft and Craig McCaw from Cellular Communications have formed a corporation called Teledisc. Despite technical and financial setbacks, this corporation is investing over $9 billion to launch over 800 low-orbit satellites by the year 2003. These satellites will hover just 435 miles above the earth and provide direct effective Internet access. Once this airborne Internet is in place, all a user will need to link up to it from any location in the world is a microcomputer with a sender/ receiver the size of a large pizza and a signal decoder.

Is there a need for this global communication system? Probably not right now. However, the Internet is growing fast and the demand for worldwide communication is growing even faster. Will Teledisc be a reality in the near future? This project requires a lot of ground-breaking technology and has had some serious financial challenges. We will have to wait and see.

VISUAL SUMMARY
Connectivity, the Wireless Revolution, and Communications

CONNECTIVITY, THE WIRELESS REVOLUTION, AND COMMUNICATIONS

Connectivity, the wireless revolution, and communications are key concepts and technologies for the twenty-first century.

Connectivity

Connectivity is a concept related to using computer networks to link people and resources. You can link or connect to large computers and the Internet providing access to extensive information resources.

The Wireless Revolution

Mobile or wireless telephones have brought dramatic changes in connectivity and communications. These wireless devices are becoming widely used for computer communication. One technology, called **Bluetooth**, allows wireless communication for nearby devices.

Communication Systems

Communication systems are electronic systems that transmit data from one location to another. Every communication system has four basic elements:

- **Sending and receiving devices**
- **Communication channel**
- **Connection devices**
- **Data transmission specifications**

COMMUNICATIONS CHANNELS

Communication channels carry data from one computer to another. Connections are either physical connections or wireless.

Physical Connections

Physical connections use a solid medium such as twisted pair telephone lines, coaxial cable, and fiber-optic cable.

- **Twisted pair**—copper wires; being replaced by other media.
- **Coaxial cable**—replaces twisted pair with a solid-copper core to provide higher transmission capacity.
- **Fiber-optic cable**—transmits data as pulses of light. Lighter and faster than coaxial cable and rapidly replacing twisted pair technology.

Wireless Connections

Wireless connections use air rather than solid substance to connect sending and receiving devices. Two primary technologies: *microwave* and *satellite*.

- **Microwave**—uses high-frequency radio waves. Called line of sight communication because radio waves travel in a straight line.
- **Satellite**—sends data long distances using rotating satellites above the earth

To be a competent end user you need to understand the concepts of connectivity, the wireless revolution, and communications. Additionally, you need to know the essential parts of communications technology including channels, connections, transmission, network architectures, and network types.

CONNECTION DEVICES

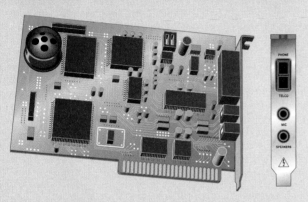

Users often connect to communication systems using standard telephone lines. These lines typically send and receive **analog signals.** Computers send and receive **digital signals.**

Modems

Modems convert digital signals to analog signals and vice versa. There are four basic types of conventional modems:

- **External**—outside the system cabinet connected by cable to serial port.
- **Internal**—card that plugs into a slot on the system board.
- **PC Card modem**—a credit card–size expansion board for portable computers.
- **Wireless**—does not connect with a cable; receives data through the air.

Other Connections

Dial-up connections connect standard telephone line to conventional modems.

Some connections are all digital. For example, **T1, T2, T3,** and **T4** support very high speed transmission without conventional modems. More affordable technologies include:

- **DSL (digital subscriber line)**—uses existing telephone lines.
- **Cable modems**—use existing cable lines.
- **Satellite/air**—uses satellites to download data.

DATA TRANSMISSION

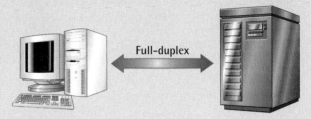

Full-duplex

Several factors affect how data is actually transmitted from one point to another:

Bandwidth

Bandwidth is a measure of a communication channel's capacity. Three bandwidths from lowest to highest are **voiceband, medium band,** and **broadband.**

Serial and Parallel Transmission

With **serial transmission,** bits flow in a single continuous stream. With **parallel transmission,** bits flow through separate lines simultaneously.

Direction of Data Transmission

Three directions or modes of data flow are:

- **Simplex communication**—data flows in only one direction.
- **Half-duplex communication**—data flows in both directions but not simultaneously.
- **Full-duplex communication**—data flows in both directions simultaneously.

Protocols

Protocols are rules for exchanging data. **TCP/IP** is the standard protocol for the Internet with two essential features:

- Identification of every computer on the Internet using unique **IP addresses (Internet Protocol addresses)** and the **domain name system (DNS).**
- Reformatting information into small **packets** to travel across the Internet and reassembling the information at its destination.

NETWORK ARCHITECTURE

Network architecture describes how a **computer network** is configured and what strategies are used.

Terms

Terms often used with networks are **node, client, server, network operating system, distributed processing,** and **host computer.**

Configurations

Networks can be configured in several ways:

- **Star network**—each device linked to a central unit; control maintained by **polling**.
- **Bus network**—each device handles its own communications along a common connecting cable called a **bus.**
- **Ring network**—each device connected to two other devices forming a ring.
- **Hierarchical network (hybrid network)**—connect smaller computers to a central host.

Strategies

Every network has a **strategy,** or way of sharing information and resources.

- **Terminal network system**—a centralized computer distributes power to several terminals.
- **Peer-to-peer network system**—each computer acts as both a server and a client.
- **Client/server network system**—client computers request resources from a server computer.

NETWORK TYPES

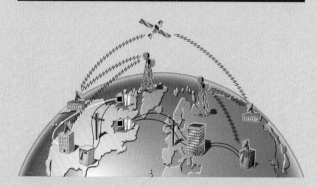

Networks can be citywide or even international using both cable and air connections. Three network types are: *local area networks, metropolitan area networks,* and *wide area networks.*

Local Area Networks

Local area networks or **LANs** connect devices that are located close to one another. Often these devices are located in the same office or floor. **Network gateways** and **bridges** link a LAN to other LANs or to larger networks.

Metropolitan Area Networks

Metropolitan area networks or **MANs** are used to link office buildings within a city. *Cellular phone systems* expand the flexibility of MANs by allowing links to car phones and portable phones.

Wide Area Networks

Wide Area Networks or **WANs** are the largest type. They span states and countries, or form worldwide networks. The Internet is the largest wide area network in the world.

analog signals (176)
asynchronous communications port (178)
bandwidth (178)
Bluetooth (172)
broadband (178)
bus (181)
bus network (181)
cable modems (177)
client (180)
client/server network system (184)
communication channel (173, 174)
communication systems (172)
computer network (180)
connection device (173)
connectivity (172)
coaxial cable (174)
data transmission specifications (173)
demodulation (176)
dial-up service (176)
digital signals (176)
digital subscriber line (DSL) (177)
distributed data processing system (181)
distributed processing (180)
domain name system (DNS) (179)
enterprise computing (184)
external modem (176)
fiber-optic cable (174)
full-duplex communication (179)
half-duplex communication (179)
hierarchical network (182)
host computer (180)
hybrid network (182)
identification (178)
internal modem (176)
IP address (Internet Protocol address) (179)
line of sight communication (174)
local area network (LAN) (185)
low bandwidth (178)
medium band (178)

metropolitan area network (MAN) (188)
microwave (174)
modem (176)
modulation (176)
network (180)
network architecture (180)
network bridge (185)
network gateway (185)
network operating system (NOS) (180)
node (180)
packets (179)
parallel data transmission (178)
PC card modem (176)
peer-to-peer network system (183)
polling (180)
protocols (179)
reformatting (179)
ring network (181)
RS-232C connector (178)
satellite (175)
satellite/air connection services (177)
sending and receiving devices (173)
serial data transmission (178)
server (180)
simplex communication (178)
star network (180)
strategy (183)
TCP/IP transmission control protocol/Internet protocol (179)
telephone lines (174)
terminal network system (183)
time-sharing system (181)
T1, T2, T3, T4 lines (177)
topology (180)
twisted pair (174)
voiceband (178)
wide area network (WAN) (188)
wireless modems (176)

CHAPTER REVIEW

MULTIPLE CHOICE

Circle the letter or fill in the correct answer.

1. Modulation and demodulation are the processes of a(n) _____.
   a. connection device
   b. node
   c. modulator
   d. modem
   e. OSI

2. Standard telephone lines and conventional modems provide what is called _____.
   a. network architecture
   b. broadband
   c. dial-up service
   d. data transmission
   e. channels

3. Voiceband is also called _____.
   a. low bandwidth
   b. medium band
   c. analog signal
   d. broadband
   e. packets

4. Microcomputers with DSL, cable, and satellite connections use _____.
   a. analog signals
   b. broadband
   c. medium band
   d. voiceband
   e. low bandwidth

5. In _____, bits flow in a series or continuous stream.
   a. parallel data transmission
   b. packets
   c. simplex communication
   d. half-duplex communication
   e. serial data transmission

6. Every computer on the Internet has a unique numeric address called a(n) _____.
   a. packet
   b. RS-232C connector
   c. IP address
   d. bandwidth
   e. network bridge

7. The standard protocol for the Internet is _____.
   a. TCP/IP
   b. OSI
   c. RS-232C
   d. DSL
   e. NOS

8. _____ describes how the network is arranged and how the resources are coordinated and shared.
   a. Topology
   b. Communication channel
   c. Sharing system
   d. Network architecture
   e. Domain name system

9. _____ controls and coordinates the activities of all computers and devices on a network.
   a. TCP/IP
   b. NOS
   c. DNS
   d. OSI
   e. none of the above

10. In a(n) _____ network, each device in the network handles its own communications control.
    a. host
    b. client
    c. bus
    d. sharing
    e. polling

MATCHING

Match each numbered item with the most closely related lettered item. Write your answers in the spaces provided.

a. coaxial cable

b. demodulation

c. analog signals

d. twisted pair

e. bandwidth

f. parallel data transmission

g. communication system

h. TCP/IP

i. distributed processing

j. Bluetooth

k. half-duplex

l. internal modem

m. packets

n. computer network

o. hybrid network

p. client

q. topology

r. star network

s. fiber optic

t. wide area network

1. Electronic system that transmits data over communication lines from one location to another. _g_

2. The type of signals that telephones typically send and receive. _c_

3. High-frequency transmission cable with a single solid-copper core. _a_

4. Uses microwaves to transmit data over short distances up to 33 feet. _j_

5. The process of converting analog to digital signals. _b_

6. Consists of a plug-in circuitboard inside the system unit. _l_

7. Cable consisting of hundreds of copper wires that culminates in a wall jack for a telephone. _d_

8. Cable that transmits data as pulses of light through tubes of glass. _s_

9 Bits per second transmission capability of a channel. _e_

10. Transmission in which bits flow through separate lines simultaneously. _f_

11. Standard protocol for the Internet. _h_

12. Broken-down parts of a message that are sent over the Internet. _m_

13. Communications system connecting two or more computers that work together to exchange information and share resources. _n_

14. A node that requests and uses resources available from other nodes. _p_

15. System in which computing power is located and shared at different locations. _i_

16. The configuration of a network. _q_

17. This type of network allows several users to share resources on a central computer. _o_

18. Several computers linked to a central host that serves as hosts to smaller computers or devices. _r_

19. Mode of data flow wherein data flows in both directions but not simultaneously. _k_

20. Countrywide and worldwide networks. _t_

OPEN-ENDED

On a separate sheet of paper, respond to each question or statement.

1. Define and discuss connectivity, the wireless revolution, and communications.
2. Identify and describe the various physical and wireless communication channels.
3. Identify the standard Internet protocol and discuss its essential features.
4. Define and discuss the four principal network topologies.
5. Define and discuss the three most common network strategies.

1 Palm

Palm is the leader in Personal Digital Assistants, or PDAs. Recent advances in technology allow PDAs like the Palm to communicate on the go. Visit our Web site at http://www.mhhe.com/oleary to link to Palm's Web site. Once connected, review the latest PDA products and then answer the following questions in a one-page paper: (a) What support for Internet connection is available? (b) What is required to connect a Palm to the Internet? (c) What type of Internet information is accessible? Is there any type which is not accessible? (d) Would you use an Internet-connected PDA? Why or why not?

2 Ricochet Internet Access

Ricochet is an innovative new technology that provides high-speed Internet access to mobile computer users. To learn more about this technology, visit our Web site at http://www.mhhe.com/oleary to connect to the Ricochet Web site. Once connected, explore the site, and then answer the following questions in a one-page paper: (a) What equipment does a user require to connect to the Ricochet network? (b) How does the Ricochet network deliver

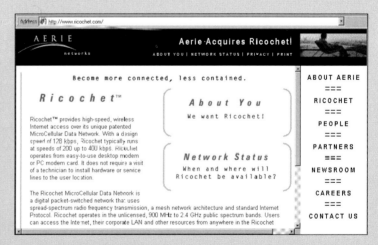

the Internet to users? (c) What are the current limitations of this technology? (d) Would you use Ricochet over a more standard Internet connection? Why?

Interactive Companion CD-ROM 1

Complete the "Network Communications" Lab located on your Interactive Companion CD-ROM, and then answer the following questions in a one-page paper: (a) What are **packets**? (b) Define the term **protocol**. Which two common protocols were mentioned in the Lab? (c) What does the acronym **modem** stand for and what are typical types of modems?

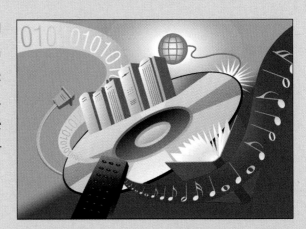

Virtual Private Networks 2

People who telecommute to work must often connect to a corporate LAN securely over the Internet. Virtual Private Networking, or VPN, is a solution for this. Conduct a Web search using the keyword "VPN" or "Virtual Private Networking" to learn more. Then answer the following questions in a one-page paper: (a) Describe what VPN is and what it does. (b) How is using VPN different from accessing files from a company Web site? (c) What advantage does this offer individuals and organizations?

1 User Connection

One of the key determinants to enjoyable and effective use of the Internet is available bandwidth. As bandwidth increases, Internet content becomes richer and more varied. Write a two-page paper titled "Internet Connections" that addresses the following: (a) Define **voiceband, medium band,** and **broadband.** (b) Describe the four types of connections that are commonly available. (c) Discuss how faster Internet connections are shaping the way in which the Internet is used. (d) Research and discuss three specific examples.

2 Electronic Monitoring

Programs known as "sniffers" are sometimes used to monitor communications on corporate networks. Recently, the FBI unveiled a technology known as Carnivore that can monitor an individual's Internet activity and eavesdrop on e-mail messages. Write a two-page paper that answers the following questions: (a) Is it a violation of an employee's privacy for an organization or corporation to use sniffer programs to monitor communications on their network? (b) Is it a violation of

privacy for a government agency such as the FBI to use programs like Carnivore to monitor communications on the Internet? (c) Under what conditions are the types of monitoring discussed in parts (a) and (b) acceptable and ethical? (d) How can these conditions be enforced?

NOTES

THE INTERNET, THE WEB, AND ELECTRONIC COMMERCE

COMPETENCIES

After you have read this chapter, you should be able to:

1

Describe Internet providers, connections, and protocols.

2

Discuss e-mail, mailing lists, newsgroups, chat groups, and instant messaging.

3

Describe search tools including search, metasearch, and specialized search engines.

4

Discuss electronic commerce including Web storefronts, auctions, and electronic payment.

5

Describe Web utilities: Telnet, FTP, plug-ins, and helper applications.

6

Discuss intranets, extranets, and firewalls.

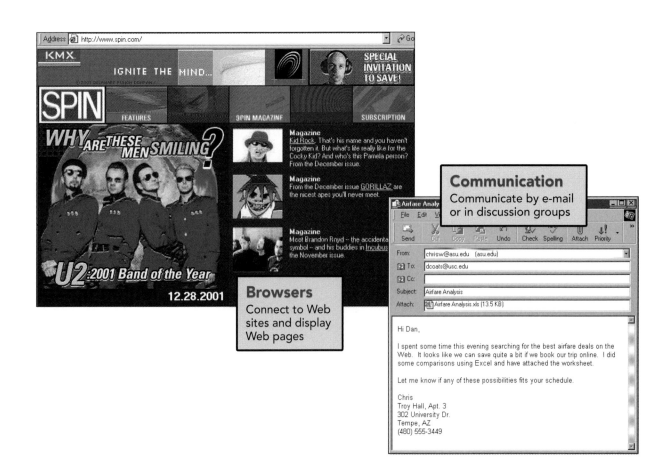

Browsers
Connect to Web sites and display Web pages

Communication
Communicate by e-mail or in discussion groups

Want to communicate with a friend across town, in another state, or even in another country? Perhaps you would like to send a drawing, a photo, or just a letter. Looking for travel or entertainment information? Perhaps you're researching a term paper or exploring different career paths. Where do you start? For these and other information-related activities, try the Internet and the Web. They are 21st-century information resources designed for all of us to use.

The Internet is like a highway that connects you to millions of other people and organizations. Unlike typical highways that move people and things from one location to another, the Internet moves your **ideas** and **information**. Rather than moving through geographic space, you move through **cyberspace**—the space of electronic movement of ideas and information. The Web provides an easy-to-use, exciting, multimedia interface to connect to the Internet and to access the resources available in cyberspace.

It has become an everyday tool for all of us to use. For example, you can create personal Web sites to share information with others and use instant messaging to chat with friends and collaborate on group projects.

Competent end users need to be aware of the resources available on the Internet and the Web. Additionally, they need to know how to access these resources, to effectively communicate electronically, to efficiently locate information, to understand electronic commerce, to use Web utilities, and to be knowledgeable about extranets, intranets, and security issues.

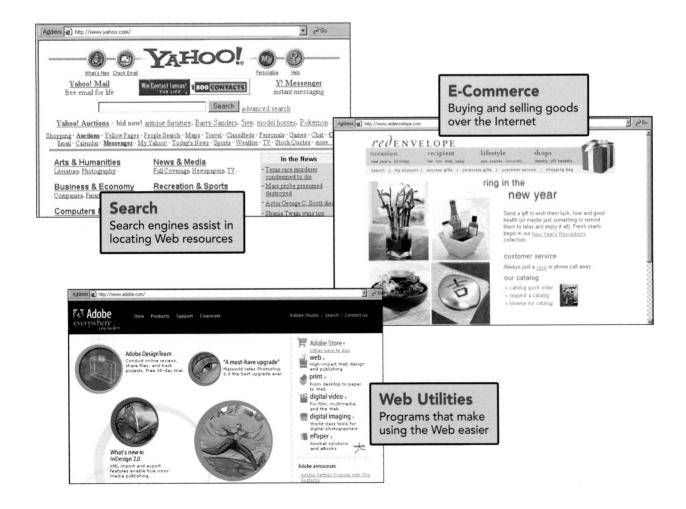

Search
Search engines assist in locating Web resources

E-Commerce
Buying and selling goods over the Internet

Web Utilities
Programs that make using the Web easier

> The Internet is a worldwide network. The Web is a multimedia interface. Internet uses include communication, electronic commerce, information gathering, entertainment, and education.

The Internet was launched in 1969 when the United States funded a project that developed a national computer network called **Advanced Research Project Agency Network (ARPANET).** The **Web,** also known as **WWW** and the **World Wide Web,** was introduced in 1992 at the **Center for European Nuclear Research (CERN)** in Switzerland. Prior to the Web, the Internet was all text—no graphics, animations, sound, or video. The Web provided a multimedia interface to resources available on the Internet. From these research beginnings, the Internet and the Web have evolved as tools for all of us to use.

It is easy to get the Internet and the Web confused, but they are not the same thing. The Internet is the actual physical network. It is made up of wires, cables, and satellites. It connects computers and resources throughout the world. The Web is a multimedia interface to resources available on the Internet.

Every day over a billion users from every country in the world use the Internet and the Web. What are they doing? The most common uses are the following.

- **Communicating** is by far the most popular activity. You can exchange e-mail with your family and friends located almost anywhere in the world. You can join and listen to discussions and debates on a wide variety of special-interest topics. You can chat "live" with others. You can even create your own personal Web page for friends and family to visit. (See Making IT Work for You: Personal Web Sites on pages 204 and 205.)

- **Shopping** or using electronic commerce is one of the fastest-growing Internet applications. You can visit a cybermall or window shop at the best stores, look for the latest fashions, search for bargains, and make purchases. (See Figure 8-1.) You can purchase goods using checks, credit cards, or electronic cash.

- **Searching** for information has never been more convenient. You can access some of the world's largest libraries directly from your home computer. You can visit virtual libraries, search through their stacks, read selected items, and even check out books.

Figure 8-1 Web storefront

Figure 8-2 E-learning site

- **Entertainment** options are nearly endless. You can find music, movies, magazines, and computer games. You will find live concerts, movie previews, book clubs, and interactive live games.

- **Education** or e-learning is another rapidly emerging Web application. (See Figure 8-2.) You can take classes on almost any subject. There are courses just for fun and there are courses for high school, college, and graduate school credit. Some cost nothing to take and others cost a lot. To learn more about e-learning, visit some of the sites presented in Figure 8-3.

The first step to using the Internet and Web is to get connected, or to gain access to the Internet.

Company	Site	Cost of Course
Dell	www.educateu.com	$30 to $1300
Digital Think	www.digitalthink.com	$99 to $1000
EduPoint.com	www.edupoint.com	$10 to $1000
Hungry Minds	www.hungryminds.com	free to $1499
Learn2.com	www.learn2.com	$20 to $100

Figure 8-3 E-Learning sites

ACCESS

The Internet and the telephone system are similar—you can connect a computer to the Internet much like you connect a phone to the telephone system. Once you are on the Internet, your computer becomes an extension of what seems like a giant computer—a computer that branches all over the world. Once provided with a connection to the Internet, you can browse the Web.

> Providers give us access to the Internet. Browsers provide access to Web resources.

PROVIDERS

The most common way to access the Internet is through a **provider** or **host computer.** The providers are already connected to the Internet and provide a path or connection for individuals to access the Internet. Your college or university most likely provides you with free access to the Internet either through their local area networks or through a dial-up or telephone connection.

PERSONAL WEB SITES

Do you have something to share with the world? Would you like a personal Web site, but don't want to deal with learning HTML and paying for server time? Many services are available to get you started—for FREE!

How It Works A service site on the Web provides access to tools to create personal Web pages. After registering with the site, you create your Web pages. Once completed, the service site acts as a host for your personal Web site and others are free to visit it from anywhere on the Web.

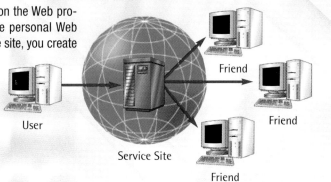

User

Service Site

Friend

Friend

Friend

Getting Started The first step to creating your own Web site is to register with a service site. One of the most popular Personal Web site services is Homestead. To connect to and register for your Web site, follow the instructions below.

1
- Connect to *www.homestead.com.*
- Select *Homestead Personal.*
- Click the *Sign Up* link.
- Complete the registration process to log in.

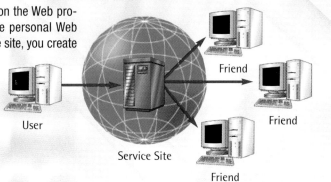

2
- Click the *Personal Homepages* link.

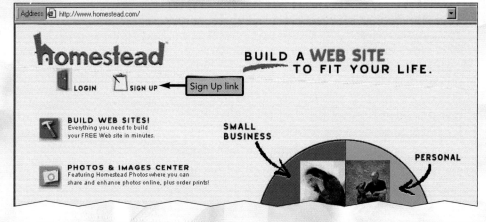

3
- Click the *Home Page* link.

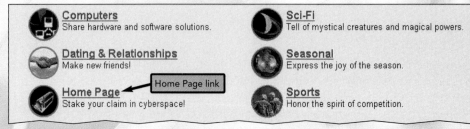

Selecting a Template Once you have registered with a Personal Web service site, you are ready to create your Web pages. Homestead offers a variety of templates to assist in the development of Web pages. For example:

1 ● Click the *Build Using Page Wizard* button.

● Select the *Basic Layout.*

● Select the *Left Navigation* link.

● Click *Next.*

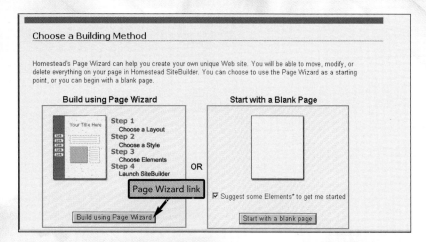

2 ● Select the *Message Board* element.

● Click *Next.*

● Click *Start Building.*

After a few moments, the template you configured with the Page Wizard is displayed.

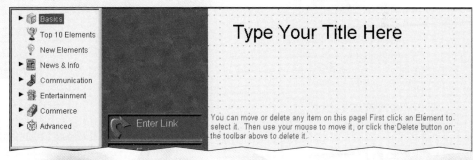

Creating Your Web Pages Once you have selected the template, you are ready to customize it by adding elements, photos, text and/or links to your Web page. After completing the page(s), save it to make it available to anyone over the Internet.

1 ● Customize your page to meet your needs by adding links, elements, text, and photos.

The Web is continually changing and some of the specifics presented in this Making IT Work for You may have changed. See our Web site at http://www.mhhe.com/oleary for possible changes and to learn more about this application of technology.

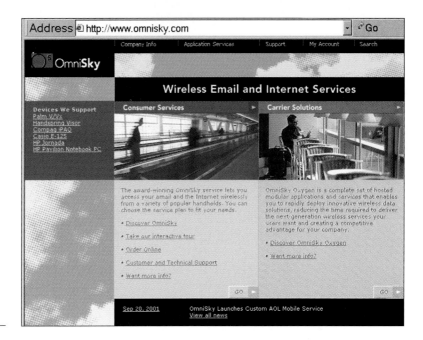

Address http://www.omnisky.com   Go

Company Info | Application Services | Support | My Account | Search

OmniSky

Wireless Email and Internet Services

Devices We Support
Palm V/Vx
Handspring Visor
Compaq iPAQ
Casio E-125
HP Jornada
HP Pavilion Notebook PC

Consumer Services   ▶   Carrier Solutions   ▶

The award-winning OmniSky service lets you access your email and the Internet wirelessly from a variety of popular handhelds. You can choose the service plan to fit your needs.

• Discover OmniSky
• Take our interactive tour
• Order Online
• Customer and Technical Support
• Want more info?

OmniSky Oxygen is a complete set of hosted modular applications and services that enables you to rapidly deploy innovative wireless data solutions, reducing the time required to deliver the next-generation wireless services your users want and creating a competitive advantage for your company.

• Discover OmniSky Oxygen
• Want more info?

GO ▶   GO ▶

Sep 20, 2001   OmniSky Launches Custom AOL Mobile Service
View all news

Figure 8-4 Wireless ISP

> **TIPS** Did you know that some Internet service providers are free? Users of free providers note numerous advertisements and sometimes slow service; however, free is free. If you're interested, check out these sites:
>
> ● **www.freeinternet.com**
> ● **www.netzero.com**

Commercial Internet service providers (ISPs) include national, regional, and wireless service providers.

● **National service providers** like America Online (AOL) are the most widely used. They provide access through standard telephone connections. Users can access the Internet from almost anywhere within the country for a standard fee without incurring long-distance telephone charges.

● **Regional service providers** also use telephone lines. Their service area, however, is smaller, typically consisting of several states. If users access the Internet from outside the regional area, they incur long-distance connection charges in addition to the service's standard fees.

● **Wireless service providers** do not use telephone lines. They provide Internet connections for computers with wireless modems and a wide array of wireless devices. (See Figure 8-4.)

To learn more about service providers, visit some of the sites presented in Figure 8-5.

As discussed in the previous chapter, users connect to ISPs using one of a variety of connection technologies including DSL, cable, and wireless modems. This creates a client/server network. The user's computer is the client that requests services from the provider's computer or server.

Provider	Type	Site
America Online (AOL)	National	www.aol.com
AT&T WorldNet	National	www.att.net
BellSouth	Regional	www.bellsouth.net
Quest Internet Service	Regional	www.quest.net
OmniSky	Wireless	www.omnisky.com
SprintPCS	Wireless	www.sprintpcs.com

Figure 8-5 Internet service providers

BROWSERS

Browsers are programs that provide access to Web resources. As we discussed in Chapter 3, this software connects you to remote computers, opens and transfers files, displays text and images, and provides in one tool an uncomplicated interface to the Internet and Web documents. Two well-known browsers are Netscape Navigator and Microsoft Internet Explorer. (See Figure 8-6.)

For browsers to connect to other resources, the location or address of the resources must be specified. These addresses are called **uniform resource locators (URLs).** Following the domain name system (DNS) introduced in Chapter 7, all URLs have at least two basic parts. (See Figure 8-7.) The first part presents the protocol used to connect to the resource. The protocol *http://* is by far the most common. The second part presents the domain name or the name of the server where the resource is located. In Figure 8-7 the server is identified as *www.aol.com.* (Many URLs have additional parts specifying directory paths, file names, and pointers.) The last part of the domain name following the dot (.) is the **domain code.** It identifies the type of organization. For example, *com* indicated a commercial site.

The URL *http://www.aol.com* connects your computer to a computer that provides information about America Online (AOL). These informational locations on the Web are called **Web sites.** Moving from one Web site to another is called **surfing.**

Once the browser has connected to a Web site, a document file is sent to your computer. This document contains **Hypertext Markup Language (HTML)** commands. The browser interprets the HTML commands and displays the document as a **Web page.** Typically, the first page of a Web site is referred to as its home page. (See Figure 8-8.) The **home page** presents information about the site along with references and **hyperlinks,** or connections to other documents that contain related information—text files, graphic images, audio, and video clips.

These documents may be located on a nearby computer system or on one halfway around the world. The references appear as underlined and colored text and/or images on the Web page. To access the referenced material, all you do is click on the highlighted text or image. A link is automatically made to the computer containing the material, and the referenced material appears.

Figure 8-6 Browser: Internet Explorer

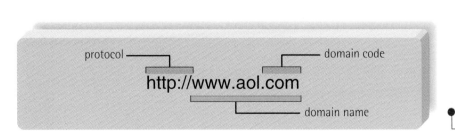

Figure 8-7 Two basic parts of a URL

Figure 8-8 Spin Magazine's online homepage

Type	Site
Horizontal	www.excite.com
Horizontal portal	www.aol.com
Vertical for sports	www.cbs.sportsline.com
Vertical for news	www.usatoday.com
Vertical for computers	www.zdnet.com

Figure 8-9 Popular Web portals

Web pages can also contain links to special programs, called **applets,** written in a programming language called **Java.** These programs can be quickly downloaded and run by most browsers. Java applets are widely used to add interest and activity to a Web site by presenting animation, displaying graphics, providing interactive games, and much more.

Some sites offer a variety of services, including e-mail, sports updates, financial data, news, and links to other selected Web sites. These sites, called **Web portals,** are designed to encourage you to visit them each time you are on the Web, to act as your home base, and to use as a gateway to their resources. There are two types of portals. **Horizontal portals** are designed to appeal to mass audiences. They offer general-interest services and links. **Vertical portals** present focused content to appeal to special-interest groups. For a list of some popular portals, see Figure 8-9.

Concept Check

✔ What is a browser?

✔ How do browsers locate/connect to other resources?

✔ What are Web portals?

s previously mentioned, communication is the most popular Internet activity. The impact of electronic communication cannot be overestimated. At a personal level, friends and family can stay in contact with one another even when separated by thousands of miles. At a business level, electronic communication has become a standard and many times preferred way to stay in touch with suppliers, employees, and customers.

> Communication by e-mail is the most common Internet activity. Discussion groups include mailing lists, newsgroups, chat groups, and instant messaging.

E-MAIL

You can communicate with anyone in the world who has an Internet address or e-mail account with a system connected to the Internet. All you need is access to the Internet and an e-mail program. Two of the most widely used e-mail programs are Microsoft's Outlook Express and Netscape's Navigator.

Suppose that you have a friend, Dan Coats, who is going to the University of Southern California. You and Dan have been planning a trip for the upcoming break. You have heard there are some inexpensive airfare deals online. To save money, you and Dan agree to research these offers and e-mail each other your findings.

A typical e-mail message has three basic elements: header, message, and signature. (See Figure 8-10.) The **header** appears first and typically includes the following information:

- **Addresses:** Addresses of the persons sending, receiving, and, optionally, anyone else who is to receive copies.
- **Subject:** A one-line description, used to present the topic of the message. Subject lines typically are displayed when a person checks his or her mailbox.
- **Attachments:** Many e-mail programs allow you to attach files such as documents and worksheets. If a message has an attachment, the file name appears on the attachment line.

> **TIPS**
>
> What if you don't know or have forgotten someone's e-mail address? You can go to e-mail address directories, also known as e-mail "white pages." These directories can be used much like you would use the telephone white pages. Here are three e-mail address directories you might try:
>
> - www.bigfoot.com
> - www.people.yahoo.com
> - www.infospace.com

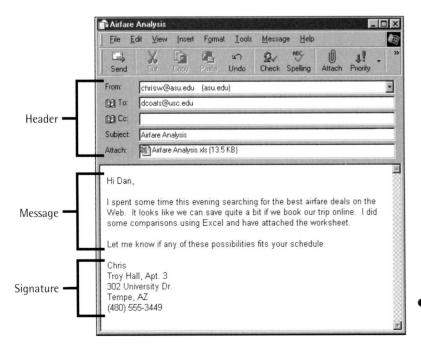

Figure 8-10 Basic elements of an e-mail message

The letter or **message** comes next. It is typically short and to the point. Finally, the **signature line** provides additional information about the sender. Typically, this information includes the sender's name, address, and telephone number.

Following the domain name system (DNS) discussed earlier, e-mail addresses have two basic parts. (See Figure 8-11.) The first part is the user's name and the second part is the domain name, which includes the domain code. In our example e-mail, *dcoats* is Dan's username. The server providing e-mail service for Dan is *usc.edu*. The domain code indicates that the provider is an educational institution.

DISCUSSION GROUPS

You can also use e-mail to communicate with people you do not know but with whom you wish to share ideas and interests. You can participate in discussions and debates that range from general topics like current events and movies to specialized forums like computer troubleshooting and Star Trek.

- **Mailing lists** allow members of a mailing list to communicate by sending messages to a **list address.** Each message is then copied and sent via e-mail to every member of the mailing list. To participate in a mailing list, you must first subscribe by sending an e-mail request to the mailing list **subscription address.** (See Figure 8-12.) Once you are a member of a list, you can expect to receive e-mail from others on the list. You may find the number of messages to be overwhelming. If you want to cancel a mailing list, send an e-mail request to "unsubscribe" to the subscription address.

- **Newsgroups,** unlike mailing lists, use a special network of computers called the **UseNet.** Each of these computers maintains the newsgroup listing. There are over 10,000 different newsgroups organized into major topic areas that are further subdivided into subtopics. (See Figure 8-13.)

Contributions to a particular newsgroup are sent to one of the computers on the UseNet. This computer saves the messages on its system and periodically shares all its recent messages with the other computers on the UseNet. Unlike mailing lists, a copy of each message is not sent to each

Figure 8-11 Two parts of an e-mail address

Description	Subscription Address
Music and bands	dbird@netinfo.com.au
Movies	moviereview-request@cuenet.com
Jokes	dailyjoke@lists.ivillage.com
Travel	tourbus@listserv.aol.com

Figure 8-12 Popular mailing lists

major topic ——————
further division
of subtopic

rec.arts.cinema

subtopic ————

Figure 8-13 Newsgroup hierarchy

Description	Newsgroups
Aerobics fitness	misc.fitness.aerobic
Cinema	rec.arts.movies
Mountain biking	rec.bicycles.off-road
Music	rec.music.hip-hop
Clip art	alt.binaries.clip-art

Figure 8-14 Popular newsgroups

member of a list. Rather, interested individuals check contributions to a particular newsgroup, reading only those of interest. There are thousands of newsgroups covering a wide variety of topic areas. (See Figure 8-14.)

- **Chat groups** allow direct "live" communication. To participate, you join a chat group, select a **channel** or topic, and communicate live with others by typing words on your computer. Other members of your channel immediately see those words on their computers and can respond in the same manner. One popular chat service is called **Internet Relay Chat (IRC)**. This software is available free from several locations on the Internet. Using the chat-client software, you log on to the server, select a channel or topic in which you are interested, and begin chatting. To participate, you need access to a server or computer that supports IRC. This is done using special chat-client software.

- **Instant messaging,** like chat groups, allows one or more people to communicate via direct, "live" communication. Instant messaging, however, provides greater control and flexibility than chat groups. (See Making IT Work for You: Instant Messaging, on pages 212–213.) To use instant messaging, you specify a list of friends, or "buddies," and register with an instant messaging server. Whenever you connect to the Internet, you use special software to tell your messaging server that you are online too. It notifies you if any of your buddies are online. At the same time, it notifies your buddies that you are online. You can then send messages back and forth to one another instantly.

Before you submit a contribution to a discussion group, it is recommended that you observe or read the communications from others. This is called **lurking.** By lurking, you can learn about the culture of a discussion group. For example, you can observe the level and style of the discussions. You may decide that a particular discussion group is not what you were looking for—in which case, unsubscribe. If the discussions are appropriate and you wish to participate, try to fit into the prevailing culture. Remember that your contributions will likely be read by hundreds of people.

For a list of some other commonly used discussion group terms, see Figure 8-15.

On the Web Explorations

Almost all ISPs and online service providers offer e-mail service to their customers. But you can get this service for free from Hotmail, Juno Online Services, USA Net Inc., and Yahoo. To learn more about these free services, visit our site at:

http://www.mhhe.com/oleary

Figure 8-15 Selected discussion–group terms

Term	Description
FAQ	Frequently asked question
Flaming	Insulting, putting down, or attacking
Lurking	Reading news but not joining in to contribute
RFD	Request for discussion
Saint	Someone who aids new users by answering questions
Thread	A sequence of ongoing messages on the same subject
Wizard	Someone who has comprehensive knowledge about a subject

INSTANT MESSAGING

Do you enjoy chatting with your friends? Are you working on a project and need to collaborate with others in your group? Perhaps instant messaging is just what you're looking for. It's easy and free with an Internet connection and the right software.

How It Works Users register with an instant messaging server and identify friends and colleagues (buddies). Whenever a user is online, the instant messaging server notifies the user of all buddies who are also online and provides support for direct "live" communication.

Getting Started The first step is to connect to one of the many Web sites that support instant messaging. Once at the site, register, download, and install instant messaging software, and create your buddy list.

For example, you can set up AOL Instant Messenger as shown below.

① • Connect your browser to *aim.aol.com*.

• Click the link to register as a new user.

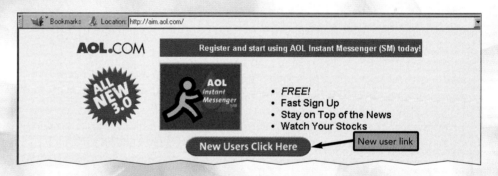

② • Complete the registration form.

• Submit the form and download the *Instant Messenger* software.

③ • Install the software by double-clicking the file you downloaded and following the on-screen instructions.

• Create your *Buddy List* using the *Add a Buddy* wizard.

Add a Buddy wizard

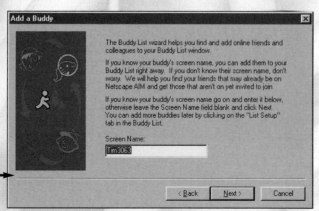

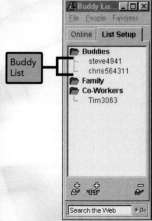

Communicating with a Friend Once you have set up your instant messaging software, you can use it to communicate, live, with your online buddies. For example, you could use AOL Instant Messenger as follows:

1
● **Double-click your friend's screen name.**

● **Enter your message into the message window.**

● **Click the *Send* button.**

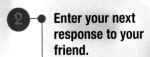
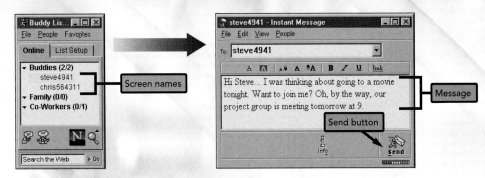

2
● **Enter your next response to your friend.**

● **Click the *Send* button.**

● **Repeat this step to continue your conversation.**

Your message is displayed along with your friend's reply.

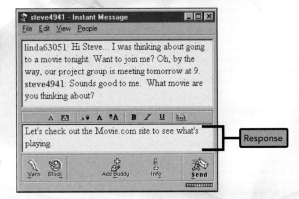

Collaborating with a Group You can just as easily communicate or collaborate with a group of people. To conduct a virtual group meeting, all group participants must be signed on and one participant acts as the coordinator.

For example, with AOL Instant Messenger, the coordinator begins as follows:

1
● **Select the screen name for each participant.**

● **Click the *Buddy Chat* button to open the *Invitation* window.**

● **Click the *Send* button to send the invitation.**

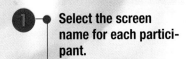
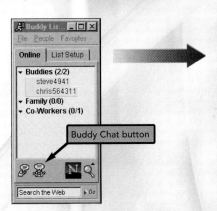
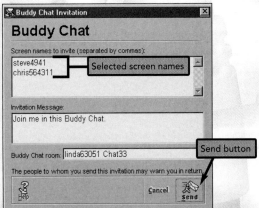

Participants join the chat room by accepting the Invitation. While the meeting is in progress, the message window on each participant's screen displays the text of the conversation of all participants. Most instant messaging servers require that all participants use the same instant messaging software. However, as standards evolve, this limitation will likely be overcome.

The Web is continually changing and some of the specifics presented in this Making IT Work for You may have changed. See our Web site at http://www.mhhe.com/oleary for possible changes and to learn more about this application of technology.

SEARCH TOOLS

Search services maintain databases and provide search engines to locate information. Metasearch engines submit search requests to several search engines simultaneously. Specialized search engines focus on subject-specific Web sites.

The Web can be an incredible resource providing information on nearly any topic imaginable. Are you planning a trip? Writing an Economics paper? Looking for a movie review? Trying to locate a long-lost friend? Information sources related to these questions, and much, much more are available on the Web.

With over two billion pages and more being added daily, the Web is a massive collection of inter-related pages. With so much available information, locating the precise information you need can be difficult. Fortunately, a number of organizations called **search services** or **search providers** can help you locate the information you need. They maintain huge databases relating to information provided on the Web and the Internet. The information stored at these databases includes addresses, content descriptions or classifications, and keywords appearing on Web pages and other Internet informational resources. Special programs called **agents, spiders,** or **bots** continually look for new information and update the search services' databases. Additionally, search services provide special programs called search engines that you can use to locate specific information of the Web.

SEARCH ENGINES

Search engines are specialized programs that assist you in locating information on the Web and the Internet. To find information, you go to the search service's Web site and use their search engine. See Figure 8-16 for a list of some of the most widely used search engines. For example, see Figure 8-17 for Yahoo!'s search engine. This search engine, like most others, provides two different search approaches.

Figure 8-16 Search engines

Search Service	Site
Alta Vista	www.altavista.com
Direct Hit	www.directhit.com
Google	www.google.com
HotBot	www.hotbot.com
NorthernLight	www.northernlight.com
Oingo	www.oingo.com
Yahoo!	www.yahoo.com

- **Keyword search**: In a **keyword search**, you enter a keyword or phrase reflecting the information you want. The search engine compares your entry against its database and returns a list of **hits** or sites that contain the keywords. Each hit includes a hyperlink to the referenced Web page (or other resource) along with a brief discussion of the information contained at that location. Many searches result in a large number of hits. For example, if you were to enter the keyword *travel*, you would get over a thousand hits. Search engines order the hits according to those sites that most likely contain the information requested and present the list to you in that order, usually in groups of ten.

- **Directory search**: Most search engines also provide a directory or list of categories or topics such as Arts & Humanities, Business & Economics, Computers & Internet. In a **directory search**, also known as an **index**

Figure 8-17 Yahoo! search engine

search, you select a category that fits the information that you want. Another list of subtopics related to the topic you selected appears. You select the subtopic that best relates to your topic and another subtopic list appears. You continue to narrow your search in this manner until a list of Web sites appears. This list corresponds to the hit list previously discussed.

As a general rule, if you are searching for general information, use the directory search approach. For example, to find general information about music, use a directory search beginning with the category Arts & Humanities. If you are searching for specific information, use the key word approach. For example, if you were looking for a specific MP3 file, use a key word search entering the album title and/or the artist's name in the text selection box.

A recent study by the NEC Research Institute found that any one search engine includes only a fraction of the informational sources on the Web. Therefore, it is highly recommended that you use more than one search engine when researching important topics. Or, you could use a special type of search engine called a metasearch engine.

Are you going to use a search tool to locate some information? Here are a few tips that might help.

1 **Start with the right approach.** For general information, use a direct search. For specific information, use a key word search.

2 **Be as precise as possible.** Use specific key words that relate directly to the topic.

3 **Use multiple words.** Use quotation marks to identify key words.

4 **Use Boolean operators.** Typically, these include words such as "and," "not," "or."

5 **Check your spelling.** Misspelling is one of the most common problems.

6 **Keep moving.** Look only at the first page of search results. If necessary, try another search using different key words.

METASEARCH ENGINES

One way to research a topic is to visit the Web site for several individual search engines. At each site, enter the search instructions, wait for the hits to appear, review the list, and visit selected sites. This process can be quite time-consuming and duplicate responses from different search engines are inevitable. Metasearch engines offer an alternative.

Metasearch engines are programs that automatically submit your search request to several search engines simultaneously. The metasearch engine receives the results, eliminates duplicates, orders the hits, and then provides the edited list to you. There are several metasearch sites available on the Web. (See Figure 8-18.) One of the best known is MetaCrawler.

Metasearch Service	Site
Mamma	www.mamma.com
MetaCrawler	www.metacrawler.com
ProFusion	www.profusion.com
Search	www.search.com

Figure 8-18 Metasearch sites

Search Tools

SPECIALIZED SEARCH ENGINES

Specialized search engines focus on subject-specific Web sites. Specialized sites can potentially save you time by narrowing your search. For example, let's say you are researching a paper about the fashion industry. You could begin with a general search engine like Yahoo! Or, you could go to a search engine that specializes specifically in fashion.

Concept Check	
✓	What is a search engine?
✓	What are the two approaches used by a search engine?
✓	How does a metasearch engine locate Web resources?

ELECTRONIC COMMERCE

Web storefronts offer goods and services. Web auctions are like traditional auctions. Electronic payment options include check, credit card, and electronic cash.

On the Web Explorations

Electronic commerce is one of the fastest growing Web applications. To learn more about it, visit our Web site at

http://www.mhhe.com/oleary

Electronic commerce, also known as **e-commerce**, is the buying and selling of goods over the Internet. Have you ever bought anything over the Internet? If you have not, there is a very good chance that you will within the next year or two. Shopping on the Internet is growing rapidly and there seems to be no end in sight. (See Figure 8-19.)

Just like any other type of commerce, electronic commerce involves two parties: businesses and consumers. There are three basic types of electronic commerce:

- **Business-to-consumer (B2C)** involves the sale of a product or service to the general public or end users. Oftentimes, this arrangement eliminates the middleman by providing manufacturers direct sales to customers. Other times, retail stores create a presence on the Web as another way to reach customers.
- **Consumer-to-consumer (C2C)** involves individuals selling to individuals. This often takes the form of an electronic version of the classified ads or an auction. Goods are described and interested buyers contact sellers to negotiate prices. Unlike traditional sales via classified ads and auctions, buyers and sellers typically never meet face-to-face.
- **Business-to-business (B2B)** involves the sale of a product or service from one business to another. This is typically a manufacturer–supplier relationship. For example, a furniture manufacturer requires raw materials such as wood, paint, and varnish. In B2B electronic commerce, manufacturers electronically place orders with suppliers and many times payment is made electronically.

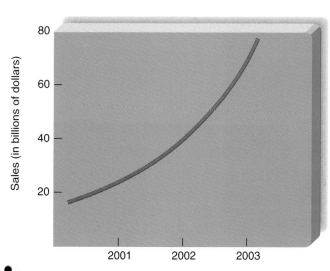

Figure 8-19 Online shopping

Figure 8-20 B2C Web storefront

WEB STOREFRONTS

Web storefronts are virtual stores for B2C electronic commerce. Shoppers visit the stores on the Web to inspect merchandise and make purchases. (See Figure 8-20.) A new type of program called **Web storefront creation packages** or **commerce servers** has recently evolved to help businesses create virtual stores. These packages create Web sites that allow visitors to register, browse, place products into virtual shopping carts, and purchase goods and services.

These programs do even more behind the scenes. They calculate taxes and shipping costs, handle a variety of payment options, update and replenish inventory, and ensure reliable and safe communications. Additionally, the storefront sites collect data about visitors and generate reports to evaluate the site's profitability.

WEB AUCTIONS

A recent trend in C2C electronic commerce is the growing popularity of Web auctions. **Web auctions** are similar to traditional auctions except that buyers and sellers seldom, if ever, meet face-to-face. Sellers post descriptions of products at a Web site and buyers submit bids electronically. Like traditional auctions, sometimes the bidding becomes highly competitive and enthusiastic. There are two basic types of Web auction sites:

- **Auction house sites** sell a wide range of merchandise directly to bidders. The auction house owner presents merchandise that is typically from a company's surplus stock. These sites operate like a traditional auction, and bargain prices are not uncommon. Auction house sites are generally considered safe places to shop.
- **Person-person auction sites** operate more like flea markets. The owner of the site provides a forum for numerous buyers and sellers to gather. While the owners of these

Figure 8-21 Web auction site: eBay

Organization	Site
Amazon	www.auctions.amazon.com
eBay	www.ebay.com
Priceline.com	www.priceline.com
Sotheby's	www.sothebys.com
Yahoo!	www.auctions.yahoo.com

Figure 8-22 Auction sites

sites typically facilitate the bidding process, they are not involved in completing transactions or in verifying the authenticity of the goods sold. (See Figure 8-21.) As with purchases at a flea market, buyers and sellers need to be cautious.

For a list of the most popular Web auction sites, see Figure 8-22.

ELECTRONIC PAYMENT

The single greatest challenge for electronic commerce is the development of fast, secure, and reliable payment methods for purchased goods. (See Figure 8-23.) The three basic payment options are check, credit card, and electronic cash.

Figure 8-23 Electronic payment

- Checks are the most traditional and perhaps the safest. Unfortunately, check purchases require the longest time to complete. After selecting an item, the buyer sends a check through the mail. Upon receipt of the check, the seller verifies that the check is good. If it is good, then the purchased item is sent out.

- Credit card purchases are faster and more convenient than check purchases. Credit card fraud, however, is a major concern for both buyers and sellers. Criminals known as **carders** specialize in stealing, trading, and using stolen credit cards over the Internet.

- **Electronic cash,** or **e-cash,** is the Internet's equivalent to traditional cash. It is also known as **cybercash** and **digital cash**. Buyers purchase e-cash from a third party (a bank that specializes in electronic currency) by transferring funds from their banks. Buyers purchase goods using e-cash.

Sellers convert the e-cash to traditional currency through the third party. Although not as convenient as credit card purchases, e-cash is more secure. For a list of e-cash providers, see Figure 8-24.

Organization	Site
PayPal	www.paypal.com
PayMe.com	www.payme.com
EmoneyMail	www.emoneymail.com

Figure 8-24 Electronic cash providers

Concept Check

✓ What are the three types of electronic commerce?

✓ Describe Web storefronts and Web auctions.

✓ What are the three basic payment options for electronic payment?

WEB UTILITIES

As discussed in Chapter 2, utilities are programs that make computing easier. **Web utilities** are specialized utility programs that make using the Internet and the Web easier and safer. Some of these utilities are Internet services for connecting and sharing resources over the Internet. Others are browser-related programs that either become part of your browser or are executed from your browser.

> Web utilities are programs that make working with the Web and the Internet easier and safer. Telnet and FTP are Internet services for connecting, running, and sharing files. Plug-ins operate as part of a browser. Helper applications are launched from a browser.

TELNET

Many computers on the Internet will allow you to connect to them and to run selected programs on them. **Telnet** is the Internet service that helps you to connect to another computer (host) on the Internet and log on to that computer as if you were on a terminal in the next room. There are hundreds of computers on the Internet that you can connect to. Some allow limited free access, and others charge fees for their use.

FTP

File transfer protocol (FTP) is an Internet service for transferring files. Many computers on the Internet allow you to copy files to your computer. This is called **downloading.** You can also use FTP to copy files from your computer to another computer on the Internet. This is called **uploading.**

Figure 8-25 Plug-in site: Adobe

PLUG-INS

Plug-ins are programs that are automatically loaded and operate as a part of your browser. (See Figure 8-25.) Many Web sites require you to have one or more plug-ins to fully experience their content. Some widely used plug-ins include:

- Acrobat Reader from Adobe, used to view and print a variety of standard forms and other documents saved in a special format called PDF.
- Cosmos from Silicon Graphics, displaying three-dimensional graphics and used in sites displaying virtual reality.

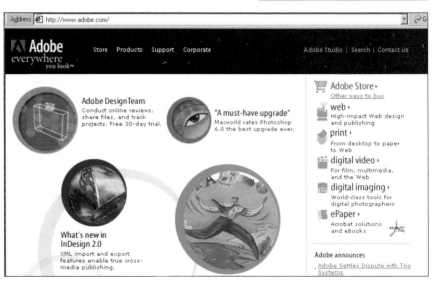

Plug-in	Source
Acrobat Reader	www.adobe.com
Cosmos Player	www.cosmos.sgi.com
Media Player	www.microsoft.com
RealPlayer	www.real.com
Shockwave	www.macromedia.com

Figure 8-26 Plug-in sites

- Media Player from Microsoft, used to play audio files (including MP3 files) and to view video.
- Quicktime from Apple, required by over 20,000 Web sites to display video and play audio.
- RealPlayer from RealNetworks, used to play and to view audio files including MP3 files and to view video.
- Shockwave from Macromedia, used for a variety of Web-based games, view concerts, and dynamic animations.

Some of these utilities are included in many of today's browsers. Others must be installed before they can be used by your browser. To learn more about plug-ins and how to download them, visit some of the sites listed in Figure 8-26.

HELPER APPLICATIONS

Also known as **add-ons, helper applications** are independent programs that can be executed or launched from your browser. There are hundreds of helper applications, most of them designed to maximize your efficiency. Three of the most common types are off-line browsers, information pushers, and filters.

- **Off-line browsers,** also known as **Web-downloading utilities** and **pull products,** can greatly reduce the time spent waiting for Web pages to download to your computer. These programs automatically connect to selected Web sites, download HTML documents, and save them to your hard disk. You can view the Web pages later without being connected to the Internet and without waiting for documents to be downloaded. Two popular off-line browsers are InContext FlashSite and Teleport Pro. (See Figure 8-27.)
- **Information pushers** are also known as **Web broadcasters** and **push products.** Imagine a personalized newspaper containing only those articles that interested you the most. That is the basic idea behind information pushers. You select topic areas known as **channels** that you are interested in. Information pushers gather information on your topics from the Web and send it to your hard disk, where you can read it whenever you want. Two well-known information pushers are Entry Point and BackWeb client.

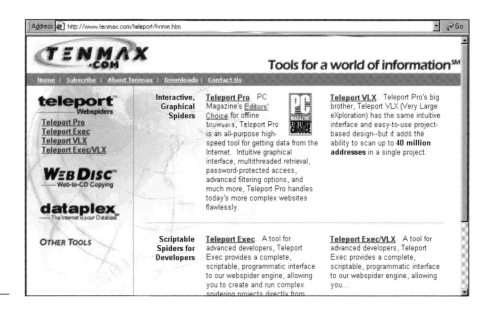

Figure 8-27 Off-line browser: Teleport

Figure 8-28 Web filter: Cybersitter

Type	Source	Site
Off-line browsers	Incontext FlashSite	www.incontext.com
	Teleport Pro	www.tenmax.com
Information pushers	Entry Point	www.entrypoint.com
	BackWeb Client	www.backweb.com
Filters	Cyber Patrol	www.cyberpatrol.com
	Cybersitter	www.cybersitter.com

Figure 8-29 Helper application sites

• **Filters** block access to selected sites. The Internet is an interesting and multifaceted arena. But one of those facets is a dark and seamy one. Parents, in particular, are concerned about children roaming unrestricted across the Internet. Filter programs allow parents as well as organizations to block out selected sites and set time limits. (See Figure 8-28.) Additionally, these programs can monitor use and generate reports detailing the total time spent on the Internet, and time spent at individual Web sites, chat groups, and newsgroups. Three well-known filters are Cyber Patrol, Cybersitter, and Net Nanny.

To learn more about helper applications, explore some of the sites presented in Figure 8-29.

Do your children or little brother or sister use the Internet a lot? While you may want them to be able to take advantage of the educational and entertainment side of the Internet, you also want to protect them from the negative side. To help protect them from viewing inappropriate material, consider the following suggestions:

1 Locate. Place the computer in a common area where children can be easily supervised.

2 Discuss. Discuss browsing with children to explain what types of content you consider to be appropriate.

3 Filter. Use a filter program and/or investigate your browser's filtering capabilities.

Recent versions of Internet Explorer, for example, include a Content Advisor program.

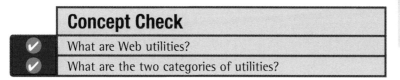

Concept Check

✓ What are Web utilities?

✓ What are the two categories of utilities?

> Intranets are private networks within an organization. Extranets are private networks connecting organizations. Firewalls use proxy servers to provide security.

Nearly every organization today uses the Internet to promote its products and to service its customers. These organizations have found the Internet and the Web to be powerful yet very easy-to-use tools for reaching the public. They have also found that they can apply Internet technologies within their organizations to connect their own employees and to connect to other organizations. (See Figure 8-30.) These networks are called intranets and extranets.

Figure 8-30 Connecting people and organizations

INTRANETS

An **intranet** is a *private* network within an organization that resembles the Internet. Like the *public* Internet, intranets use browsers, Web sites, and Web pages. Intranets typically provide e-mail, mailing lists, newsgroups, and FTP services accessible only to those within the organization.

Organizations use intranets to provide information to their employees. Typical applications include electronic telephone directories, e-mail addresses, employee benefit information, internal job openings, and much more. Employees find surfing their organizational intranets to be as easy and as intuitive as surfing the Internet.

EXTRANETS

An **extranet** is a *private* network that connects *more than one* organization. Many organizations use Internet technologies to allow suppliers and others limited access to their networks. The purpose is to increase efficiency and reduce costs. For example, General Motors has thousands of suppliers for the parts that go into making an automobile. By having access to the production schedules, suppliers can schedule and deliver parts as they are needed at the General Motors assembly plants. In this way, General Motors can be assured of having adequate parts without maintaining large inventories.

FIREWALLS

Organizations have to be very careful to protect their information systems. A **firewall** is a security system designed to protect an organization's network against external threats. It consists of hardware and software that control access to a company's intranet or other internal networks.

Typically a firewall includes a special computer called a **proxy server.** This computer is a gatekeeper. All communications between the company's internal networks and the outside world must pass through it. By evaluating the source and the content of each communication, the proxy server decides whether it is safe to let a particular message or file pass into or out of the organization's network. (See Figure 8-31.)

Of course, end users have security issues as well. We are subject to many of the same types of security concerns that face organizations. Additionally, we need to be concerned about the privacy of our personal information. As we will discuss in Chapter 9, "Security and Privacy," personal firewalls are also used to protect personal privacy and security.

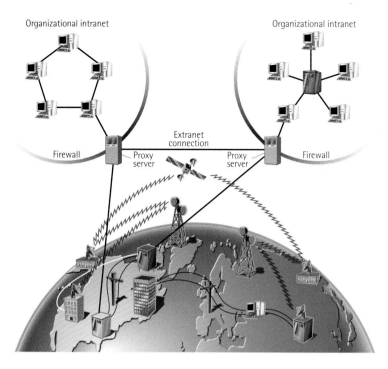

Figure 8-31 Intranets, extranets, firewalls, and proxy servers

A Look to the Future

Internet2 Will Be a Private High-Performance Internet

Have you ever been unable to connect to the Internet? Have you ever had a long wait before a Web page or a graphic appeared on your screen? Almost all of us have experienced busy servers and slow access. Unfortunately, Internet service is expected to get worse. For organizations that depend on the Internet to reach customers and conduct other business activities, this trend is very concerning.

To address this concern, a separate private Internet called Internet2 is being developed. It will be a high-speed network capable of dazzling feats that far exceed today's Internet capabilities. Expected to be fully operational by the end of next year, Internet2 will have limited access to those willing to pay more to get more. Access to today's Internet will remain public and available for a nominal fee.

The primary beneficiaries of Internet2 will be federal agencies and major corporations. Each will pay an annual fee of $500,000 for access to this network that combines high performance with tightly controlled security. One of the first to take advantage of Internet2 will be online publishers of books, photographs, and original artwork. Advanced virtual reality interfaces, called "nanomanipulators," are expected to be available. Researchers from different parts of the world will be able to share devices such as atomic microscopes and to jointly study, experience, and move within realistic virtual subatomic environments.

Will moving power users to Internet2 increase the performance of the public Internet? Do you think Internet2 will have any effect on you? We will have to wait and see.

VISUAL SUMMARY
The Internet, the Web, and Electronic Commerce

ACCESS

Once connected to the Internet, your computer seemingly becomes an extension of a giant computer that branches all over the world.

Providers

The most common access is through a **provider** or **host computer.** Three widely used providers are:

- **National service providers**—like AOL, use standard telephone lines.
- **Regional service providers**—offer access within a specific geographic area.
- **Wireless service providers**—do not require any type of connecting lines to wireless devices.

Browsers

Browsers access the Web and provide Internet services. Some related terms are:

- **URLs**—addresses to Web resources.
- **Surfing**—moving from one Web site to another.
- **HTML**—commands that display Web pages.
- The **home page**—typically the first page at a Web site.
- **Hyperlinks**—connections to related sites and documents.
- **Java**—programming language for creating special programs called **applets**.
- **Web portals (horizontal and vertical)**—sites that provide a variety of services.

COMMUNICATION

Communication is the most popular Internet activity. Two categories are e-mail and discussion groups.

E-mail

An e-mail has three basic elements:

- **Header** including addresses, subject line, and attachments.
- **Message** or text.
- **Signature line** providing sender information.

Discussion Groups

Discussion groups are ways to communicate electronically with one or more individuals. This type of communication includes:

- **Mailing lists**—use e-mail subscription and **list addresses.**
- **Newsgroups**—are organized by major topic areas and use the **UseNet** network.
- **Chat groups**—allow direct "live" communication.
- **Instant messaging**—provides greater flexibility than chat groups.

Terms associated with discussion groups include: **FAQ, flaming, lurking, RFD, saint, thread,** and **wizard.**

To be a competent end user you need to be aware of resources available on the Internet and Web, to be able to access these resources, to effectively communicate electronically, to efficiently locate information, to understand electronic commerce, and to use Web browsers and utilities. Also, competent end users need to be aware of organizational intranets and extranets.

SEARCH TOOLS

Search tools locate information on the Web. **Search services** or **search providers** maintain huge Web site databases. **Agents, spiders,** or **bots** are programs that update these databases.

Search Engines

Search engines locate information on the Web. Most search engines provide two search approaches:

- **Keyword search**—a keyword(s) is entered and a list of **hits** or sites containing the keywords is presented. Good for locating specific information

- **Directory search**—also known as an **index search**; selections are made from a succession of topics and subtopics until a list of Web sites appears. Good for locating general information.

Metasearch Engines

Metasearch engines submit search requests to several search engines simultaneously. Duplicate sites are eliminated, hits are ordered, and a composite hit list is presented.

Specialized Search Engines

Specialized search engines focus on subject-specific Web sites.

ELECTRONIC COMMERCE

Electronic commerce, or **e-commerce,** is the buying and selling of goods over the Internet. Three basic types are:

- **Business-to-consumer (B2C)**—involves the sale of a product or service to the general public or end users.

- **Consumer-to-consumer (C2C)**—involves individuals selling to individuals.

- **Business-to-business (B2B)**—involves the sale of a product or service from one business to another.

Web Storefronts

Web storefronts are virtual stores for B2B electronic commerce. **Web storefront creation packages** or **commerce servers** are programs for creating virtual stores.

Web Auctions

Web auctions are C2C electronic commerce. They are similar to traditional auctions except that buyers and seller rarely meet face-to-face. Two basic types are **auction house sites** and **person-to-person sites.**

Electronic Payment

Three basic payment options are check, credit card, and **electronic cash** (also known as **e-cash, cybercash,** and **digital cash**).

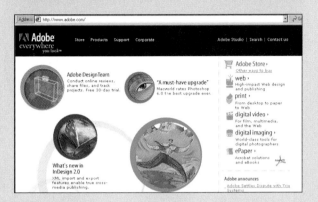

Web utilities are specialized programs that make using the Internet and the Web easier and safer.

Telnet

Telnet is an Internet service that provides terminal access to host computers.

FTP

FTP (file transfer protocol) is an Internet service for **uploading** and **downloading** files.

Plug-ins

Plug-ins are automatically loaded and operate as part of a browser. Some are included in many of today's browsers; other must be installed.

Helper Applications

Helper applications (add-ons, help applications) are independent applications that can be executed from a browser. There are three types: **offline browsers (Web-downloading utilities** or **pull products), information pushers (Web broadcasters, push products)**, and **filters**.

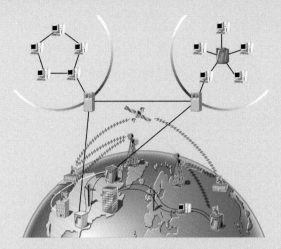

Many organizations use Internet technologies in their private networks. These include **intranets, extranets,** and **firewalls.**

Intranets

Intranets are *private* networks within an organization that resemble the Internet. They use browsers, Web sites, and Web pages that are available only to those within the organization.

Extranets

Extranets are similar to intranets, except that extranets connect more than one organization. Extranets are often used to connect suppliers and producers.

Firewalls

A **firewall** is a security system to protect against external threats. It consists of both hardware and software. All communications into and out of an organization pass through a special security computer called a **proxy server**.

KEY TERMS

add-ons (220)
address (209)
Advanced Research Project Agency Network
   (ARPANET) (202)
agents (214)
applets (208)
attachment (209)
auction house sites (217)
bots (214)
browser (207)
business-to-business (B2B) (216)
business-to-consumer (B2C) (216)
carders (218)
Center for European Nuclear Research (CERN)
   (202)
channel (211, 220)
chat group (211)
commerce servers (217)
consumer-to-consumer (C2C) (216)
cybercash (218)
cyberspace (218)
digital cash (218)
directory search (214)
domain code (207)
downloading (219)
e-cash (218)
e-commerce (216)
electronic cash (218)
electronic commerce (216)
extranet (222)
file transfer protocol (FTP) (219)
filter (221)
firewall (222)
header (209)
helper applications (220)
hits (214)
home page (207)
horizontal portal (208)
host computer (203)
hyperlinks (207)
Hypertext Markup Language (HTML) (207)
index search (214)
information pushers (220)
instant messaging (211)
Internet Relay Chat (IRC) (211)

intranet (222)
Java (208)
keyword search (214)
list address (210)
lurking (211)
mailing list (210)
message (210)
metasearch engine (215)
national service provider (206)
newsgroup (210)
off-line browsers (220)
person-person auction site (217)
plug-in (219)
provider (203)
proxy server (222)
pull products (220)
push products (220)
regional service provider (206)
search engines (214)
search providers (214)
search services (214)
signature line (210)
specialized search engine (216)
spiders (214)
subject (209)
subscription address (210)
surfing (207)
Telnet (219)
uniform resource locator (URL) (207)
uploading (219)
UseNet (210)
vertical portal (208)
Web (202)
Web auctions (217)
Web broadcasters (220)
Web-downloading utilities (220)
Web page (207)
Web portals (208)
Web sites (207)
Web storefront creation packages (217)
Web storefronts (217)
Web utilities (219)
wireless service provider (206)
World Wide Web (202)
WWW (202)

CHAPTER REVIEW

MULTIPLE CHOICE

Circle the letter or fill in the correct answer.

1. The Internet was launched in 1969 when the U.S. funded a project to develop a national computer network called _____.
   a. ARPANET
   b. CERN
   c. WWW
   d. the Web
   e. IRC

2. _____ use telephone lines and service an area consisting of several states.
   a. Wireless service providers
   b. National service providers
   c. Local service providers
   d. Regional service providers
   e. Commercial ISPs

3. _____ present focused content to appeal to special-interest groups.
   a. Agents
   b. Horizontal portals
   c. Vertical portals
   d. Web portals
   e. UseNets

4. To participate in a chat group, select a _____ and communicate live with others.
   a. signal
   b. index
   c. engine
   d. list
   e. channel

5. Bots are also known as _____ and _____.
   a. indexes, hits
   b. agents, spiders
   c. providers, hits
   d. agents, providers
   e. spiders, hits

6. In a directory or _____ search, you select a category that fits the information you want.
   a. packet
   b. keyword
   c. index
   d. specialized
   e. subject

7. In _____ commerce, individuals sell to other individuals without ever meeting face to face.
   a. C2C
   b. B2C
   c. B2B
   d. C2I
   e. I2I

8. _____ are programs that are automatically loaded and operate as a part of your browser.
   a. Add-ins
   b. Plug-ins
   c. Helpers
   d. Utilities
   e. Providers

9. _____ are independent programs that can be executed or launched from your browser.
   a. Plug-ins
   b. Add-ons
   c. Providers
   d. Agents
   e. Applets

10. _____ are programs that automatically connect to Web sites, download HTML documents, and save them to your hard disk.
    a. Off-line browsers
    b. Web-downloading utilities
    c. Pull products
    d. (a) and (b)
    e. all of the above

MATCHING

Match each numbered item with the most closely related lettered item. Write your answers in the spaces provided.

a. Web portal
b. cyberspace
c. surfing
d. header
e. lurking
f. subscription address
g. Web auction
h. provider
i. metasearch engine
j. Web storefronts
k. commerce server
l. URLs
m. applets
n. IRC
o. hits
p. e-cash
q. signature line
r. bots
s. e-commerce
t. carders

1. The space of electronic movement of ideas and information. _____
2. The most common way to access the Internet. _____
3. Addresses of Web resources. _____
4. Moving from one Web site to another. _____
5. Special programs written in Java. _____
6. Sites that offer a variety of services and are designed to act as a home base for users on the Web. _____
7. Part of an e-mail message that includes the subject, address, and attachments. _____
8. Typically includes the sender's name, address, and telephone number. _____
9. To participate in a mailing list, you must send a request to this address. _____
10. The most popular chat service. _____
11. Reading and observing discussions without participating. _____
12. Special programs that look for new information and update a search service database. _____
13. The list of sites that contain the keywords of a keyword search. _____
14. Program that automatically submits a search request to several search engines simultaneously. _____
15. Buying and selling goods over the Internet. _____
16. Program for creating Web sites for virtual stores. _____
17. Virtual stores where shoppers inspect goods and make purchases. _____
18. Similar to a traditional auction, but buyers and sellers interact only on the Web. _____
19. Criminals that specialize in stealing, trading, and using stolen credit cards over the Internet. _____
20. Internet equivalent to traditional cash. _____

OPEN-ENDED

On a separate sheet of paper, respond to each question or statement.

1. Discuss the uses of the Internet. Which activities have you participated in? Which one do you think is the most popular?
2. Explain the differences between the three types of providers.
3. What are the basic elements of an e-mail message?
4. What are the types of discussion groups? Describe any groups you participate in.
5. Describe the different types of search engine. What kinds of information does each return? Give an example of the type of search each engine is best for.

1 Instant Messaging

Do you enjoy chatting with your friends? Are you working on a project and need to collaborate with others in your group? Perhaps instant messaging is just what you're looking for. It's easy and free with an Internet connection and the right software. To learn more about instant messaging, review Making IT Work for You: Instant Messaging on pages 212 and 213. Then visit our Web site at http://www.mhhe.com/oleary, play the videos, and answer the following questions in a one-page paper: (a) What is the URL for creating a new AOL Instant Messenger account? (b) What users appear in the buddy list? (c) What users enter the newly created chat room?

2 Online Shopping

Shopping on the Internet can be fast and convenient. Connect to our Web site at http://www.mhhe.com/oleary to link to a popular shopping site. Once there, try shopping for one or two products, and answer the following questions in a one-page paper: (a) What are the pros and cons of shopping online versus a traditional store? (b) What assurance does the site provide that personal information such as your credit card number

will be secure when purchasing online? (c) What is this site's return policy? (d) Would you buy items from this site? Why or why not?

Interactive Companion CD-ROM 1

Complete the "Internet Overview" Lab located on your Interactive Companion CD-ROM, and then answer the following questions in a one-page paper: (a) What types of Internet communications software are reviewed in the Lab? (b) What are **plug-ins**, and why are they useful? (c) In what ways is cable modem service different from DSL?

E-cash 2

Using e-cash is one way to add a level of security to online purchases. Research two or three companies that specialize in e-cash, and then answer the following questions in a one-page paper: (a) How is e-cash more secure than paying by cash, check, or credit card? (b) What does e-cash cost? Are there fees for the buyer? What about the seller? (c) How widely accepted is e-cash? Do all sites accept it? (d) Would you use e-cash for an online purchase today? Why or why not?

1 Electronic Commerce

Electronic commerce is one of the most exciting Web applications. Write a two-page paper titled "Electronic Commerce" that addresses the following: (a) Define electronic commerce including B2C, C2C, and B2B. Provide examples. (b) What types of businesses and consumers are most affected by electronic commerce today? What types will be affected in the future? Discuss and justify your positions. (c) What are the greatest challenges to future developments in electronic commerce? Discuss and justify your conclusions.

2 Free Speech Online

Some feel that there is too much objectionable material allowed on the Internet, whereas others argue that the Internet should be completely uncensored. Consider these two viewpoints and answer the following questions in a two-page paper: (a) Should religious groups be allowed to distribute information over the Internet? What about groups that advocate hatred or oppression? (b) Is there any material you feel should not be freely available on the Web? What

about child pornography? (c) If you think some regulation is required, who should determine what restrictions should be imposed? (d) The Internet is not "owned" by a particular group or country. What limitations does this impose on enforcement of restrictions?

PRIVACY AND SECURITY

COMPETENCIES

After you have read this chapter, you should be able to:

1 Describe the most significant negative effects associated with computer technology.

2 Discuss the privacy issues raised by the presence of large databases, electronic networks, the Internet, and the Web.

3 Describe the security threats posed by computer criminals, computer crime, and other hazards.

4 Discuss ways that individuals and organizations protect their security.

5 Describe the common types of physical and mental risks associated with computer use and ways to protect yourself against these risks.

6 Discuss what the computer industry is doing, and what you can do, to protect the environment.

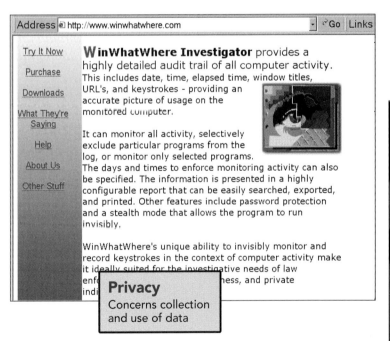

Address http://www.winwhatwhere.com   Go   Links

Try It Now
Purchase
Downloads
What They're Saying
Help
About Us
Other Stuff

WinWhatWhere Investigator provides a highly detailed audit trail of all computer activity. This includes date, time, elapsed time, window titles, URL's, and keystrokes - providing an accurate picture of usage on the monitored computer.

It can monitor all activity, selectively exclude particular programs from the log, or monitor only selected programs. The days and times to enforce monitoring activity can also be specified. The information is presented in a highly configurable report that can be easily searched, exported, and printed. Other features include password protection and a stealth mode that allows the program to run invisibly.

WinWhatWhere's unique ability to invisibly monitor and record keystrokes in the context of computer activity make it ideally suited for the investigative needs of law enfo...   ness, and private indi...

Privacy
Concerns collection and use of data

Security
Keeping private information safe from criminals and natural hazards

The tools and products of the information age do not exist in a world by themselves. As we said in Chapter 1, a computer system consists not only of software, hardware, data, and procedures but also of **people**. Because of people, computer systems may be used for both good and bad purposes.

There are more than 300 million microcomputers in use today. What are the consequences of the widespread presence of this technology? Does technology make it easy for others to invade our personal privacy? When we apply for a loan or for a driver's license, or when we check out at the supermarket, is that information about us being distributed and used without our permission? When we use the Web, is information about us being collected and shared with others?

Does technology make it easy for others to invade the security of business organizations like our banks or our employers? What about health risks to people who use computers? What about the environment? Do computers pose a threat to our ecology?

This technology prompts lots of questions—very important questions. Perhaps these are some of the most important questions for the twenty-first century. Competent end users need to be aware of the potential impact of technology on people and how to protect themselves on the Web. They need to be sensitive to and knowledgeable about personal privacy, organizational security, ergonomics, and the environmental impact of technology.

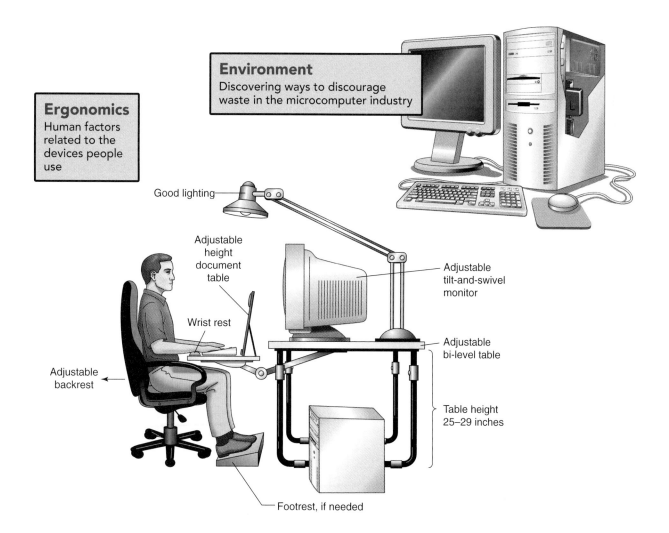

Environment
Discovering ways to discourage waste in the microcomputer industry

Ergonomics
Human factors related to the devices people use

Good lighting

Adjustable height document table

Adjustable tilt-and-swivel monitor

Wrist rest

Adjustable bi-level table

Adjustable backrest

Table height 25–29 inches

Footrest, if needed

PEOPLE

Information systems consist of people, procedures, software, hardware, and data. The most significant concerns for people are privacy, security, ergonomics, and the environment.

As we have discussed, information systems consist of people, procedures, software, hardware, and data. (See Figure 9-1.) This chapter focuses on people. While most everyone agrees that technology has had a very positive impact on people, it is important to recognize the negative or potentially negative impacts as well.

Effective implementation of computer technology involves maximizing its positive effects while minimizing its negative effects. The most significant concerns are:

- **Privacy:** What are the threats to personal privacy and how can we protect ourselves?
- **Security:** How can access to sensitive information be controlled and how can we secure hardware and software?
- **Ergonomics:** What are the physical and mental risks to technology and how can these risks be eliminated or controlled?
- **Environment:** What can individuals and organizations do to minimize the impact of technology on our environment?

Let us begin by examining privacy.

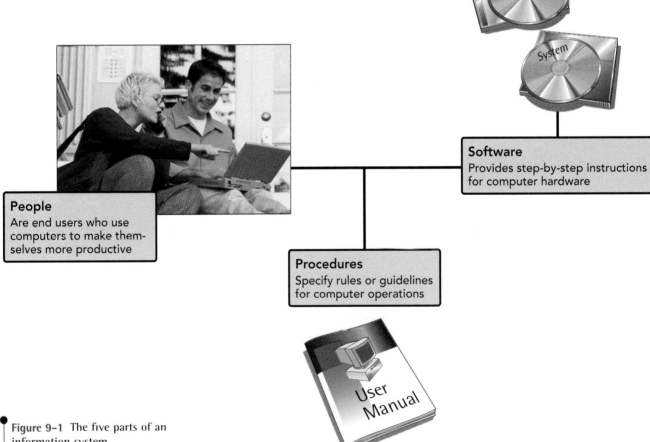

People
Are end users who use computers to make themselves more productive

Procedures
Specify rules or guidelines for computer operations

Software
Provides step-by-step instructions for computer hardware

Figure 9-1 The five parts of an information system

PRIVACY

What do you suppose controls how computers can be used? You probably think first of laws. Of course that is right, but technology is moving so fast that it is very difficult for our legal system to keep up. The essential element that controls how computers are used today is ethics.

> Every computer user should be aware of ethical matters, including how databases and networks are used and the major privacy laws.

Ethics, as you may know, are standards of moral conduct. **Computer ethics** are guidelines for the morally acceptable use of computers in our society. There are four primary computer ethics issues:

- **Privacy** concerns the collection and use of data about individuals.
- **Accuracy** relates to the responsibility of those who collect data to ensure that the data is correct.
- **Property** relates to who owns data and rights to software.

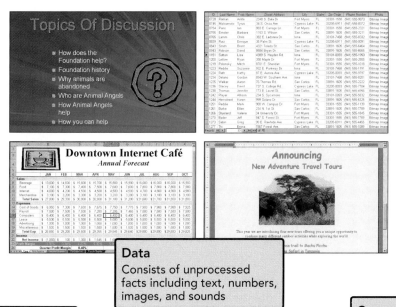

Data
Consists of unprocessed facts including text, numbers, images, and sounds

Hardware
Includes keyboard, mouse, monitor, system unit, and other devices

Connectivity
Allows computers to share information and to connect to the Internet

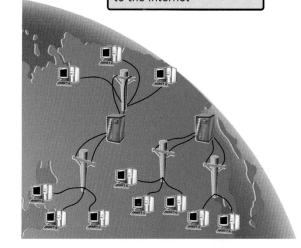

- **Access** relates to the responsibility of those who have data to control and who is able to use that data.

We are all entitled to ethical treatment. This includes the right to keep personal information, such as credit ratings and medical histories, from getting into unauthorized hands. Many people worry that this right is severely threatened. Let us see what some of the concerns are.

LARGE DATABASES

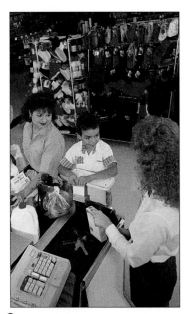

Figure 9-2 Large organizations are constantly compiling information about us, such as the kinds of products we buy

Large organizations are constantly compiling information about us. The federal government alone has over 2,000 databases. Our social security numbers have become a national identification number. This number has become a standard field in all kinds of databases including employment records, medical records, credit card records, and on and on. The vast majority of forms we fill out today require our social security number. Indeed, even children are now required to have social security numbers. Shouldn't we be concerned that cross-referenced information might be used for the wrong purposes?

Every day, data is gathered about us and stored in large databases. For example, for billing purposes, telephone companies compile lists of the calls we make, the numbers called, and so on. A special telephone directory (called a **reverse directory**) lists telephone numbers followed by subscriber names. Using it, government authorities and others could easily get the names, addresses, and other details about the persons we call. Credit card companies keep similar records. Supermarket scanners in grocery checkout counters record what we buy, when we buy it, how much we buy, and the price. (See Figure 9-2.) Publishers of magazines, newspapers, and mail-order catalogs have our names, addresses, phone numbers, and what we order.

A vast industry of data gatherers or "information resellers" now exists that collects such personal data. They then sell it to direct marketers, fund-raisers, and others. Did you know that for a nominal fee someone could obtain a copy of your monthly bank and credit card statements? If you own stocks, bonds, and/or mutual funds, they could also obtain a list of your financial holdings along with specific account numbers.

Your personal information including preferences, habits, and financial data has become a marketable commodity. This raises many issues, including:

- **Spreading information without personal consent:** How would you feel if your name and your taste in movies were made available nationwide? For a while, Blockbuster, a large video rental company, considered doing just this.

  What if a great deal of information about your shopping habits—collected about you without your consent—was made available to any microcomputer user who wanted it? Before dropping the project, Lotus Development Corporation and Equifax Inc. planned to market disks containing information on 120 million American consumers. (Lotus claimed it was providing small businesses with the same information currently available to larger organizations.)

  How would you feel if an employer were using your *medical* records to make decisions about hiring, placement, promotion, and firing? A University of Illinois survey found that half the Fortune 500 companies were using employee medical records for that purpose.

- **Spreading inaccurate information:** How accurate is the information being circulated? Mistakes that creep into one computer file may find their way into other computer files. For example, credit records may be in error. Moreover, even if you correct an error in one file, the correction may not be made in other files. Indeed, erroneous information may stay in computer files for years. It's important to know, therefore, that you have some recourse.

The law allows you to gain access to those records about you that are held by credit bureaus. Under the Freedom of Information Act (described shortly), you are also entitled to look at your records held by government agencies. (Portions may be deleted for national security reasons.)

PRIVATE NETWORKS

Suppose you use your company's electronic mail system to send a co-worker an unflattering message about your supervisor. Later you find the boss has been spying on your exchange. Or suppose you are a subscriber to an online discussion group. You discover that the company that supports the discussion group screens all your messages and rejects those it deems inappropriate. Both these situations have actually happened.

The first instance, of firms eavesdropping on employees, has inspired attempts at federal legislation. One survey revealed that over 20 percent of businesses search employees' electronic mail and computer files using so-called **snoopware.** (See Figure 9-3.) These programs can record virtually everything you do on your computer. Currently this is legal. One proposed law would not prohibit electronic monitoring but would require employers to provide prior written notice. They would also have to alert employees during the monitoring with some sort of audible or visual signal.

The second instance, in which online information services restrict libelous, obscene, or otherwise offensive material, exists with most commercial services. In one case, the Prodigy Information Service terminated the accounts of eight members who had been using the electronic mail system to protest Prodigy's rate hikes. Prodigy executives argued that the U.S. Constitution does not give members of someone's private network the right to express their views without restrictions. Opponents say that the United States is becoming a nation linked by electronic mail. Therefore, the government has to provide protection for users against other people reading or censoring their messages.

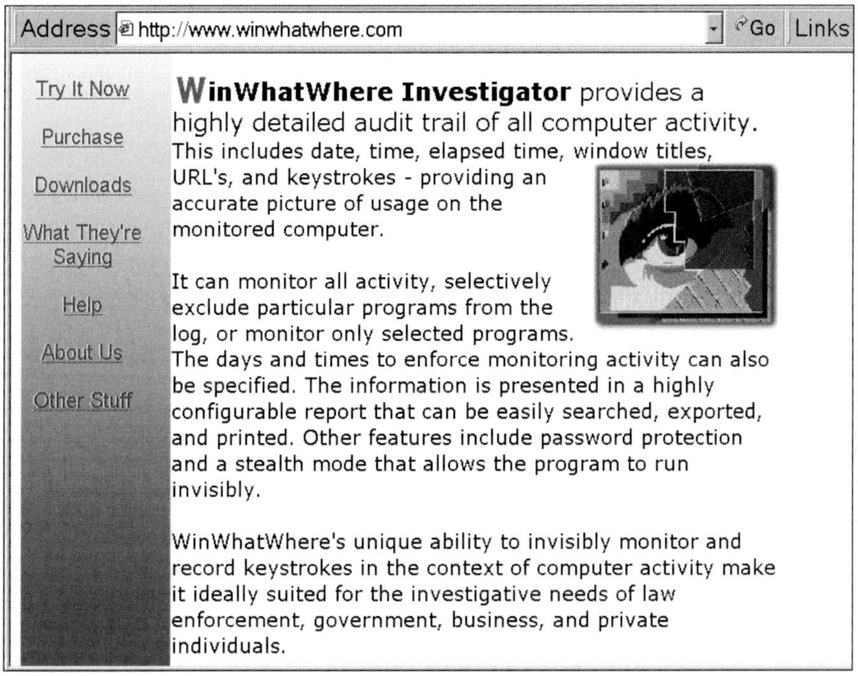

TIPS

Do you suppose any of your medical records are publicly available? If so, what information do you suppose is included? Here's one way to find out: Make a written request to the Medical Information Bureau. Their address is:

● **Medical Information Bureau (MIB)**
  P.O. Box 105
  Essex Station
  Boston, MA 02112

Another way is to visit their Web site at:

● **http://www.mib.com**

Address http://www.winwhatwhere.com   ▾ ⟳Go Links

Try It Now

Purchase

Downloads

What They're Saying

Help

About Us

Other Stuff

WinWhatWhere Investigator provides a highly detailed audit trail of all computer activity. This includes date, time, elapsed time, window titles, URL's, and keystrokes - providing an accurate picture of usage on the monitored computer.

It can monitor all activity, selectively exclude particular programs from the log, or monitor only selected programs. The days and times to enforce monitoring activity can also be specified. The information is presented in a highly configurable report that can be easily searched, exported, and printed. Other features include password protection and a stealth mode that allows the program to run invisibly.

WinWhatWhere's unique ability to invisibly monitor and record keystrokes in the context of computer activity make it ideally suited for the investigative needs of law enforcement, government, business, and private individuals.

Figure 9-3 Snoopware

THE INTERNET AND THE WEB

When you send e-mail on the Internet or browse the Web, do you have any concerns about privacy? Most people do not. They think as long as they are selective about disclosing their name or other personal information, then little can be done to invade their personal privacy. Experts call this the **illusion of anonymity** that the Internet brings.

As discussed earlier, it is a common practice in many organizations to monitor e-mail content on messages sent within their private electronic networks. Likewise, for some unscrupulous individuals, it is also a common practice to eavesdrop or snoop into the content of e-mail sent across the Internet.

Furthermore, when you browse the Web, your activity is monitored. Whenever you visit a Web site, your browser stores critical information onto your hard disk, typically without your permission or knowledge. For example, your browser creates a **history file** that includes the locations of sites visited by your computer system.

Another way your Web activity is monitored is by **cookies** or specialized programs that are deposited on your hard disk. Typically, these programs are deposited without your knowledge or consent. These programs record what sites you visit, what you do at the sites, and other information you provide such as credit card numbers. There are two basic types of cookies: *traditional* and *net* cookies.

- **Traditional cookies** monitor your activities at a single site. When you first visit a site, a cookie is deposited and begins to monitor your activities. When you leave the site, the cookie becomes dormant. When you revisit, the cookie is reactivated and sends the previously collected information to the site and continues recording your activities. These cookies are intended to provide customized service. For example, when you revisit an electronic commerce site, you can be greeted by name, customized advertising banners, and directed to Web pages promoting items you have previously purchased.

- **Ad network cookies** monitor your activities across all sites you visit. Once deposited onto your hard drive, they are continually active collecting information on your Web activities. These cookies are deposited by organizations that compile and market the information including individual personal profiles, mailing lists, and e-mail addresses. Two such organizations are DoubleClick and Avenue A. (See Figure 9-4.)

Fortunately, for those individuals who object to cookies, most browsers include settings to block and control cookies. Specialized programs, called **cookie-cutter programs,** allow users to selectively filter or block the most intrusive ad network cookies while allowing selective traditional cookies to operate. One of the best-known cookie-cutter programs is WebWasher. (See Figure 9-5.)

MAJOR LAWS ON PRIVACY

Some federal laws governing privacy matters have been created (see Figure 9-6). However, privacy is primarily an *ethical* issue, for many records stored by nongovernment organizations are not covered by existing laws. Yet individuals have shown that they are concerned about controlling who has the right to personal information and how it is used. A Code of Fair Information Practice is summarized in Figure 9-7. The code was recommended in 1977 by a committee established by

TIPS What can you do to protect your privacy while on the Web? Here are a few suggestions.

1. **Encrypt sensitive e-mail.** Encrypt or code sensitive e-mail using special encryption programs.

2. **Shield your identity.** Use an anonymous remailer or special Web site that forwards your e-mail without disclosing your identity.

3. **Block cookies.** Use browsers or cookie cutter programs that allow you to block Web sites from depositing cookies on your hard disk.

4. **Notify providers.** Instruct your service provider or whomever you use to link to the Internet not to sell your name or any other personal information.

5. **Be careful.** Never disclose your telephone number, passwords, or other private information to strangers.

Figure 9-4 Avenue A

Figure 9-5 WebWasher

Law	Year	Protection
Fair Credit Reporting Act	1970	Gives right to review and correct personal credit records; restricts sharing of personal credit histories.
Freedom of Information Act	1970	Gives right to see personal files collected by federal agencies.
Privacy Act	1974	Prohibits use of federal information for purposes other than original intent.
Right to Financial Privacy Act	1979	Limits federal authority to examine personal bank records.
Computer Fraud and Abuse Act	1986	Allows prosecution of unauthorized access to computers and databases.
Electronic Communications Privacy Act	1986	Protects privacy on public electronic-mail systems.
Video Privacy Protection Act	1988	Prevents sale of video-rental records.
Computer Matching and Privacy Protection Act	1988	Limits government's authority to match individual's data.
Computer Abuse Amendments Act	1994	Outlaws transmission of viruses
National Information Infrastructure Protection Act	1996	Protects computer systems, networks, and information.
No Electronic Theft (NET) Act	1997	Prevents unauthorized distribution of copyrighted software on the Internet.
Child Online Protection Act (COPA)	1998	Prohibits commercial distribution of materials harmful to minors.

Figure 9-6 Summary of privacy laws

former Secretary of Health, Education, and Welfare Elliott Richardson. It has been adopted by many information-collecting businesses, but privacy advocates would like to see it written into law.

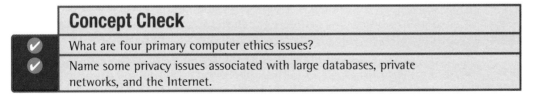

Concept Check

✓ What are four primary computer ethics issues?

✓ Name some privacy issues associated with large databases, private networks, and the Internet.

Principle	Description
No secret databases	There must be no record-keeping systems containing personal data whose very existence is kept secret.
Right of individual access	Individuals must be able to find out what information about them is in a record and how it is used.
Right of consent	Information about individuals obtained for one purpose cannot be used for other purposes without their consent.
Right to correct	Individuals must be able to correct or amend records of identifiable information about them.
Assurance of reliability and proper use	Organizations creating, maintaining, using, or disseminating records of identifiable personal data must make sure the data is reliable for its intended use. They must take precautions to prevent such data from being misused.

Figure 9-7 Principles of the Code of Fair Information Practice

SECURITY

> Threats to computer security are computer crimes including viruses, electronic break-ins, and natural and other hazards. Security measures consist of encryption, restricting access, anticipating disasters, and making backup copies.

We are all concerned with having a safe and secure environment to live in. We are careful to lock our car doors and our homes. We are careful about where we walk at night and whom we talk to. This is physical security. What about computer security? Does it matter if someone gains access to personal information about you? What if someone learns your credit card number or your checking account number? What if a mistake is made and your credit history shows a number of large unpaid loans? What if all your school records are lost? These are just a few of the reasons to be concerned about computer security. (See Figure 9-8.)

THREATS TO COMPUTER SECURITY

Keeping information private depends on keeping computer systems safe from criminals, natural hazards, and other threats.

Computer Criminals

A **computer crime** is an illegal action in which the perpetrator uses special knowledge of computer technology. Computer criminals are of four types:

- **Employees:** The largest category of computer criminals consists of those with the easiest access to computers—namely, employees. Sometimes the employee is simply trying to steal something from the employer—equipment, software, electronic funds, proprietary information, or computer time. Sometimes the employee may be acting out of resentment and is trying to get back at the company.
- **Outside users:** Not only employees but also some suppliers or clients may have access to a company's computer system. Examples are bank customers who use an automated teller machine. Like employees, these authorized users may be able to obtain confidential passwords or find other ways of committing computer crimes.
- **Hackers and crackers:** Some people think of these two groups as being the same, but they are not. **Hackers** are people who gain unauthorized

Figure 9-8 There are numerous threats to computer security

access to a computer system for the fun and challenge of it. **Crackers** do the same thing but for malicious purposes. They may intend to steal technical information or to introduce what they call a bomb—a destructive computer program—into the system.

- **Organized crime:** Members of organized crime groups have discovered that they can use computers just as people in legitimate businesses do, but for illegal purposes. For example, computers are useful for keeping track of stolen goods or illegal gambling debts. In addition, counterfeiters and forgers use microcomputers and printers to produce sophisticated-looking documents such as checks and driver's licenses.

- **Terrorists:** Knowledgeable terrorist groups and hostile governments could potentially crash satellites and wage economic warfare by disrupting navigation and communication systems. The Department of Defense reports that its computer systems are probed approximately 250,000 times a year by unknown sources.

Computer Crime

The FBI estimates that businesses lost $1.5 trillion in the past year from computer crimes. The number of these crimes has tripled in the past two years. Computer crime can take various forms:

- **Damage:** Disgruntled employees sometimes attempt to destroy computers, programs, or files. Hackers and crackers are notorious for creating and distributing malicious programs known as viruses.

  Viruses are programs that migrate through networks and operating systems and attach themselves to different programs and databases. There are four basic types of viruses: boot sector, file, Trojan horse, and macro. Creating and knowingly spreading a virus is a very serious crime and a federal offense punishable under the Computer Abuse Amendments Act of 1994.

  A variant on the virus is the **worm.** This destructive program fills a computer system with self-replicating information, clogging the system so that its operations are slowed or stopped. One of the most infamous to date is known as the Code Red. In 2001, it traveled across the world, stopping tens of thousands of computers along its way. Another variant is the **denial of service attack** in which Web sites are overwhelmed with data. The result is that users are unable to access the Web site.

  Viruses and worms typically find their way into microcomputers through copied floppy disks or programs downloaded from the Internet. Because viruses can be so serious—certain "disk-killer" viruses can destroy all the information on one's system—computer users are advised to exercise care in accepting new programs and data from other sources. See Figure 9-9 for a list of common viruses.

  Detection programs called **virus checkers** are available to alert users when certain kinds of viruses enter the system. (See Making IT Work for You: Virus Protection on pages 244–245.) Four of the most widely used

Name	Description
Apology-B	follows every outgoing e-mail with a second e-mail containing virus
KuKworm	automatically attaches to outgoing e-mail
Love Bug	recreates itself through Microsoft Outlook; renames files
Stages-A	copies itself on all available network drives
Thus	deletes data on December 13th

Figure 9-9 Commonly encountered viruses

Worried about computer viruses? Did you know that others could be intercepting your private e-mail? It is even possible for them to gain access and control over your computer system. Fortunately, Internet security suites are available to help ensure your safety while you are on the Internet.

How It Works Internet security suites are collections of programs that create a protective barrier around your computer system. These suites, such as Norton AntiVirus and eSafe, are designed to protect against computer viruses and to ensure security and privacy of computer system resources.

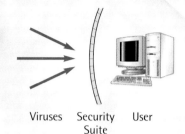

Viruses   Security   User
Suite

Getting Started The first step is to install an Internet security suite. Once installed, the software will continually work to ensure security and privacy. One such suite, eSafe, has a version available free from the Internet. To install this suite, follow the instructions below.

1 ● Connect to *www.ealaddin.com/esafe* and click *Downloads.*

● Select *Downloads.*

● Select *Home Users.*

● Click the *eSafe* link.

● Complete the registration form.

● Download the *eSafe* software.

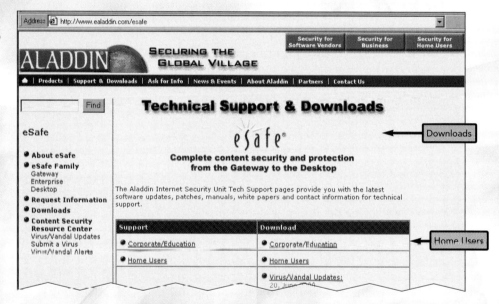

2 ● Double-click the download file.

● Follow the on-screen instructions to install *eSafe Desktop.*

eSafe Numerous security files have been installed. One of these, Desktop Watch, runs continually to search for privacy and security violations to the computer system. Another program, Desktop Configuration, provides a menu to access some of eSafe's most powerful applications including Sandbox, Personal Firewall, and Anti-Virus.

Sandbox

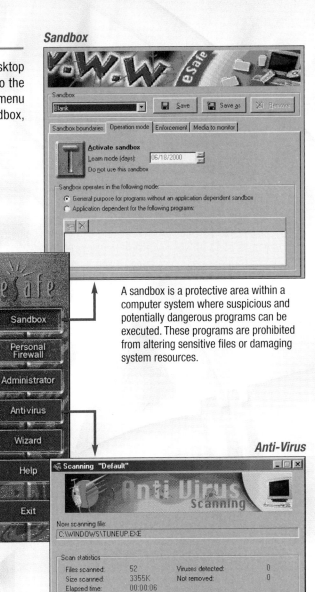

Personal Firewall

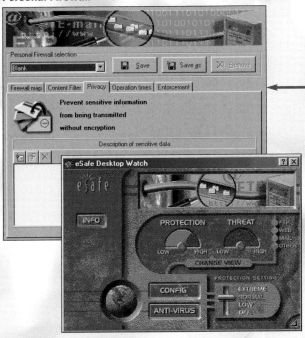

A sandbox is a protective area within a computer system where suspicious and potentially dangerous programs can be executed. These programs are prohibited from altering sensitive files or damaging system resources.

Anti-Virus

Personal Firewalls are programs that monitor all inbound and outbound traffic to a computer system. They limit access to only authorized users, automatically check files for viruses, and filter out unwanted content.

Anti-Virus controls how frequently the computer system is searched for computer viruses. When a file is checked, it is compared to the profile of over 6,000 known viruses. Once a virus is detected, it is typically either eliminated from the file or the entire file is deleted.

The Web is continually changing and some of the specifics presented in this Making IT Work for You may have changed. See our Web site at http://www.mhhe.com/oleary for possible changes and to learn more about this application of technology.

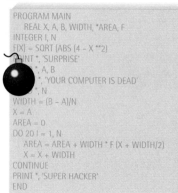

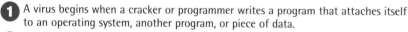

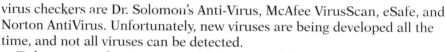

1 A virus begins when a cracker or programmer writes a program that attaches itself to an operating system, another program, or piece of data.

2 The virus travels via floppy disk or downloading from the Internet or other networks or bulletin boards anywhere that the operating system, program, or data travels.

3 The virus is set off. A nondestructive virus may simply print a message ("Surprise!"). A destructive virus may erase data, destroy programs, and even (through repeated reading and writing to one location) wear out a hard disk. The virus may be set off either by a time limit or by a sequence of operations by the user.

Figure 9-10 How a computer virus can spread

virus checkers are Dr. Solomon's Anti-Virus, McAfee VirusScan, eSafe, and Norton AntiVirus. Unfortunately, new viruses are being developed all the time, and not all viruses can be detected.

To learn more about viruses and how you could get one, study Figure 9-10.

- **Theft:** Theft can take many forms—of hardware, of software, of data, of computer time. Thieves steal equipment, of course, but there are also white-collar crimes. Thieves steal data in the form of confidential information such as preferred-client lists. They also use (steal) their company's computer time to run another business.

Unauthorized copying of programs for personal gain is a form of theft called **software piracy.** According to the **Software Copyright Act of 1980,** it is legal for a program owner to make only his or her own backup copies of that program. *It's important to note that none of these copies may be legally resold or given away. This may come as a surprise to those who copy software from a friend, but that's the law.*

Pirated software accounts for over 40 percent of software used in the United States. The incidence of pirated software is even higher overseas in such countries as Italy (82 percent) and Thailand (92 percent). Penalties for violating this law are up to $250,000 in fines and five years in prison.

- **Manipulation:** Finding entry into someone's computer network and leaving a prankster's message may seem like fun, which is why hackers do it. It is still against the law. Moreover, even if the manipulation seems harmless, it may cause a great deal of anxiety and wasted time among network users.

Are you concerned about catching a virus? Here are a few suggestions that might help:

1 Use an antivirus program. Install antivirus programs on all computer systems you use and run them frequently.

2 Check disks. Before using any floppy or CD, check for viruses.

3 Enable write protection. Protect data and programs on floppy disks by enabling write protection.

4 Check all downloads. Check all files downloaded from the Internet.

5 Update your antivirus program. New viruses are being developed daily, and the virus programs are continually being revised. Update your antivirus program frequently.

The Computer Fraud and Abuse Act of 1986 makes it a crime for unauthorized persons even to *view*—let alone copy or damage—data using any computer across state lines. It also prohibits unauthorized use of any government computer or computer used by any federally insured financial institution. Offenders can be sentenced to up to 20 years in prison and fined up to $100,000.

Of course, using a computer in the course of performing some other crime, such as selling fraudulent products, is also illegal.

Other Hazards

There are plenty of other hazards to computer systems and data besides criminals. They include the following:

- **Natural hazards:** Natural forces include fires, floods, wind, hurricanes, tornadoes, and earthquakes. Even home computer users should store backup disks of programs and data in safe locations in case of fire or storm damage.

- **Civil strife and terrorism:** Wars, riots, and other forms of political unrest are real risks in some parts of the world. Even people in developed countries, however, must be mindful that acts of sabotage are possible.

- **Technological failures:** Hardware and software don't always do what they are supposed to do. For instance, too little electricity, caused by a brownout or blackout, may cause the loss of data in primary storage. Too much electricity, as when lightning or other electrical disturbance affects a power line, may cause a **voltage surge,** or **spike.** This excess of electricity may destroy chips or other electronic components of a computer.

  Microcomputer users should use a **surge protector,** a device that separates the computer from the power source of the wall outlet. When a voltage surge occurs, it activates a circuit breaker in the surge protector, protecting the computer system.

  Another technological catastrophe occurs when a hard-disk drive suddenly "crashes," or fails, perhaps because it has been bumped inadvertently. If the user has forgotten to make backup copies of data on the hard disk, data may be lost. (See Figure 9-11.)

- **Human errors:** Human mistakes are inevitable. Data-entry errors are probably the most commonplace. Programmer errors also occur frequently. Some mistakes may result from faulty design, as when a software manufacturer makes a deletion command closely resembling another command. Some errors may be the result of sloppy procedures. One such example occurs when office workers keep important correspondence under file names that no one else in the office knows.

Figure 9-11 Crashes can result in lost data

Figure 9-12 Disasters—both natural and manmade—can play havoc with computers

MEASURES TO PROTECT COMPUTER SECURITY

Security is concerned with protecting information, hardware, and software. They must be protected from unauthorized use as well as from damage from intrusions, sabotage, and natural disasters. (See Figure 9-12.) Considering the numerous ways in which computer systems and data can be compromised, we can see why security is a growing field. Some of the principal measures to protect computer security are the following.

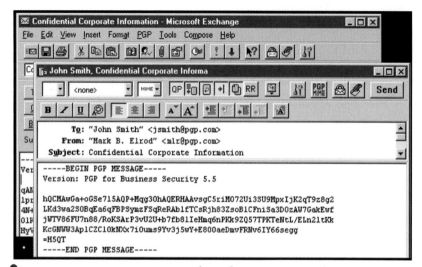

Figure 9-13 Encrypted e-mail

Encrypting Messages

Whenever information is sent over a network, the possibility of unauthorized access exists. The longer the distance the message has to travel, the higher the security risk is. For example, an e-mail message on a LAN meets a limited number of users operating in controlled environments such as offices. An e-mail message traveling across the country on the information superhighway affords greater opportunities for the message to be intercepted.

Businesses have been **encrypting,** or coding, messages for years. They have become so good at it that some law enforcement agencies are unable to wiretap messages from suspected criminals. Some federal agencies have suggested that a standard encryption procedure be used so that law enforcement agencies can monitor suspected criminal communications. The government is encouraging businesses that utilize the Internet to use a special encryption program. This program is available on a processor chip called the Clipper chip and is also known as the Key Escrow chip.

Individuals are also using encryption programs to safeguard their private communications. One of the most widely used personal encryption programs is Pretty Good Privacy. (See Figure 9-13.)

Restricting Access

Security experts are constantly devising ways to protect computer systems from access by unauthorized persons. Sometimes security is a matter of putting guards on company computer rooms and checking the identification of everyone admitted. Oftentimes it is a matter of being careful about assigning passwords to people, and of changing them when people leave a company. **Passwords** are secret words or numbers that must be keyed into a computer system to gain access. In some dial-back computer systems, the user telephones the computer, punches in the correct password, and hangs up. The computer then calls back at a certain preauthorized number.

As mentioned in Chapter 8, most major corporations today use special hardware and software called **firewalls** to control access to their internal computer networks. Firewalls act as a security buffer between the corporation's private network and all external networks, including the Internet. All electronic communications coming into and leaving the corporation must be evaluated by the firewall. Security is maintained by denying access to unauthorized communications. (See Figure 9-14.)

Anticipating Disasters

Companies (and even individuals) that do not make preparations for disasters are not acting wisely. **Physical security** is concerned with protecting hardware from possible human and natural disasters. **Data security** is concerned with protecting software and data from unauthorized tampering or damage. Most large organizations have a **disaster recovery plan** describing ways to continue operating until normal computer operations can be restored.

Hardware can be kept behind locked doors, but often employees find this restriction a hindrance to their work, so security is lax. Fire and water (including the water from ceiling sprinkler systems) can do great damage to equipment. Many companies therefore will form a cooperative arrangement

Figure 9-14 Restricting access is one way to protect computer systems

to share equipment with other companies in the event of catastrophe. Special emergency facilities called **hot sites** may be created that are fully equipped backup computer centers. They are called **cold sites** if they are empty shells in which hardware must be installed.

Backing Up Data

Equipment can always be replaced. A company's *data,* however, may be irreplaceable. Most companies have ways of trying to keep software and data from being tampered with in the first place. They include careful screening of job applicants, guarding of passwords, and auditing of data and programs from time to time. The safest procedure, however, is to make frequent backups of data and to store them in remote locations.

Security for Microcomputers

If you own a microcomputer system, there are several procedures to follow to keep it safe:

- **Avoid extreme conditions:** Don't expose the computer to extreme conditions. Direct sun, rain from an open window, extreme temperatures, cigarette smoke, and spilled drinks or food are harmful to microcomputers. Clean your equipment regularly. Use a surge protector to protect against voltage surges.

- **Guard the computer:** Put a cable lock on the computer. If you subscribe or belong to an online information service, do not leave passwords nearby in a place accessible to others. Etch your driver's license number into your equipment. That way it can be identified in the event it is recovered after theft.

- **Guard programs and data:** Store disks properly, preferably in a locked container. Make backup copies of all your important files and programs. Store copies of your files in a different—and safe—location from the site of your computer.

See Figure 9-15 for a summary of the different measures to protect computer security.

Measure	Description
Encrypting	Coding all messages sent over a network
Restricting	Limiting access to authorized persons using such measures as passwords, dial-back systems, and firewalls
Anticipating	Preparing for disasters by ensuring physical security and data security through a disaster recovery plan
Backing up	Routinely copying data and storing it at a remote location
Securing	Protecting a microcomputer by avoiding extreme conditions, guarding the computer, programs, and data

Figure 9-15 Measures to protect computer security

Concept Check

✓ Give examples of threats to computer security that involve computer crimes.

✓ Give examples of other hazards that can threaten computer security.

✓ What are some of the measures taken to ensure computer security?

> Ergonomics helps computer users take steps to avoid physical and mental health risks and to increase productivity.

Even though computers have decreased significantly in cost, they are still expensive. Why have them, then, unless they can make workers more effective? Ironically, there are certain ways in which computers may actually make people *less* productive. Many of these problems will most likely affect workers in positions that involve intensive data entry, such as clerks and word processor operators. However, they may also happen to anyone whose job involves heavy use of the computer. As a result, there has been great interest in a field known as ergonomics.

Ergonomics (pronounced "er-guh-*nom*-ix") is defined as the study of human factors related to things people use. It is concerned with fitting the job to the worker rather than forcing the worker to contort to fit the job. As computer use has increased, so has interest in ergonomics. People are devising ways that computers can be designed and used to increase productivity and avoid health risks.

PHYSICAL HEALTH

Sitting in front of a screen in awkward positions for long periods may lead to physical problems. These can include eyestrain, headaches, and back pain. Users can alleviate these problems by taking frequent rest breaks and by using well-designed computer furniture. Some recommendations by ergonomics experts for the ideal microcomputer setup are illustrated in Figure 9-16.

The physical health matters related to computers that have received the most attention recently are the following:

- **Avoiding eyestrain and headache:** Our eyes were made for most efficient seeing at a distance. However, monitors require using the eyes at closer range for a long time, which can create eyestrain, headaches, and double vision.

  To make the computer easier on the eyes, take a 15-minute break every hour or two. Avoid computer screens that flicker. Keep computer screens

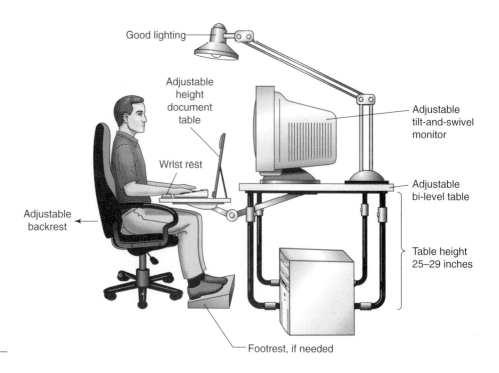

Figure 9-16 Recommendations for the ideal microcomputer work environment

away from windows and other sources of bright light to minimize reflected glare on the screen. Special antiglare screen coatings and glare shields are also available. Make sure the screen is three to four times brighter than room light. Keep everything you're focusing on at about the same distance. For example, the computer screen, keyboard, and a document holder containing your work might be positioned about 20 inches away. Clean the screen of dust from time to time.

Figure 9-17 Back and neck pain

- **Avoiding back and neck pain:** Many people work at monitors and keyboards that are in improper positions. The result can be pains in the back and neck. (See Figure 9-17.)

   To avoid such problems, make sure equipment is adjustable. You should be able to adjust your chair for height and angle, and the chair should have good back support. The table on which the monitor stands should also be adjustable, and the monitor itself should be of the tilt-and-swivel kind. The monitor should be at eye level or slightly below eye level. Keyboards should be detachable. Document holders should be adjustable.

- **Avoiding effects of electromagnetic fields:** Like many household appliances, monitors generate invisible electromagnetic field (EMF) emissions, which can pass through the human body. Some observers feel that there could be a connection between these EMF emissions and miscarriages (and even some cancers). A study by the government's National Institute of Occupational Safety and Health found no statistical relationship between monitors and miscarriages. Even so, several companies have introduced low-emission monitors. They state that no health or safety problems exist with older monitors; rather, they are merely responding to market demands.

   One recommendation is that computer users should follow a policy of "prudent avoidance" in reducing their exposure to EMF emissions. They should try to sit about 2 feet or more from the computer screen and 3 feet from neighboring terminals. The strongest fields are emitted from the sides and backs of terminals. Pregnant women should be particularly cautious and are encouraged to consult with their physician.

- **Avoiding repetitive strain injury:** Data-entry operators may make as many as 23,000 keystrokes a day. Some of these workers and other heavy keyboard users have fallen victim to a disorder known as repetitive strain injury.

   Repetitive strain injury (RSI)—also called **repetitive motion injury** and **cumulative trauma disorder**—is the name given to a number of injuries. These result from fast, repetitive work that can cause neck, wrist, hand, and arm pain. RSI is by far the greatest cause of workplace illnesses in private industry. It accounts for *billions* of dollars in compensation claims and lost productivity every year. Some RSI sufferers are slaughterhouse, textile, and automobile workers, who have long been susceptible to the disorder. One particular type of RSI, **carpal tunnel syndrome,** found among heavy computer users, consists of damage to nerves and tendons in the hands. (See Figure 9-18.) Some victims report the pain is so intense that they cannot open doors or shake hands and that they require corrective surgery.

   Before the computer, typists would stop to change paper or make corrections, thus giving themselves short but frequent rest periods. Ergonomically correct keyboards have recently been developed to help prevent injury from heavy computer use. (See Figure 9-19.) But, in addition, because RSI is caused by repetition and a fast work pace, you should

Figure 9-18 Carpal tunnel syndrome

Figure 9-19 Ergonomic keyboard

remember to take frequent short rest breaks. Experts also advise getting plenty of sleep and exercise, watching your weight, sitting up straight, and learning stress-management techniques.

MENTAL HEALTH

Computer technology offers not only ways of improving productivity but also some irritants that may be counterproductive.

- **Avoiding noise:** Computing can be quite noisy. Voice input and output can be distracting for co-workers. Working next to a printer for several hours can leave one with ringing ears. Also, users may develop headaches and tension from continual exposure to the high-frequency, barely audible squeal produced by cooling fans and vibrating parts inside the system unit. This is particularly true for women, who hear high-frequency sounds better than men do. They may be affected by the noise even when they are not conscious of hearing it.

  Head-mounted microphones and earphones greatly reduce the effect of voice input and output. Acoustical tile and sound-muffling covers are available for reducing the noise from co-workers and impact printers. Tightening loose system unit components will reduce high-frequency noise.

- **Avoiding stress from excessive monitoring:** Research shows that workers whose performance is monitored electronically suffer more health problems than do those watched by human supervisors. For instance, a computer may monitor the number of keystrokes a data-entry clerk completes in a day. It might tally the time a customer-service person takes to handle a call. The company might then decide to shorten the time allowed and to continue monitoring employees electronically. By so doing, it may force a pace leading to physical problems, such as RSI, and mental health difficulties. One study found that electronically monitored employees reported more boredom, tension, extreme anxiety, depression, anger, and severe fatigue than those who were not electronically monitored.

  Recently it has been shown that electronic monitoring actually is not necessary. For instance, both Federal Express and Bell Canada replaced electronic monitoring with occasional monitoring by human managers. They found that employee productivity stayed up and even increased.

  A new word—*technostress*—has been proposed to describe the stress associated with computer use that is harmful to people. **Technostress** is the tension that arises when we have to unnaturally adapt to computers rather than having computers adapt to us.

DESIGN

Electronic products from microwave ovens to VCRs to microcomputers offer the promise of more efficiency and speed. Often, however, the products are so overloaded with features that users cannot figure them out. Because a microprocessor chip handles not just one operation but several, manufacturers feel obliged to pile on the bells and whistles. Thus, many home and office products, while being fancy technology platforms, are difficult for humans to use.

A recent trend among manufacturers is to deliberately strip down the features offered, rather than to constantly do all that is possible. In appliances, this restraint is shown among certain types of high-end audio equipment, which come with fewer buttons and lights. In computers, there are similar trends. Surveys show that consumers want plug-and-play equipment—machines that they can simply turn on and quickly start working. Thus, computers are being made easier to use, with more menus, windows, icons, and pictures.

For a summary of ergonomic concerns, see Figure 9-20.

Problem	Remedy
Eyestrain and headache	Take frequent breaks, avoid screen glare, place object at fixed focal distance
Back and neck pain	Use adjustable equipment
Electromagnetic field	Sit 2 feet or more from screen emissions
Repetitive strain injury	Use ergonomically correct keyboards, take frequent breaks
Noise	Use head-mounted microphones and earphones, install acoustical tile and sound-muffling covers, tighten system unit components
Stress from excessive monitoring	Remove electronic monitoring

Figure 9-20 Summary of ergonomic concerns

Concept Check

✓ What is ergonomics and why is it important?

✓ What are some of the most significant physical and mental health concerns?

THE ENVIRONMENT

What do you suppose uses the greatest amount of electricity in the workplace? Microcomputers do. They account for 5 percent of the electricity used. Increased power production translates to increased air pollution, depletion of nonrenewable resources, and other environmental hazards.

> Computer industry has responded to the Energy Star program with the Green PC. You can help by conserving, recycling, and educating.

The Environmental Protection Agency (EPA) has created the **Energy Star** program to discourage waste in the microcomputer industry. Along with over 50 manufacturers, the EPA has established a goal of reducing power requirements for system units, monitors, and printers. The industry has responded with the concept of the **Green PC.** (See Figure 9-21.)

THE GREEN PC

The basic elements of the Green PC are:

- **System Unit:** Using existing technology from portable computers, the system unit (1) uses an energy-saving microprocessor that requires a minimal amount of power, (2) employs microprocessor and hard-disk drives that shift to an energy-saving or sleep mode when not in operation, (3) replaces the conventional supply unit with an adapter that requires less electricity, and (4) eliminates the cooling fan.
- **Display:** Displays have been made more energy efficient by using (1) flat panels that require much less energy than the

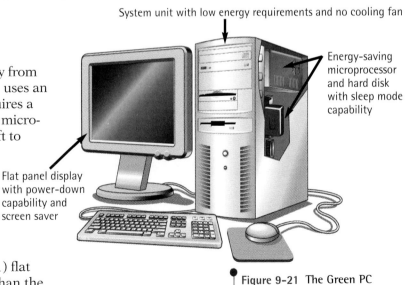

System unit with low energy requirements and no cooling fan

Energy-saving microprocessor and hard disk with sleep mode capability

Flat panel display with power-down capability and screen saver

Figure 9-21 The Green PC

traditional monitors, (2) special power-down monitors that automatically reduce power consumption when not in use, and (3) screen-saver software that clears the display whenever it is not in use.

- **Manufacturing:** Computer manufacturers such as Intel, Apple, Compaq, and others are using fewer harmful chemicals in production. Particular attention is given to **chlorofluorocarbons (CFCs)** in solvents and cleaning agents. (CFCs can travel into the atmosphere and are suspected by some in the scientific community to deplete the earth's ozone layer.) Toxic nickel and other heavy metals are being eliminated or reduced in the manufacturing processes.

Of course, not all of these technologies and manufacturing processes are used for all microcomputers. But more and more of them are.

PERSONAL RESPONSIBILITY

Some of the things that you, as a computer user, can do to help protect the environment are the following:

- **Conserve:** The EPA estimates that 30 to 40 percent of computer users leave their machines running days, nights, and weekends. When finished working for the day, turn off all computers and other energy-consuming devices. The EPA also estimates that 80 percent of the time a monitor is on, no one is looking at it. Use screen-saver programs that blank the computer screen after three to five minutes of inactivity.

- **Recycle:** U.S. businesses use an enormous amount of paper each year—a pile 48,900 miles high. Much of that, as well as the paper we throw out at home, can be recycled. Other recyclable items include computer boxes, packaging material, printer cartridges, and floppy disks. Last year over 24 million computers were thrown away. Only 14 percent were recycled. Recycle discarded computers by contacting any one of the groups listed in Figure 9-22.

- **Educate:** Be aware of and learn more about ecological dangers of all types. Make your concerns known to manufacturers and retail agencies. Support ecologically sound products.

Organization	Web Site
Computers for Schools Association	www.detwiler.org
Computers for Youth	www.cfy.org
National Cristina Foundation	www.cristinak.org
Share Technology	www.sharetechnology.org

Figure 9-22 Computer recycling groups

Concept Check

✔ What is a Green PC?

✔ What are the basic elements of the Green PC?

✔ What other actions can you take to help protect the environment?

A Look to the Future

New Legislation Will Be Needed to Define Government's Relationship to New Technology

Technology often has a way of outracing existing social and political institutions. For instance, citizens have a right to request government records under the Freedom of Information Act. But even in its most recent amendment, in 1986, the act does not mention the word computer or define the word record. Can the government therefore legally deny, as one agency did, a legitimate request for data on corporate compliance with occupational safety and health laws? Access laws lag behind even as the government collects more information than ever.

In addition, there has been a rise in computer-related crimes. These include bank and credit card fraud, viruses, and electronic break-ins of government and private computer systems. Law-enforcement agencies continue to crack down on these computer crimes. Yet they may also be jeopardizing the rights of computer users who are not breaking the law. Such users may be suffering illegal searches and violation of constitutional guarantees of free speech. However, it is unclear how the First Amendment protects speech and the Fourth Amendment protects against searches and seizures in this electronic world.

One professor of constitutional law has proposed a new amendment to the Constitution. This amendment would extend the other freedoms in the Bill of Rights, those on free speech and search and seizure restrictions. Under this amendment, all new technology and media for generating, storing, and altering information would be covered.

PRIVACY

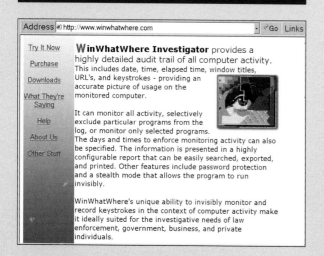

PRIVACY

Computer ethics are guidelines for moral computer use. Four computer ethics issues:

- **Privacy** concerns collection and use of data about individuals.
- **Accuracy** relates to the responsibility of those who collect data to ensure correctness.
- **Property** relates to who owns the data.
- **Access** relates to the responsibility of those who have data to control who is able to use it.

Large Databases

Large organizations are constantly compiling information about us. **Reverse directories** are special telephone directories that list telephone numbers followed by subscriber names. Two key personal privacy issues are:

- Spreading information without personal consent.
- Spreading inaccurate information.

Private Networks

Many organizations monitor employee e-mail and computer files using special software called **snoopware.** Most online information services restrict libelous, obscene, or other offensive material.

Internet and the Web

Many people believe that while using the Web as long as they are selective about disclosing their name and other personal information, little can be done to invade their privacy. This is an **illusion of anonymity.**

Created by browsers, history files record locations of sites visited by a computer system. Cookies are specialized programs deposited onto you computer system that records sites visited, activity at sites, and other information.

Two types of cookies:

- **Traditional cookies**—monitor activities at a single site.
- **Ad network cookies**—monitor activities across all sites visited.

Cookie-cutter programs selectively filter or block most ad network cookies while allowing selective traditional cookies to operate.

Major Privacy Laws

There are numerous federal laws governing privacy matters. Privacy is an ethical issue subject to the Code of Fair Information Practice. This code is not a law.

To be a competent end user you need to be aware of the potential impact of technology on people. You need to be sensitive to and knowledgeable about personal privacy, organizational security, ergonomics, and the environmental impact of technology.

SECURITY

Threats to Computer Security

Keeping information private depends on keeping computers safe from computer criminals including:

- Employees—the largest category of computer criminals.
- Outside users—often suppliers or clients that may have access to computer systems.
- Hackers and crackers—**hackers** gain access for the fun and challenge while **crackers** do it for malicious purposes.
- Organized crime—including counterfeiting and forgery.
- Terrorists—potentially crash satellites and wage economic warefare.

Common computer crimes include:

- Damage—**viruses** are programs that cause damage, **worms** fill computer systems with self-replicating information, and **denial of service attacks** shut down Web sites.
- Theft—unauthorized copying of programs is called software **piracy** and protected by the **Software Copyright Act of 1980.**
- Manipulation—changing data or leaving prank messages is illegal under the **Computer Fraud and Abuse Act of 1986.**

SECURITY

- Other hazards—including natural disasters, civil strife, terrorism, technological failures, and human error.

Voltage surges or **spikes** are excess electricity that may destroy electronic components. **Surge protectors** provide safety against such damage.

Measures to Protect Computer Security

Security is concerned with keeping hardware, software, data, and programs safe from unauthorized personnel. Some measures are:

- **Encrypting** or encoding all messages including personal e-mail.
- Restricting access to computer systems by using **passwords** and **firewalls.**
- Anticipating disasters by ensuring **physical** and **data security. Disaster recovery plans** describe procedures to continue operations following a disaster. **Hot sites** are special emergency facilities. **Cold site**s are empty shells in which hardware must be installed.
- Backing up data, which unlike hardware cannot always be replaced.
- Securing microcomputers including avoidance of extreme conditions, installing cables, using passwords, and permanently marking equipment.

ERGONOMICS

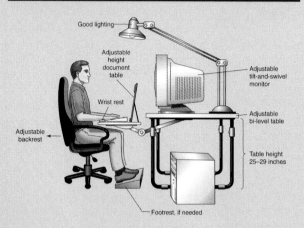

THE ENVIRONMENT

Ergonomics is the study of human factors related to things people use, including computers.

Physical Health

Physical health problems and their solutions include:

- Eyestrain and headache—take frequent breaks; avoid glare on the monitor.
- Back and neck pains—use adjustable chairs, tables, monitor stands, keyboards.
- Electromagnetic fields—sit 2 feet from the screen, 3 feet from adjacent computers.
- **Repetitive strain injury (RSI)** including **carpal tunnel syndrome**—avoid with frequent breaks; good posture; healthy lifestyle; and ergonomic keyboards.

Mental Health

Counterproductive mental irritations include:

- Noise from clattering printers and high-frequency squeal from computers.
- Stress from excessive monitoring. Unnatural adaptation to computers can cause **technostress.**

Design

Computers are being designed for easier and healthier use. There is a trend toward simplifying features offered on new models.

Microcomputers are the greatest users of electricity in the workplace. The EPA has established the **Energy Star** program to promote energy-efficient computer use. The computer industry has responded with the concept of the **Green PC.**

The Green PC

The basic elements of the Green PC include:

- System units with energy-saving processors, sleep-mode capability, efficient adapters, and no cooling fans.
- Display units that replace CRT displays with flat panels, use special power-down monitors, and use screen-saver software.
- Manufacturing that eliminates or reduces the use of harmful chemicals such as **chlorofluorocarbons (CFCs),** nickel, and other heavy metals.

Personal Responsibility

As a responsible computer user, you can help protect the environment by:

- Conserving energy by turning off computer systems at night and using screen-savers.
- Recycling paper, computer boxes, packaging materials, printer cartridges, and floppy disks.
- Educating yourself and others about ecological dangers and using ecologically sound products.

KEY TERMS

access (238)
accuracy (237)
ad network cookies (240)
carpal tunnel syndrome (251)
chlorofluorocarbons (CFCs) (254)
cold site (249)
Computer Abuse Amendments Act of 1994 (241)
computer crime (242)
computer ethics (237)
Computer Fraud and Abuse Act of 1986 (241)
Computer Matching and Privacy Protection Act of 1988 (241)
cookie-cutter programs (240)
cookies (240)
cracker (243)
cumulative trauma disorder (251)
data security (248)
denial of service attack (243)
disaster recovery plan (248)
Electronic Communications Privacy Act of 1986 (241)
encrypting (248)
Energy Star (253)
environment (236)
ergonomics (236, 250)
ethics (237)
Fair Credit Reporting Act of 1970 (241)
firewall (248)
Freedom of Information Act of 1970 (241)
Green PC (253)

hacker (242)
history file (240)
hot site (249)
illusion of anonymity (240)
National Information Infrastructure Protection Act of 1996 (241)
No Electronic Theft (NET) Act of 1997 (241)
password (248)
physical security (248)
privacy (236, 237)
Privacy Act of 1974 (241)
property (237)
repetitive motion injury (251)
repetitive strain injury (RSI) (251)
reverse directory (238)
Right to Financial Privacy Act of 1979 (241)
security (236, 247)
snoopware (239)
Software Copyright Act of 1980 (246)
software piracy (246)
spike (247)
surge protector (247)
technostress (252)
traditional cookies (240)
Video Privacy Protection Act of 1988 (241)
virus (243)
virus checker (243)
voltage surge (247)
worm (243)

CHAPTER REVIEW

MULTIPLE CHOICE

Circle the letter or fill in the correct answer.

1. The ethical issue that relates to the responsibility of those who collect data to ensure that the data is correct is _____.
   a. privacy
   b. accuracy
   c. property
   d. access
   e. ethics

2. The ethical issue that concerns the collection and use of data about individuals is _____.
   a. privacy
   b. accuracy
   c. property
   d. access
   e. ethics

3. The largest category of computer criminals is _____.
   a. crackers
   b. hackers
   c. agents
   d. organized criminals
   e. employees

4. _____ is/are concerned with protecting information, hardware, and software.
   a. Users
   b. FBI agents
   c. Security
   d. The Department of Defense
   e. Protection Programs

5. The Clipper Chip and the Key Escrow chip provide _____ to companies.
   a. safety
   b. disaster protection plans
   c. ergonomics
   d. encryption
   e. data security

6. _____ is concerned with protecting hardware from possible human and natural disasters.
   a. Physical security
   b. Data security
   c. The FBI
   d. Encryption
   e. Energy Star

7. _____ is concerned with fitting the job to the worker rather than forcing the worker to contort to fit a job.
   a. Human Resources
   b. Ergonomics
   c. Energy Star
   d. RSI
   e. An HMO

8. _____ is also called repetitive motion injury and cumulative trauma disorder.
   a. RSI
   b. ARD
   c. TVT
   d. EMI
   e. BRM

9. _____ describes the stress that is associated with computers.
   a. RSI
   b. EMI
   c. Technostress
   d. Computer Use Distress
   e. Cumulative TechStress

10. Environmentally friendly system units, display, and manufacturing are the basic elements of the _____.
    a. Energy Star
    b. Green PC
    c. Standard System
    d. Millennium Plan
    e. EarthTech Program

Match each numbered item with the most closely related lettered item. Write your answers in the spaces provided.

a. snoopware

b. computer crime

c. ad network cookies

d. property

e. hacker

f. disaster recovery plan

g. cookie-cutter program

h. cold site

i. cookie

j. ethics

k. firewall

l. viruses

m. reverse directory

n. worm

o. denial of service attack

p. encrypting

q. virus checkers

r. spike

s. illusion of anonimity

t. cracker

1. Standards of moral conduct. _____

2. Relates to who owns data and rights to software. _____

3. Directory that lists subscriber names followed by telephone numbers. _____

4. Programs that record virtually every activity on a computer system. _____

5. Belief that there is little threat to personal privacy via the Internet. _____

6. Specialized programs that record information on Web site visitors. _____

7. Cookies that continually monitor Web activity and report information back to marketing organizations. _____

8. Program that blocks the most intrusive ad network cookies. _____

9. Illegal action involving special knowledge of computer technology. _____

10. Person who gains unauthorized access to a computer system for the fun and challenge of it. _____

11. Person who gains unauthorized access to a computer system for malicious purposes. _____

12. Hidden instructions that migrate through networks and operating systems and become embedded in different programs. _____

13. Fills a computer system with self-replicating information. _____

14. Type of virus that overwhelms Web sites with data making them inaccessible to users. _____

15. Programs that alert users when certain viruses enter a system. _____

16. Excess of electricity that may destroy chips or other electronic computer components. _____

17. Coding information so that only authorized users can read or use it. _____

18. Security hardware and software that controls access to internal computer networks. _____

19. Plan used by large corporations describing ways to continue operations following a disaster until normal computer operations can be restored. _____

20. Special emergency facility in which hardware must be installed but which is available to a company in a the event of a disaster. _____

OPEN-ENDED

On a separate sheet of paper, respond to each question or statement.

1. Discuss the relationship between databases and privacy.

2. Discuss the principles of the Code of Fair Information Act. Why do you think this Act has not been made into law?

3. Discuss the various kinds of computer criminals.

4. What are the principal measures used to protect computer security? What is encryption? How is it used by corporations and individuals?

5. What is ergonomics? How does computer use impact mental health? Physical health? What steps can be taken to alleviate technostress? What is ergonomic design?

1 Virus Protection

Worried about computer viruses? Did you know that others could be intercepting your private e-mail? It is even possible for them to gain access and control over your computer system. Fortunately, Internet security suites are available to help ensure your safety while you are on the Internet. To learn more about this technology, review Making IT Work for You: Virus Protection on pages 244 and 245. Then visit our Web site at http://www.mhhe.com/oleary. Once at that site, play the videos and answer the following questions in a one-page paper: (a) Describe the process for downloading and installing eSafe. (b) What settings were demonstrated for the Personal Firewall? (c) Describe the function of the Sandbox.

2 Anonymous Web Browsing

Are you concerned about others tracking your online activities? Did you know that it is possible to review all the Web sites you visited on a particular computer or network? The Anonymizer is one solution. Visit our site at http://www.mhhe.com/oleary to link to the Anonymizer Web site. Browse a couple of Web sites anonymously, and then answer these questions in a one-page paper: (a) How does Anonymizer ensure anonymity? (b) What are the drawbacks to using Anonymizer for all of your Web activities? (c) What type of monitoring cannot be averted by Anonymizer? (d) Would you use anonymous Web browsing? Why or why not?

Interactive Companion CD-ROM 1

Complete the "Workplace Issues" Lab located on your Interactive Companion CD-ROM, and then answer the following questions in a one-page paper: (a) List and briefly define the security concerns presented in this Lab. (b) What is the most common way hackers gain unauthorized passwords, according to the Lab? (c) Explain the steps that Pretty Good Privacy (PGP) uses to protect data.

Online Backup 2

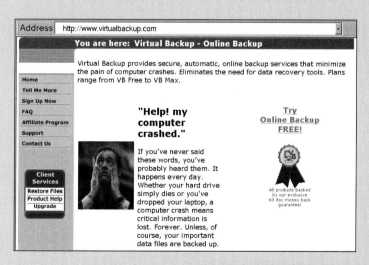

One of the best ways to safeguard important personal or corporate data is to use an online backup service. Research three or four online backup services, and then answer the following questions in a one-page paper: (a) What are the general features of online backup services? (b) What types of emergencies do online backups help with that other backup methods do not? (c) How are backups scheduled? (d) Is this service a replacement for making backups locally? Why or why not?

1 Firewalls

Firewalls are a necessary component of complete computer security. They consist of hardware and software that control access to internal networks. A firewall usually includes a proxy server as a gatekeeper. Write a two-page paper titled "Firewall Security" that addresses the following: (a) Define the term **firewall.** (b) What types of computer crime do firewalls protect against? (c) What types of computer crime are firewalls unable to protect against? Why? (d) What type of firewall protection might a corporation use? (e) What firewall protection is available for home users?

2 Plagiarism

Suspicious of cheating, a professor at the University of Virginia developed a program to compare the term papers of his current and past students. Alarmingly, he found that 122 students' work suggested plagiarizing. Consider the implications of this case, and then answer the following questions in a two-page paper: (a) With more and more academic submissions being stored in an electronic format, how is the ease of copying another's work easier? (b) For the same rea-

son, how is detecting an unoriginal work easier? (c) Have you ever copied and pasted text from a Web site or other electronic document and passed it off as your own? (d) How does "borrowing" work in this way affect other students? What about the original author? Explain.

YOUR FUTURE AND INFORMATION TECHNOLOGY

After you have read this chapter, you should be able to:

1

Explain why it's important to have an individual strategy in order to be a "winner" in the information age.

2

Describe how technology is changing the nature of competition.

3

Discuss three ways people may react to new technology.

4

Describe how you can use your computer competence to stay current and to take charge of your career.

5

Discuss what computer trainers, database administrators, network managers, programmers, systems analysts, technical writers, and Webmasters do.

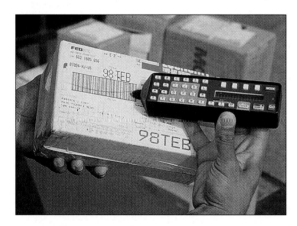

Technology and Organizations
Technology forces organizational change by introducing new ways for businesses to compete

Technology and People
Some people react negatively to technological change by being cynical, naive, or frustrated but the most positive reaction to technological change is to be proactive

Throughout this book, we have emphasized practical subjects that are useful to you now or will be very soon. Accordingly, this final chapter is not about the far future, say, 10 years from now. Rather, it is about today and the near future—about developments whose outlines we can already see. It is about how organizations adapt to technological change. It is also about what you as an individual can do to keep your computer competency up to date.

Are the times changing any faster now than they ever have? It's hard to say. People who were alive when radios, cars, and airplanes were being introduced certainly lived through some dramatic changes. Has technology made our own times even more dynamic? Whatever the answer, it is clear we live in a fast-paced age. The challenge for you as an individual is to devise ways to stay current and to use technology to your advantage. For example, you can use the Web to locate job opportunities.

To stay competent, end users need to recognize the impact of technological change on organizations and people. They need to know how to use change to their advantage and to be winners. Although end users do not need to be specialists in information technology, they should be aware of career opportunities in the area.

Careers in Information Systems
Are varied and command some of the best salaries and job security

Title	Description
Systems analyst	Analyzes, designs, and implements information system
Webmaster	Designs, creates, monitors, and evaluates corporate Web sites
Database administrator	Structures, coordinates, links, and maintains databases
Programmer	Revises existing software and creates new software
Network manager	Monitors existing networks and implements new networks
Technical writer	Creates user manuals and documentation for information systems
Computer trainer	Provides classes and support for computer users

Be a Winner
By staying current, developin specialties, and being aler organizational changes opportunities for inn

> To be a winner in the informa-
> tion revolution, you need an
> individual strategy.

Most businesses have become aware that they must adapt to changing technology or be left behind. Many organizations are now making formal plans to keep track of technology and implement it in their competitive strategies. For example, banks have found that automated teller machines (ATMs) are vital to retail banking. (See Figure 10-1.) Not only do they require fewer human tellers, but they can also be made available 24 hours a day. More and more banks are also trying to go electronic, doing away with paper transactions wherever possible. Thus, ATM cards can now be used in many places to buy gas or groceries. Many banks are also trying to popularize home banking so that customers can use microcomputers for certain financial tasks. In addition, banks are exploring the use of some very sophisticated application programs. These programs will accept cursive writing (the handwriting on checks) directly as input, verify check signatures, and process the check without human intervention.

Figure 10-1 Automated teller machines are examples of technology used in business strategy

Clearly, such changes do away with some jobs—those of many bank tellers and cashiers, for example. However, they create opportunities for other people. New technology requires people who are truly capable of working with it. These are not the people who think every piece of equipment is so simple they can just turn it on and use it. Nor are they those who think each new machine is a potential disaster. In other words, new technology needs people who are not afraid to learn it and are able to manage it. The real issue, then, is not how to make technology better. Rather, it is how to integrate the technology with people.

You are in a very favorable position compared with many other people in industry today. After reading the previous chapters, you have learned more than just the basics of hardware, software, connectivity, and the Internet. You have learned the most *current* technology. You are therefore able to use these tools to your advantage—to be a winner.

How do you become and stay a winner? In brief, the answer is: You must form your own individual strategy for dealing with change. First let us look at how businesses are handling technological change. Then let's look at how people are reacting to these changes. Finally, we will offer a few suggestions that will enable you to keep up with—and profit from—the information revolution.

Concept Check

Cite examples of ways computers are changing the business world.

What are the human requirements of new technology?

CHAPTE

and Information Technology

Technology can introduce new ways for businesses to compete with each other. Some of the principal changes are as follows.

> Technology changes the nature of competition by introducing new products, new enterprises, and new relationships among customers and suppliers.

NEW PRODUCTS

Technology creates products that operate faster, are priced cheaper, are often of better quality, or are wholly new. Indeed, new products can be individually tailored to a particular customer's needs. For example, financial services company Merrill Lynch took advantage of technology to launch a cash management account. This account combines information on a person's checking, savings, credit card, and securities accounts into a single monthly statement. It automatically sets aside "idle" funds into interest-bearing money market funds. Customers can access their accounts on the Web and get a complete picture of their financial condition at any time. However, even if they don't pay much attention to their statements, their surplus funds are invested automatically.

NEW ENTERPRISES

Information technology can build entirely new businesses. Two examples are Internet service providers and Web site development companies.

* Just a few years ago, the only computer connectivity options available to individuals were through online service providers like America Online and through colleges and universities. Now, hundreds of national service providers and thousands of local service providers are available.
* Thousands of small companies specializing in Web site development have sprung up in the past three years. These companies help small- to medium-sized organizations by providing assistance in evaluating, creating, and maintaining Web sites. Large organizations employ specialists called **Webmasters** to provide this type of support.

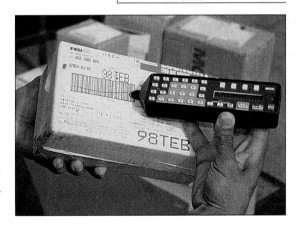

Figure 10-2 New technology helps Federal Express maintain customer loyalty

NEW CUSTOMER AND SUPPLIER RELATIONSHIPS

Businesses that make their information systems easily available may make their customers less likely to take their business elsewhere. For instance, Federal Express, the overnight package delivery service, does everything possible to make its customers dependent on it. Upon request, customers receive airbills with their name, address, and account number preprinted on them, making shipping and billing easier. Package numbers are scanned into the company's information system so that they can be tracked from pickup point to destination. (See Figure 10-2.) Thus, apprehensive customers can be informed very quickly of the exact location of their package as it travels toward its destination.

Concept Check

 How does technology change the nature of competition among businesses?

 What role do Webmasters play in an organization?

> People may be cynical, naïve, frustrated, or proactive in response to technology.

Clearly, recent technological changes, and those sure to come in the near future, will produce significant changes and opportunities in the years ahead. How should we be prepared for them?

People have different coping styles when it comes to technology. It has been suggested, for instance, that people react to changing technology in one of four ways. These ways are *cynicism, naïveté, frustration,* and *proactivity.*

Figure 10-3 The cynic: "These gadgets are overrated."

CYNICISM

The **cynic** feels that, for a manager at least, the idea of using a microcomputer is overrated. (See Figure 10-3.) Learning and using it take too much time, time that could be delegated to someone else. Doing spreadsheets and word processing, according to the cynic, are tasks that managers should understand. However, the cynic feels that such tasks take time away from a manager's real job of developing plans and setting goals for the people being supervised.

Cynics may express their doubts openly, especially if they are top managers. Or, they may only pretend to be interested in microcomputers, when actually they are not interested at all.

NAIVETE

Many **naïve** people are unfamiliar with computers. They may think computers are magic boxes capable of solving all kinds of problems that computers really can't handle. In contrast, some naïve persons are actually quite familiar with computers. However, such people underestimate the difficulty of changing computer systems or of generating information.

FRUSTRATION

The **frustrated** person may already be quite busy and may hate having to take time to learn about microcomputers. Such a person feels it is an imposition to have to learn something new. Often she or he is too impatient to try to understand the manuals explaining what hardware and software are supposed to do. The result, therefore, is continual frustration. (See Figure 10-4.) Some people are frustrated because they try to do too much. Or they're frustrated because they find manuals difficult to understand. Oftentimes they feel stupid when actually the manuals are at fault.

PROACTIVITY

Webster's Collegiate Dictionary defines **proactive**, in part, as "acting in anticipation of future problems, needs, or changes." A proactive person looks at technology in a positive realistic way. (See Figure 10-5.) They are not cynics, underestimating the likely impact of technology on their lives. They are not naïve, overestimating the ability of technology to solve the world's or their problems. They do not easily become frustrated and give up using technology. Proactive people are positive in their outlook and look at new technology as providing new tools that when correctly applied can positively impact their lives.

Most of us fall into one of the four categories. Cynicism, naïveté, frustration, and proactivity are common human responses to change. Do you see yourself or others around you responding to technology in any of these ways?

Figure 10-4 The frustrated: "This stuff doesn't make sense half the time."

Figure 10-5 The proactive: "How can I use this new tool?"

For those who respond negatively, just being aware of their reaction can help them become more positive and proactive to tomorrow's exciting new changes in technology.

Concept Check

 Describe four ways people cope with technological changes in the workplace.

How do proactive people view technological change?

HOW YOU CAN BE A WINNER

So far we have described how progressive organizations are using technology in the information age. Now let's concentrate on you as an individual. (See Making IT Work for You: Locating Job Opportunities Online on pages 396–397.) How can you stay ahead? Here are some ideas.

> Individuals need to stay current, develop specialties, and be alert to organizational changes and opportunities for innovation.

STAY CURRENT

Whatever their particular line of work, successful professionals keep up both with their own fields and with the times. We don't mean you should try to become a computer expert and read a lot of technical magazines. Rather, you should concentrate on your profession and learn how computer technology is being used within it.

Every field has trade journals, whether the field is interior design, personnel management, advertising, or whatever. Most such journals regularly present articles about the uses of computers. It's important that you also belong to a trade or industry association and go to its meetings. Many associations sponsor seminars and conferences that describe the latest information and techniques.

LOCATING JOB OPPORTUNITIES ONLINE

Did you know that you could use the Internet to find a job? You can browse through job listings, post resumes for prospective employers, and even use special agents to continually search for that job that's just right for you.

How It Works There are several Web sites designed to bring together prospective employers and employees. These sites maintain a database of available jobs and a database of resumes. Individuals are able to post resumes and to search through available jobs. Organizations are able to post job opportunities and to search through individual resumes.

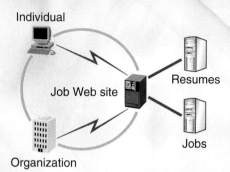

Browsing Jobs Listings Three well-known job search sites on the Web are hotjobs.com, yahoo!jobs, and monster.com. You can connect to these sites and browse through job opportunities.

For example, after connecting to monster.com, you can search for a job by following the steps similar to those shown below.

1
● Connect to *www.monster.com.*
● Click the *Search Jobs* link.

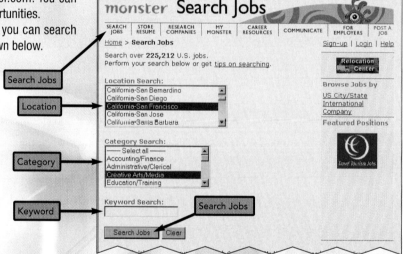

2
● Select a location to search.
● Select a category to search.
● Optionally, enter any keywords to search.
● Click *Search Jobs.*

3
● Select a job title to learn more about a job posting.

A detailed job posting, including description, company information, and contact information is displayed.

Posting Your Resume To make your qualifications known to prospective employers, you can post your resume at the job search site.

1
- Select *My Monster*.
- Select *Create a new account*.
- Follow the on-screen instructions to create an account.

2
- Log onto your new account.
- Select *Submit Resume*.
- Complete the on-screen resume form.
- Click *Submit Resume*.

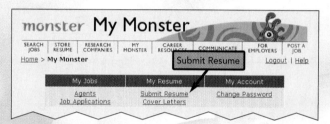

Creating an Agent You can automate the job search process by creating an agent. The agent monitors new job listings and notifies you by e-mail whenever a new job fits your criteria.

1
- Log onto your account.
- Select *Agents*.

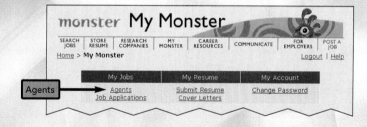

2
- Enter keyword to describe the job you want.
- Respond to a series of drop-down boxes to specify location preference, job categories, and how often you would like to be notified of new job listings.

Your agent will search new job listings and alert you to new opportunites by e-mail.

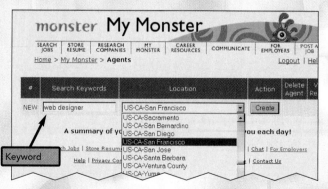

The Web is continually changing and some of the specifics presented in this Making IT Work for You may have changed. See our Web site at http://www. mhhe.com/oleary for possible changes and to learn more about this application of technology.

Figure 10-6 PC World on the Web

Another way to stay current is by participating electronically with special-interest newsgroups on the Internet.

MAINTAIN YOUR COMPUTER COMPETENCE

Actually, you should try to stay *ahead* of the technology. Books, journals, and trade associations are the best sources of information about new technology that applies to your field. The general business press—*Business Week, Fortune, Inc., The Wall Street Journal,* and the business section of your local newspaper—also carries computer-related articles.

However, if you wish, you can subscribe to a magazine that covers microcomputers and information more specifically. Examples are *InfoWorld, PC World,* and *MacWorld.* You may also find it useful to look at newspapers and magazines that cover the computer industry as a whole. An example of such a periodical is *ComputerWorld.* Most of these magazines also have an online version available on the Web. (See Figure 10-6.)

DEVELOP PROFESSIONAL CONTACTS

Besides being members of professional associations, successful people make it a point to maintain contact with others in their field. They stay in touch by telephone, e-mail, and newsgroups and go to lunch with others in their line of work. Doing this lets them learn what other people are doing in their jobs. It tells them what other firms are doing and what tasks are being automated. Developing professional contacts can keep you abreast not only of new information but also of new job possibilities. (See Figure 10-7.) It also offers social benefits. An example of a professional organization found in many areas is the local association of realtors.

DEVELOP SPECIALTIES

Figure 10-7 Professional organizations and contacts help you keep up in your field

Develop specific as well as general skills. You want to be well-rounded within your field, but certainly not a "jack of all trades, master of none." Master a trade or two *within* your profession. At the same time, don't become identified with a specific technological skill that might very well become obsolete.

The best advice is to specialize to some extent. However, don't make your specialty so tied to technology that you'll be in trouble if the technology shifts. For example, if your career is in marketing or graphics design, it makes sense to learn about desktop publishing and Web page design. (See Figure 10-8.) That way you can learn to make high-quality, inexpensive graphics layouts. It would not make as much sense for you to become an expert on, say, the various types of monitors used to display the graphics layouts, because such monitors are continually changing.

Expect to take classes during your working life to keep up with developments in your field. Some professions require more keeping up than others— a computer specialist, for example, compared to a human resources manager. Whatever the training required, always look for ways to adapt and improve your skills to become more productive and marketable. There may be times when you are tempted to start all over again and learn completely new skills. However, a better course of action may be to use emerging technology to improve your present base of skills. This way you can build on your current strong points and then branch out to other fields from a position of strength.

BE ALERT FOR ORGANIZATIONAL CHANGE

Every organization has formal lines of communication—for example, supervisor to middle manager to top manager. However, there is also the *grapevine*—informal lines of communication. (See Figure 10-9.) Some service departments will serve many layers of management and be abreast of the news on all levels. For instance, the art director for advertising may be aware of several aspects of a companywide marketing campaign. Secretaries and administrative assistants know what is going on in more than one area.

Being part of the office grapevine can alert you to important changes—for instance, new job openings—that can benefit you. However, you always have to assess the validity of what you hear on the grapevine. Moreover, it's not advisable to be a contributor to office gossip. Behind-the-back criticisms of other people have a way of getting back to the person criticized.

Be especially alert for new trends within the organization—about future hiring, layoffs, automation, mergers with other companies, and the like. Notice which areas are receiving the greatest attention from top management. One tip-off is to see what kind of outside consultants are being brought in. Independent consultants are usually invited in because a company believes it needs advice in an area with which it has insufficient experience.

LOOK FOR INNOVATIVE OPPORTUNITIES

You may understand your job better than anyone—even if you've only been there a few months. Look for ways to make it more efficient. How can present procedures be automated? How can new technology make your tasks easier? Discuss your ideas with your supervisor, the training director, or the head of the information systems department. Or discuss them with someone else who can see that you get the recognition you deserve. (Co-workers may or may not be receptive and may or may not try to take credit themselves.)

A good approach is to present your ideas in terms of saving money rather than "improving information." Managers are generally more impressed with ideas that can save dollars than with ideas that seem like potential breakthroughs in the quality of decisions.

In general, it's best to concentrate on the business and organizational problems that need solving. Then look for a technological way of solving them. That is, avoid becoming too enthusiastic about a particular technology and then trying to make it fit the work situation.

Figure 10-8 Desktop publishing: a good specialty to develop for certain careers

Figure 10-9 Informal communication can alert you to important organizational changes

Concept Check

✔ Outline the strategies you can use to stay ahead and be successful in your career.

✔ Discuss the advantages and disadvantages of specialization.

Employment opportunities in information systems are excellent.

Being a winner does not necessarily mean having a career in information systems. There are, however, several jobs within information systems that you might like to consider. Some are *systems analyst, Webmaster, database administrator, programmer, network manager,* and *computer support specialist.*

SYSTEMS ANALYST

The occupation of **systems analyst** is one of the fastest growing and is expected to almost double by the year 2005. As a systems analyst, you would work with other individuals within an organization to evaluate their information needs, design computer software and hardware to meet those needs, and then implement the information systems.

WEBMASTER

One of the newest and highest-demand occupations is **Webmaster.** As a Webmaster, your duties would focus on designing, creating, monitoring, and evaluating corporate Web sites. As organizations are using more intranets and extranets, the importance and demand for Webmasters will continue to increase. Webmasters combine technical Internet skills with design and layout expertise. (See Figure 10-10.)

Figure 10-10 Webmaster at work

DATABASE ADMINISTRATOR

Database administrators play a critical role in large organizations. They are responsible for structuring, coordinating, linking, and maintaining internal databases. Additionally, they are involved with selecting and monitoring external databases including Internet databases. As a database administrator, you likely would use specialized database techniques such as data mining and data warehousing.

PROGRAMMER

Another high-demand profession is that of **programmer.** Programmers typically work closely with a systems analyst to either create new software or to revise existing programs. As a programmer you likely would use programming languages like C++ and Java.

NETWORK MANAGER

Nearly all information systems within an organization are connected by networks. **Network managers** ensure that existing information and communication systems are operating effectively and that new communication systems are implemented as needed. (See Figure 10-11.) The importance of this occupation within most organizations is increasing dramatically as the Internet plays a larger role in corporate communications. As a network manager, you would also be responsible for ensuring computer security and individual privacy.

Figure 10-11 Network managers monitor and develop new communication systems

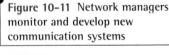

COMPUTER SUPPORT SPECIALISTS

The demand for **computer support specialists** is expected to double in the next few years. These specialists include technical writers, computer trainers, computer technicians, and help desk specialists.

- **Technical writers** explain, in writing, how information systems and programs work.

Figure 10-12 Computer trainers teach others about new systems and software

Title	Description
Systems analyst	Analyzes, designs, and implements information systems
Webmaster	Designs, creates, monitors, and evaluates corporate Web sites
Database administrator	Structures, coordinates, links, and maintains databases
Programmer	Revises existing software and creates new software
Network manager	Monitors existing networks and implements new networks
Technical writer	Creates user manuals and documentation for information systems
Computer trainer	Provides classes and support for computer users

Figure 10-13 Careers in information systems

- **Computer trainers** prepare and present classes to teach application software and to instruct users on how to use the organization's information systems. (See Figure 10-12.)
- **Computer technicians** install hardware and software as well as trouble-shoot problems for users.
- **Help desk specialists** typically provide telephone support for end users within the organization. They respond to a variety of requests including advice on how to use specific software applications and how to use the organization's networks.

For a summary of careers in information systems, see Figure 10-13.

Concept Check

✓ What are some employment opportunities in the field of information systems?

✓ Describe the various types of computer support specialists.

A Look to the Future

Being Computer Competent Means Taking Positive Control of the Rest of Your Life

This is not the end; it is the beginning. Being a skilled computer end user —being computer competent—is not a matter of thinking "Someday I'll have to learn all about that." It is a matter of living in the present and keeping an eye on the future. It is also a matter of having the discipline to keep up with the prevailing technology. It is not a matter of focusing on vague "what ifs." It is a matter of concentrating on your goals and learning how the computer can help you achieve them. Being an end user, in short, is not about trying to avoid failure. Rather, it is about always moving toward success—about taking control over the exciting new tools available to you.

A Look to the Future

TECHNOLOGY AND ORGANIZATIONS

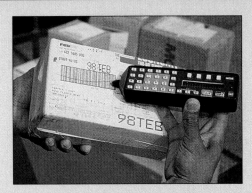

Technology can introduce new ways for businesses to compete with each other. They can compete by creating *new products,* establishing *new enterprises,* and developing *new customer and supplier relationships.*

New Products

Technology creates products that operate faster, are priced more cheaply, are often better quality, or are wholly new. New products can be individually tailored to a particular customer's needs.

New Enterprises

Technology can build entirely new businesses. Two examples:

- Internet service providers—just a few years ago, only a few Internet service providers like America Online were available. Now, thousands of national and local providers are available.
- Web site development companies—thousands of small companies specializing in developing Web sites have sprung up in just the past three years.

New Customer and Supplier Relationships

Businesses that make their information systems easily available may make their customers less likely to take their business elsewhere (e.g., overnight delivery services closely track packages and bills).

TECHNOLOGY AND PEOPLE

People have different coping styles when it comes to technology. Four common reactions to new technology are *cynicism, naïveté, frustration,* and *proactivity.*

Cynicism

The cynics feel that new technology is overrated and too troublesome to learn. Some cynics openly express their doubts. Others pretend to be interested.

Naïveté

Naïve people may be unfamiliar or quite familiar with computers. Unfamiliar ones tend to think of computers as magic boxes. Even those familiar with technology often underestimate the time and difficulty of using technology to generate information.

Frustration

Frustrated users are impatient and irritated about taking time to learn new technology. Often these people have too much to do, find manuals difficult to understand, and/or feel stupid.

Proactivity

A proactive person looks at technology in a positive and realistic way. He or she is not cynical, naïve, or frustrated regarding new technology. Proactive people are positive and look at new technology as providing new tools that can positively impact their lives.

To stay competent, you need to recognize the impact of technological change on organizations and people. You need to know how to use change to your advantage and to become a winner. Although you do not need to be a specialist in information technology, you should be aware of career opportunities in the area.

HOW YOU CAN BE A WINNER

Six ongoing activities that can help you be successful are the following.

Stay Current

Read trade journals and the general business press, join professional associations, and participate in interest groups on the Internet.

Maintain Your Computer Competency

Stay current by being alert for computer-related articles in the general business press and in trade journals in your particular profession.

Develop Professional Contacts

Stay active in your profession and meet people in your field. This provides information about other people, firms, job opportunities, and social contacts.

Develop Specialties

Develop specific as well as general skills. Expect to take classes periodically to stay current with your field and technology.

Be Alert for Organizational Change

Use formal and informal lines of communication. Be alert for new trends within the organization.

Look for Innovative Opportunities

Look for ways to increase efficiency. Present ideas in terms of saving money rather than "improving information."

CAREERS IN INFORMATION SYSTEMS

Being a winner does not necessarily mean having a career in information systems. There are, however, some excellent employment opportunities in information systems, including the following.

Systems Analyst

Systems analysts analyze, design, and implement information systems.

Webmaster

Webmasters design, create, monitor, and evaluate corporate Web sites.

Database Administrator

Database administrators structure, coordinate, link, and maintain databases.

Programmer

Programmers revise existing programs and create new software.

Network Managers

Network managers monitor existing networks and implement new ones.

Computer Support Specialist

- **Technical writers**—create documents to explain how information systems and programs work.
- **Computer trainers**—prepare and present classes on software and information systems.
- **Computer technicians**—install hardware and software and troubleshoot problems for users.
- **Help desk specialists**—provide telephone support for end users.

KEY TERMS

computer support specialist (400)
computer technician (401)
computer trainer (401)
cynic (394)
database administrator (400)
frustrated (394)
help desk specialist (401)

naïve (394)
network manager (400)
proactive (394)
programmer (400)
systems analyst (400)
technical writer (400)
Webmaster (393, 400)

CHAPTER REVIEW

MULTIPLE CHOICE

Circle the letter or fill in the correct answer.

1. The real issue with technology is _____.
   a. finding qualified individuals
   b. making it better
   c. integrating it with people
   d. teaching it to students
   e. summarizing it for the general society

2. The principal changes technology brings to business are _____, new enterprises, and new customer and supplier relationships.
   a. new computers
   b. new problems
   c. new agencies
   d. new laws
   e. new products

3. The _____ user believes that learning and using computers take time away from their real jobs.
   a. cynical
   b. proactive
   c. frustrated
   d. confused
   e. naïve

4. The _____ user believes all problems can be solved by computers.
   a. proactive
   b. optimistic
   c. frustrated
   d. naïve
   e. cynical

5. The _____ user does not easily become frustrated and give up using technology.
   a. proactive
   b. cynical
   c. naïve
   d. inexperienced
   e. advanced

6. The best advice in regard to specializing is _____.
   a. don't do it
   b. it is a necessity in today's business world
   c. learn one program and learn it well
   d. learn a little about every program
   e. do so to some extent

7. The field of _____ is expected to almost double by the year 2005.
   a. network manager
   b. systems analyst
   c. Webmaster
   d. programmer
   e. technical writer

8. As organizations are using more intranets and extranets, the importance of and demand for _____ will continue to increase.
   a. network managers
   b. systems analysts
   c. Webmasters
   d. programmers
   e. technical writers

9. The importance of _____ within most organizations is increasing dramatically as the Internet plays a larger role in corporate communications.
   a. network managers
   b. systems analysts
   c. Webmasters
   d. programmers
   e. technical writers

10. The demand for _____ is expected to double in the next few years.
   a. computer support specialists
   b. Webmasters
   c. programmers
   d. network managers
   e. database administrators

Match each numbered item with the most closely related lettered item. Write your answers in the spaces provided.

a. computer technician

b. database administrator

c. computer trainer

d. technical writer

e. proactive

f. systems analyst

g. network manager

h. computer support specialists

i. programmer

j. cynic

k. help desk specialist

l. frustrated

m. Webmaster

1. A computer specialist employed to evaluate, create, and maintain Web sites. _____

2. Computer user who feels the idea of using microcomputers is overrated. _____

3. Computer user who feels it is an imposition to have to take the time to understand technology. _____

4. Computer user who looks at technology in a positive and realistic way. _____

5. Computer professional who studies an organization's systems to determine what actions to take and how to use computer technology to assist them. _____

6. Computer specialist responsible for structuring, coordinating, linking, and maintaining internal databases. _____

7. Computer specialist who creates new software or revises existing software. _____

8. Computer professional who ensures that existing information and communication systems are operating effectively. _____

9. Technical writers, computer trainers, computer technicians, and help desk specialist. _____

10. Computer professional who explains, in writing, how information systems and programs work. _____

11. Computer professional who prepares and presents classes to teach application software. _____

12. Computer professional who installs hardware and software and troubleshoots problems for users. _____

13. Computer professional who provides telephone support for end users within an organization. _____

On a separate sheet of paper, respond to each question or statement.

1. Why is strategy important to individual success in the information age? What is your strategy?

2. Describe how technology changes the nature of competition.

3. How can your computer competencies help you get ahead in today's market?

4. Discuss the role of computer support specialists. What is the difference between a computer technician and a help desk specialist?

5. What does *proactive* mean? What is a proactive computer user? What advantages does this type of user have over the other types?

Jobs Online **1**

Did you know that you can use the Internet to find a job? You can browse through job listings, post resumes for prospective employers, and even use special agents to continually search for that job that's just right for you. To learn more about online job searches, review Making IT Work for You: Locating Job Opportunities Online on pages 396 and 397. Then visit our Web site at http://www.mhhe.com/oleary. Once at that site, play the videos and answer the following questions in a one-page paper: (a) What locations and categories were selected for the job search? (b) Describe the process for posting a resume. (c) What search criteria were used to set up the job search agent?

Maintain Computer Competence **2**

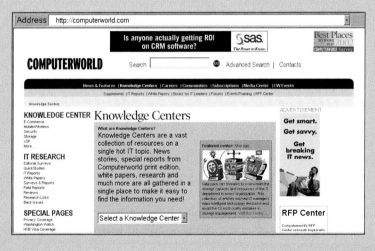

There are several sources of information to help keep you up to date on current computing trends. Visit our Web site at http://www.mhhe.com/oleary to link to a few computing sites. Connect to each and explore, and then answer the following questions in a one-page paper: (a) List the sites you visited and describe the focus of each. (b) Which of these sites was most useful? Why? (c) Which of these sites was least useful? Why? (d) What are other ways you can stay in step with current computing issues?

1 Interactive Companion CD-ROM

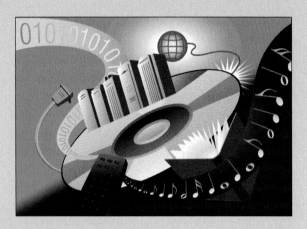

Complete the "Purchasing Decisions" Lab located on your Interactive Companion CD-ROM, and then answer the following questions in a one-page paper: (a) What is the first step in determining what type of computer to buy? (b) What considerations are there for buying a printer? (c) What does "UPS" stand for, and what does a UPS do?

2 Resume Advice

There are several excellent resources available online to help you write a winning resume. Conduct a Web search using the keywords "resume help" to learn more. Review at least five sites, and then compose a sample resume for yourself applying the information from the sites.

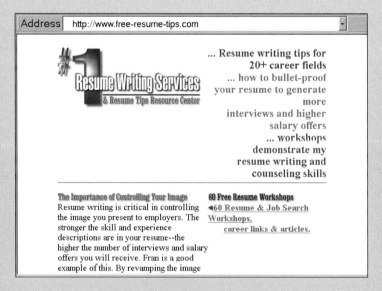

Information Systems Careers 1

The U.S. government is anticipating a need for over one million information systems workers in the next five years. Write a two-page paper titled "Careers in Information Systems" that addresses the following: (a) List and describe the seven types of careers available in IS. (b) Of those seven, single out one that is of particular interest to you and research it further. What types of companies are seeking this type of employee? What are the job requirements?

Job Offers 2

Consider this scenario, and then answer the questions that follow in a two-page paper: You are at a new job for about six months and have stopped actively seeking new employment when you receive an unsolicited offer for a job that seems a better opportunity. (a) What are your obligations to your present company? (b) What are your obligations to yourself? (c) What would you do in this situation? Defend your answer.

THE EVOLUTION OF THE COMPUTER AGE

Many of you probably can't remember a world without computers, but for some of us, computers were virtually unknown when we were born and have rapidly come of age during our lifetime.

Although there are many predecessors to what we think of as the modern computer—reaching as far back as the 18th century, when Joseph Marie Jacquard created a loom programmed to weave cloth and Charles Babbage created the first fully modern computer design (which he could never get to work)—the Computer Age did not really begin until the first computer was made available to the public in 1951.

The modern age of computers spans almost 50 years (thus far), which is typically broken down into five generations. Each generation is marked by a significant advancement in technology:

- **First Generation (1951–57):** During this generation, computers were built with vacuum tubes—electronic tubes that were made of glass and were about the size of light bulbs.

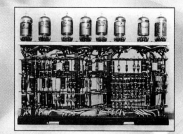

- **Second Generation (1958–63):** This generation begins with the first computers built with transistors—small devices that transfer electronic signals across a resistor. Because transistors are much smaller, use less power, and create less heat than vacuum tubes, the new computers were faster, smaller, and more reliable than the first-generation machines were.

- **Third Generation (1964–69):** In 1964, computer manufacturers began replacing transistors with integrated circuits. An integrated circuit (IC) is a complete electronic circuit on a small chip made of silicon (one of the most abundant elements in the earth's crust). These computers were more reliable and compact than computers made with transistors, and they cost less to manufacture.

- **Fourth Generation (1970–90):** There are many key advancements that were made during this generation, the most significant of which was the use of the microprocessor—a specialized chip developed for computer memory and logic. This revolutionized the computer industry by making it possible to use a single chip to create a smaller "personal" computer (as well as digital watches, pocket calculators, copy machines, and so on).

- **Fifth Generation (1991–2000 and beyond):** Our current generation has been referred to as the "Connected Generation" because of the industry's massive effort to increase the connectivity of computers. The rapidly expanding Internet, World Wide Web, and intranets have created an information superhighway that has enabled both computer professionals and home computer users to communicate with others across the globe.

This appendix provides you with a timeline that describes some of the most significant events in each generation.

First Generation
The Vacuum Tube Age

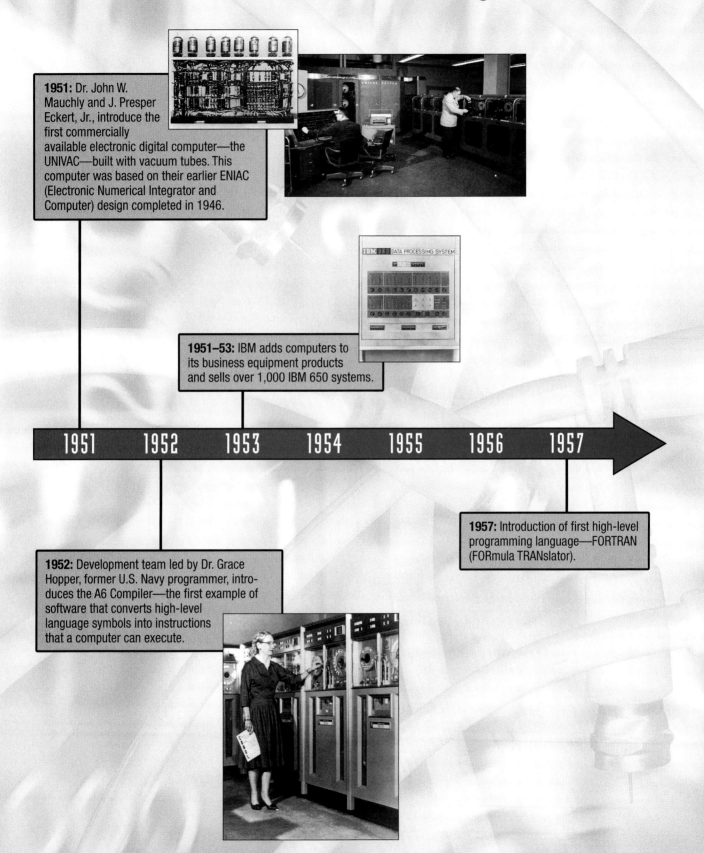

1951: Dr. John W. Mauchly and J. Presper Eckert, Jr., introduce the first commercially available electronic digital computer—the UNIVAC—built with vacuum tubes. This computer was based on their earlier ENIAC (Electronic Numerical Integrator and Computer) design completed in 1946.

1951–53: IBM adds computers to its business equipment products and sells over 1,000 IBM 650 systems.

| 1951 | 1952 | 1953 | 1954 | 1955 | 1956 | 1957 |

1957: Introduction of first high-level programming language—FORTRAN (FORmula TRANslator).

1952: Development team led by Dr. Grace Hopper, former U.S. Navy programmer, introduces the A6 Compiler—the first example of software that converts high-level language symbols into instructions that a computer can execute.

Second Generation
The Transistor Age

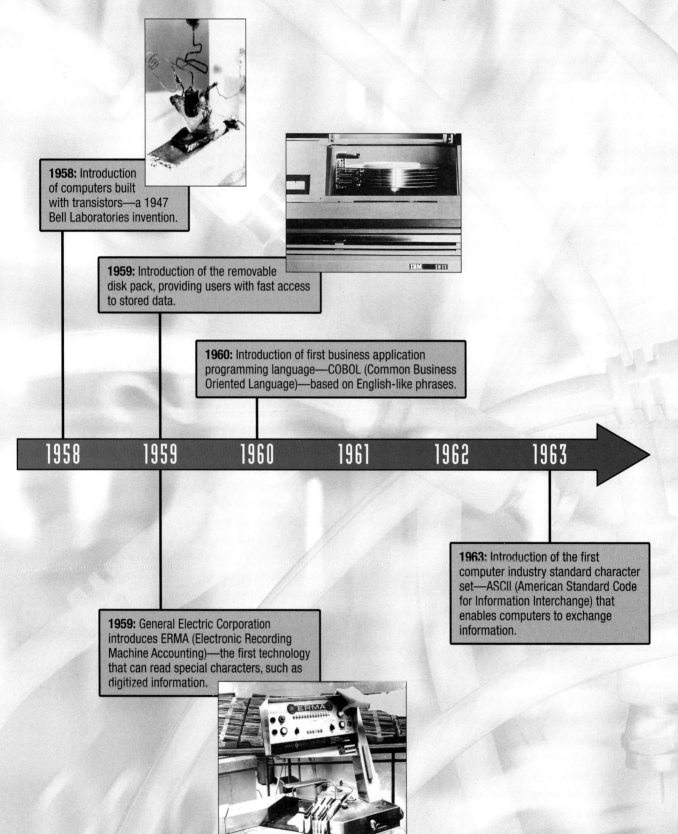

1958: Introduction of computers built with transistors—a 1947 Bell Laboratories invention.

1959: Introduction of the removable disk pack, providing users with fast access to stored data.

1960: Introduction of first business application programming language—COBOL (Common Business Oriented Language)—based on English-like phrases.

1958 1959 1960 1961 1962 1963

1963: Introduction of the first computer industry standard character set—ASCII (American Standard Code for Information Interchange) that enables computers to exchange information.

1959: General Electric Corporation introduces ERMA (Electronic Recording Machine Accounting)—the first technology that can read special characters, such as digitized information.

Third Generation
The Integrated Circuit Age

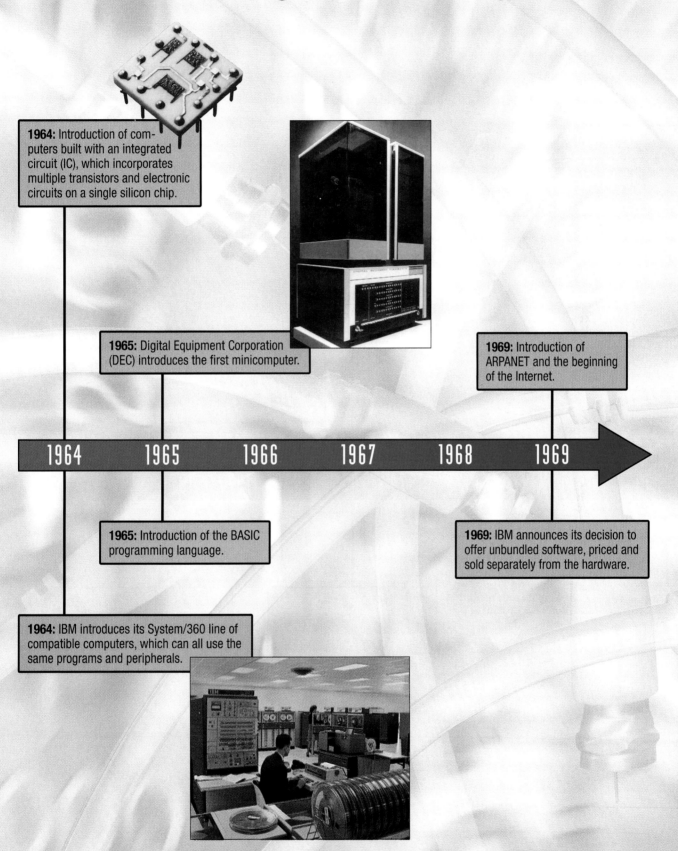

1964: Introduction of computers built with an integrated circuit (IC), which incorporates multiple transistors and electronic circuits on a single silicon chip.

1965: Digital Equipment Corporation (DEC) introduces the first minicomputer.

1969: Introduction of ARPANET and the beginning of the Internet.

1964   1965   1966   1967   1968   1969

1965: Introduction of the BASIC programming language.

1969: IBM announces its decision to offer unbundled software, priced and sold separately from the hardware.

1964: IBM introduces its System/360 line of compatible computers, which can all use the same programs and peripherals.

Fourth Generation
The Microprocessor Age

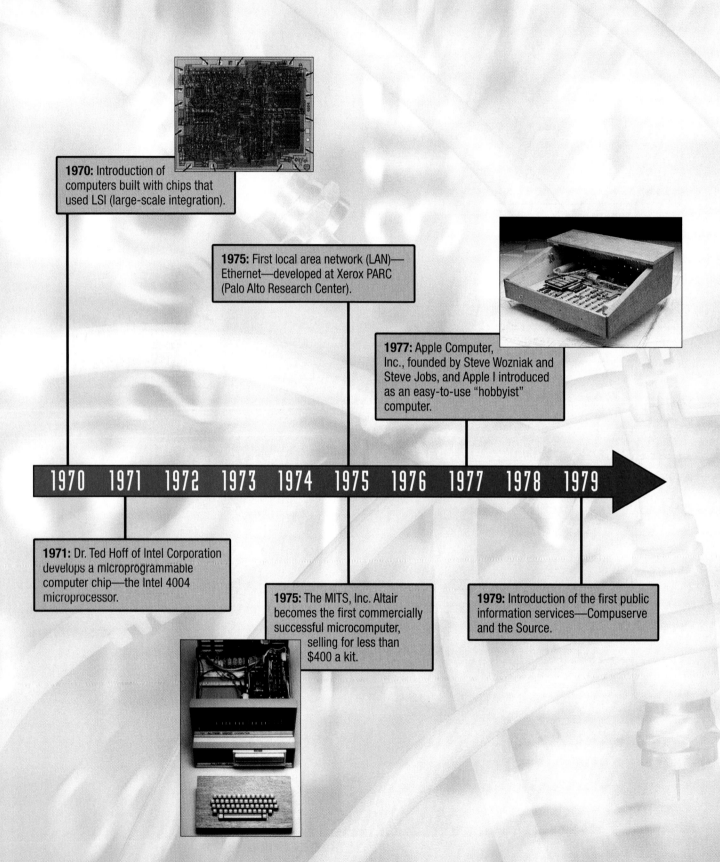

1970: Introduction of computers built with chips that used LSI (large-scale integration).

1975: First local area network (LAN)—Ethernet—developed at Xerox PARC (Palo Alto Research Center).

1977: Apple Computer, Inc., founded by Steve Wozniak and Steve Jobs, and Apple I introduced as an easy-to-use "hobbyist" computer.

1970 1971 1972 1973 1974 1975 1976 1977 1978 1979

1971: Dr. Ted Hoff of Intel Corporation develops a microprogrammable computer chip—the Intel 4004 microprocessor.

1975: The MITS, Inc. Altair becomes the first commercially successful microcomputer, selling for less than $400 a kit.

1979: Introduction of the first public information services—Compuserve and the Source.

1980: IBM asks Microsoft founder, Bill Gates, to develop an operating system—MS DOS—for the soon-to-be released IBM personal computer.

1981: Introduction of the IBM PC, which contains an Intel microprocessor chip and Microsoft's MS-DOS operating system.

1989: Introduction of Intel 486—the first 1,000,000 transistor microprocessor.

| 1980 | 1981 | 1982 | 1983 | 1984 | 1985 | 1986 | 1987 | 1988 | 1989 | 1990 |

1984: Apple introduces the Macintosh Computer, with a unique, easy-to-us graphical user interface.

1985: Microsoft introduces their Windows graphical user interface.

1990: Microsoft releases Windows 3.0, with an enhanced graphical user interface and the ability to run multiple applications.

Fifth Generation
The Age of Connectivity

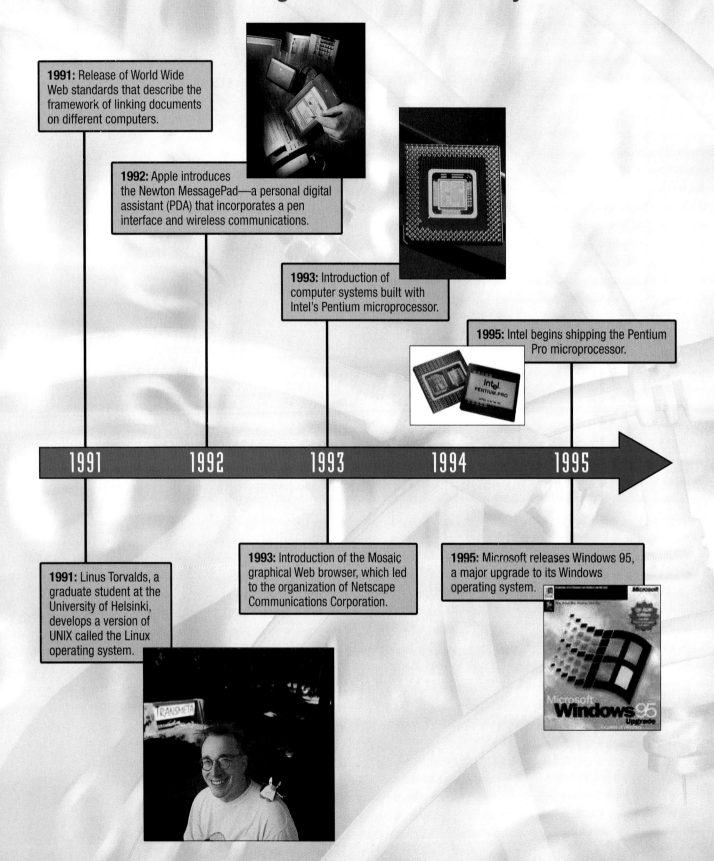

1991: Release of World Wide Web standards that describe the framework of linking documents on different computers.

1992: Apple introduces the Newton MessagePad—a personal digital assistant (PDA) that incorporates a pen interface and wireless communications.

1993: Introduction of computer systems built with Intel's Pentium microprocessor.

1995: Intel begins shipping the Pentium Pro microprocessor.

1991   1992   1993   1994   1995

1991: Linus Torvalds, a graduate student at the University of Helsinki, develops a version of UNIX called the Linux operating system.

1993: Introduction of the Mosaic graphical Web browser, which led to the organization of Netscape Communications Corporation.

1995: Microsoft releases Windows 95, a major upgrade to its Windows operating system.

The Evolution of the Computer Age

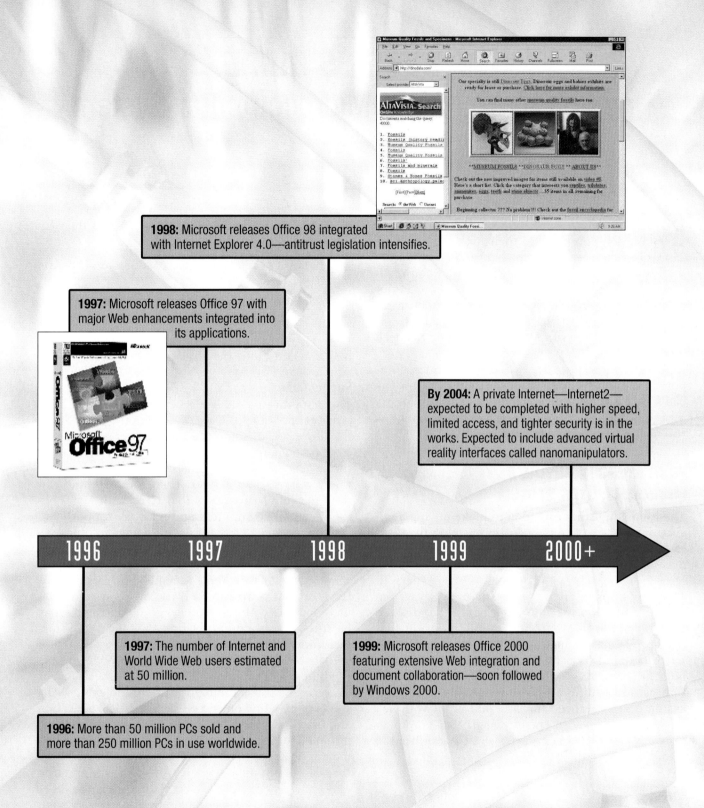

1998: Microsoft releases Office 98 integrated with Internet Explorer 4.0—antitrust legislation intensifies.

1997: Microsoft releases Office 97 with major Web enhancements integrated into its applications.

By 2004: A private Internet—Internet2—expected to be completed with higher speed, limited access, and tighter security is in the works. Expected to include advanced virtual reality interfaces called nanomanipulators.

1996   1997   1998   1999   2000+

1997: The number of Internet and World Wide Web users estimated at 50 million.

1999: Microsoft releases Office 2000 featuring extensive Web integration and document collaboration—soon followed by Windows 2000.

1996: More than 50 million PCs sold and more than 250 million PCs in use worldwide.

Fifth Generation: The Age of Connectivity

Some people make snap judgments about some of the biggest purchases in their lives: cars, college educations, houses. People have been known to buy such things based solely on an ad, a brief conversation, or a one-time look. They may be making an impulsive decision about something costing thousands of dollars. Who is to blame, then, if they are disappointed later? They simply didn't take time to check it out.

The same concerns apply in buying a microcomputer system. You can make your choice on the basis of a friend's enthusiasm or a salesperson's promises. Or you can proceed more deliberately, as you would, say, in looking for a job.

FOUR STEPS IN BUYING A MICROCOMPUTER SYSTEM

The following is not intended to make buying a microcomputer an exhausting experience. Rather, it is to help you clarify your thinking about what you need and can afford.

The four steps in buying a microcomputer system are presented on the following pages. We divided each step into two parts on the assumption that your needs may change, but so may the money you have to spend on a microcomputer. For instance, later in your college career or after college graduation, you may want a far more powerful computer system than you need now. At that point you may have more money to spend. Or, if your employer provides you with a computer, you may not need to spend money at all.

STEP 1

What Needs Do I Want a Computer to Serve?

The trick is to distinguish between your needs and your wants. Sure, you *want* a cutting-edge system powerful enough to hold every conceivable program you'll ever need. And you want a system fast enough to process them all at the speed of light. But do you

need this? Your main concern is to address the two-part question:

- What do I need a computer system to do for me today?
- What will I need it to do for me in another year or two?

The questionnaire at the end of this guide will help you determine the answers to both questions.

Suggestions

The first thing to establish is whether you need a computer at all. Some colleges offer computer facilities at the library or in some dormitories. Or perhaps you can borrow a roommate's. The problem, however, is that when you are up against a term-paper deadline, many others may be also. Then, the machine you want may not be available. To determine the availability of campus computers and network support, call the computer center or the dean of students' office.

Another matter on which you might want advice is what type of computer is popular on campus. Some schools favor Apple Macintoshes, others favor IBMs or IBM-compatibles. If you own a system that's incompatible with most others on campus, you may be stuck if your computer breaks down. Ask someone knowledgeable, who is a year or two ahead of you, if your school favors one system over another.

Finally, look ahead and determine whether your major requires a computer. Business and engineering students may find one a necessity, physical education and drama majors may not. Your major may also determine the kind of computer that's best. A journalism major may want an IBM or IBM-compatible notebook that can be set up anywhere. An architecture major may want a powerful desktop Macintosh with a laser printer that can produce elaborate drawings. Ask your academic advisor for some recommendations.

Example

Suppose you are a college student beginning your sophomore year, with no major declared. Looking at the courses you will likely take this year, you decide you will probably need a computer mainly for word processing. That is, you need a system that will help you write short (10- to 20-page) papers for a variety of courses.

By this time next year, however, you may be an accounting major. Having talked to some juniors and seniors, you find that courses in this major, such as financial accounting, will require you to use elaborate spreadsheets. Or maybe you will be a fine arts or architecture major. Then you may be required to submit projects for which drawing and painting desktop publishing software would be helpful. Or perhaps you will be out in the job market and will be writing application letters and résumés. In that case, you'll want them to have a professional appearance.

STEP 2

How Much Money Do I Have to Spend on a Computer System?

When you buy your first computer, you are not necessarily buying your last. Thus, you can think about spending just the bare-bones amount for a system that meets your needs while in college. Then you might plan to get another system later on. After all, most college students who own cars (quite often used cars) don't consider those the last cars they'll own.

You know what kind of money you have to spend. Your main concern is to answer this two-part question:

- How much am I prepared to spend on a computer system today?
- How much am I prepared to spend in another year or two?

The questionnaire at the end of this guide asks you this.

Suggestions

You can probably buy a good used computer of some sort for under $300 and a printer for under $50. On the other hand, you might spend $1,000 to $2,500 on a new state-of-the-art system. When upgraded, this computer could meet your needs for the next five years.

There is nothing wrong with getting a used system, if you have a way of checking it out. For a reasonable fee, a computer-repair shop can examine it prior to your purchase. Look at newspaper ads and notices on campus bulletin boards for good buys on used equipment. Also try the Internet. Often the sellers will include a great deal of software and other items (disks, reference materials) with the package. If you stay with recognized brands such as Apple,

IBM, Compaq, or Dell, you probably won't have any difficulties. The exception may be with printers, which, since they are principally mechanical devices, may get a lot of wear and tear. This is even more reason to tell the seller you want a repair shop to examine the equipment before you buy.

If you're buying new equipment, be sure to look for student discounts. Most college bookstores, for instance, offer special prices to students. Mail-order houses also steeply discount their products. These firms run ads in such periodicals as *Computer Shopper* (sold on newsstands) and other magazines as well as the Internet. However, using mail and telephone for repairs and support can be a nuisance. Often you can use the prices advertised by a mail-order house to get local retail computer stores to lower their prices.

Example

Perhaps you have access to a microcomputer at the campus student computing center, the library, or the dormitory. Or you can borrow a friend's. However, this computer isn't always available when it's convenient for you. Moreover, you're not only going to college but also working, so both time and money are tight. Having your own computer would enable you to write papers when it's convenient for you. Spending more than $350 might cause real hardship, so a new microcomputer system may be out of the question. You'll need to shop the newspaper classified ads or the campus bulletin boards to find a used but workable computer system.

Or, maybe you can afford to spend more now—say, between $1,000 and $2,000—but probably only $500 next year. By this time next year, however, you'll know your major and how your computer needs have changed. For example, if you're going to be a finance major, you need to have a lot more computer memory (primary storage). This will hold the massive amounts of data you'll be working with in your spreadsheets. Or maybe you'll be an architecture major or graduating and looking for a job. In that case, you may need a laser printer to produce attractive-looking designs or application letters. Thus, whatever system you buy this year, you'll want to upgrade it next year.

STEP 3

What Kind of Software Will Best Serve My Needs?

Most computer experts urge that you determine what software you need before you buy the hardware. The reasoning here is that some hardware simply won't run the software that is important to you. This is certainly true once you get into *sophisticated* software. Examples include specialized programs available for certain professions (such as certain agricultural or retail-management programs). However, if all you are interested in today are the basic tools of software—word processing, spreadsheet, and communications programs—these are available for nearly all microcomputers. The main caution is that some more recent versions of application software won't run on older hardware. Still, if someone offers you a free computer, don't say no because you feel you have to decide what software you need first. You will no doubt find it sufficient for many general purposes, especially during the early years in college.

That said, you are better served if you follow step 3 after step 2—namely, finding the answers to the two-part question:

- What kind of software will best serve my needs today?
- What kind will best serve my needs in another year or two?

The questionnaire at the end of this guide may help you determine your answers.

Suggestions

No doubt some kinds of application software are more popular on your campus—and in certain departments on your campus—than others. Are freshman and sophomore students mainly writing their term papers in Word, WordPerfect, or Word Pro? Which spreadsheet is most often used by business students: Excel, Lotus 1-2-3, or Quattro Pro? Which desktop publishing program is most favored by graphic arts majors: PageMaker, Ventura Publisher, or Freehand? Do many students use their microcomputers to access the Internet, and, if so, which communications software is the favorite? Do engineering and architecture majors use their own machines for CAD/CAM applications? Start by asking other students and your academic advisor.

If you're looking to buy state-of-the-art software, you'll find plenty of advice in various computer magazines. Several of them rate the quality of newly issued programs. Such periodicals include *Info-World, PC World, PC/Computing,* and *MacWorld.*

Example

Suppose you determine that all you need is software to help you write short papers. In that case, nearly any kind of word processing program would do. You could even get by with some older versions or off-brand kinds of word processing software. This might happen if such software was included in the sale of a used microcomputer that you bought at a bargain price.

But will this software be sufficient a year or two from now? Looking ahead, you guess that you'll major in theater arts and minor in screenwriting, which you may pursue as a career. At that point a simple word processing program won't do. You learn from juniors and seniors in that department that screenplays are written using special screenwriting programs. This is software that's not available for some computers. Or, as an advertising and marketing major, you're expected to turn word-processed promotional pieces into brochures. For this, you need desktop publishing software. Or, as a physics major, you discover you will need to write reports on a word processor that can handle equations. In short, you need to look at your software needs not just for today but also for the near future. You especially want to consider what programs will be useful to you in building your career.

STEP 4

What Kind of Hardware Will Best Serve My Needs?

A bare-bones hardware system might include a three-year-old desktop or notebook computer with a 3½-inch floppy disk drive and a hard-disk drive. It should also include a monitor and a printer. With a newer system, the sky's the limit. On the one hand, as a student—unless you're involved in some very specialized activities—it's doubtful you'll really need such things as voice-input devices, touch screens, scanners, and the like. On the other hand, you will probably need speakers and a CD-ROM or DVD-ROM drive. The choices of equipment are vast.

As with the other steps, the main task is to find the answers to a two-part question:

- What kind of hardware will best serve my needs today?

- What kind will best serve my needs in another year or two?

There are several questions on the questionnaire at the end of this guide to help you determine answers to these concerns.

Suggestions

Clearly, you should let the software be your guide in determining your choice of hardware. Perhaps you've found that the most popular software in your department runs on a Macintosh rather than an IBM-compatible. If so, that would seem to determine your general brand of hardware.

Whether you buy IBM or Macintosh, a desktop or a notebook, we suggest you get a 3½-inch floppy disk drive, a hard-disk drive with at least 2 gigabytes of storage, a DVD-ROM drive, at least 128 megabytes of memory, and an ink-jet printer.

As with software, several computer magazines not only describe new hardware but also issue ratings. See *InfoWorld*, *PC World*, and *MacWorld*, for example.

Example

Right now, let's say, you're mainly interested in using a computer to write papers, so almost anything would do. But you need to look ahead.

Suppose you find that Word seems to be the software of choice around your campus. You find that Word 97 will run well on a Pentium machine with 8 megabytes of memory and a 1-gigabyte hard disk. Although this equipment is now outdated, you find from looking at classified ads that there are many such used machines around. Plus, they cost very little—well under $500 for a complete system.

If you're a history or philosophy major, maybe this is all the hardware and software you need. Indeed, this configuration may be just fine all the way through college. However, some majors, and the careers following them, may require more sophisticated equipment. Your choice then becomes: Should I buy an inexpensive system now that can't be upgraded, then sell it later and buy a better one? Or should I buy at least some of the components of a good system now and upgrade it over the next year or so?

As an advertising major, you see the value of learning desktop publishing. This will be a useful if not essential skill once you embark on a career. In exploring the software, you learn that Word includes some desktop publishing capabilities. However, the hardware you previously considered simply isn't sufficient. Moreover, you learn from reading about software and talking to people in your major that there are better desktop publishing programs. Specialized desktop publishing programs like Ventura Publisher are considered more versatile than Word. Probably the best software arrangement, in fact, is to have Word as a word processing program and Ventura Publisher for a desktop publishing program.

To be sure, the campus makes computers that will run this software available to students. If you can afford it, however, you're better off having your own. Now, however, we're talking about a major expense. A computer running a Pentium III microprocessor, with 256 megabytes of memory, a 3½-inch disk drive, a DVD-ROM disk drive, and a 10-gigabyte hard disk, plus a modem, color monitor, and laser printer, could cost in excess of $1,500.

Perhaps the best idea is to buy now, knowing how you would like your system to grow in the future. That is, you will buy a microcomputer with a Pentium III microprocessor. But at this point, you will buy only an ink-jet printer and not buy a DVD-ROM drive. Next year or the year following, you might sell off the less sophisticated peripheral devices and add a DVD-ROM drive and a laser printer.

DEVELOPING A PHILOSOPHY ABOUT COMPUTER PURCHASING

It's important not to develop a case of "computer envy." Even if you bought the latest, most expensive microcomputer system, in a matter of months, something better will come along. Computer technology is still in a very dynamic state, with more powerful, versatile, and compact systems constantly hitting the marketplace. So what if your friends have the hottest new piece of software or hardware? The main question is: Do you need it to solve the tasks required of you or to keep up in your field? Or can you get along with something simpler but equally serviceable?

VISUAL SUMMARY
The Buyer's Guide:
How to Buy Your Own Microcomputer System

NEEDS

What do I need a computer system to do for me today? In another year or two?

I wish to use the computer for:

	Today	1–2 years
Word processing—writing papers, letters, memos, or reports	❏	❏
Business or financial applications—balance sheets, sales projections, expense budgets, or accounting problems	❏	❏
Record-keeping and sorting—research bibliographies, scientific data, or address files	❏	❏
Graphic presentations—of business,scientific, or social science data	❏	❏
Online information retrieval—to campus networks, service providers, or the Internet	❏	❏
Publications, design, or drawing—for printed newsletters, architectural drawing, or graphic arts	❏	❏
Multimedia—for video games, viewing, creating, presenting, or research	❏	❏
Other—(specify): _____	❏	❏

BUDGET

How much am I prepared to spend on a system today? In another year or two?

I can spend:

	Today	1–2 years
Under $500	❏	❏
Up to $1,000	❏	❏
Up to $1,500	❏	❏
Up to $2,000	❏	❏
Up to $2,500	❏	❏
Over $3,000 (specify): _____	❏	❏

Buying a Microcomputer System	
Step	**Questions**
1	*My needs:* What do I need a computer system to do for me today? In another year or two?
2	*My budget:* How much am I prepared to spend on a system today? In another year or two?
3	*My software:* What kind of software will best serve my needs today? In another year or two?
4	*My hardware:* What kind of hardware will best serve my needs today? In another year or two?

To help clarify your thinking about buying a microcomputer system, complete the questionnaire by checking the appropriate boxes.

SOFTWARE

What kinds of software will best serve my needs today? In another year or two?

The application software I need includes:

	Today	1–2 years
Word processing—Word, WordPerfect, Word Pro, or other (specify): _____	❏	❏
Spreadsheet—Excel, Lotus 1-2-3, Quattro Pro, or other (specify): _____	❏	❏
Database—Access, Paradox, Approach, or other (specify): _____	❏	❏
Presentation graphics— PowerPoint, Freelance, CorelPresentations, or other (specify): _____	❏	❏
Browsers—Netscape Navigator, Microsoft Internet Explorer, or other (specify): _____	❏	❏
Other—integrated packages, software suites, graphics, multimedia, Web Authoring, CAD/CAM, other (specify): _____	❏	❏

The system software I need:

	Today	1–2 years
Windows 98	❏	❏
Windows 2000	❏	❏
Windows XP	❏	❏
Mac OS	❏	❏
UNIX	❏	❏
Other (specify): _____	❏	❏

HARDWARE

What kinds of hardware will best serve my needs today? In another year or two?

The hardware I need includes:

	Today	1–2 years
Microprocessor—Pentium III, Pentium II, Power PC, other (specify): _____	❏	❏
Memory—(specify amount): _____	❏	❏
Monitor—size (specify): _____	❏	❏
Floppy disk drives—3½" and/or Zip (specify): _____	❏	❏
Optical disk drive—CD-ROM, DVD-ROM (specify type, speed, and capacity): _____	❏	❏
Hard-disk drive—(specify capacity): _____	❏	❏
Portable computer—laptop, notebook, subnotebook, personal digital assistant (specify): _____	❏	❏
Printer—ink-jet, laser, color (specify): _____	❏	❏
Other—modem, speakers, fax, surge protector (specify): _____	❏	❏

THE UPGRADER'S GUIDE
How to Upgrade Your Microcomputer System

If you own a microcomputer, chances are that your machine is not the latest and greatest. Microcomputers are always getting better—more powerful and faster. While that is a good thing, it can be frustrating trying to keep up.

What can you do? If you have lots of money, you can simply buy a new one. Another alternative is to upgrade or add new components to increase the power and speed of your current microcomputer. You probably can increase your system's performance at a fraction of the cost of a new one.

THREE STEPS IN UPGRADING A MICROCOMPUTER SYSTEM

The following is not intended to detail specific hardware upgrades. Rather, it is intended to help you clarify your thinking about what you need and can afford.

The three steps in upgrading a microcomputer system are presented on the following pages. Each step begins by asking a key question and then provides some suggestions or factors to consider when responding to the question.

Step 1

Is It Time to Upgrade?

Almost any upgrade you make will provide some benefit; the trick is determining if it is worth the monetary investment. It is rarely practical to rebuild an older computer system into a newer model piece by piece. The cost of a complete upgrade typically far exceeds the purchase price of a new system. But if your system is just a piece or two away from meeting your needs, an upgrade may be in order.

Clearly defining what you hope to gain with an upgrade of some of your system's hardware will enable you to make the most relevant and cost-effective selections. Before deciding what to buy, decide what goal you hope to accomplish. Do you want to speed up your computer's performance? Do you need more space to save your files? Is it a new component you'd like to add, such as a DVD-ROM drive?

Suggestions

A good place to start is the documentation on the packaging of any software you use or plan to use. Software manufacturers clearly label the minimum requirements to use their product. These requirements are usually broken down into categories that relate to specific pieces of hardware. For instance, how much RAM (random access memory) does a new program require? How much hard disk space is needed? Keep in mind these ratings are typically the bare minimum. If your system comes very close to the baseline in any particular category, you should still consider an upgrade.

Another thing to investigate is whether there is a software solution that will better serve your needs. For instance, if you are looking to enhance performance or make more room on your hard disk, there are diagnostic and disk optimization utility programs that may solve your problem. In Chapter 3, we discuss a variety of utility programs, such as Norton SystemWorks, that monitor, evaluate, and enhance system performance and storage capacity.

Typical objectives of an upgrade are to improve system performance, increase storage capacity, or add new technology.

Step 2

What Should I Upgrade?

Once you have clearly defined your objectives, the focus shifts to identifying specific components to meet those objectives.

Suggestions

If your objective is to improve performance, three components to consider are RAM, the microprocessor, and expansion cards. If your objective is to increase storage capacity, two components to consider are hard disk drive and Zip disk drive. If you are adding new technology, consider the capability of your current system to support new devices.

Performance

If you want to increase the speed of your computer, consider increasing the amount of RAM. In most cases, this upgrade is relatively inexpensive and will yield the highest performance result per dollar invested. How much your system's performance will increase depends on how much RAM you start with, the size of programs you run, and how often you run large programs.

Another way to increase speed is to replace your system's microprocessor. Processor speed is measured in megahertz (MHz). This rating is not a direct measurement of how fast the processor works, but rather gives you a general idea of how it compares to other processors. (Computing magazines such as PC World often publish articles comparing the relative effectiveness of different processors.) The concept behind a microprocessor upgrade is simple: A faster processor will process faster. This is often an expensive upgrade and not as cost-effective as increasing RAM.

If you are looking at upgrading for a specific type of application, perhaps an expansion card is your answer. Expansion cards connect to slots on the system board, provide specialized support, and often free up resources and increase overall system performance. For example, if you run graphics-intensive programs, such as a drafting program or a video game, a video-card upgrade may be a good buy. An upgraded video card can be used to support higher resolution displays, handle all video data, and speed up overall system performance.

Storage Capacity

It's not hard to know when it's time to upgrade your storage capacity. If you frequently have to delete old files to make way for new ones, then it is probably time for more space. A larger or an additional hard drive is usually the solution. Two things to consider when comparing new hard drives are (1) size, which is usually rated in gigabytes (GB) of data the drive can hold, and (2) seek time, which is a rating of the average time it takes the drive to access any particular piece of data.

If you are storing a lot of data that you no longer use, such as old term papers, you might consider adding a Zip drive. This is usually cheaper and is a good way to archive and transport data. Access time is slower than from a hard drive, so this is an option best suited for infrequently used data or for backing up data.

New Technology

Perhaps you are not looking to modify existing hardware, but would like to add a new device. Examples include large high-resolution monitors, DVD-ROM drives, and high-speed printers.

The key consideration is whether the new device will work with your existing hardware. The requirements for these devices are typically printed on the outside packaging. If not, then refer to the product's operating manuals. Obviously, if your current system cannot support the new technology, you need to evaluate the cost of the new device plus the necessary additional hardware upgrades.

Step 3

Who Should Do the Upgrade?

Once you've decided that the cost of the upgrade is justified and you know what you want to upgrade, the final decision is who is going to do it. Basically, there are two choices. You can either do it yourself or pay for professional installation.

Suggestions

The easiest way, and many times the best way, is to have a professional perform the upgrade. If you select this option, be sure to include the cost of installation in your analysis. If you have had some prior hardware experience or are a bit adventurous, you may want to save some money and do it yourself.

Visit a few computer stores that carry the upgrades you have selected. Most stores that provide the parts will install them as well. Talk with their technical people, describe your system (better yet, bring your system unit to the store), and determine the cost of professional installation. If you are thinking of doing it yourself, ask for their advice. Ask if they will provide assistance if you need it.

If you decide to have the components professionally installed, get the total price in writing and inquire about any guarantees that might exist. Before leaving your system be sure that it is carefully tagged with your name and address. After the service has been completed, pay by credit card and thoroughly test the upgrade. If it does not perform satisfactorily, contact the store and ask for assistance. If the store's service is not satisfactory, you may be able to have your credit card company help to mediate any disputes.

VISUAL SUMMARY
The Upgrader's Guide:
How to Upgrade Your Microcomputer System

Upgrading a Microcomputer System

Step	Questions
1	Needs: Is it time to upgrade? What do I need that my current system is unable to deliver?
2	Analysis: What should I upgrade? Will the upgrade meet my needs and will it be cost effective?
3	Action: Who should do the upgrade? Should I pay a professional or do it myself?

NEEDS

Is it time to upgrade? What do I need that my current system is unable to deliver?

I am considering an upgrade to:
- ❏ **Improve performance because**
  - ❏ My programs run too slow
  - ❏ I cannot run some programs I need
- ❏ **Increase storage capacity because**
  - ❏ I don't have enough space to store all my files
  - ❏ I don't have enough space to install new programs
  - ❏ I need a secure place to back up important files
  - ❏ I'd like to download large files from the Internet
- ❏ **Add new technology**
  - ❏ Zip Drive
  - ❏ DVD-ROM
  - ❏ High-performance monitor
  - ❏ Printer
  - ❏ TV tuner card
  - ❏ Enhanced video card
  - ❏ Enhanced sound card
  - ❏ Other _____

ANALYSIS

What should I upgrade? Will the upgrade meet my needs and will it be cost effective?

I will improve:
- ❏ **Performance by**
  - ❏ Adding random-access memory (RAM)
    Current RAM (MB) _____
    Upgrade to _____
    Cost $_____
    Expected improvement _____
    Other factors _____
  - ❏ Replacing the current microprocessor
    Current processor _____
    Upgrade processor _____
    Cost $_____
    Expected improvement _____
    Other factors _____
  - ❏ Adding an expansion card
    Type _____
    Purpose _____
    Cost $_____
    Expected improvement _____
    Other factors _____
- ❏ **Storage capacity by**
  - ❏ Adding a hard disk drive
    Current size (GB) _____
    Upgrade size (GB) _____
    Cost $_____
    Expected improvement _____
    Other factors _____
  - ❏ Adding a Zip disk drive
    Upgrade size (GB) _____
    Cost $_____
    Type _____
    Expected improvement _____
    Other factors _____
- ❏ **Functionality by adding**
    New technology _____
    System requirements _____
    Cost $_____
    Expected improvement _____
    Other factors _____

To help clarify your thinking about upgrading a microcomputer system, complete the questionnaire by checking the appropriate boxes.

ACTION

Who should do the upgrade? Should I do it myself or should I pay a professional?

The two choices are:

❏ **Professional installation**

The easiest way, and many times the best way, is to have a professional perform the upgrade. If you select this option, be sure to include the cost of installation in you analysis. Pay with a credit card, and make sure your system is tagged with your name and address before you part with it.

❏ **Do-it-yourself installation**

If you have had some prior hardware experience or are a bit adventurous, you may want to save some money and do it yourself. Avoid touching sensitive electronic parts and be sure to ground yourself by touching an unpainted metal surface in your computer.

Glossary

A

Accelerated Graphics Port (AGP): A type of bus line that is dedicated to the acceleration of graphics performance.

Access: Refers to the responsibility of those having data to control who is able to use that data.

Access time: The period between the time the computer requests data from a secondary storage device and the time the transfer of data is completed.

Accounting: The organizational department that records all financial activity from billing customers to paying employees.

Accounts payable: The activity that shows the money a company owes to its suppliers for the materials and services it has received.

Accounts receivable: The activity that shows what money has been received or is owed by customers.

Accuracy: Relates to the responsibility of those who collect data to ensure that the data is correct.

Active desktop: The Windows dektop view in which "active content" from Web pages is displayed.

Active-matrix: Type of flat-panel monitor in which each pixel is independently activated. More colors with better clarity can be displayed.

Ad network cookies: Cookies that monitor your activities across all sites you visit, continually active in collecting information on your Web activities.

Adapter card: *See* Expansion card.

Add-on: *See* Helper applications.

Address: Located in the header of an e-mail message, the e-mail address of the persons sending, receiving, and optionally, anyone else who is to receive copies.

Advanced application: Also known as a special-purpose application, this type of application includes thousands of programs that are narrowly focused on specific disciplines and occupations.

Advanced Research Project Agency Network (ARPANET): A national computer network from which the Internet developed.

Agent: Program for updating search engine. Also called bot or spider.

Analog signal: Signal that represents a range of frequencies, such as the human voice.

Analytical graphs or charts: Form of graphics used to put numeric data into forms that are easier to analyze, such as bar charts, line graphs, and pie charts.

Animation: Feature involving special visual and sound effects.

Antivirus programs: Programs that guard a computer system from viruses or other damaging programs.

Applets: Java programs used on Web pages.

Application generator: Software with modules that have been preprogrammed to accomplish various tasks, such as calculation of overtime pay.

Applications: Programs such as word processing and spreadsheets.

Application software: Software that can perform useful work, such as word processing, cost estimating, or accounting tasks.

Arithmetic-logic unit (ALU): The part of the CPU that performs arithmetic and logical operations.

arithmetic operations: Fundamental math operations: addition, subtraction, multiplication, and division.

Artificial intelligence (AI): A field of computer science that attempts to develop computer systems that can mimic or simulate human thought processes and actions.

Artificial reality: *See* Virtual reality.

ASCII (American Standard Code for Information Interchange): Binary coding scheme widely used on all computers, including microcomputers.

Assembly language: Second generation of programming languages. These languages use abbreviations for program instructions.

Asynchronous communications port: *See* Serial port.

Attachment: A file, such as a document or worksheets, that is attached to an e-mail message.

Attributes: In an object-oriented database, the description of entities.

Auction house sites: Web sites that operate like a traditional auction to sell merchandise to bidders.

Audio-output devices: Devices, such as speakers and headphones, that translate audio information from the computer into sounds that people can recognize and understand.

Automated design tool: Software package that evaluates hardware and software alternatives according to requirements given by the systems analyst.

B

Backup: A utility program that helps protect you from the affects of a disk failure by making a copy of selected or all files that have been saved onto a disk.

Backup programs: Programs that make copies of files to be used in case the originals are lost or damaged.

Backup tape cartridge unit: *See* Magnetic tape streamer.

Balance sheet: Lists the overall financial condition of an organization.

Bandwidth: Bits-per-second transmission capability of a channel.

Bar code: Code consisting of vertical zebra-striped marks printed on product containers; read with a bar-code reader.

Bar-code reader: Photoelectric scanner that reads bar codes for processing.

Basic applications: *See* General-purpose applications.

Batch processing: Processing performed all at once on data that has been collected over several days.

Beta testing: Testing by a select group of potential users in the final stage of testing a program.

Binary coding schemes: The representation of characters as 0s and 1s, or "off" and "on" electrical states, in a computer.

Binary system: Numbering system in which all numbers consist of only two digits—0 and 1.

Bit (binary digit): A 0 or 1 in the binary system.

Bitmap file: Graphic file in which image is made up of thousands of dots (pixels).

Bluetooth: Recent wireless technology that allows nearby devices to communicate.

Bot: *See* Agent.

Broadband: Bandwidth that includes microwave, satellite, coaxial cable, and fiber-optic channels. It is used for very high speed computers.

Browser: Special Internet software that allows users to effortlessly jump from one computer's resources to another computer's resources.

Bus: A data roadway along which bits travel.

Bus line: Electronic data roadway, connecting the parts of the CPU to each other and linking the CPU with other important hardware, along which bits travel. Also, the common connecting cable in a bus network.

Bus network: Network in which all communications travel along a common path. Each device in the network handles its own communications control. There is no host computer or file server.

Business-to-business (B2B): A type of electronic commerce that involves the sale of a product or service from one business to another.

Business-to-consumer (B2C): A type of electronic commerce that involves the sale of a product or service to the general public or end users.

Button: A special area you can click to make links and "navigate" through a presentation.

Byte: Unit consisting of eight bits. There are 256 possible bit combinations in a byte.

C

Cable: Cords used to connect input and output devices to the system unit.

Cable modem: Allows all digital communication; speed of 27 million bps.

Cache memory: Area of random-access memory (RAM) set aside to store the most frequently accessed information. Acts as a temporary high-speed holding zone between memory and CPU.

Carder: Criminal who steals credit cards over the Internet.

Carpal tunnel syndrome: Disorder found among frequent computer users, consisting of damage to nerves and tendons in the hands. *See also* Repetitive strain injury.

Cathode-ray tube (CRT): Desktop-type monitor built in the same way as a television set. The most common type of monitor for the office and the home. These monitors are typically placed directly on the system unit or on the top of the desk.

CD: *See* Compact disc.

CD-R: Optical disk that can be written to once. After that it can be read many times without deterioration and cannot be written on or erased.

CD-ROM (compact disc-read-only memory): Optical disk that allows data to be read but not recorded.

CD-RW (compact disc-rewritable): Optical disk that is not permanently altered when data is recorded.

Cell: The space created by the intersections of a vertical column and a horizontal row in a worksheet.

Center for European Nuclear Research (CERN): In Switzerland; where the Web was introduced in 1992.

Central processing unit (CPU): Part of the computer that holds data and program instructions for processing the data. The CPU consists of the control unit and the arithmetic-logic unit. In a microcomputer, the CPU is on a single electronic component, the microprocessor chip.

Chain printer: An expensive high-speed machine typically used within organizations to serve several computers connected by a network or a mainframe computer requiring large quantities of printed output.

Channel: Topic for discussion in a chat group.

Character: A single letter, number, or special character such as a punctuation mark or $.

Character and mark recognition device: Specialty devices that are able to recognize special characters and marks.

Chassis: *See* System unit.

Chat group: An online discussion group that allows direct "live" communication.

Checklist: List of questions that helps in guiding the systems analyst and end user through key issues for the present system.

Child node: A node one level below the node being considered in a hierarchical database or network.

Chip: A tiny circuit board etched on a small square of sandlike material called silicon.

Chlorofluorocarbons (CFCs): Toxic chemicals found in solvents and cleaning agents. Chlorofluorocarbons can travel into the atmosphere and deplete the earth's ozone layer.

CISC: *See* Complex instruction set computer chip.

Clarity: Indicated by the resolution, or amount of pixels, on a monitor. The greater the resolution, the better the clarity.

Classes: In an object-oriented database, similar objects grouped together.

Client: A node that requests and uses resources available from other nodes.

Client operating system: A type of desktop operating system that works with a network's NOS to share and coordinate resources.

Client/server network system: Network in which one powerful computer coordinates and supplies services to all other nodes on the network. Server nodes coordinate and supply specialized services, and client nodes request the services.

Closed architecture: Computer manufactured in such a way that users cannot easily add new devices.

Coaxial cable: High-frequency transmission cable that replaces the multiple wires of telephone lines with a single solid-copper core.

Code: Write a program using the appropriate computer language.

Coding: Actual writing of a computer program.

Cold site: Special emergency facility in which hardware must be installed but which is available to a company in the event of a disaster to its computer system. *Compare* Hot site.

Column: A vertical block of cells one cell wide in a worksheet.

Combination key: Keys such as the *Ctrl* key that perform an action when held down in combination with another key.

Commerce server: *See* Web storefront creation packages.

Common data item: In a relational database, all related tables must have a common data item or key field.

Common user database: Company database that contains selected information both from the common operational database and from outside (proprietary) databases.

Communication channel: The actual connecting medium that carries the message between sending and receiving devices.

Communication systems: Electronic systems that transmit data over communications lines from one location to another.

Compact disc (CD): Widely used optical disk format.

Compact disc rewritable: *See* CD-RW,

Compact disc-read only memory: *See* CD-ROM.

Compiler: Software that converts the programmer's procedural-language program (source code) into machine language (object code).

Complementary metal-oxide semiconductor (CMOS): A CMOS chip provides flexibility and expandability for a computer system; unlike RAM, it does not lose its contents if power is turned off; unlike ROM, its contents can be changed.

Complex instruction set computer (CISC) chip: The most common type of microprocessor that has thousands of programs written specifically for it.

Computer Abuse Amendments Act of 1994: Outlaws transmission of viruses and other harmful computer code.

Computer-aided design (CAD): Type of program that manipulates images on a screen.

Computer-aided manufacturing (CAM): Type of program that controls automated factory equipment, including machine tools and robots.

Computer-aided software engineering (CASE) tool: *See* Automated design tool

Computer crime: Illegal action in which a perpetrator uses special knowledge of computer technology. Criminals may be employees, outside users, hackers and crackers, and organized crime members.

Computer ethics: Guidelines for the morally acceptable use of computers in our society.

Computer Fraud and Abuse Act of 1986: Law allowing prosecution of unauthorized access to computers and databases.

Computer Matching and Privacy Protection Act of 1988: Law setting procedures for computer matching of federal data for verifying eligibility for federal benefits or for recovering delinquent debts.

Computer network: Communications system connecting two or more computers and their peripheral devices.

Computer support specialist: Specialists including technical writers, computer trainers, computer technicians, and help desk specialists.

Computer technician: Specialist who installs hardware and software as well as trouble-shoots problems for users.

Computer trainer: Computer professional who provides classes to instruct users.

Connection device: A device that acts as an interface between the sending and receiving devices and the communication channel.

Connectivity: Capability of the microcomputer to use information from the world beyond one's desk. Data and information can be sent over telephone or cable lines and through the air.

Consumer-to-consumer (C2C): A type of electronic commerce that involves individuals selling to individuals.

Continuous-speech recognition system: Voice-recognition system used to control a microcomputer's operations and to issue commands to special application programs.

Controller card: *See* Expansion card.

Control unit: Section of the CPU that tells the rest of the computer how to carry out program instructions.

Cookie-cutter programs: Specialized programs that allow users to selectively filter or block the most intrusive ad network cookies while allowing selective traditional cookies to operate.

Cookies: Programs that record information on Web site visitors.

Cordless or wireless mouse: A battery-powered mouse that typically uses radio waves or infrared light waves to communicate with the system unit.

Cracker: One who gains unauthorized access to a computer system for malicious purposes.

Cumulative trauma disorder: *See* Repetitive strain injury.

Cybercash: *See* Electronic cash.

Cyberspace: The space of electronic movement of ideas and information.

Cynic: Individual who feels that the idea of using a microcomputer is overrated and too troublesome to learn.

D

Data: Raw, unprocessed facts that are input to a computer system.

Data banks: *See* Proprietary database.

Data bus: *See* Bus line.

Data dictionary: Dictionary containing a description of the structure of the data in a database.

Data flow diagram: Diagram showing the data or information flow within an information system.

Data integrity: A database characteristic relating to the consistency and accuracy of data.

Data mining: Technique of searching data warehouses for related information and patterns.

Data projector: Specialized devices, similar to slide projectors, that connect to microcomputers and project computer output.

Data processing system (DPS): Transaction processing system that keeps track of routine operations and records these events in a database.

Data redundancy: A common database problem in which data is duplicated and stored in different files.

Data security: Protection of software and data from unauthorized tampering or damage.

Data transmission specifications: The rules and procedures that coordinate sending and receiving devices and the communication channels.

Data warehouse: Special type of database that supports data mining.

Data workers: People involved with the distribution and communication of information, such as secretaries and clerks.

Database: A collection of related files.

Database administrator (DBA): Person responsible for structuring, coordinating, linking, and maintaining databases.

Database file: File containing highly structured and organized data.

Database management system (DBMS): *See* Database manager.

Database manager: Software package used to set up, or structure, a database.

DataPlay: An optical write-once format, similar to CD-R, designed for optical disks with a capacity of 500 MB or enough to hold 5 hours of CD-quality sound.

Debugging: Programmer's word for testing and then eliminating errors in a program.

Decision support system (DSS): Flexible tool for analysis that helps managers make decisions about unstructured problems, such as the effect of events and trends outside the organization.

Decision table: Table showing the decision rules that apply when certain conditions occur and what action should take place as a result.

Demand report: The opposite of a scheduled report. A demand report is produced on request.

Demodulation: Process performed by a modem in converting analog signals to digital signals.

Denial of service attack: A variant virus in which Web sites are overwhelmed with data, resulting in the inability for users to access the Web site.

Desk checking: Process of checking out a computer program by studying the program listing line by line, looking for syntax and logic errors.

Desktop: Windows user interface.

Desktop computer: Computer small enough to fit on top or along the side of a desk and yet too big to carry around.

Desktop operating systems: *See* Stand-alone operating systems.

Desktop publishing: Program that allows you to mix text and graphics to create publications of professional quality.

Desktop system unit: A system unit that typically contains the system's electronic components and selected secondary storage devices.

Destination file: A document in which a linked object is inserted.

Device driver: Specialized program designed to allow particular input or output devices to communicate with the rest of the computer program.

Dial-up service: Method of accessing the Internet using a high-speed modem and standard telephone lines.

Digital camera: Similar to a traditional camera except that images are recorded digitally in the camera's memory rather than on film.

Digital cash: *See* Electronic cash.

Digital notebook: An input device that records and stores pen movements.

Digital signal: Signal that represents the presence or absence of an electronic pulse.

Digital subscriber line (DSL): Provides high-speed connection using existing telephone lines.

Digital versatile disc: *See* DVD.

Digital versatile disc-read only memory: A type of DVD disk that can provide over two hours of very high-quality video and sound.

Digital versatile disk (DVD): Similar to CD-ROMs except that more data can be packed into the same amount of space.

Digital video camera: Input device that records motion digitally.

Digital video disc: *See* DVD (digital versatile disc).

Direct access: A fast approach to external storage, provided by disks, where information is not in a set sequence.

Direct approach: Approach for systems implementation whereby the old system is simply abandoned for the new.

Direct file organization: File organization that makes use of key fields to go directly to the record being sought rather than reading records one after another.

Directory search: A search engine option that provides a directory or list of categories or topics to choose from, followed by subtopics that help you narrow your search until a list of Web sites appears.

Disaster recovery plan: Plan used by large organizations describing ways to continue operations following a disaster until normal computer operations can be restored.

Discrete-speech recognition system: Voice-recognition system that allows users to dictate directly into a microcomputer using a microphone.

Disk: *See* Floppy disk; Hard disk; Optical disk.

Disk caching: Method of improving hard-disk performance by anticipating data needs. It requires a combination of hardware and software.

Disk cleanup: Windows utility that eliminates nonessential files.

Disk defragmenter: Windows utility that optimizes disk performance by eliminating unnecessary fragments and by rearranging files.

Diskette: *See* Floppy disk.

Distributed data processing system: In a network, computers that perform processing tasks at their own dispersed locations whiles also sharing programs, data, and other resources with each other.

Distributed database: Database that can be made accessible through a variety of communications networks, which allows portions of the database to be located in different places.

Distributed processing: System in which computing power is located and shared at different locations.

Document: Any kind of text material.

Documentation: Written descriptions and procedures about a program and how to use it.

Document file: File created by a word processor to save documents such as letters, research papers, and memos.

Domain code: Last part of an Internet address, which identifies the geographical description or organizational identification.

Domain name system (DNS): Internet addressing method that assigns names and numbers to people and computers.

DO UNTIL structure: Loop structure in programming that appears at the end of a loop. The DO UNTIL loop means that the loop statements will be executed at least once.

DO WHILE structure: Loop structure in programming that appears at the beginning of a loop. The DO WHILE loop will keep executing as long as there is information to be processed.

Dot-matrix printer: A type of printer that forms characters and images using a series of small pins on a print head. Used where high-quality output is not required.

Downloading: Process of transferring information from a remote computer to the computer one is using.

Draw program: Program used to help create artwork for publications. *See also* Illustration program.

Driver: *See* Device driver.

Dual-scan monitor: *See* Passive-matrix monitor.

Dumb terminal: Terminal that can be used to input and receive data but cannot process data independently.

DVD (digital versatile, or video, disc): Similar to CD-ROMs except that more data can be packed into the same amount of space.

DVD-random-access memory (DVD-RAM): A type of reusable DVD disk.

DVD-recordable (DVD-R): A recordable DVD disk.

DVD-rewritable (DVD-RW): A type of reusable DVD disk.

DVD-ROM: Digital versatile disc-read-only memory.

E

EBCDIC (Extended Binary Coded Decimal Interchange Code): Binary coding scheme that is a standard for minicomputers and mainframe computers.

E-book: Handheld, book-sized devices that display text and graphics.

E-book reader: *See* E-book.

Economic feasibility: Condition in which costs of designing a new sytem will be justified by the benefits it will provide.

Electronic cash (e-cash): Currency for Internet purchases.

Electronic commerce (e-commerce): Buying and selling of goods over the Internet.

Electronic Communications Privacy Act of 1986: Law protecting the privacy of users on public electronic-mail systems.

Electronic mail (e-mail): Similar to an electronic bulletin board, but provides confidentiality and may use special communications rather than telephone lines.

Electronic spreadsheet: *See* Spreadsheet.

Electrostatic plotter: Plotter that uses electrostatic charges to create images made up of tiny dots on specially treated paper.

E-mail: *See* Electronic mail.

Embedded object: Information inserted into a destination file of another application that becomes part of this file but can be edited within the destination file using the server application.

Embedded operating system: An operating system that is completely stored within the ROM memory of the device that it is in; used for hand-held computers and smaller devices like PDAs.

Encrypting: Coding information so that only the user can read or otherwise use it.

End user: Person who uses microcomputers or has access to larger computers.

Energy Star: Program created by the Environmental Protection Agency to discourage waste in the microcomputer industry.

Enterprise computing: Integrating an organization's networks.

Entities: In an object-oriented database, a person, place, thing, or event that is to be described.

Erasable optical disk: Optical disk on which the disk drive can write information and also erase and rewrite information.

Ergonomics: Study of human factors related to things people use.

Ethics: Standards of moral conduct.

Exception report: Report that calls attention to unusual events.

Executive information system (EIS): Sophisticated software that can draw together data from an organization's databases in meaningful patterns.

Executive support system (ESS): *See* Executive information system.

Expansion card: Optional device that plugs into a slot inside the system unit. Ports on the board allow cables to be connected from the expansion board to devices outside the system unit.

Expert system: Computer program that provides advice to decision makers who would otherwise rely on human experts.

External data: Data gathered from outside an organization.

External modem: Modem that stands apart from the computer and is connected by a cable to the computer's serial port. Another cable connects the modem to the telephone wall jack.

Extranet: Private network that connects more than one organization.

F

Fair Credit Reporting Act of 1970: Law prohibiting credit agencies from sharing credit information with anyone but authorized customers and giving consumers the right to review and correct their credit records.

Fax machine: Device that scans an image and sends it electronically over telephone lines to a receiving fax machine, which converts the electronic signals back to an image and recreates it on paper.

Fiber-optic cable: Special transmission cable made of glass tubes that are immune to electronic interference. Data is transmitted through fiber-optic cables in the form of pulses of light.

Field: Each column of information within a record is called a field. A field contains a set of related characters.

File: A collection of related records.

File compression: Process of reducing the storage requirements for a file.

File compression programs: Programs that reduce the size of files.

File decompression: Process of expanding a compressed file.

File transfer protocol (FTP): Internet service for transferring files.

Filter: Program to block selected Web sites, set time limits, monitor use, and generate reports on use.

Find: In word processing, a command that allows the user to locate any character, word, or phrase in a document.

Firewall: Security hardware and software.

FireWire port: Used to connect high-speed printers and even videocameras to system unit.

Firmware: *See* ROM.

Fixed disk: *See* Internal hard disk.

Flash memory: *See* Flash RAM.

Flash memory card: A solid state storage device widely used in notebook computers.

Flash RAM: RAM chips that retain data even when power is disrupted.

Flatbed scanner: An input device similar to a copying machine.

Flexible disk: *See* Floppy disk.

Floppy: *See* Floppy disk.

Floppy disk: Flat, circular piece of magnetically treated mylar plastic that rotates within a jacket.

Floppy-disk cartridge: Include Zip disks, SuperDisks, and HiFD disks, all competing to become the next higher capacity floppy disk standard.

Folder: A named area on a disk that is used to store related subfolders and files.

Formatting: The process of adapting a floppy disk to the type of microcomputer and disk drive that you are using.

Formatting toolbar: A collection of buttons used as shortcuts to commands that enhance the appearance of a document.

Formula: Instructions for calculations in a spreadsheet.

Fragmented: Storage technique that breaks up large files and stores the parts wherever space is available.

Freedom of Information Act of 1970: Law giving citizens the right to examine data about them in federal government files, except for that restricted for national security reasons.

Frustrated: Person who feels it is an imposition to have to learn something new like computer technology.

Full-duplex communication: Mode of communication in which data is transmitted back and forth at the same time.

Function: In a spreadsheet, a built-in formula that performs calculations automatically.

Fuzzy logic: Used by expert systems to allow users to respond by using qualitative terms such as *great* and *OK*.

G

General ledger: Activity that produces income statements and balance sheets based on all transactions of a company.

General-purpose applications: Applications designed to be used by most people doing the most common tasks, such as browsers and word processors.

Generations of programming languages: The five generations are machine languages, assembly languages, procedural languages, problem-oriented languages, and natural languages.

Gigahertz: Billions of beats per second.

Grammar checker: In word processing, a tool that identifies poorly worded sentences and incorrect grammar.

Graphic tablet: Records sketches and tracings using a special graphics surface or tablet and a special stylus.

Graphical map: Diagram of a Web site's overall design.

Graphical user interface (GUI): Special screen that allows software commands to be issued through the use of graphic symbols (icons) or pull-down menus.

Graphics suite: Group of graphics programs offered at lower cost than if purchased separately.

Green PC: Microcomputer industry concept of an environmentally friendly, low-power-consuming machine.

Grid chart: Chart that shows the relationship between input and output documents.

Group decision support system (GDSS): System used to support the collective work of a team addressing large problems.

H

Hacker: Person who gains unauthorized access to a computer system for the fun and challenge of it.

Half-duplex communication: Mode of communication in which data flows in both directions, but not simultaneously.

Handheld computer: *See* Personal digital assistant (PDA).

Hard copy: Images output on paper by a printer or plotter.

Hard disk: Enclosed disk drive that contains one or more metallic disks. A hard disk has many times the capacity of a floppy disk.

Hard-disk cartridge: Hard disk that is easily removed.

Hard-disk pack: Several platters aligned one above the other, thereby offering much greater storage capacity.

Hardware: Equipment that includes a keyboard, monitor, printer, the computer itself, and other devices.

Hashing: Program that uses mathematical operations to convert the key field's numeric value to a particular storage address.

Head crash: Occurs when the surface of the read-write head or particles on its surface contact the magnetic disk surface.

Header: The first element of an e-mail message.

Help: A feature in most application software providing options that typically include an index, a glossary, and a search feature to locate reference information about specific commands.

Help desk specialist: Specialist who provides telephone support for end users within the organization.

Helper applications: Independent programs that can be executed by a browser. Also called add-ons.

Hierarchical database: Database in which fields or records are structured in nodes.

Hierarchical network: Network consisting of several computers linked to a central host computer. The computers linked to the host are themselves hosts to other computers or devices.

HiFD disk: High-capacity floppy disk manufactured by Sony.

High performance serial bus (HPSB): *See* FireWire port.

Higher level: Programming languages that are closer to the language humans use.

High-definition television (HDTV): All-digital television that delivers a much clearer and more detailed widescreen picture.

History file: Created by browser to store information on Web sites visited.

Hits: The sites that a search engine returns with after running a keyword search, ordered from most likely to least likely to contain the information requested.

Home page: Top-level or opening page of Web site.

Horizontal portal: Web portal designed to appeal to mass audiences.

Host computer: A large centralized computer. A common way of accessing the Internet. The host computer is connected to the Internet and provides a path or connection for individuals to access the Internet.

Hot site: Special emergency facility consisting of a fully equipped computer center available to a company in the event of disaster to its computer system. *Compare* Cold site.

HTML editor: *See* Web authoring program.

Human resources: The organizational department that focuses on the hiring, training, and promoting of people, as well as any number of human center activities within the organization.

Hybrid network: *See* Hierarchical network.

Hyperlink: A hypertext link.

Hypermedia: *See* Multimedia.

Hypertext Markup Language (HTML): Programming language for the document files that are used to display Web pages.

I

Icon: Graphic object on the desktop used to represent commonly used features.

Identification: The unique numeric address, or IP address, on every computer on the internet.

I-drive: *See* Internet hard drive.

IF-THEN-ELSE structure: Logical selection structure whereby one of two paths is followed according to IF, THEN, and ELSE statements in a program.

Illusion of anonymity: The misconception that being selective about disclosing personal information on the Internet can prevent an invasion of personal privacy.

Illustration program: Used to modify vector images and thus create line art, 3-D models, and virtual reality. Also called draw program.

Image capturing device: A device, such as a digital camera or a digital video camera, that creates or captures original images.

Image editor: Used to create and modify bitmap files. Also called paint program.

Income statement: A statement that shows a company's financial performance – income, expenses, and the difference between them for a specific time period.

Index search: *See* Directory search.

Index sequential file organization: Compromise between sequential and direct file organization. Records are stored sequentially, but an index is used to access a group of records directly.

Individual database: Collection of integrated records useful mainly by just one person.

Industrial robots: Robots used in factories to perform a variety of tasks. For example, machines used in automobile plants to do painting and polishing.

Industry Standard Architecture (ISA): Bus-line standard developed for the IBM Personal Computer. It first consisted of an 8-bit-wide data path, then a 16-bit-wide data path.

Information: Data that has been processed by a computer system.

Information pusher: Program that automatically gathers information on topics of your choice and saves it on your hard disk. Also called push product and Web Broadcaster utility.

Information system: Collection of hardware, software, people, data, and procedures that work together to provide information essential to running an organization.

Information technology (IT): Computer systems, either large or microcomputers, which provide understanding to the end user.

Information utilities: *See* Proprietary database.

Information worker: Employee that creates, distributes, and communicates information.

Initializing: *See* Formatting.

Ink-jet printer: Printer that sprays small droplets of ink at high speed onto the surface of the paper.

Input: Any data or instructions that are used by a computer.

Input device: Piece of equipment that puts data into a form a computer can process.

Instant messaging: Communication and collaboration tool for direct, "live," connections over the Internet.

Integrated circuit: *See* Silicon chip.

Integrated package: Collection of computer programs that work together and share information.

Intelligent terminal: Terminal that includes a processing unit, memory, secondary storage, communications software, and a telephone hookup or other communications link.

Interactivity: User participation in a multimedia presentation.

Interface card: *See* Expansion card.

Internal data: Data from within an organization.

Internal hard disk: Storage device consisting of one or more metallic platters sealed inside a container. Internal hard disks are installed inside the system cabinet of a microcomputer.

Internal modem: *See* Modem card.

Internet: A huge computer network available to nearly everyone with a microcomputer and a means to connect to it. It is a resource for information about an infinite number of topics.

Internet hard drive: A special service site on the Web which provides users with free or low cost storage, allowing for access to the information from any computer that is connected to the Internet.

Internet relay chat (IRC): Leading type of chat group service.

Internet service provider (ISP): Provides access to the Internet.

Internet telephony: *See* Telephony.

Internet terminal: Provides access to the Internet and displays Web pages on a standard television set. Also called Web terminal.

Interpreter: Software that converts a procedural language one statement at a time into machine language just before the statement is executed.

Intranet: Like the Internet but privately owned by an organization.

Inventory: Material or products that a company has in stock.

Inventory control system: A system that keeps records of the number of each kind of part or finished good in the warehouse.

IP address (Internet Protocol address): The unique numeric address of a computer on the Internet that facilitates the delivery of e-mail.

J

Java: A portable programming language.

Joystick: Popular input device for computer games.

K

Keyboard: Input device that looks like a typewriter keyboard but has additional keys.

Key field: The common field by which tables in a database are related to each other.

Keyword search: A type of search option that causes the search engine to compare your entry against its database and return with a list of sites, or hits, that contain the keyword you entered.

Knowledge-based systems: Programs that duplicate human knowledge

Knowledge work system (KWS): Specialized information system used to create information in a specific area of expertise.

Knowledge workers: People involved in the creation of information, such as engineers and scientists.

L

Lands: *See* Lands and pits.

Lands and pits: Flat and bumpy areas, respectively, that represent 1s and 0s on the optical disk surface to be read by a laser.

Language translator: Converts programming instructions into a machine language that can be processed by a computer.

Laser printer: Printer that creates dotlike images on a drum, using a laser beam light source.

Layout files: Sample presentation files.

Levels: Generations of programming languages.

Line of sight communication: Microwave communication using high-frequency radio waves.

Link: A connection to related information.

Linked object: Information created in a source file from one application and inserted into a destination file of another application while maintaining a link between files.

Linux: Type of Unix operating system initially developed by Linus Torvalds.

Liquid crystal display (LCD): Display consisting of liquid crystal molecules whose optical properties can be altered by an applied electric field.

List address: Internet mailing list address. Members of a mailing list communicate by sending messages to the list address.

Local area network (LAN): Network consisting of computers and other devices that are physically near each other, such as within the same building.

Logic error: Error that occurs when a programmer has used an incorrect calculation or left out a programming procedure.

Logic structure: Structure that controls the logical sequence in which computer program instructions are executed. The three structures are sequence, selection, and loop.

Logical operations: Comparing two pieces of data to see whether one is equal to (=), less than (<), or greater than (>) the other.

Loop structure: Logic structure in which a process may be repeated as long as a certain condition remains true.

Low bandwidth: *See* Voiceband.

Lower level: Programming language closer to the language the computer itself uses.

Lurking: Observing or reading communications from others on an Internet discussion group without participating.

M

Machine language: Language in which data is represented in 1s and 0s.

Mac OS: Operating system designed for Macintosh computers.

Magnetic-ink character recognition (MICR): Direct-entry scanning device used in banks. This technology is used to automatically read the futuristic-looking numbers on the bottom of checks.

Magnetic tape reels: Typically ½-inch wide and ½-mile long, this type of magnetic tape is used by mainframe computers due to its massive storage capacity.

Magnetic tape streamer: Device that allows duplication (backup) of the data stored on a microcomputer hard disk.

Mailing list: Type of discussion group available on the Internet.

Main board: *See* System board.

Mainframe: Computer that can process several million program instructions per second. Large organizations rely on these room-size systems to handle large programs with lots of data.

Maintenance programmer: Programmers who maintain software by updating it to protect errors, improve usability, standardize, and adjust to organizational changes.

Management information system (MIS): Computer-based information system that produces standardized reports in summarized, structured form. It is used to support middle managers.

Many-to-many relationship: In a network database, each child node may have more than one parent node and vice versa.

Mark sensing: *See* Optical-character recognition.

Marketing: The organizational department that plans, prices, promotes, sells, and distributes the organization's goods and services.

Master file: Complete file containing all records current up to the last update.

Mechanical mouse: Traditional and most widely used type of mouse. It has a ball on the bottom and is attached with a cord to the system unit.

Medium band: Bandwidth of special leased lines, used mainly with minicomputers and mainframe computers.

Memory: Part of the microcomputer that holds data for processing, instructions for processing the data, and information (processed data) waiting to be output or sent to secondary storage.

Menu: List of commands.

Menu bar: A bar that displays the menu names that can be selected.

Message: The content portion of e-mail correspondence.

Metasearch engine: Program that automatically submits your search request to several indices and search engines, then creates an index from received information.

Methods: In an object-oriented database, descriptions of how the data is to be manipulated.

Metropolitan area network (MAN): Network linking office buildings in a city.

Microcomputer: Small, low-cost computer designed for individual users.

Microcomputer database: *See* Individual database.

Microprocessor: The central processing unit of a microcomputer. The microprocessor is contained on a single integrated circuit chip.

Microsecond: One-millionth of a second.

Microwave: Communication using high-frequency radio waves that travel in straight lines through the air.

Middle management: Middle-level managers deal with control and planning. They implement the long-term goals of the organization.

Midrange computer: *See* Minicomputer.

Minicomputer: Desk-sized machine falling in between microcomputers and mainframes in processing speed and data-storing capacity.

Mobile robots: Robots that act as transports.

Modem: Communications device that translates the electronic signals from a computer into electronic signals that can travel over a telephone line.

Modem card: Also know as an internal modem, a card that allows distant computers to communicate with one another by converting electronic signals from within the system unit into electronic signals that can travel over telephone lines and other types of connections.

Modulation: Process of converting digital signals to analog signals.

Module: *See* Program module.

Monitor: Output device like a television screen that displays data processed by the computer.

Morphing: Special effect in which one image seems to melt into another.

Motherboard: *See* System board.

Mouse: Device that typically rolls on the desktop and directs the cursor on the display screen.

Multifunctional devices: Devices that typically combine the capabilities of a scanner, printer, fax, and copying machine.

Multimedia: Technology that can link all sorts of media into one form of presentation.

Multitasking: Operating system that allows a single user to run several application programs at the same time.

N

Naïve: People who underestimate the difficulty of changing computer systems or generating information.

Nanomanipulator: Advanced virtual reality interface.

National Information Infrastructure Protection Act of 1996: Provides penalties for trespassing on computer systems, threats made against computer networks, and theft of information.

National service provider: Internet service providers such as America Online (AOL) that provide access through standard telephone connections and allow users to access the Internet from almost anywhere within the country for a standard fee.

Natural language: Language designed to give people a more human connection with computers.

Net personal computer (Net PC): Low-cost type of intelligent terminal that typically has only one type of secondary storage and no expansion slots.

Network: The arrangement in which various communications channels are connected.

Network adapter card: Connects the sytem unit to a cable that connects to other devices on the network.

Network architecture: Describes how a network is arranged and how the resources are shared.

Network bridge: Connects networks of the same configuration.

Network computer: *See* Network terminal.

Network database: Database with a hierarchical arrangement of nodes, except that each child node may have more than one parent node.

Network gateway: Connection by which a local area network may be linked to other local area networks or to larger networks.

Network manager: Computer professional who ensures that existing information and communication systems are operating effectively and that new ones are implemented as needed. Also responsible for meeting security and privacy requirements.

Network operating system (NOS): Software that interacts with applications and computers, and also coordinate activities between computers on a network.

Network server: *See* Network operating system.

Network terminal: Low-cost alternative to intelligent terminal; relies on host computer or server for software. *Also* called network computer.

Node: Any device connected to a network. Also, points in a hierarchical database connected like the branches of an upside-down tree.

No Electronic Theft (NET) Act of 1997: Provides penalties for unathorized distribution of copyrighted materials (software) on the Internet.

Nonvolatile storage: Permanent storage used to preserve data and programs.

Norton AntiVirus: Collection of antivirus programs from Symantec.

Norton CleanSweep: Collection of programs to safely remove files and programs from Symantec.

Norton CrashGuard: Collection of programs that protect against system crashes from Symantec.

Norton Utilities: Collection of 17 troubleshooting utilities from Symantec.

Norton Web Services: Service from Symantec that monitors a computer system for out-of-date software.

Notebook computer: Portable computer weighing between 5 and 10 pounds.

Notebook system unit: A small, portable system unit that contains electronic components, selected secondary storage devices and input devices.

Numeric entry: In a worksheet or spreadsheet, typically used to identify numbers or formulas.

O

Object: An element such as a text box that can be added to a workbook and that can be selected, sized, and moved.

Object code: Machine language code converted by a compiler from source code.

Object linking and embedding (OLE): Powerful feature of many application programs that allows sharing of information.

Objectives: The problems you are trying to solve.

Objects: In an object-oriented database, items that contain both data and instructions to manipulate the date.

Object-oriented database: Keep track of objects, which are entities that contain both data and the action that can be taken on data.

Object-oriented programming (OOP): Methodology in which a program is organized into objects, each containing both the data and processing operations necessary to perform a task.

Object-oriented software development: Software development approach that focuses less on the tasks and more on defining the relationships between previously defined procedures or objects.

Office automation system (OAS): System designed primarily to support data workers. It focuses on managing documents, communicating, and scheduling.

Off-line browser: Program that automatically connects to selected Web sites, downloads HTML documents, and saves them to your hard disk. Also called pull product and Web-downloading utility.

One-to-many relationship: In a hierarchical database, each entry has one parent node, and a parent may have several child nodes.

1.44 MB 3¹/₂-inch disk: The most widely used floppy disk.

Online storage: *See* Internet hard drive.

Open architecture: Microcomputer architecture allowing users to expand their systems by inserting optional devices known as expansion cards.

Operating system: Software that interacts between application software and the computer. The operating system handles such details as running programs, storing data and programs, and processing data.

Operational model: A decision model that helps lower-level managers accomplish the organization's day-to-day activities, such as evaluating and maintaining quality control.

Operational feasibility: Condition in which the design of a new system will be able to function within the existing framework of an organization.

Operators: Individuals needing documentation of error messages.

Optical-character recognition (OCR): Scanning device that uses special preprinted characters, such as those printed on utility bills, that can be read by a light source and changed into machine-readable code.

Optical disk: Storage device that can hold 650 megabytes of data. Lasers are used to record and read data on the disk.

Optical-mark recognition (OMR): Device that senses the presence or absence of a mark, such as a pencil mark.

Optical mouse: A type of mouse that emits and senses light to detect mouse movement.

Optical scanner: *See* Scanner.

Organization chart: Chart showing the levels of management and formal lines of authority in an organization.

Output: Processed data or information from a computer.

Output device: Equipment that translates processed information from the central processing unit into a form that can be understood.

P

Packaged program: Application program also referred to as a prewritten program.

Packet: Before a message is sent on the Internet, it is broken down into small parts called packets. Each packet is then sent separately over the Internet. At the receiving end, the packets are reassembled into the correct order.

Paint program: *See* Image editor.

Palmtop computer: *See* Personal digital assistant (PDA).

Parallel approach: Systems implementation in which old and new systems are operated side by side until the new one has shown it is reliable.

Parallel port: Used to connect external devices that send or receive a lot of data over a short distance. Mostly used to connect printers to system unit.

Parent node: Node one level above the node being considered in a hierarchical database or network.

Passive-matrix monitor: Monitor that creates images by scanning the entire screen.

Password: Special sequence of numbers or letters that limits access to information, such as electronic mail.

Payroll: Activity concerned with calculating employee paychecks.

PC card: *See* Personal Computer Memory Card International Association (PCMCIA) card.

PC Card hard disk: A hard disk cartridge for a notebook computer.

PC card modem: a credit card–size expansion board that is inserted into portable computers. A telephone cable connects the modem to the telephone wall jack.

Peer-to-peer network system: Network in which nodes can act as both servers and clients. For example, one microcomputer can obtain files located on another microcomputer and can also provide files to other microcomputers.

People: End users, the most important of the five components of an information system.

Perception systems: Robots that imitate some of the human senses.

Peripheral Component Interconnect (PCI): Bus architecture that combines the capabilities of MCA and EISA with the ability to send video instructions at speeds to match the microprocessor.

Personal Computer Memory Card International Association (PCMCIA) card: Credit card–sized expansion cards developed for portable computers.

Personal digital assistant (PDA): A device that typically combines pen input, writing recognition, personal organizational tools, and communication capabilities in a very small package. Also called Handheld PC and palmtop computer.

Personal laser printer: Inexpensive laser printer widely used by single users to produce black-and-white documents.

Personal video recorder card: *See* TV tuner card.

Person-to-person auction site: A type of Web auction site where the owner provides a forum for numerous buyers and sellers to gather.

Phased approach: Systems implementation in which the new system is implemented gradually over a period of time.

Photo printer: A special-purpose ink jet printer designed to print photo-quality images from digital cameras.

Physical security: Activity concerned with protecting hardware from possible human and natural disasters.

Pilot approach: Systems implementation in which the new system is tried out in only one part of the organization. Later it is implemented throughout the rest of the organization.

Pits: *See* Lands and pits.

Pixel: Smallest unit on the screen that can be turned on and off or made different shades.

Platform scanner: Handheld direct-entry device used to read special characters on price tags.

Plotter: Special-purpose output device for producing bar charts, maps, architectural drawings, and three-dimensional illustrations.

Plug and Play: Set of hardware and software standards developed to create operating systems, processing units, and expansion cards, as well as other devices, that are able to configure themselves.

Plug-in: Program that is automatically loaded and operates as part of a browser.

Plug-in board: *See* Expansion card.

Pointer: For a monitor, a pointer is typically displayed as an arrow and controlled by a mouse. For a database, a pointer is a connection between parent node and child node in a hierarchical database.

Pointing stick: Device used to control the pointer by directing the stick with your finger.

Polling: Process whereby a host computer or file server asks each connecting device whether it has a message to send and then allows the message to be sent.

Port: Connecting socket on the outside of the system unit. Used to connect input and output devices to the system unit.

Portable language: Language that can be run on more than one kind of computer.

Portable scanner: Handheld input device for scanning images and text.

Preliminary investigation: First phase of systems analysis and design. It involves defining the problem, suggesting alternative systems, and preparing a short report.

Presentation file: A file created by presentation graphics programs to save presentation materials.

Presentation graphics: Graphics used to communicate a message or to persuade other people.

Prewritten program: Application program also referred to as a packaged program.

Primary storage: *See* Memory.

Printer: Device that produces printed paper output.

Privacy: Computer ethics issue concerning the collection and use of data about individuals.

Privacy Act of 1974: Law designed to restrict the way federal agencies share information about American citizens. It prohibits federal information collected for one purpose from being used for a different purpose.

Proactive: Person who looks at technology in a positive realistic way.

Problem-oriented language: Programming language designed to solve specific problems.

Procedural language: Programming language designed to express the logic that can solve problems.

Procedures: Rules or guidelines to follow when using hardware, software, and data.

Processing rights: Refers to which people have access to what kind of data.

Processor: *See* Central processing unit.

Production: The organizational department that actually creates finished goods and services using raw materials and personnel.

Program: List of instructions for the computer to follow to process data. *See also* Software.

Program analysis: *See* Program specification.

Program code: Program is written or coded using a programming language.

Program definition: *See* Program specification.

Program design: Creation of a solution using programming techniques such as top-down program design, pseudocode, flowcharts, logic structures, object-oriented programming, and CASE tools.

Program flowchart: Flowchart graphically presenting the detailed sequence of steps needed to solve a programming problem.

Program maintenance: Activity of updating software to correct errors, improve usability, standardize, and adjust to organizational changes.

Programmer: Computer professional who creates new software or revises existing software.

Programming: Six-step procedure for creating a program.

Program module: Logically related program statements.

Program specification: Programming step in which objectives, outputs, inputs, and processing requirements are determined.

Program test: Program debugged by looking for syntax and logic errors.

Project manager: Software that enables users to plan, schedule, and control the people, resources, and costs needed to complete a project on time.

Property: Computer ethics issue relating to who owns data and rights to software.

Proprietary database: Enormous database an organization develops to cover certain particular objects. Access to this type of database is usually offered for a fee.

Proprietary operating system: A network operating system that is owned and licensed by a company.

Protocol: Rules for exchanging data between computers.

Provider: *See* Host computer.

Proxy server: Computer that acts as a gateway or checkpoint in an organization's firewall.

Pseudocode: Narrative form of the logic of a computer program.

Pull product: *See* Off-line browser.

Purchase order: A form that shows the name of the company supplying the material or service and what is being purchased.

Purchasing: Buying of raw materials and services.

Push product: *See* Information pusher.

Q

Query language: Easy-to-use language understandable to most users. It is used to search and generate reports from a database.

R

RAM (random-access memory): Volatile storage that holds the program and data the CPU is presently processing.

RAM cache: *See* Cache memory.

Range: A selection consisting of two or more cells in a worksheet.

Rapid applications development (RAD): Involves the use of powerful development software and specialized teams as an alternative to the systems development life cycle approach.

Reader/sorter: A special purpose input device that reads characters made of ink containing magnetized particles.

Read-only: Formatting that prevents the user from writing any new data onto a disc or from erasing any data imprinted by the publisher.

Real-time processing: Processing that occurs when data is processed at the same time the transaction occurs.

Record: Each line of information in a database is a record. A record is a collection of related fields.

Reduced instruction set computer (RISC) chip: Powerful microprocessor chip found in workstations.

Redundant arrays of inexpensive disks (RAIDs): Groups of inexpensive hard-disk drives related or grouped together using networks and special software. They improve performance by expanding external storage.

Reformatting: The reassembly of packets sent or transmitted across the Internet.

Regional service provider: An Internet service provider that provides access through standard telephone connections in a specific area, typically several states for a standard fee. If users access the Internet from outside the regional area, they incur long-distance connection charges.

Relation: Table in a relational database in which data elements are stored.

Relational database: A widely used database structure, in which data is organized into related tables.

Repetitive motion injury: *See* Repetitive strain injury.

Repetitive strain injury (RSI): Category of injuries resulting from fast, repetitive work that causes neck, wrist, hand, and arm pain.

Replace: In word processing, command that enables the user to search for a word and replace it with another.

Research: The organizational department that identifies, investigates, and develops new products and services.

Resolution: A measurement in pixels of a monitor's clarity.

Resources: Coordinated by the computer's operating system, these include the keyboard, mouse, printer, monitor, storage devices, and memory.

Reverse directory: A special telephone directory that lists telephone numbers followed by subscriber names.

Right to Financial Privacy Act of 1979: Law setting strict procedures that federal agencies must follow when seeking to examine customer records in banks.

Ring network: Network in which each device is connected to two other devices, forming a ring. There is no host computer, and messages are passed around the ring until they reach the correct destination.

Robot: Machine used in factories and elsewhere that can be reprogrammed to do more than one task.

Robotics: Field of study concerned with developing and using robots.

Roller ball: *See* Trackball.

ROM (read-only memory): Refers to chips that have programs built into them at the factory. The contents of such chips cannot be changed by the user.

Row: A horizontal block of cells one cell high in a worksheet.

RS-232C connector: Serial port, a port set up for serial data transmission.

S

Sales order processing: Activity that records the demands of customers for a company's products or services.

Satellite/air connection services: Connection services that use satellites and the air to download or send data to users at a rate seven times faster than dial-up connections.

Scanner: Device that identifies images on a page and automatically converts them to electronic signals that can be stored in a computer.

Search: *See* Find.

Search engine: Search tool that lets you search by entering key words or phrases.

Search provider: *See* Search services.

Search services: Organizations that maintain databases relating to information provided on the Web and the Internet and provide search engines to help you locate information.

Secondary storage: Permanent storage used to preserve programs and data, including floppy disks, hard disks, and magnetic tape.

Sector: Section shaped like a pie wedge that divides the tracks on a disk.

Security: The protection of information, hardware, and software.

Selection structure: Logic structure that determines which of two paths will be followed when a decision must be made by a program.

Semiconductor: Silicon chip through which electricity flows with some resistance.

Sending and receiving devices: Often a computer or specialized communication device that sends as well as accepts messages in the form of data, information, and/or instructions.

Sequence structure: Logic structure in which one program statement follows another.

Sequential access: An approach to external storage, provided by magnetic tape, where information is stored in sequence.

Sequential file organization: File organization in which records are stored physically one after another in predetermined order.

Serial data transmission: Method of transmission in which bits flow in a series, one after another.

Serial port: Used to connect external devices that send or receive data one bit at a time over a long distance. Used for mouse, keyboard, modem, and many other devices.

Server: A connection to the Internet that stores document files used to display pages.

Service program: *See* Utility.

Shared laser printer: More expensive laser printer used by a group of users to produce black-and-white documents.

Sheet: *See* Worksheet.

Signature line: Provides additional information about a sender of an e-mail message, such as name, address, and telephone number.

Silicon chip: Tiny circuit board etched on a small square of sandlike material called silicon. Chips are mounted on carrier packages, which then plug into sockets on the system board.

Simplex communication: Mode of communication in which data travels in one direction only.

Size: In a monitor, indicated by the length of the viewing area.

Slot: Area on a system board that accepts cards to expand a computer system's capabilities.

Smart card: Card about the size of a credit card containing a tiny built-in microprocessor. It can be used to hold such information as frequent flier miles.

Snoopware: Programs that record virtually every activity on a computer system.

Soft copy: Images or characters output on a monitor screen.

Software: Computer program.

Software Copyright Act of 1980: Law allowing owners of programs to make copies for backup purposes, and to modify them to make them useful, provided they are not resold or given away.

Software development: *See* Programming.

Software engineer: Computer programming professionals.

Software piracy: Unauthorized copying of programs for personal gain.

Software suite: Individual application programs that are sold together as a group.

Solid-state storage: A secondary storage device that has no moving parts. Data is stored and retrieved electronically.

Sorting: Arranging objects numerically or alphabetically.

Source code: Programmers' procedural language program converted into object code by a compiler.

Source document: Original version of a document before any processing has been performed on it.

Source file: The document that stores the data for the linked object.

Special purpose application: Programs that are narrowly focused on specific disciplines and occupations. *See* Advanced applications.

Specialized search engine: Search engines that focus on subject-specific Web sites.

Spelling checker: Program used with a word processor to check the spelling of typed text against an electronic dictionary.

Spider: *See* Agent.

Spike: *See* Voltage surge.

Spreadsheet: Computer-produced spreadsheet based on the traditional accounting "worksheet" that has rows and columns that can be used to present and analyze data.

Stand-alone systems: Also called desktop operating systems, a type of operating system that controls a single desktop or notebook computer.

Standard toolbar: A collection of buttons used as shortcuts to the most frequently used menu commands.

Star network: Network of computers or peripheral devices linked to a central computer through which all communications pass. Control is maintained by polling.

Start menu: A Windows menu listing commands used to gain access to information, change hardware settings, find information, get online help, run programs, log off a network, and shut down the computer system.

Story boards: Design tool for planning and structuring a multimedia presentation.

Strategic models: A decision model that assists top-managers in long-range planning, such as stating company objectives or planning plant locations.

Strategy: A way of coordinating the sharing of information and resources.

Streaming audio: The delivery of sound files in which the multimedia files are first compressed before they are requested and then converted and played while they are being received.

Streaming multimedia: Technologies for the delivery of Web content in which multimedia files are first compressed before they are requested and then converted and played while they are being received.

Streaming video: The delivery of video files in which the multimedia files are first compressed before they are requested and then converted and played while they are being received.

Structured problem: A problem which can be broken down into a series of well-defined steps.

Structured program: Program that uses logic structures.

Structured programming techniques: Techniques that consist of top-down program design, pseudocode, flowcharts, and logic structures.

Structured query language (SQL): Program control language used to create sophisticated database applications.

Subject: Located in the head of an e-mail message, a one-line description used to present the topic of the message.

Subscription address: Mailing list address. To participate in a mailing list, you must first subscribe by sending an e-mail request to the mailing list subscription address.

Supercomputer: Fastest calculating device ever invented, processing billions of program instructions per second.

SuperDisk: High-capacity floppy disk manufactured by Imation.

Supervisor: Manager responsible for managing and monitoring workers. Supervisors have responsibility for operational matters.

Surfing: Moving from one Web site to another.

Surge protector: Device separating the computer from the power source of the wall outlet. When a voltage surge occurs, a circuit breaker is activated, protecting the computer system.

SVGA: Refers to a resolution standard that displays 800 by 600 pixels.

SXGA: Refers to a resolutuion standard of 1,280 by 1,024 pixels.

Syntax error: Violation of the rules of whatever language a computer program is written in.

System: Collection of activities and elements designed to accomplish a goal.

System board: Flat board that usually contains the CPU and some memory chips.

System cabinet: *See* System unit.

System clock: Clock that controls how fast all the operations within a computer take place.

System flowchart: Flowchart that shows the kinds of equipment used to handle the data or information flow.

System software: "Background" software that enables the application software to interact with the computer.

It includes programs that help the computer manage its own internal resources.

System unit: Part of a microcomputer that contains the CPU.

Systems analysis: Determining the requirements for a new system. Data is collected about the present system, analyzed, and new requirements are determined.

Systems analysis and design: Six-phase problem-solving procedure for examining an information system and improving it.

Systems analysis report: Report prepared for higher management describing the current information system, the requirements for a new system, and a possible development schedule.

Systems analyst: Computer professional who studies an organization's systems to determine what actions to take and how to use computer technology to assist them.

Systems audit: A systems audit compares the performance of a new system to the original design specifications to determine if the new procedures are actually improving productivity.

Systems design: Phase consisting of designing alternative systems, selecting the best system, and writing a systems design report.

Systems design report: Report prepared for higher management describing alternative designs, presenting cost versus benefits and outlining the effects of alternative designs on the organization.

Systems development: Phase consisting of developing software, acquiring hardware, and testing the new system.

Systems life cycle: Phases of systems analysis and design.

Systems maintenance: Consists of a systems audit and periodic evaluation.

T

Table (in database): The list of records in a database.

Tactical models: A decision model that assists middle-level managers to control the work of the organization, such as financial planning and sales promotion planning.

Technical feasibility: Condition in which hardware, software, and training will be available to facilitate the design of a new system.

Technical writer: Computer professional who explains in writing how a computer program works.

Technostress: Tension that arises when humans must unnaturally adapt to computers.

Telephone lines: A transmission medium for both voice and data.

Telephony: Communication that uses the Internet rather than traditional communication lines to connect two or more people via telephone.

Television board: Contains a TV tuner and video converter that changes the TV signal into one that can be displayed on your monitor.

Telnet: Internet service that helps to connect computers on the Internet and to run programs on remote computers.

Templates: Model presentations.

Terminal: Form of input (and output) device that consists of a keyboard, a monitor, and a communications link.

Terminal network system: Network system in which processing power is centralized in one large computer, usually a mainframe. The nodes connected to this host computer are terminals with little or no processing capabilities.

Text entry: In a worksheet or spreadsheet, typically used to identify or label information.

Thermal printer: Printer that uses heat elements to produce images on heat-sensitive paper.

Thin client: *See* Network terminal.

Thin film transistor (TFT) monitor: Type of flat-panel monitor that activates each pixel independently.

Time-sharing system: System that allows several users to share resources in the host computer.

Toggle key: On-off key.

T1, T2, T3, T4 lines: High-speed lines that support all digital communications, provide very high capacity, and are very expensive.

Toolbar: Bar located typically below the menu bar. It contains icons or graphical representations for commonly used commands.

Top-down analysis method: Method used to identify the top-level component of a system and break this component down into smaller components for analysis.

Top-down program design: Process of identifying the top element (module) for a program and then breaking the top element down into smaller pieces in a hierarchical fashion.

Top management: Top-level managers are concerned with long-range (strategic) planning. They supervise middle management.

Topology: The configuration of a network.

Touch screen: Monitor screen that allows actions or commands to be entered by the touch of a finger.

Touch surface: Typically part of a portable computer, similar to a mouse.

Track: Closed, concentric ring on a disk on which data is recorded.

Trackball: Device used to control the pointer by rotating a ball with your thumb.

Traditional cookies: Intended to provide customized service, programs that record information on Web site visitors on a specific site. When you leave the site, the cookie becomes dormant, and is reactivated when you revisit the site.

Transaction file: File containing recent changes to records that will be used to update the master file.

Transaction processing system (TPS): System that records day-to-day transactions.

Transmission control protocol/Internet protocol (TCP/IP): The two standard protocols for all communications on the Internet.

Troubleshooting programs: Programs that recognize and correct computer related problems.

Twisted pair: Copper-wire telephone line.

2HD: Two-sided, double-density disk.

TV tuner card: *See* Television board.

U

Unicode: A 16-bit code designed to support international languages like Chinese and Japanese.

Uniform resource locator (URL): Addresses of resources on the Web.

Unix: An operating system originally developed for minicomputers. It is now important because it can run on many of the more powerful microcomputers.

Uploading: Process of transferring information from the computer the user is operating to a remote computer.

Uninstall program: Programs that safely and completely remove unwanted programs and related files.

Universal serial bus (USB): Combines with a PCI bus on the system board to support several external devices without inserting cards for each device.

Universal serial bus (USB) port: Expected to replace serial and parallel ports.

Unstructured problem: A problem that requires the use of intuition, reasoning, and memory.

UseNet: Special network of computers that support newsgroups.

User: *See* End user.

User interface: Means by which users interact with programs and hardware.

Utility: Performs specific tasks related to managing computer resources or files.

UXGA: Refers to a resolution standard of 1,600 by 1,200 pixels.

V

Vector file: Composed of a collection of objects such as lines, rectangles, and ovals.

Vector image: Graphics file made up of a collection of objects such as lines, rectangles, and ovals.

Vertical portal: Web portal designed to appeal to special-interest groups.

Very high level: Problem-orientated languages that require little special training on the part of the user.

Videoconferencing systems: Computer systems that allow people located at various geographic locations to have in-person meetings.

Video display screen: *See* Monitor.

Video Privacy Protection Act of 1988: Law preventing retailers from selling or disclosing video-rental records without the customer's consent or a court order.

Virtual environment: *See* Virtual reality.

Virtual memory: Feature of an operating system that increases the amount of memory available to run programs.

Virtual reality: Interactive sensory equipment (headgear and gloves) that allows users to experience alternative realities to the physical world.

Virtual reality modeling language (VRML): Used to create real-time animated 3-D scenes.

Virus: Hidden instructions that migrate through networks and operating systems and become embedded in different programs. They may be designed to destroy data or simply to display messages.

Virus checker: Detection programs that alert users when certain kinds of viruses enter the system.

Voiceband: Bandwidth of a standard telephone line.

Voice-input device: Direct-entry device that converts speech into a numeric code that can be processed by a computer.

Voice recognition system: *See* Voice-input device.

Volatile storage: Temporary storage that destroys the current data when power is lost or new data is read.

Voltage surge (spike): Excess of electricity, which may destroy chips or other electronic computer components.

VR: *See* Virtual reality.

W

Wand reader: Special-purpose handheld device used to read OCR characters.

Web: A service that provides a multimedia interface to resources on the Internet. *See also* World Wide Web.

Web appliance: *See* Internet terminal.

Web auction: Similar to traditional auctions except that buyers and sellers meet only on the Web.

Web authoring: Creating a Web site.

Web authoring program: Word processing program for generating Web pages. Also called HTML editor; Web page editor.

Web broadcaster: *See* Information pusher.

Web cam: Specialized digital video camera for capturing images and broadcasting to the Internet.

Webmaster: Person who designs, creates, monitors, and evaluates corporate Web sites.

Web page: Browsers interpret HTML documents to display Web pages.

Web portal: Site that offers a variety of services such as e-mail, news, and sports updates.

Web site: A location on a server.

Web site address: *See* Uniform resource locator (URL).

Web storefront creation packages: Programs for creating Web sites for virtual stores.

Web storefronts: Virtual stores where shoppers can go to inspect goods and make purchases.

Web terminal: *See* Internet terminal.

Web utilities: Specialized utility programs that make using the Internet and the Web easier and safer.

Web-downloading utility: *See* Off-line browser.

What-if analysis: Spreadsheet feature in which changing one or more numbers results in the automatic recalculation of all related formulas.

Wide area network (WAN): Countrywide network that uses microwave relays and satellites to reach users over long distances.

Window: A rectangular area containing a document or message.

Windows: An operating environment that extends the capability of DOS.

Wireless modem: Modem that connects to the serial port but does not connect to telephone lines. It receives through the air.

Wireless revolution: A revolution that is expected to dramatically affect the way we communicate and use computer technology.

Wireless service provider: Provides Internet connections for computers with wireless modems and a wide array of wireless devices.

Word: Unit that describes the number of bits in a common unit of information.

Word processing: Use of a computer to create, edit, save, and print documents composed of text.

Word wrap: Feature of word processing that automatically moves the cursor from the end of one line to the beginning of the next.

Workbook: The file in which you work and store sheets created in Excel.

Worksheet file: File created by an electronic spreadsheet.

World Wide Web (WWW, the Web): Internet service that uses hypertext to jump from document to document and from computer to computer. The Web is accessed by browsers.

Worm: Variant on computer virus, a destructive program that fills a computer system with self-replicating information, clogging the system so that its operations are slowed or stopped.

WORM (write once, read many): Form of optical disk that allows data to be written only once but read many times without deterioration.

Write-protect notch: Notch on a floppy disk used to prevent the computer from destroying data or information on the disk.

X

XGA (extended graphics array): Circuit board that can be inserted into a microcomputer and offers up to 256 colors under normal circumstances and more than 65,000 colors with special equipment.

Z

Zip disk: High capacity floppy disk manufactured by Sony.

Credits

Index